HOMICIDE AND VIOLENT CRIME

SOCIOLOGY OF CRIME, LAW AND DEVIANCE

Series Editor: Mathieu Deflem

Recent Volumes:

Volumes 1–5:	Jeffrey T. Ulmer
Volume 6:	Ethnographies of Law and Social Control, edited by Stacey Lee Burns, 2005
Volume 7:	Sociological Theory and Criminological Research, Views from Europe and United States, edited by Mathieu Deflem, 2006
Volume 8:	Police Occupational Culture: New Debates and Directions, edited by Megan O'Neill, Monique Marks, and Anne- Marie Singh, 2007
Volume 9:	Crime and Human Rights, edited by Stephan Paramentier and Elmar Weitekamp, 2007
Volume 10:	Surveillance and Governance: Crime Control and Beyond, edited by Mathieu Deflem, 2008
Volume 11:	Restorative Justice: From Theory to Practice, edited by Holly Ventura Miller, 2008
Volume 12:	Access to Justice, edited by Rebecca Sandefur, 2009
Volume 13:	Immigration, Crime and Justice, edited by William F. McDonald, 2009
Volume 14:	Popular Culture, Crime and Social Control, edited by Mathieu Deflem, 2010
Volume 15:	Social Control: Informal, Legal and Medical, edited by James J. Chriss, 2010
Volume 16:	Economic Crisis and Crime, edited by Mathieu Deflem, 2011
Volume 17:	Disasters, Hazards and Law, edited by Mathieu Deflem, 2012
Volume 18:	Music and Law, edited by Mathieu Deflem, 2013
Volume 19:	Punishment and Incarceration: A Global Perspective, edited by Mathieu Deflem, 2013
Volume 20:	Terrorism and Counterterrorism Today, edited by Mathieu Deflem, 2015
Volume 21:	The Politics of Policing: Between Force and Legitimacy, edited by Mathieu Deflem, 2016
Volume 22:	Race, Ethnicity and Law, edited by Mathieu Deflem, 2017

SOCIOLOGY OF CRIME, LAW AND DEVIANCE VOLUME 23

HOMICIDE AND VIOLENT CRIME

EDITED BY

MATHIEU DEFLEM

University of South Carolina, USA

emerald PUBLISHING

United Kingdom – North America – Japan
India – Malaysia – China

Emerald Publishing Limited
Howard House, Wagon Lane, Bingley BD16 1WA, UK

First edition 2018

British Library Cataloguing in Publication Data
A catalogue record for this book is available from the British Library

ISBN: 978-1-78714-876-5 (Print)
ISBN: 978-1-78714-875-8 (Online)
ISBN: 978-1-78743-940-5 (Epub)

ISSN: 1521-6136 (Series)

Printed and bound by CPI Group (UK) Ltd, Croydon, CR0 4YY

ISOQAR
REGISTERED
Certificate Number 1985
ISO 14001

ISOQAR certified Management System, awarded to Emerald for adherence to Environmental standard ISO 14001:2004.

INVESTOR IN PEOPLE

CONTENTS

PART III
POLICE AND STATE POWER

PART IV
ACROSS THE GLOBE

LIST OF CONTRIBUTORS

Ericka B. Adams	Department of Justice Studies, San José State University, CA, USA.
Kayla Allison	Departments of Criminal Justice and Sociology, Indiana University, IN, USA
Melissa J. Tetzlaff-Bemiller	Department of Social Sciences, Augusta University, GA, USA
Denise Paquette Boots	Program in Criminology and Criminal Justice University of Texas at Dallas, TX, USA
Timothy Bray	Program in Criminology and Criminal Justice, University of Texas at Dallas, TX, USA
Claire Chabot	School of Criminology, University of Montreal, QC, Canada
Mathieu Deflem	University of South Carolina, Department of Sociology, SC, USA
Daniel Adrian Doss	Computer Information Systems, University of West Alabama, AL, USA
Laura M. Gulledge	School of Criminal Justice, The University of Southern Mississippi, MS, USA
Malcolm D. Holme	Department of Sociology, University of Wyoming, WY, USA
Alesa Liles	Department of Government and Sociology, Georgia College and State University, GA, USA
Stacy Moak	Department of Social Work, University of Alabama Birmingham, AL, USA
Marc Ouime	École de Criminologie, Université de Montréal, QC, Canada
James B. Pratt, Jr	Department of Criminology, Law and Society, University of California, CA, USA

Wendy C. Regoeczi	Department of Criminology, Anthropology, and Sociology, Cleveland State University, OH, USA
Claudio G. Vera Sanchez	Department of Justice Studies, San José State University, CA, USA
Mateus Rennó Santos	Department of Criminology and Criminal Justice, University of Maryland, MD, USA
Danielle Sutton	Sociology and Anthropology, University of Guelph, ON, Canada
Alexander Testa	Department of Criminology and Criminal Justice, University of Maryland, MD, USA
Paige Vaughn	Department of Criminology and Criminal Justice, University of Missouri – St. Louis, MO, USA
Jennifer Wareham	Department of Criminal Justice, Wayne State University, MI, USA

INTRODUCTION: STUDYING VIOLENCE AND KILLING

Mathieu Deflem

The archetypical representation of the criminal in the nineteenth century, and for centuries earlier, was that of the violent offender who was lacking in civilization, humanity, and intelligence. From at least the nineteenth century onward, this criminological image has been replaced by that of the cunningly intelligent modern criminal who took advantage, better than the police had done as one official once expressed, of the new means and opportunities afforded by various technological advances (Deflem, 2002; Pasquino, 1991). In the development of the criminological sciences this transformation is reflected in the move from a preoccupation with the anomalies of the body, exemplarily expressed in the work of Cesare Lombroso, toward the opportunities offered in and the pressures exerted by various social conditions that produced deviant and criminal behavior as its normal or rational outcome. Briefly stated, one might expect today that violent crime and homicide should largely be a thing of the past. But this is not the case. We are not, it would seem, quite as civilized as we all too routinely think we are. Or, more precisely stated, civilization and more and less lethal forms of violence are indeed not necessarily the antagonists we like to and often do presume (Rojas, 2002).

This volume in the series *Sociology of Crime, Law and Deviance* is devoted to the social-scientific study of violence and homicide, not only because of the peculiar stubbornness of these offenses in contemporary times, but even more sharply so because a multitude of incidents of violence and killing, simply stated and striking to observe, are often in the news. Ranging from concerns over accusations of domestic abuse to killings in our cities and across the world, violent crime and homicide have stayed with us, not as mere remnants of a past we cannot shake, but as expressions of certain dynamics and strains of our world of today. The chapters in this volume tackle some of these important issues and questions with a variety of theoretical frameworks and methodological tools as applied to a number of relevant offenses.

Homicide and Violent Crime
Sociology of Crime, Law and Deviance, Volume 23, 1–3

ISSN: 1521-6136/doi:10.1108/S1521-613620180000023001

In Part I of this volume, chapters comprise those concerning the role of family and gender. Melissa J. Tetzlaff-Bemiller focuses her chapter on the dramatic concept and reality of child murder. Using statistical data, she shows the value of a more proper and methodical study of the killing of children that can allow for more adequate relevant criminal policies. Denise Paquette Boots, Laura M. Gulledge, Timothy Bray, and Jennifer Wareham examine the Dallas Domestic Violence Task Force about the response to domestic violence. They highlight the findings of the project and detail its policy recommendations. In a third and final chapter concerning family and gender issues, Alesa Liles and Stacy Moak argue that theory and intervention suggestions on offending have to be gender-specific to account for the role of women. The authors derive their conclusions on the basis of an examination of historical research on female offending.

Part II pays attention to a variety of institutions and identity aspects in matters concerning violent crime. Danielle Sutton relies on the work of classical sociologist Emile Durkheim to analyze dynamics of the Manson Family as a quasi-religious group. The chapter contributes to discussing religion as an appropriate framework for our understanding of violence. In a chapter on the deterrence and mitigation for campus violence, Daniel Adrian Doss studies violence on college campuses from a phenomenological framework. The author suggests ways to develop preventive and control strategies toward the establishment of a lasting campus safety. Kayla Allison discusses serious forms of bias violence on the basis of identity fusion theory. Focused on the Charleston church shooting, the author shows the value of using publicly available sources for the use of social-psychological theories that can be applied to the study of discriminatory violence.

Centered on the role of police and other state institutions, Part III of this volume begins with a chapter by Wendy C. Regoeczi concerning the conditions of evidence examining and explanation trends in homicide clearances. She specifically examines the level of support for existing explanatory frameworks of why some criminal killings are more likely to be solved than others. Malcolm D. Holmes's chapter examines the pressing problems of police violence involving minority citizens in the United States. The research shows that the incidence of police violence is higher in segregated minority neighborhoods. Seeking to account for the effect of police on violence, Paige Vaughn formulates a multi-level theory to account for how police typically respond to incidents of violence. This perspective reveals how police not responding to violence and the institution not being perceived as legitimate will affect violent offending. James B. Pratt, Jr extends the perspective to problematize the notion of the American Dream and its role in institutional anomie theory. Pratt argues that one must critically engage with the United States' legacy of racial violence and racialized social conditioning.

In the final part of this book, global and comparative dimensions are reflected upon to expand, usefully, beyond the borders of the United States. Studying international trends of homicide, Mateus Rennó Santos and Alexander Testa review the relevant literature on the basis of data from the World Health Organization. The authors reveal a general but uneven drop in homicide across the globe, which they attribute to factors beyond local phenomena. Claire Chabot and Marc Ouimet analyze 145 countries of the world and argue that especially impoverished countries have relatively high homicide rates. Indeed, the authors argue that economic determinants, especially inequality, and also formal mechanisms of social control as dependent on poverty and wealth, are important factors to consider. In the final chapter of this volume, Ericka B. Adams and Claudio G. Vera Sanchez study homicide in the country of Trinidad and Tobago. They find homicide concentrated among young men of African descent who live in underprivileged and demographically dense communities.

Taking the various chapters of this book as a whole, then, the authors make a useful contribution to the social-scientific study of violent crime and homicide in our world today. In this sense, the authors respond collectively and individually to take seriously the need to examine the conditions, causes, and consequences of some of the most problematic behaviors in, not despite of, the age of modernity. The chapters presented here are hoped to thoughtfully contribute to unravel some of the reasons why violence and homicide have until today persisted in various forms and manifestations.

REFERENCES

Deflem, M. (2002). Technology and the internationalization of policing: A comparative-historical perspective. *Justice Quarterly*, *19*(3), 453–475.

Pasquino, P. (1991). Criminology: The birth of a special knowledge. In G. Burchell, C. Gordon, & P. Miller (Eds.), *The Foucault effect* (pp. 235–250). Chicago, IL: University of Chicago Press.

Rojas, C. (2002). *Civilization and violence: Regimes of representation in nineteenth-century Colombia.* Minneapolis, MN: University of Minnesota Press.

PART I

FAMILY AND GENDER

CHAPTER 1

THE MURDERING OF CHILDREN

Melissa J. Tetzlaff-Bemiller

ABSTRACT

Purpose – *This chapter aims to present an overview of what constitutes child murder, including definitions, history, prevalence, risk factors, offender motivations, and theoretical understanding.*

Design/methodology/approach – *The author uses secondary data from the National Incident-Based Reporting System, Uniformed Crime Reports, and Vital Statistics to show comparisons with previously conducted research. This allows for an overview of child murder.*

Findings – *There are numerous inconsistencies due to methodological issues. It is hard to find studies where a large sample was used. Definitions of child vary between studies, as does the age categories used. In addition, child homicide is predicted to be grossly underrepresented due to lack of communication between agencies, lack of formalized training, lack of a formalized classification system, and lack of reporting.*

Originality/value – *Research on child homicide can be instrumental in many areas including policy creation, implementation, and evaluation. It can serve as a benefit for those attempting to provide preventative measures. It may also help law enforcement with investigation. It is only through continued analysis of these types of cases and vigilant research, policy, and practice that society can more effectively protect young children from exposure to potentially murderous outcomes.*

Keywords: Child homicide; fatal child abuse; child victimization; violent crime

Homicide and Violent Crime
Sociology of Crime, Law and Deviance, Volume 23, 7–24

ISSN: 1521-6136/doi:10.1108/S1521-613620180000023002

INTRODUCTION

Child murder has existed for a very long time. Spinelli (2005) mentions that Babylonian and Chaldeon civilizations left abnormal infants on the roadside to die, and in the seventeenth century mothers were punished by the church if they were found to have murdered their infant. Further accounts of child murder from as early as the 1600s are given by many scholars (Caron, 2010; Meyer, Oberman, & White, 2001). Child murder seems to bring both interest and hesitation in the research community. There has been research conducted on child murder, but it relatively is in its infancy especially when compared to adult homicide and hence requires more attention.

Nevertheless, there is a sizable amount of research regarding child murder. In most cases, research examines the characteristics of the offender and victim that are psychological or biological in nature, as well as characteristics of the crime. When analyzing the offender, it has been suggested that children are more likely to be murdered by a parent from the age of birth to 4 years of age (Davies, 2005). Concerning the manner of death, research indicates that abandonment, excessive force, suffocation, or poison (Shelton, Corey, Donaldson, & Dennison, 2011) is common when a mother commits infanticide, and firearms (Davies, 2005) are more common when the father commits the murder. Most research looks at why the murder happened, with many scholars pointing to stigma, not wanting the child, a form of depression, or financial issues (Finkel, Burke, & Chaves, 2000; Shelton et al., 2011; Spinelli, 2005). Research details the events leading up to the murder, the murder itself, and the psychological/biological state of both the offender and victim. Chapter 2 will discuss what constitutes child murder – the prevalence of child murder, sociodemographic and culture characteristics, risk factors, offender motivations, criminological theoretical explanations, and limitations.

WHAT IS CHILD MURDER?

Although many categories of child murder exist most scholars tend to agree with and use the following definitions: neonaticide – murder of a newborn within the first 24 hours of birth; infanticide – murder of an infant child who is less than 1 year old; and filicide – murder of one's own child, including both step-children and adult children (Alt & Wells, 2010; Barlow & Clayton, 1996; Davies, 2005; Lyman et al., 2003). However, not all agree with the above definitions. For example, while some scholars use the maximum age of 18 when discussing filicides (Lucas et al., 2002), others include any child murdered by a parent regardless of age. In addition, there is also differing opinions about neonaticide. Jason, Gilliland, and Tyler (1983) suggested that neonaticide includes children from birth to 1 week in age (Jason et al., 1983) as opposed to being limited to the first 24 hours of the child's life. Furthermore, various scholars have also suggested other terms to account for child murder such as prolicide – murder of one's offspring, including infants and fetuses in-utero (Davies, 2005) and familicide – murder of the entire family (Alt & Wells, 2010).

Thus, as noted above, there is not a single globally accepted definition of child murder in the research literature. Generally, when studying child murder, researchers create age categories in order to compare and contrast or focus on a more specific age group. This is because the circumstances for the murder of a 17-year-old will most likely be drastically different from those of a murdered 2-year-old. For example, some scholars categorize the age of victims as less than 1 year, 1–5 years, 6–10 years, and 11–14 years (Strang, 1996). Other scholars use the categories of less than 1 year, 1–4 years, 5–9 years, 10–14 years, and 15 years and older (Chew, McCleary, Lew, & Wang, 1999; Christoffel, 1984). Still, some scholars categorize each year individually from birth to 4 years (Ewigman, Kivlahan, & Land, 1993), or use birth to 1 month, 1–12 months, 13–24 months, 2–5 years, and 6–12 years (Crittenden & Craig, 1990). The lack of universally accepted definitions, as well as differing age categories can make researching child homicide, especially when focusing on younger children, somewhat difficult. This tends to be an issue for scholars who examine the literature for comparative purposes.

According to the United States Government, a child is a person who has not reached his 18th birthday. Therefore, child murder could include any person under the age of 18 who has been murdered. However, for this chapter, the age range focused on will be from birth to 5 years of age.

HISTORY OF CHILD HOMICIDE

Child murder can be traced throughout history (Barlow & Clayton, 1996). Meyer et al. (2001) declare that there is every reason to believe that infanticide is as old as human society itself and that no culture has been immune to it. Moreover, infanticide was legal throughout the ancient civilizations of Mesopotamia, Greece, and Rome, and justified on grounds ranging from population control, to eugenics, to illegitimacy (Meyer et al., 2001). According to Spinelli (2005), "in Babylonian and Chaldeon civilizations abnormal infants, considered to be children of witches who consummated with animals or demons, were left on the roadside to die. In the Greek and Roman eras, birth control and eugenic reasons were the primary causes for infant murder by fathers who had absolute rule in the family" (p. 15). Infants were often times sacrificed and unwanted newborns, or those thought to be too weak, were exposed to the elements as a means to controlling the population (Meyer et al., 2001). Over time, inheritance, illegitimacy, and stigma became grounds for infant murder (Lagaipa, 1990; Meyer et al., 2001).

In 1647, Russia became the first country to adopt a more humane attitude and by 1888, all European states established a legal distinction between infanticide and murder and gave more lenient penalties to infanticide offenders (Spinelli, 2004). Meyer et al. (2001) discussed that infanticide was considered a crime committed exclusively by unmarried women, and even in societies with infanticide laws that governed all citizens, it was speculated that married women who committed infanticide generally avoided punishment. Spinelli (2005) alleged that certain cultures began to see women as biologically vulnerable around the time of birth. This is one reason for probation or medical treatment of the offenders in the early 1900s to be allowed as opposed to strictly incarceration. Meyer et al. (2001) furthers this thought by discussing how:

> [...] medicalization of infanticide was embraced in England where they recognized infanticide as a distinct form of homicide due to the impact of pregnancy and birth upon the mother's mental status. (p. 11)

It is further suggested that the defendant's culpability for the crime is limited and that the maximum crime in which the mother can be charged with is manslaughter, instead of murder (Meyer et al., 2001).

In the 1900s, different countries began expressing contrasting views concerning child murder. Whereas countries such as the United Kingdom held lenient views due to the thought that the murder was the outcome of an illness, the response in the United States was harsh because it was seen as murder. The United States did not have any laws regarding infanticide (Meyer et al., 2001); it was seen as a type of murder. Individuals found guilty of child murder were convicted without regard to the age of the victim (Caron, 2010; Finkel et al., 2000). However, individual states within the United States had the freedom to decide on mitigating and aggravating circumstances, which in turn led to differing convictions and punishments for an individual who kills a child (Spinelli, 2005). Therefore, an offender may be treated more leniently or harshly for the murder of his child depending on local community views. The sentence could also differ depending upon the age of the victim. For example, if an individual kills a child who was less than a year old, his punishment may be harsher (Spinelli, 2005). There are some arguments concerning the United States federal and state statutes. One major issue is that the United States does not recognize types of mental illness such as postpartum depression or postpartum psychosis (Spinelli, 2005). Many studies have shown this to be reasons why some mothers kill their young (Finkel et al., 2000; Shelton et al., 2011; Spinelli, 2005). If a state does not recognize postpartum depression or psychosis, then they may be placing individuals who need treatment in prisons. However, Spinelli (2005) does mention that the incident rates are not much different when comparing a place like the United States, which focuses on punishment, to other nations that focus on treatment.

As the literature suggests, ideas concerning child murder change with culture. Defective infants, female infants, motherless or illegitimate infants, closely spaced children, and children resulting from multiple births have all been at risk for infanticide in some cultures at some point in time (Crittenden & Craig, 1990). It appears that cultures viewed the murdering of children differently throughout history. Some cultures condone it (the well-known population control and sex selection) while some treat the offenders (by putting them in medical settings), and still others disapprove and convict harsh sentences.

PREVALENCE

The reported prevalence of child murder tends to fluctuate. For example, in 1990, the worldwide prevalence of violent deaths for children 4 years old and under accounted for 1,926 out of 17,472 violent deaths (Murray & Lopez, 1996).

Shelton et al. (2011) contend that the United States has the fourth highest rate, behind Japan, Austria, and Finland, of infant homicide relative to population size. According to the Uniform Crime Reports, there were 428 children aged birth to 4 years old murdered out of a total of 9,616 killings in 2015; 168 were under 1 year old and 260 were between 1 and 4 years old (Federal Bureau of Investigation, 2015). According to the Centers for Disease Control and Prevention (CDC, 2016), homicide was the fourth leading cause of death in the United States for children (all races and both sexes) between the ages of 1 and 4 years in 2016. However, when averaged for the years of 1999–2016, homicide was the third leading cause of death in the United States for children (all races and both sexes) aged 1–4 years (CDC, 1999–2016). While gender does not seem to make much of a difference, when one examines race, for 2016, homicide is the second leading cause of death for Black children aged 1–4 years.

Child homicide is a rare crime in Western societies (Putkonen et al., 2011), but research points out that both child murder and fatal cases of child abuse are severely undercounted (Herman-Giddens et al., 1999; Jason & Andereck, 1983; Overpeck, 2002). This undercounting is accounted for by poor documentation, infanticides reported as SIDS (sudden infant death syndrome) deaths, lack of death certificates, unfound corpses, and undocumented births due to pregnancy denial (Herman-Giddens et al., 1999; Spinelli, 2005). Lyman et al. (2003) say that the:

> [...] underascertainment is due to restrictions into inaccuracies in coding causes of death, incomplete or inaccurate information on death certificates or police reports, variable case definitions, and the absence of a national system for reviewing child homicides. (p. 1064)

Other reasons for inaccurate estimations could be that investigators may lack certain skills, failure to communicate findings, and lack access to additional professional records. Overall, it can be assumed that child murder, like other crime, is grossly underestimated in secondary official data. According to data from the National Child Abuse and Neglect Data System, an estimated 1,670 children died from abuse or neglect in 2015, a 5.7% increase from 2011 (Child Welfare Information Gateway, 2015). Of these nearly three-quarters of the children were between birth and 3 years old with 49.4% being younger than 1 year old (Child Welfare Gateway Information, 2015).

Because of underreporting, accurate data are difficult to obtain and, when data are collected, reporting methods vary (Alt & Wells, 2010). "Data collection and reporting procedures among health, law enforcement, and social service agencies are not uniform, standardized, or coordinated" (Ewigman et al., 1993, p. 335). Ewigman et al. (1993), who studied underreporting of maltreatment as a cause of death, found significant underreporting in all the data used, including vital statistics, FBI – UCR homicide data, and the child protective service information.

SOCIODEMOGRAPHIC/CULTURAL CHARACTERISTICS AND RISK FACTORS

Research concerning risk factors for child homicide has reported some contradictory findings. Some of these inconsistencies can be attributed to sampling differences (Chew et al., 1999). Most research (Abel, 1986; Chew et al., 1999; Ewigman et al., 1993; Lucas et al., 2002) is based on small local samples of child homicide, which tend to be rather site-specific. Some studies (Chew et al., 1999; Clifford et al., 2017, Jason et al., 1983) are based on larger samples, but contradictions still tend to be prevalent. Therefore, it may be that the population from which the sample was drawn significantly influences the risk factors discussed, and hence the same must be acknowledged.

Victim Gender

One factor that is inconsistent is the gender of the victim. While some research indicates an even distribution between male and female child homicide victims (Chew et al., 1999; Silverman, Reidel, & Kennedy, 1990), others conclude that the majority are male victims (Brewster et al., 1998; Clifford et al., 2017; Ewigman et al., 1993; Klevens & Leeb, 2010; Putkonen et al., 2011; Shelton et al., 2011; U.S. Department of Health and Human Services, 2015), and yet others report predominately female victims (Abel, 1986; Crittenden & Craig, 1990; Lyman et al., 2003). One other observation that has been made is that the difference in sex may be characterized by age (Chew et al., 1999; Lucas et al., 2002) where males are more vulnerable in one age group and females in another.

Offender Gender

Similar to research on victims, there are contradictions concerning the offender's gender. Some research indicates that males, most likely the father, are more likely to be the offenders (Brewster et al., 1998; Clifford et al., 2017; Ewigman et al., 1993; Schnitzer & Ewigman, 2005), while others claim that females, most likely the mother, are more likely to be the offenders (Abel, 1986; Crittenden & Craig, 1990; Friedman, Horwitz, & Resnick, 2005; Goetting, 1988; Putkonen et al., 2011; U.S. Department of Health and Human Services, 2015). It has also been suggested that the age of the victim tends to differentiate the sex of the offender, with females more likely to be the offenders when children are less than 1 year old (Brewster et al., 1998; Jason et al., 1983; Lucas et al., 2002).

Victim Race/Ethnicity

There is also disagreement concerning the race and ethnicity of the victims in existing research. Findings from some studies indicate that African Americans tend to be overrepresented among the victims of child homicide (Abel, 1986; Goetting, 1988; Lyman et al., 2003), while others report that Caucasians are more commonly the victims of child homicide (Brewster et al., 1998; Clifford et al., 2017; Ewigman et al., 1993; Lucas et al., 2002; Shelton et al., 2011). According to the U.S. Department of Health and Human Services publication (Child Maltreatment, chapter 4, Fatalities [2015]), there is a racial disparity where the rate of Black children murdered is overrepresented with a rate of 4.63 per 100,000 compared to White children murdered at a rate of 1.86 per 100,000. Unfortunately, there seems to be little inclusion of other ethnicities.

When studies include Hispanics, they are usually found to be the least represented among victims (Lucas et al., 2002; Shelton et al., 2011). Chew et al. (1999) argue that child homicide victimization closely resembles the composition of the general population.

Offender Race/Ethnicity

The literature acknowledges a discrepancy pertaining to the offender's race/ethnicity as well. While some studies have found that the offender is more likely to be African American (Crittenden & Craig, 1990; Goetting, 1988), others have found that the offender is more likely to be Caucasian (Brewster et al., 1998; Shelton et al., 2011). Similar to the research on victims, rarely are other race/ethnicities included. The racial distribution of homicide perpetrators and victims is most likely similar because murders tend to be intraracial (Huff-Corzine, Corzine, & Moore, 1991).

Victim Age

Children under the age of five tend to be at the greatest risk for death (Abel, 1986; Levine, Compann, & Freeman, 1995; McClain et al., 1994). Abel (1986) affirmed that children aged 1–4 years contained highest number of homicide victims; while Christoffel (1984) remarks that a homicide is most prevalent during infancy. Further, it was acknowledged that "historical and cross-cultural evidence suggests that infanticide is a separate entity from later child homicide and from child abuse" (Christoffel, 1984, p. 68), which may lead to the death of a child. Children seem to be most vulnerable at young ages and may even depend fully upon their parents. In fact, it has been indicated that the greatest number of child homicides occur among infants (under age 1), young children (ages 1–4), and in teenagers (ages 13–17) (Abel, 1986; Chew et al., 1999; Cristoffel, 1984; Crittenden & Craig, 1990). In Crittenden and Craig's (1990) study, it was determined that the rate of homicide was highest during the first month of life, dropped dramatically after the first month, and slowly decreased as the child got older. In Clifford et al.'s (2017) study, 45% of the sample were 1 year old and under. Scholars agree that younger children are more at risk; they just use different groupings of age.

Offender Age

When studies examine the age of the offender, it is generally agreed that the offenders tend to be young adults. Brewster et al. (1998) found the mean age of the female offender to be about 23 years and the male offender to be about 24 years. Chew et al. (1999) found that as the victim's age, the offenders tend to be older. In a study conducted by Lucas et al. (2002) the mean age of mothers who murdered their children (who were between 1 and 4 years old) were approximately 26 years old and the fathers mean age was approximately 29 years old. Clifford et al. (2017) noted that the mean age of offenders was 27.69 while the median age was 26 years old. However, Putkonen et al. (2011) found that the mean age of mothers was approximately 32 years old, while the mean age of fathers was approximately 38 years old. A possible reason the offenders are older in Putkonen et al. (2011), may be related to the fact that the study consisted of children under the age of 18 years and was not specific to younger children under the age of 5 years. Still, consistent with other studies, female offenders tended to be younger than males. Shelton et al. (2011) found the mean age of female offenders to be approximately 22 years old. Goetting (1988) found the mean age of female offenders to be 26 years. Most scholars find that the offenders are in their twenties. This may be related to the time (age) in which individuals usually have their children.

Victim/Offender Relationship

A common finding of child murder is the observation that children are most likely to be murdered by someone they know, usually a parental figure (Brewster et al., 1998; Clifford et al., 2017; Crittenden & Craig, 1990; Douglas, 2013; Mayhew, 2007). According to Alt and Wells (2010) only 3% of children murdered are actually killed by strangers. The U.S. Department of Health and Human Services publication (Child Maltreatment, chapter 4, Fatalities [2015]) over three-quarters of the perpetrators are parents. Chew et al. (1999) provide an explanation for this expressing that in early childhood, most of the child's time is spent in the company of primary caretakers and other household members. When children reach a certain age, they enter school and no longer spend as much time in the company of their parents or other household members.

The discrepancy exists when considering whether it is the mother or father who is mostly involved with the murder. Some research suggests that the mother is more likely to be the offender (Abel, 1986; Crittenden & Craig, 1990; Goetting, 1988; Jason et al., 1983; Putkonen et al., 2011) while others suggest the father is most likely to be the offender (Brewster et al., 1998; Ewigman et al., 1993; Strang, 1996). Mothers are more likely to be the offender when the child is less than 1 year old (Brewster et al., 1998; Crittenden & Craig, 1990; Jason et al., 1983; Lucas et al., 2002; Mayhew, 2007).

Drug and Alcohol Use

Research has also explored whether or not offenders were intoxicated prior to the murdering of a child. Substance abuse has been found to exist in 40–80% of the homes where children are abused (National Council on Child Abuse and Family Violence, 2014). However, the association between violence and substance abuse tends to be complex. Most studies that examined substance use looked at both alcohol and drugs. According to Putkonen et al. (2011), fathers were more often diagnosed with a substance abuse or dependency. Approximately 42% of fathers were intoxicated while only 11% of mothers were intoxicated at the time of the crime (Putkonen et al., 2011). The U.S. Department of Health and Human Services (2017) also found that perpetrators had risk factors for alcohol (nearly 7%) or drug use (18%). Clifford et al. (2017) found that nearly 80% of offenders were not under the influence of drugs or alcohol at the time of the incident.

Weapons

Children are significantly more likely to be murdered with the use of a personal weapon (Chew et al., 1999; Lucas et al., 2002; Lyman et al., 2003; Mayhew, 2007). In a study conducted by Abel (1986) it was found that most children were beaten with the hands, feet, or blunt objects. In a study conducted by Brewster et al. (1998), 58% of the sample had head trauma. Mayhew (2007) also indicates beatings as being the primary cause of child murder, but mentions that neonaticide generally occurs from suffocation (being wrapped in a towel or placed in a box), abandonment, drowning (especially if born into a toilet), or from other forms of physical abuse. The most common weapon used in Shelton et al. (2011) was an asphyxiant, but the authors mention that this is not always done manually and could entail the use of a plastic bag, water, ligature strangulation, etc. Crittenden and Craig (1990) obtained similar findings: the most common way a neonate was murdered was through suffocation, and children aged 1–5 years old were most likely to be murdered by beatings. According to Clifford et al.'s (2017) study, the most used was personal weapons (35%). When a non-personal weapon is used, the weapon most used tends to be a knife (Brewster et al., 1998) or anything that is not bolted down and could be used as a weapon of opportunity (such as a lamp or remote) (Mayhew, 2007). Guns may also be used, but this is generally more prevalent in murder-suicide, familicide, or related to domestic violence (Mayhew, 2007) and is more likely to be used by a male perpetrator (Crittenden & Craig, 1990).

Seasons, Days, and Hours

Some characteristics of the time of the incident have also been examined. When observing seasonal trends, Abel (1986) found that 43.5% of the child murders occurred during spring/fall, followed by summer (29%), and winter (27.5%). McCleary and Chew (2002) found that the risk for infants, toddlers, and preschool children peaks in the winter season, while the risk for older individuals peaks in the summer season.

When discussing the days in which child murder is most likely to occur, there are mixed results. One study found that 53% of the child murders occurred from Tuesday through Thursday, 47% occurred on the weekend, and none occurred on Monday or Friday (Brewster et al., 1998). Abel (1986) found that 24% of the homicides occurred on Saturday, about 18% on Monday, about 15% occurred on both Friday and Sunday, only 8% on Wednesday, and nearly 7% on Thursday. Putkonen et al. (2011) found that filicide occurring on the weekdays was evenly distributed, but Sunday was the most common day for fathers to commit filicide. Lucas et al. (2002) discussed that for children aged 1–4 years old, the weekend was most prevalent.

A commonality among much research is concerning the time of day. Midday tends to be when most child homicides take place (Brewster et al., 1998; Lucas et al., 2002). Putkonen et al. (2011) concluded that mothers commit filicide throughout the course of the day while fathers predominantly committed filicide during the morning or evening. This was also confirmed in Clifford et al. (2017) when the majority of child homicides were committed by males (66.4%) and occurred between the hours of 4.00 p.m. and 3.59 a.m. (55.5%). This may be due to the employment status of the offenders. Further, Goetting (1988) found no discernible pattern concerning month, day, or hour of the homicides.

Location

When location has been included, it has been found that most child homicides happen at home (Abel, 1986; Brewster et al., 1998; Goetting, 1988; Putkonen et al., 2011; Shelton et al., 2011). Brewster et al. (1998) found that 71% occurred in the home; Abel (1986) found 74% occurred in the child's personal residence. The majority of the murders in Putkonen et al. (2011) study were committed at home, with the bathrooms being most common. Shelton et al. (2011) also found child murder in the bathroom (65%) but limited their sample to neonates.

Abuse and Neglect

Some scholars have suggested that violence toward children is a continuum of violence that ranges from the mildest forms, such as neglect or physical punishment, to the most severe forms, such as murder. As it is well known among homicide researchers, "The difference between assault and homicide is often as simple as luck, aim, or the presence/absence of a weapon" (Gelles, 1991, p. 60). Statistics also show that up to one in five child homicides occur in the context of domestic violence in the home (Jaffe, Campbell, Hamilton, & Juodis, 2012). According to the U.S. Department of Health and Human Services (2015), 14.4% of children murdered were exposed to domestic violence. In addition, children aged 4 years and younger are the most likely victims of child homicide caused by maltreatment and account for 77% of the child fatalities due to abuse and neglect (Child Welfare Information Gateway, 2015).

Putkonen et al. (2011) found that 34% of fathers but only 8% of mothers had previously abused the victim prior to the murder. Brewster et al. (1998) described the victims in their study as being relatively normal at birth (having had normal gestational periods and birth weights); however, by the time of their death, they were substantially smaller in their weight and length compared to other babies of the same age. This may be characteristic of neglect. Usually child murder is related to beatings, but neglect can co-occur with abuse or be the sole cause of the murder. Brewster et al. (1998) found that over half of the sample of infants suffered from some form of physical trauma before their fatal injury. According to Herman-Giddens et al. (1999) 80–90% of murder among children younger than 6 years of age result from child abuse. Moreover, more than 90% of fatal child abuse cases were among children younger than 5 years old, with more than 40% occurring in infants (McClain et al., 1994). Mayhew (2007), who is a child death investigator, positioned that abusive head trauma and abdominal trauma are both usually caused by beatings, which tend to be primarily caused by personal weapons (hands, feet, etc.) or a weapon of opportunity (anything not bolted down). Not all studies have included a measure for prior abuse as it is not available in many secondary data sources.

Poverty and Employment Status

Research has found that there is a direct relationship between the incidence of child homicide and economic conditions. Specifically, the typical families with child abuse fatalities are poor, rural, and white (Jason & Andereck, 1983). Findings also suggest that "the higher the number of [child] homicides, the higher the unemployment and percentage of families living below the poverty level" (Abel, 1986, p. 711).

Abel (1986) suggests that more murders occurred in places with higher unemployment rates. However, Putkonen et al. (2011) reported that nearly half of the fathers who committed filicide were employed, whereas only approximately one-fourth of the mothers worked outside the home. Brewster et al. (1998) found that 77% of offenders were employed at the time of the incident, whereas in Goetting's (1988) study, 70% of the offenders were unemployed and 25% of the offenders were on welfare. Approximately 45% of offenders were on Medicaid in Ewigman et al. (1993) study.

Geographical Location

An additional area of exploration is geographical location. McClain et al. (1994) proposes that homicide rates in the United States differ according to geographic location. They examined the occurrence of fatal child abuse or neglect of children aged birth to 5 years for each state in the United States from 1979 to 1988 and found the highest incidence in the South and West, and the lowest in Northeast (McClain et al., 1994). Jason et al. (1983) findings suggested that homicide among infants aged 1 week or less occur more often in rural areas with the regional distribution being higher in the Northeast and South; homicide among infants aged 1 week to 1 year was highest in the North Central region. Still, Gelles et al. (1991) find that although the rate of adult homicide is highest in the South, infant and toddler homicide rate is highest in the West. Clifford et al. (2017) also found that the majority of child homicides (51.3%) occurred in the South followed by the Midwest (28.6%)

Marital Status

Lucas et al. (2002) found that families were most likely composed of married households, but the families of the youngest victims were represented by single, separated, or divorced parents. Putkonen et al. (2011), furthers this with their findings that family disintegration seemed relevant. This was truer for fathers than for mothers. Lyman et al. (2003) also found that the majority of offenders were single.

Sociocultural factors, such as poverty and preexisting social relationships, "explain almost all state to state differences in adult homicide rates, but they do not explain differences among states and homicide deaths of infants" (Gelles, 1991, p. 64). Scholars have attempted to include some sociocultural issues in their research. It has been acknowledged that an unfavorable social environment is considered vulnerability (Putkonen et al., 2011). Risk factors can be difficult to assess accurately and measure, which can cause challenges when researching child murder. Lyman et al. (2003) declares that the impact of community level factors and social stressors has not been addressed much in previous literature and the inclusion of these ecological variables in an appropriate analysis may increase understanding of how contextual factors translate into differences in individual level risk.

OFFENDER MOTIVATIONS FOR CHILD MURDER

Deaths in early infancy tends to be indicative of discarding rather than punishing, and deaths in early childhood are usually more indicative of attempts to manage child behavior, punishing rather than discarding (Crittenden & Craig, 1990). It has been determined that many child deaths that occur in early childhood seem to be more closely related to child abuse and neglect. This is a time period when physical discipline is most often used (Crittenden & Craig, 1990). Mayhew (2007) claims that most child homicides are a result of frustration and lack of appropriate expectations of children, but others are calculated acts of violence. The number one trigger is usually crying with the risk of harm rising if the baby is colicky; other triggers are toilet training and feeding time (Mayhew, 2007). However, the methods of the homicide change as the child ages. This trend can be attributed to a variety of factors including the size and age of the victim, the size of the perpetrator, the reaction by the caregiver to the child's behaviors, and the accessibility of weapons (Mayhew, 2007).

When research is conducted on child murder, usually the scholars look for risk factors. Thus, some scholars have attempted to create offender motivation classifications. There are many classifications, but the following tends to be seen most often within research: (1) pathological, (2) unwanted child, (3) accidental, (4) revenge/retaliation, (5) altruistic, (6) nonaccidental, and (7) religious.

Pathological child murder is when the offender has an altered state of mind, a homicide–suicide, or when a parent or caregiver was suffering from a mental illness, depression, or acute psychosis (Alt & Wells, 2010; Bourrget & Bradford, 1990; Resnick, 1969). According to Alt and Wells (2010) some parents or caregivers suffer from a mental illness and have gone mad when the event occurred; some even heard voices telling them to commit the murder. Mothers may have delusions about the child or hear voices telling them how to kill their child (Schwartz & Isser, 2007). Depression tends to be another reason why individuals murder children. At least two forms of depression may affect women after giving birth: postpartum distress and postpartum psychosis. According to Alt and Wells (2010), postpartum psychosis is the most severe form. Some defense attorneys for those who have committed child murder, especially neonaticide or infanticide, claim that the woman was suffering from a reactive psychosis or postpartum depression, which made her kill (Schwartz & Isser, 2007) and therefore attempt to lessen her culpability.

Unwanted child murder is when the mother denies or conceals the pregnancy prior to the neonaticide (Alt & Wells, 2010; Bourrget & Bradford, 1990;

Resnick, 1969). At times, the birth of an unwanted child can lead to the murdering of that child. This may be caused by an extramarital affair; if the spouse/partner does not want the child it is also plausible that the woman considered an abortion but waited too long, could not afford one, or could not locate an abortion provider (Alt & Wells, 2010). Young girls who become pregnant may fear that they will be excluded by their families if it is discovered that they have had sex and are pregnant (Schwartz & Isser, 2007). There are still cultures and religions where a child born out of wedlock creates shame for the family. Mayhew (2007) suggests that not all deaths of neonates are from murder; many natural deaths occur during this time.

Accidental child murder includes various forms of abuse and neglect such as shaken baby syndrome or battered child syndrome (Alt & Wells, 2010; Bourrget & Bradford, 1990; Resnick, 1969). There are different definitions constituting abuse and neglect (Ewigman et al., 1993), as well as the fact that such abuse can range in severity. Often times, child murder is caused by overzealous corporal punishment (Schwartz & Isser, 2007), which can be triggered by noxious behavior (Mayhew, 2007), but the intent may have only been the punishment and not death.

Revenge or retaliation child murder involves revenge or retaliation against the spouse or girl/boyfriend (Alt & Wells, 2010; Bourrget & Bradford, 1990; Resnick, 1969). This type of child murder is a deliberate attempt to make the other parent suffer. The murder usually occurs when the male (especially the father) does not want the child, or when he wants to punish the female for infidelity (Schwartz & Isser, 2007).

Altruistic child murder may occur if a child has a disability, physical or mental. The offender, usually a parent, may be concerned about the child being stigmatized by others in their community or have difficulties caring for the child (Alt & Wells, 2010). Further, such motive may happen if an offender decides to commit suicide and fears the child will not have anyone left to care for them (Alt & Wells, 2010). This form of murder may be seen as a mercy killing (Schwartz & Isser, 2007).

Nonaccidental child murder would include sudden infant death syndrome or Munchausen Syndrome by Proxy. Alt and Wells (2010) suggest that SIDS is a common death among infants. SIDS usually occurs in infants younger than 1 year old. While SIDS is not always murder, it can be. Shwartz and Isser (2007) claim that when the cause of death is SIDS and no explanation can be found for it, the death may actually be a murder. Another type of death that would fit into this motive category could be Munchausen Syndrome by Proxy. This is when a parent usually the mother (Schwartz & Isser, 2007) – uses her child to gain attention by either causing her child to become ill or reporting pseudo ailments (Alt & Wells, 2010; Mayhew, 2007). The continued cause of ailments could lead to the death of the child. Some of the intentional ailments include, but are not limited to, feeding the child poison to induce stomach pain, aggravating an existing sore, inducing apnea by smothering, or twisting or breaking bones. One issue with this syndrome is that often times the mothers uses different hospitals, pediatricians, or emergency clinics to avoid being discovered (Schwartz & Isser, 2007).

A final classification motive is religion. Religion is still a large part of society and Alt and Wells (2010) suggest that religion may play a role with child murder. They continue by addressing the fact that some cultures avoid medical intervention and try to heal through using prayer alone. Schwartz and Isser (2000) also discuss how certain religious sects, or cults, may prohibit medical intervention.

While the above classifications have been useful for trying to explain why individuals (usually parents) murder their young, they by no means represent an all-inclusive or exhaustive list. Due to the extent of this unfortunate phenomena (differences with age, geographic location, motive, cause of death, etc.), it seems nearly impossible to develop an all-inclusive and exhaustive list of classifications. For example, a motive that is not listed above could be that it is instrumental to murder a child. Such a death may be associated with personal gain; especially if a life insurance was taken out on the child. It is also evident that some categories may overlap.

THEORETICAL EXPLANATIONS

Various criminological theories have been used to explain child murder. Research primarily applies micro-level theories (Brewster et al., 1998; Goetting, 1988; Jason & Andereck, 1983; McClain et al., 1994; Putkonen et al., 2011; Schwartz & Isser, 2007; Shelton et al., 2011). Some of the theories that have been relied on to pull variables from are routine activities theory, control theory, anomie theory, and social disorganization theory. Studies applying such theories offer a wealth of information. It is because of these theories that child homicide classifications, individual risk factors, etc., are known. The following theories are the ones that tend to appear the most, but by no means are the only ones used.

Child murder can be explained using a routine activities framework (Cohen & Felson, 1979; Felson, 1995). It applies to child murder when examining the context in which it occurs. First, the motivated offender (usually a parent) is present. Second, a suitable target (the young child) is present. Third, there is a lack of a capable guardian (perhaps the parent is alone with the child). Research has included variables to measure the capable guardian, such as the presence of a witness and previous contact with the Department for Children and Families (Shelton et al., 2011). Shelton et al. (2011) found that in 75% of the cases examined, another adult or child was in the same living space, but 88% of them were unaware that the murder had occurred.

Control and anomie theories examine offenders. Control theory discusses how weak or broken social bonds with members of conventional society will increase the likelihood of criminal involvement (Hirschi, 1969). Child murder may result from situations such as a strained or broken relationship, or from a young female's fear of being disowned by her family or friends. Another type of control, self-control, emphasizes the lack of individual self-control leading to crime. Crime is contingent upon a set of conditions or opportunities, which lead individuals, particularly those with low self-control, to violate norms (Gottfredson & Hirschi, 1990). Child murder may result from revenge or retaliation caused by strained or broken relationships from infidelity or other social issues. Measures for this would include prior abuse (Brewster et al., 1998; McClain et al., 1994; Putkonen et al., 2011).

Anomie theory is relevant when exploring how negative emotions generate pressure for corrective action. This may lead to criminal acts meant to escape strain, such as seeking revenge against the sources of strain or trying to suppress negative emotions through the use of illegal drugs. Mayhew (2007) suggests that often a noxious behavior triggers child murder; for example, a baby that cries all the time. The murder could also be triggered by an unwanted child (Shelton et al., 2011). The child may lead to strained relationships, as well, and therefore be murdered.

Deviance is attributed to social disorganization when a community cannot supervise and control deviance appropriately. Social disorganization applies to the community characteristics in which child murder occurs. Shaw and McKay (1969 [1942]) suggest that social disorganization is an approach that emphasizes neighborhood structural differences instead of individual traits. The usual methods of social control are not evident in these areas, resulting in higher levels of deviant and lawless acts (Park & Burgess, 1924). Individuals who reside in areas that are characterized by impoverished conditions, evidenced by decaying housing, broken families, substance abuse, and low income and education levels, among other social issues, are more likely to experience higher rates of deviance than more socially organized areas. Social disorganization theory helps explain the distribution of neighborhood crime (Bellair & Browning, 2010). Studies have looked at female-headed households, residential stability, and other community-level indicators. Some of the measures used are poverty, crowding (Goetting, 1988; Jason & Andereck, 1983), and employment rates (Putkonen et al., 2011), to name a few. Even though these measures could be micro-level or macro-level, scholars have used them to examine individual family characteristics.

As previously mentioned, many criminological theories have been used to try and explain child murder. Due to child murder being a rare event (compared to nonchild murder), most of the studies are small scale and researchers approach their study from a micro-level perspective. These individual characteristics are noteworthy, but we may be able to get a more complete picture by using a macro-level approach, which could offer a more conservative statistical estimates of child murder.

CONCLUSION

As noted throughout the chapter, there are some issues when it comes to understanding child murder. To begin, the murdering of children – especially the age range this chapter focuses on – tends to be rare when compared to all other murder. This could be due to several issues. It may be the lack of communication between agencies (medical, law enforcement, researchers, etc.), the cause of death may be misclassified (SIDS), lack of a universal classification system, and lack of universal training and reporting methods offer some ideas. According to the

U.S. Department of Health and Human Services (2015), the passage of the Child and Family Services Improvement and Innovation Act in 2010 has led many states to change their reporting practices. For example, several states implemented new or expanded the scope of child death reviews, while other states began investigating all unexplained infant deaths regardless of whether there was an allegation of maltreatment.

Another concern is the definition of child murder. As previously mentioned, there are several age classifications for child murder. Another point of contention is if abortions should be counted. Different studies tend to use different age categories, which makes comparisons difficult. Concerning research, studies tend to use a relatively small sample and focus on micro-level variables. It has been noted that several sociodemographic and cultural characteristics of child homicide probably closely resemble the area the sample was drawn from. There are very few studies that use a large, more representative sample.

Despite the shortcomings, research in this area is notable and should continue. Studies of child homicide can help in several areas including policy creation and improvement, investigative procedures, as well as prevention programs. It is only through continued analysis of these types of cases and vigilant research, policy, and practice that society can more effectively protect young children from exposure to potentially murderous outcomes.

REFERENCES

Abel, E. L. (1986). Childhood homicide in Erie County, New York. *Pediatrics*, *77*, 709–713.

Alt, B. S., & Wells, S. (2010). *When caregivers kill: Understanding child murder by parents and other guardians*. Lanham, MD: Rowman & Littlefield.

Barlow, S. H., & Clayton, C. L. (1996). When mothers murder: Understanding infanticide by females. In H. V. Hall (Ed.), *Lethal violence* 2000 (pp. 203–229). Kamuela, HI: Pacific Institute for the Study of Conflict and Aggression.

Bellair, P. E., & Browning, C. R. (2010). Contemporary disorganization research: An assessment and further test of the systemic model of neighborhood crime. *Journal of Research in Crime and Delinquency*, *47*, 496–521.

Brewster, A., Nelson, J., Hymel, K., Colby, D., Lucas, D., McCanne, R., & Milner, J. (1998). Victim, perpetrator, family and incident characteristics of 32 infant maltreatment deaths in the United States Air Force. *Child Abuse and Neglect*, *22*, 91–101.

Caron, S. (2010). Killed by its mother: Infanticide in Providence County, Rhode Island 1870–1938. *Journal of Social History*, *44*(1), 217–241.

Centers for Disease Control and Prevention. (2016). *National Vital Statistics System, National Center for Health Statistics, CDC. Office of Statistics and Programming, National Center for Injury Prevention and Control, CDC using WISQARS*. Retrieved from https://webappa.cdc.gov/sasweb/ncipc/leadcause.html

Chew, K., McCleary, R., Lew, M., & Wang, J. (1999). The epiderniology of child homicide in California, 1981 through 1990. *Homicide Studies*, *3*, 151–169.

Child Welfare Information Gateway. (2015). *Child abuse and neglect fatalities 2012: Statistics and interventions*. Washington, DC: US Department of Health and Human Services, Children's Bureau.

Christoffel, K. (1984). Homicide in childhood: A public health problem in need of attention. *American Journal of Public Health*, *74*(3), 68–70.

Clifford, J. E., Tetzlaff-Bemiller, M. J., Jarvis, J. P., Huff-Corzine, L., Weaver, G. S., & Corzine, J. (2017). Fatal factors for preschoolers: Victims, offenders, and context. *Homicide Studies*, *21*(1), 3–20.

Cohen, L., & Felson, M. (1979). Social change and crime rate trends: A routine activity approach. *American Sociological Review*, *44*, 588–608.

Crittenden, P., & Craig, S. (1990). Developmental trends in the nature of child homicide. *Journal of Interpersonal Violence*, *5*, 202–216.

Davies, K. (2005). *The Murder Book*. Upper Saddle River, NJ: Pearson Prentice Hall.

Douglas, E. M. (2013). Case, service and family characteristics of household that experience child maltreatment fatality in the United States. *Child Abuse Review*, *22*, 311–326.

Ewigman, B., Kivlahan, C., & Land, G. (1993). The Missouri child fatality study: Underreporting of maltreatment fatalities among children younger than five years of age, 1983 through 1986. *Pediatrics*, *91*, 330–337.

Federal Bureau of Investigation. (2015). *Crime in the United States: Uniform crime reports*. Washington, DC: Department of Justice. Retrieved from https://ucr.fbi.gov/crime-in-the-u.s/2015/crime-in-the-u.s.-2015/tables/expanded_homicide_data_table_9_murder_victims_by_age_by_weapon_2015.xls

Felson, M. (1995). Those who discourage crime. In J. E. Eck & D. Weisburd (Eds.), *Crime prevention studies, Vol. 4: Crime and place* (pp. 53–66). Monsey, NY: Willow Tree Press.

Finkel, N. J., Burke, J. E., & Chavez, L. J. (2000). Commonsense judgments of infanticide: Murder, manslaughter, madness, or miscellaneous. *Psychology, Public Policy, and Law* *6*(4), 1113–1137.

Friedman, S. H., Horwitz, S. M., & Resnick, P. J. (2005). Child murder by mothers: A critical analysis of the current state of knowledge and a research agenda. *American Journal of Psychiatry*, *162*, 1578–1587.

Gelles, R. (1991). Physical violence, child abuse, and child homicide: A continuum of violence, or distinct behaviors? *Human Nature*, *2*(1), 59–72.

Goetting, A. (1988). When parents kill their young children: Detroit, 1982–1986. *Journal of Family Violence*, *3*(4), 339–346.

Gottfredson, M. R., & Hirschi, T. (1990). *A general theory of crime*. Stanford, CA: Stanford University Press.

Herman-Giddens, M. E., Brown, G., Verbiest, S., Carlson, P. J., Hooten, E. G., Howell, E., & Butts, J. D. (1999). Underascertainment of child abuse mortality in the United States. *JAMA*, *282*, 463–467.

Hirschi, T., (1969). *Causes of delinquency*. Berkeley, CA: University of California Press.

Huff-Corzine, L., Corzine, J., & Moore, D. C. (1991). Deadly connections: Culture, poverty, and the direction of lethal violence. *Social Forces*, *69*, 715–732.

Jason, J., & Andereck, N. D. (1983). Fatal child abuse in Georgia: The epidemiology of severe physical child abuse. *Child Abuse and Neglect*, *7*, 1–9.

Jason, J., Gilliland, J. C., & Tyler, C. W. (1983). Homicide as a cause of pediatric mortality in the United States. *Pediatrics*, *72*, 191–197.

Jaffe, P. G., Campbell, M., Hamilton, L. H., & Juodis, M. (2012). Children in danger of domestic homicide. *Child Abuse and Neglect*, *36*, 71–74.

Klevens, J., & Leeb, R. T. (2010). Child maltreatment fatalities in children under age 5: Findings from the National Violent Death Reporting System. *Child Abuse and Neglect*, *34*, 262–266.

Lucas, D., Wezner, K., Milner, J., McCanne, T., Harris, I., Monroe-Posey, C., & Nelson, J. (2002). Victim, perpetrator, family and incident characteristics of infant and child homicide in the United States Air Force. *Child Abuse and Neglect*, *26*, 167–186.

Lagaipa, S. J. (1990). Suffer the little children: The ancient practice of infanticide as a modern moral dilemma. *Issues in Comprehensive Pediatric Nursing*, *13*, 241–251.

Levine, M., Compann, C., & Freeman, J. (1995). Maltreatment-related fatalities: Issues of policy and prevention. *Law and Policy*, *16*, 449–471.

Lyman, L., McGwin, G., Malone, D., Taylor, A., Brissie, R., Davis, G., & Rue, L. (2003). Epidemiology of child homicide in Jefferson County, Alabama. *Child Abuse* and *Neglect*, *27*, 1603–1073.

Mayhew, L. (2007). *Child death investigations: Interdisciplinary techniques from cradle to court*. Durham, NC: Carolina Academic Press.

McClain, P., Sacks, J., Ewigman, B., Smith, S., Mercy, J., & Sniezek, J. (1994). Geographic patterns of fatal abuse or neglect in children younger than 5 years old, United States, 1979 to 1988. *Archives of Pediatrics and Adolescent Medicine*, *148*, 82–86.

McClearly, R., & Chew, K. Y. (2002). Winter is the infanticide season: Seasonal risk for child homicide. *Homicide Studies*, *6*(3), 228–239.

Meyer, C. L., Oberman, M., & White, K. (2001). *Mothers who kill their children: Understanding the acts of moms from Susan Smith to the "Prom Mom."* New York, NY: New York University Press.

Murray, C. J. K., & Lopez, A. D. (1996). *The global burden of disease* (p. 576). Boston, MA: Harvard University Press.

National Council on Child Abuse and Family Violence. (2014). *Parental substance abuse a major factor in child abuse and neglect.* Retrieved from http://www.nccafv.org/parentalsubstanceabuse.htm

Overpeck, M. D. (2002). Epidemiology of infanticide. In M. Spinelli (Ed.), *Infanticide: Psychosocial and legal perspectives on mothers who kill* (pp. 3–18). Washington, DC: American Psychiatric Press.

Park, R. E., & Burgess, E. W. (1924). *Introduction to the science of sociology* (2nd ed.). Chicago, IL: University of Chicago Press.

Putkonen, H., Amonc, S., Eronena, M., Klier, C., Almirone, M., Yourstone Cederwallf, J., & Weizmann-Heneliusa, G. (2011). Gender differences in filicide offense characteristics: A comprehensive register-based study of child murder in two European countries. *Child Abuse and Neglect, 35*, 319–328.

Schnitzer, P., & Ewigman, B. (2005). Child deaths resulting from inflicted injuries: Household risk factors and perpetrator characteristics. *Pediatrics*, *116*, 687–693.

Schwartz, L. L., & Isser, N. (2007). *Child homicide: Parents who kill.* Boca Raton, FL: CRC/Taylor & Francis.

Schwartz, L. L., & Isser, N. (2000). *Endangered children: Neonaticide, infanticide, filicide*. Boca Raton, FL: CRC Press.

Shaw, C. R., & McKay, H. D. (1969 [1942]). *Juvenile delinquency and urban areas*. Chicago, IL: University of Chicago Press.

Shelton, J. L., Corey, T., Donaldson, W. H., & Dennison, E. H. (2011). Neonaticide: A comprehensive review of investigative and pathological aspects of 55 cases. *Family Violence*, *26*, 263–276.

Silverman, R., Riedel, M., & Kennedy, L. (1990). Murdered children: A comparison of racial differences across two jurisdictions. *Journal of Criminal Justice*, *18*, 401–416.

Spinelli, M. (2004). Maternal infanticide associated with mental illness: Prevention and the promise of saved lives. *American Journal of Psychiatry, 161*(9), 1–10.

Spinelli, M. (2005). Infanticide: Contrasting views. *Womens Mental Health, 8*(15), 15–24.

Strang, H. (1966). Children as victims of homicide. *Australian Institute of Criminology: Trends and Issues in Crime and Criminal Justice*, *53*, 1–6.

Resnick, P. J. (1969). Child murder by parents: A psychiatric review of filicide. *American Journal of Psychiatry*, *126*(3), 325–334.

U.S. Department of Health and Human Services, Administration for Children and Families, Administration on Children, Youth and Families, Children's Bureau. (2015). *Child maltreatment 2015*. Retrieved from https://www.acf.hhs.gov/sites/default/files/cb/cm2015.pdf#page=66

CHAPTER 2

COORDINATED COMMUNITY RESPONSE: TOWARD A MORE SYSTEMATIC RESPONSE TO DOMESTIC VIOLENCE IN AN URBAN SETTING

Denise Paquette Boots, Laura M. Gulledge, Timothy Bray and Jennifer Wareham

ABSTRACT

Purpose – *Presents metrics and policy recommendations from the Dallas Domestic Violence Task Force (DDVTF) concerning the systemic response to domestic violence (DV) within this community.*

Design/methodology/approach – *In June 2017, 47 private citizens, nonprofit, criminal justice, social service and religious organizations, and governmental officials who participated on the task force were invited via email to participate in an electronic Qualtrics survey.*

Findings – *Both general annual metrics are offered as well as detailed monthly metrics and long-term trends for shelter and advocacy providers, police, the district and city attorney's offices, and courts. In 2016–2017 alone, roughly 15,000 people were educated on DV, 246 victims were sheltered in emergency beds each night on average, roughly 8,000 victims were turned away due to lack of space, over 15,500 DV-related calls were handled by police, 11,000 county*

Homicide and Violent Crime
Sociology of Crime, Law and Deviance, Volume 23, 25–42

ISSN: 1521-6136/doi:10.1108/S1521-613620180000023003

criminal cases were filed, and 7 intimate partner homicides occurred within the city of Dallas. Policy recommendations are offered.

Originality/value – *The DDVTF annual report is one of the largest and most comprehensive reports of its kind in the United States, with over 3,000 variables collected across the partners. Now in its third reporting year, this chapter offers an overview of key findings and policy recommendations and highlights the work of this coordinated community response team.*

Keywords: Domestic violence; task force; community-coordinated response; intimate partner violence; family violence; coordinated community response team

INTRODUCTION

Domestic violence (DV) is a pervasive problem and a public health epidemic that affects millions of people across the United States regardless of race, age, gender, religion, education, or socioeconomic status. Although there is some variance in the exact definition of DV, it is generally referred to as, "the willful intimidation, physical assault, battery, sexual assault, and/or other abusive behavior as part of a systematic pattern of power and control perpetrated by one intimate partner against another" (National Coalition Against Domestic Violence (NCADV), 2015a).

Obtaining accurate prevalence rates of DV is difficult because these acts are often times hidden and underreported (Alhabib, Nur, & Jones, 2010). Nonetheless, national statistics indicate that an average of 20 people are physically abused by an intimate partner (IP) every minute. This equates to more than 10 million abuse victims annually in the United States alone (NCADV, 2015b). Indeed, DV accounts for 21% of all violent crime in the United States (Truman & Morgan, 2014). According to the National Intimate Partner and Sexual Violence Survey (NIPSVS, 2010), 1 in 3 women and 1 in 4 men have been the victim of some form of physical violence by an IP in their lifetime, and nearly 1 in 2 women and 1 in 5 men have experienced sexual victimization, other than rape, in their lifetime (Black et al., 2011).

Approximately 19% of DV involves a weapon (Truman & Morgan, 2014). However, the presence of a gun in a DV situation has been estimated to increase the risk of homicide by 500% (Campbell et al., 2003). On average nationally, 1 in 3 female murder victims and 1 in 20 male murder victims are killed by an IP (Bridges, Tatum, & Kunselman, 2008). In 2013 alone, 941 women were killed by a male IP; with most of these homicides involving a firearm (Violence Policy Center, 2015). A recent 10-city study found that one-fifth of homicide victims with temporary protective orders are murdered within two days of obtaining the order and one-third are murdered within the first month (Vittes & Sorensen, 2008).

The shattering consequences of DV can have both short- and long-term effects on these populations. The DV victimization is correlated with higher rates of depression, anxiety, low self-esteem, insomnia, social dysfunction, suicidal ideation, substance abuse, post-traumatic stress disorder symptoms, and homelessness, as well as numerous types of other health consequences and physical injuries (Anderson, Suanders, Yoshihama, Bybee, & Sullivan, 2003; Clarke & Wydall, 2013; Nathanson, Shorey, Tirone, & Rhatigan, 2012; Salazar, Wingood, DiClemente, Lang, & Harrington, 2004; Truman & Morgan, 2014). Additionally, adults are not the only victims of DV. Children who are exposed to DV are often victimized as adults themselves and develop issues with anxiety and depression (Bacchus et al., 2017; Lyon, Perilla, & Menard, 2016). Consequently, the economic costs of DV are staggering and exceed $8 billion annually (Rothman, Hathaway, Stidsen, & de Vries, 2007). It is estimated that victims of DV lose approximately eight million days of paid work each year; with 20–60% of victims losing a job due to abuse-related reasons (Rothman et al., 2007). It is evident that the effects of DV are far-reaching and include not only physical injury, but psychological trauma, economic hardship, and even death.

LITERATURE REVIEW

Without question, DV is a pervasive problem in the United States, with lifelong consequences that threaten not only individuals, but families, as well as society as a whole. Until recently, there have been limited attempts to accurately measure and analyze the full nature and scope of this vast public health and safety issue at the community level. However, the creation of task forces across the United States to address community responses to DV has improved not only research on the topic, but ways in which to better service victims and hold offenders accountable.

DV Task Forces

A DV task force is a collaborative group of organizations that can include police departments, local/district/state/US attorney's offices, courts, probation departments, corrections departments, advocacy groups, DV shelters, DV hotline or crisis centers, medical centers, batterer intervention programs, faith-based organizations, and other community and nonprofit organizations. Although DV task forces have many different names, they share goals as a coordinated community response (CCR) team toward eradicating DV, promoting education, and disseminating best practices.

For reporting purposes across these entities, data collection processes may vary considerably. For example, while some are comprehensive in scope, others may use surveys to collect data across a selective range of public, advocate groups, and shelters, while others present data from the courts, police, and private sources. Data may include types of offenses committed, number of arrests, basic data and case dispositions from local or county police departments and criminal justice offices, as well as medical and social service systems. Data are typically aggregated and cover specific time-periods. Some task forces gather primary data via interviews with victims and their relatives, as well as victims' doctors, counselors, and lawyers. The majority of task force recommendations can be broken down into the following broad areas: policy improvement, increases in the funding of programs and organizations, increases in collaboration between organizations, greater public education on DV, and improvements in the methods and efficiency with which services are delivered. In general, recommendations tend to focus on understanding the causes of DV, however, many reports lack specific recommendations for change or do not specify the organizations that should be implementing those changes.

Community Coordinated Response Movement

A major commonality among task forces is that their success hinges on collaboration, both within task force committees, and between local governments and other organizations. While collaboration across multiple agencies and organizations is often times agreed upon as an effective tool in the fight against DV, this has not always been the case. The United States has a history of using the criminalization of certain acts as a form of assistance and mediation, regardless of whether empirical evidence shows that this criminalization is effective or not. This is especially true in the case of DV (Allen et al., 2013; Kim, 2012). Historically, law enforcement agents, prosecutors, and judges have been reluctant to get involved in domestic disputes, choosing instead to let victims and perpetrators sort things out among themselves (DePrince, Belknap, Labus, Buckingham, & Gover, 2012). Victims of these crimes were generally ignored by the criminal justice system, as the system was concerned with punishing offenders and focusing on the rights of the imprisoned (Hirschel, 2012). When agents of the criminal justice system did assist victims, their main solution was typically to provide orders of protection to victims (Shorey, Tirone, & Stuart, 2014).

However, simply utilizing legal sanctions and agents within the criminal justice system is not a complete or comprehensive solution to effectively deal with the complexities of DV (Clarke & Wyndall, 2013). This disconnect between the legal system and the needs of victims of DV necessitated the development of other methods. In response to common punitive and judicial measures, some state governments use social programs to aid female victims of DV, yet, many of these programs have not been supported as effective by empirical evidence (Allen et al., 2013). More recently, CCR teams have received increased research attention, and it is likely that continued investigations will aid in efforts to effectively reduce and respond to DV (DePrince et al., 2012; Shorey et al., 2014).

Although there is not a standardized protocol for implementation (Klevens, Baker, Shelley, & Ingram, 2008), a CCR generally involves utilizing best practices in both justice and human service systems and engaging a wide range of community partners such as criminal justice, human service, business, education, and faith-based organizations to address two main goals: promote victims safety and increase offender accountability (Sullivan, 2006). Indeed, this type of approach calls for different institutions, including advocacy groups, criminal justice, child protection, and healthcare agencies, as well as vocational and educational organizations joining resources and efforts; together, this CCR team seeks justice through the criminal justice system for victims of DV and also offers coordinated strategies and resources to support survivors as they extricate themselves from dangerous relationships.

Highlighted further in the chapter, the Dallas DV Task Force (DDVTF) is a prime example of the emergence of urban-based CCRs, which brings together various agencies, nonprofits, and government offices across the DFW Metroplex with similar missions to end DV and heal victims of IP violence. The DDVTF is unique in the way that it collaboratively involves partners across the courts, policing, as well as the nonprofit sectors. Since 2015, the task force has conducted an annual survey of all members to document the response to DV across each sector of the greater Dallas community and coordinate efforts. While the scope of this work is comprehensive, the DDVTF is unique in that it has a CCR team with a collaborative, intercooperative spirit. Although it has taken time to build trust in sharing metrics for nonprofit and elected officials alike, this large urban task force has members who share a mission of serving victims of DV while simultaneously holding offenders accountable.

Texas Statistics on DV

Findings from a recent report by the Institute on Domestic Violence and Sexual Assault revealed that Texas families experienced significant levels of IP abuse (Busch-Armendariz, Heffron, & Bohman, 2011). Regarding the prevalence of DV, approximately one in three adult Texans (or a total of 5,353,434) experienced intimate partner violence (IPV) in their lifetimes and 6% were currently in an abusive relationship. Considering gender, these numbers included an estimated three million plus women and over two million men who were survivors of DV. According to the Texas Council on Family Violence (TCFV, 2016), family violence programs statewide served nearly 70,000 victims of DV and their families. However, the needs of Texans for DV services are believed to be far greater than these numbers suggest. Family violence programs received 172,573 hotline calls in 2016 (TCFV, 2016), with victims reporting multiple types of abuse including emotional/verbal abuse (92%), physical abuse (69%), and sexual abuse (8%) (The National Domestic Violence Hotline, 2016). Regarding the status of relationships that participants had with abusive partners, a majority indicated that the perpetrators were former partners, with only 20% reporting being currently involved in an abusive relationship. These statistics suggest that, contrary to popular belief, many victims leave their abusive partners. This is a potentially dangerous time for survivors, as DV homicide statistics show. In 2016 alone, 146 Texan women were murdered by their male IPs (TCFV, 2016). Of these women, 40% had ended the relationship, were separated from their partners, or were in the process of leaving when they were murdered. As these statistics convey, DV continues to be a pervasive and deadly threat to Texans.

History of DDVTF

The DDVTF was created in 1987 to investigate and monitor the city's response to DV and has maintained an active presence in the community since its inception. Comprising elected officials and representatives of law enforcement, courts, and corrections, as well as members of the nonprofit advocacy sector (including victim transportation, outreach and education, therapy, and shelter organizations), religious, and media organizations, this CCR team has established itself as the voice of DV-related community safety concerns and activism in the Dallas area. In addition to general task force, in 2013 Dallas Mayor Mike Rawlings created the DDVTF Executive Committee under the leadership of Dallas City Council member Jennifer Staubach Gates. Comprising a smaller number of key partners, these members meet quarterly to discuss emerging issues while simultaneously helping to coordinate and guide public policy responses. As part of this effort, Council member Gates was charged with gathering metrics to highlight community and government efforts in raising awareness. Toward this end, in 2014, she invited the lead author Dr Denise Paquette Boots (program head, associate professor of criminology, and senior research fellow at the Institute for Urban Policy Research (IUPR) at the University of Texas at Dallas) to join the Executive Committee and general task force to spearhead this ambitious data collection. Dr Boots and the IUPR research team consult frequently with all Executive Committee members, including the Dallas Police Department (DPD), four shelter/advocacy partners (The Family Place, Genesis Women's Shelter & Support, Mosaic Family Services, and Salvation Army), government officials from the City of Dallas Mayor's Office and Dallas City Council, the Dallas County District Attorney's (DA) Office and City of Dallas Attorney's Office, as well as misdemeanor and felony court judges.

For the inaugural reporting cycle across 2014–2015, Dr Boots met with DDVTF partners over an 18-month period to ensure reliability and rigor in collection of measures across numerous partners; these agencies and organizations voluntarily contributed significant efforts and manpower to inform each annual report. Released in October 2017, the DDVTF *Annual Summary Report: 2016–2017* builds and expands upon the previous two annual reports to provide annual and multiple-year trends related to organizational membership, activities, and a host of selective variables that are specific to each organizations' primary mission. Feedback from both general and executive committee meetings were integrated into new iterations of the survey each year to expand the metrics and illuminate emerging policy issues of interest. The survey features two main sections: a general portion already presented and the current section relaying detailed metrics from executive committee partners on the task force. Similar to previous annual reports, the 2016–2017 reporting period covers June 1, 2016 through May 31, 2017, to allow for the release of the report in October (which is DV awareness month). With 3,112 variables captured in the final data set, these data present a cumulative picture of the systemic response to DV in the community and offer a preliminary glimpse into the year-over-year changes that drive policy and criminal justice initiatives moving forward.

METHODOLOGY

In June 2017, all 64 attendees of the general DDVTF meetings (including executive committee members) were invited via email to participate in an electronic Qualtrics survey about their activities over the previous year. In total, 47 individuals (or organizational members) started the survey and 43 completed it, yielding a 68% response rate and a 91% completion rate.

The survey asked respondents for information about themselves, their organizations (if applicable), and their involvement in the DDVTF. Those respondents who indicated that they represented the interests of an organization, such as a nonprofit or government agency, were subsequently asked about their organization's employment, characteristics, mission, and purpose. Respondents whose organizations provided shelter services were asked about shelter capacity. Respondents voluntarily participated and were free to answer all, some, or none of the questions. No incentives or financial assistance in data collection were provided to respondents. To maintain integrity, missing data were not imputed, and no entries were changed from the original data entered by participants once the survey was finalized. Due to space limitations here, only select general and detailed monthly metrics are highlighted in the present chapter, however, the full 72-page report is available for viewing online (see Boots, Bray, & Galvan, 2017).

FINDINGS

General Task Force Survey Findings

A total of 26 different organizations and 2 individuals (without organizational affiliation) responded to the demographic portion of the survey. One organization represented a for-profit entity, and one was a higher education/research institution. The remaining organizations were nonprofits, offices of elected officials, and government agencies. As in previous years, nonprofits were the most common and increasing type of responding organization, representing over half of all respondents. Organizations tended to have a lengthy period of involvement on the DDVTF overall, with roughly one-third participating for 5–9 years and 18% being an active member for 10 or more years. This metric shows the continuity and sustainability of involvement on an organizational level, even across leadership changes within these organizations.

Services provided by agencies. Respondents representing agencies/organizations were asked about the services their agencies provide to victims of DV. Law enforcement grew slightly in representation of the organizations that responded when comparing this year to the last, moving from 10% to 13%. Victim services, advocacy, and counseling continued to have the largest number of organizational respondent representation, with a 20% increase compared to last year; 63% of respondents identified this service as a main function of their respective organizations. Other services provided by significant numbers of organizations include public education and outreach at 38%, emergency shelter and transitional housing support at 29%, legal representation and prosecution at 25%, victim transportation at 21%, involvement in battering intervention and prevention programs at 21%, while 8% offered job training and educational support for DV survivors.

Training and education provided. Combined, agencies conducted 548 individual training sessions (or more than 45 per month), and reached a combined 14,748 people in the Dallas-Fort Worth area. These impressive numbers suggest that task force partners are providing a high level of outreach services to victims of DV as well as using considerable efforts and resources to educate people regarding the causes, consequences, and signs of DV. Such efforts are essential to the community in battling the myths that persist regarding DV as a whole, increasing outreach to vulnerable populations, and encouraging support for victims within their neighborhoods, places of faith, schools, and workspaces.

Reported shelter capacities. All task force members who reported providing shelter services provided details about their shelter capacity for both on- and off-site shelters. *On-site shelter* refers to the capacity to house victims of DV within the facility itself. In essence, reporting organizations own and manage the facilities that provide on-site shelter. Off-site shelters make use of facilities not controlled by the serving organization. For the majority of the reporting organizations, off-site capacity refers to motel or hotel rooms that the organization reserved and paid for as needed. Capacity can further be broken down into emergency shelters and transitional housing. An emergency shelter is defined here as one that provides victims of DV with immediate and short-term shelter directly after an incident has occurred. Transitional housing is defined as service that provides long-term housing assistance to clients, as well as subsidized housing and services to rebuild clients' lives after leaving an abusive relationship. The following data represent an aggregation of five shelters that responded to the general survey and include the four executive committee shelter partners: Genesis Women's Shelter and Support, Mosaic Family Services, Salvation Army, and The Family Place, plus the general task force member Hope's Door.

These five shelters reported a total emergency capacity (for on- and off-site locations) of 116 rooms and 562 beds for victims. For these emergency housing metrics, partners allocated 87 rooms and 530 beds dedicated to women and children, with an additional 29 rooms and 32 beds for men and children. On-site transitional housing showed capacities of 99 rooms and 225 beds for women and children (or a 43% increase from 2015 to 2016), plus five rooms and 10 beds for male victims and their children.

Restrictions to service. For a host of reasons, organizations may place various restrictions on the types of clients they will accept for service. Some organizations face limits imposed by their use of federal funding, while others enforce restrictions on client acceptance due to private funding, their internal bylaws or board oversight requirements, or potential liabilities to minimize risk to the populations they serve. For shelter referral organizations (who assist in finding beds for victims and their children), partners reported that key barriers to victim placement included having an older male child or custody of a large number of minor children. Other barriers to placement are lack of English fluency, having a pet, criminal history restrictions, being disabled or having special needs, and taking prescription medication not allowed by the shelter. All replying shelters reported having some restrictions on the clients they assist, and most of the restrictions were similar to those reported by the referral agencies. These included restrictions for victims who have active drug use or drug dependency, having older children, not being able to house male victims, restrictions barring placement for individuals with serious medical conditions, severe physical or emotional disabilities, and a lack of available translation services.

A Detailed Analysis of Agency Metrics

As stated previously, the executive committee members agreed to provide monthly data across a large number of key variables, thereby permitting a more detailed inspection of monthly trends and across reporting years. Shelters, DPD, the Dallas County DA, the Dallas City Attorney, Dallas courts, and City of Dallas elected officials provided data for the 2016–2017 annual report.

Shelters. The shelter metrics provide detailed monthly information from four nonprofit organizations in Dallas: Genesis Women's Shelter & Support, Mosaic Family Services, Salvation Army, and The Family Place. The majority of the victims assisted by the four shelters were women and children, which is a demographic group that historically tends to have higher needs for shelter (NCADV, 2016). Note that only four shelter partners report in this section, rather than the five who reported data for the general survey portion of this report. Therefore, these metrics cannot be combined or compared to the general task force metrics presented earlier.

Reported capacity of emergency and transitional beds and rooms. For the reporting period between June 1, 2016 and May 31, 2017, the total emergency shelter capacity for both on- and off-site was 60 rooms and 229 beds. Of these emergency shelter assets, 55 rooms and 221 beds were dedicated to female victims and their children, plus another five rooms and eight beds for men and children. The four shelters also reported a total of 63 rooms and 219 beds for transitional housing, including both on- and off-site. These transitional totals included 58 rooms and 203 beds for women and children and five rooms and 10 beds for men and children.

In last year's report, the executive committee shelter partners reported dedicated rooms and beds for male victims and their children in only off-site emergency shelters. Men and children had rooms and beds available in both on- and off-site emergency shelters as well as on-site transitional housing in 2016–2017. No shelter partners reported capacity for adult male victims or their children in off-site transitional housing this report cycle. A significant increase in services appears when comparing transitional housing numbers between 2015–2016 and 2016–2017. Specifically, on-site transitional housing for women and children increased from 163 beds in 2015–2016 to 203 beds in 2016–2017, or a 25% increase. In 2016–2017, no female victims were housed in off-site transitional housing. In the coming year, the level of service for adult male victims and their children will be dramatically impacted due to the opening of a new shelter by The Family Place. On May 8, 2017 (at the end of the reporting cycle), The Family Place opened the first shelter for male victims of DV in Texas. With 20 beds, it offers on-site emergency housing for men and their children of any age, which meets a critical need within the community.

Unserved due to lack of space. From June 2016 to May 2017, the executive committee shelter partners turned away a total of 7,950 women, children, and men due to a lack of space. This figure represents a 22% decrease from the previous reporting period, which saw 10,154 clients unserved due to space, but slightly higher than the 7,567 reported in 2014–2015. While the numbers for total unserved victims due to lack of space were lower in the 2016–2017 reporting cycle, the reasons behind this decrease or the sustainability of this trend in the number of victims unserved are unknown. This departure from previous years may be the result of an expansion in facility sizes, thereby allowing for more victim services, and thus decreasing the number of victims turned away. Alternatively, it has been posited that at-risk populations such as undocumented victims are afraid to seek services and may be impacting numbers of victims seeking assistance from shelter partners.

Average monthly capacity. Overall, the 2016–2017 reporting period experienced an average capacity utilization of 97%, representing a small increase from the previous reporting period. From November 2016 to May 2017, the shelters remained closer to full capacity than in the previous two years. Across all three reporting years, shelter capacity remains close to 100% in November and December. In totality, the demand continues to exceed the capacity of beds and rooms available; this is evidenced by the number of unserved victims who could not find placement.

Average nightly emergency population. The average monthly number of victims in emergency shelters was 246 in the 2016–2017 reporting cycle. This represented a robust 37% increase from the previous year by an average of 67 additional victims per month (with 179 victims in emergency shelters monthly), and an increase of 94 more victims placed in emergency shelters per month (or 61%) compared to 2014–2015. It should be noted that beds can turn over many times within a monthly period, so it is possible that more clients could be served in a month than the shelter partners show as the available bed count.

Average nightly transitional populations. In addition to providing emergency shelter for victims, several shelters also provided transitional housing services. Transitional services included long-term housing, job training, financial education, and counseling support for victims, all aimed at helping them to reenter their normal lives and preventing homelessness. Transitional housing victims are frequently long-term clients, with services provided from several months to years, depending on the unique needs of the victim and the capacity of the provider. The average monthly number of victims in transitional housing for 2016–2017 was 162, or a 10% decrease from the previous reporting year by an average of 17 victims a month.

Police response. Over the past three years, the DPD has provided detailed metrics to the DDVTF and has been an invaluable member. For the 2016–2017 reporting cycle, DPD provided detailed monthly metrics on the following items: (a) numbers of reported offenses determined to be DV related; (b) DV arrests, with a breakdown between misdemeanor and felony offenses; (c) family violence cases filed; (d) protective order violation offenses; and (e) family violence and IP murders, some of which are reported here in detail.

DV offenses, arrests, and case filings. Over the past three years, the number of reported offenses determined to be related to DV have gradually increased. Between June 1, 2016 and May 31, 2017, alone, DPD determined that 15,566 calls were DV-related, which represented a roughly 3% increase from the 15,124 calls reported in the previous reporting year. These calls include Class C misdemeanors and miscellaneous incident reports, which are calls involving DV but that do not result in a DV incident report.

Case filings. DPD filed 11,371 family violence cases over the past three years. The number of cases filed in 2016–2017 accounted for the lowest yearly total for any of the years that the annual report has summarized metrics, with 3,527 cases filed. After a 5% increase from 2014–2015 to 2015–2016, there was a 12% decrease between 2015–2016 numbers and those reported in 2016–2017. Court orders of protection, commonly called protection orders, are documents that legally restrict the behavior of known or suspected DV perpetrators. The provisions of these orders may include limitations to communication, distance to be maintained from the victim, and other stipulations specific to the case. Since 2014, DPD reported 538 protective order violations, 211 of which occurred during the 2016–2017 reporting period. This represents a 19% increase from the 178 violations reported during 2015–2016 and a 41% increase compared to the 149 violations reported during the 2014–2015 reporting period.

Misdemeanor arrests. Overall, there has been a slight but gradual decrease in the number of misdemeanor DV arrests reported by DPD. During the previous three years, DPD made 17,305 arrests on misdemeanor DV charges. In 2016–2017 there were 5,601 misdemeanor DV arrests, which is 164 fewer arrests (or a 3% decrease) from the 2015–2016. DPD leadership noted that this decline in arrests overall may be partially due to a decrease in patrol officers, which in turn has led to an increase in response times and opportunities for offenders to leave the location. As such, more suspects may become at-large, making these cases difficult to file, especially if the officers were unable to reach the victim to verify facts.

Felony arrests. Overall, there has been a decreasing trend in felony arrests as well. However, when considering the annual 2016–2017 data, the reported 1,545 arrests represented a 6% increase from the previous year's 1,458 felony arrests. Over the three-year period, DPD has reported 4,668 felony DV arrests. Monthly, DPD makes between 500 and 700 arrests for misdemeanor and felony DV. This figure translates to more than 16 DV-related arrests each day of the year.

Lethality reduction program. In 2012, DPD received a grant to implement the DV lethality assessment developed by the Maryland Model (Maryland Network Against Domestic Violence, 2017). The instrument assesses the likelihood of lethal violence based on 11 protective factors, and is an evidence-based instrument considered a best practice for increasing victim safety and preventing IP homicides. These lethality assessments represent a critical tool for DPD in reducing the likelihood of domestic homicides and identifying high-risk cases within the community once they are reported to police. DPD has conducted 13,213 lethality assessments since first providing data on this metric in 2015–2016. In 2016–2017 alone, DPD conducted 6,052 lethality assessments, which is down 15% from 2015–2016.

Using data indicators from the lethality assessment tool, DPD seeks to identify DV victims who are at higher risk for lethal violence. They subsequently follow up with these victims by conducting a home visit where they can assess safety, discuss the facts of the case, and offer information on community resources to these victims, if needed. During the 2016–2017 reporting cycle, DPD attempted 338 home visits or contacts, which is a 19% decrease from 2015–2016 (418). However, the 161 home visit contacts completed by the DV unit represent a 58% increase over the previous year (102). In fact, the percentage of home visits that resulted in a successful victim contact nearly doubled over these two years, rising from just 24% in 2015–2016 to 47% in 2016–2017. This dramatic rise in completed home visits is indicative of greater efficiency in the unit, despite significant shortages in personnel, when compared to the previous year. As these high-risk victims are thought to be in the greatest danger of lethality from their abuser, this is a significant finding and one that merits praise for DPD's efforts.

Family violence and IP homicides. It should be noted that within this chapter, family violence murders comprise *all* family-involved murders, not just those committed by former or current IPs. Since June 1, 2014 through May 31, 2017, 52 family violence murders have occurred within the city of Dallas. Within this larger number, 24 of these were deemed to be IP homicides in Dallas over same three-year period (with 11, six, and seven IP murders annually, respectively).

Of the 16 family violence murders reported by DPD in 2016–2017, almost half (seven, or 44%) involved IPs. With 11 intimate homicides recorded in Dallas in 2014–2015 (the highest year since metrics were reported in annual reports), the 2016–2017 figure of seven victims represented a 36% drop. Fig. 1 presents a schematic characteristics of the seven IP homicide offenses committed between June 1, 2016 and May 31, 2017. Contrary to the national data on IP homicides, which shows that most domestic homicides overwhelmingly involve male offenders killing female victims, four of the seven homicides (or 57%) involved female killers. Three of these male victims were Black and one was White; three males were killed by their girlfriends, while one male victim was killed by his wife. In the remaining three cases, the killers were male. The White female victim was killed by her husband, while the two African American female victims were killed by boyfriends.

Table 1 presents the demographic characteristics across the combined 24 offenses involving IP homicide victims and offenders in Dallas. When considering multi-year trends, some interesting similarities and differences emerged. The average age of the victims rose from 39 to 44 from 2014–2015 to 2015–2016 before

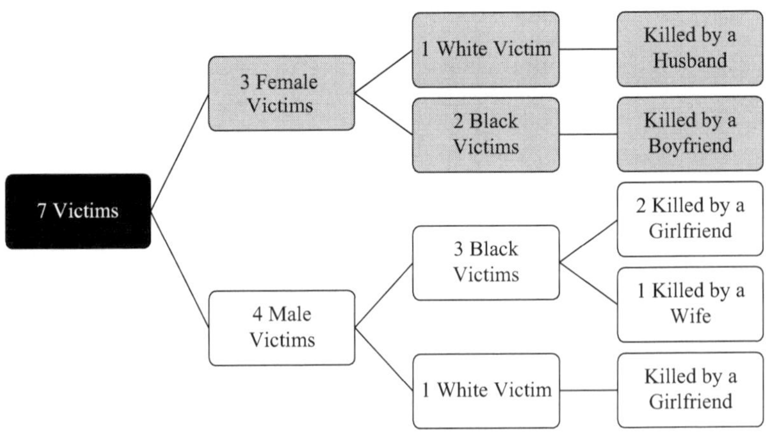

Fig. 1. IP Homicide Characteristics, DPD, 2016–2017.

Table 1. Demographic Characteristics of IP Homicide Victims and Offenders, City of Dallas, 2014–2017.

Demographic Characteristics	2014–2015	2015–2016	2016–2017
Total offenses	11	6	7
Victim demographics:			
Average age	39	44	40
Black	45%	67%	71%
Latino/a	36%	17%	0%
White	18%	17%	29%
Male	18%	17%	57%
Female	82%	83%	43%
Average number of prior victimizations	0.2	0.5	0.8
Offender demographics:			
Average age	40	46	41
Black	64%	67%	71%
Latino/a	36%	17%	14%
White	0%	17%	14%
Male	82%	83%	43%
Female	18%	17%	57%
Average prior offenses	11.0	7.5	11.0

falling again to 40 in 2016–2017. Black and Latino/a victims continue to be overrepresented as IP homicide victims, with Blacks accounting for 45%, 67%, and 71%, respectively, of all victims across the three reporting periods. As expected, and keeping with national statistics on these crimes, females account for the vast majority of victims (at over 80% each), except in 2016–2017 when they were 43% of all victims. As the total sample size is quite small with only seven offenses, these data should be interpreted with caution. Prior victimizations also rose each consecutive year for victims, from an average of 0.2 in 2014–2015 to 0.8 in 2016–2017. Regarding offender demographics, the average IP killer was in his or her early- to mid-40s. These offenders were predominately Black (followed by Latino/a) and male; an anomaly again was in reporting year 2016–2017 when only 43% of IP killers were male.

In assessing where offenses occurred by reporting period, in keeping with prior research, victims were overwhelmingly targeted at their place of residence (75% of all victimizations), with 42% and 25% of all IP homicides occurring in apartments or single-family homes across the three-year period. When breaking down IP homicides by sex of the victim and weapon type (for the 20 IP homicides for which weapon type could be determined), firearms were the weapon of choice for most IP killers, with 65% using this weapon. Knives, used in 20% of these murders, were the second most common weapon. Interesting variation can be seen by gender. Female victims were far more likely than males to be killed by firearm (85% compared to 29%). For male victims, the weapon use shows much more variance, with no single weapon type predominant. Additionally, regarding the presence of witnesses to these IP homicides, for the 22 IP homicides for which the presence or absence of witnesses could be established between 2014 and 2017, victims were killed without witnesses present in over three-quarters of

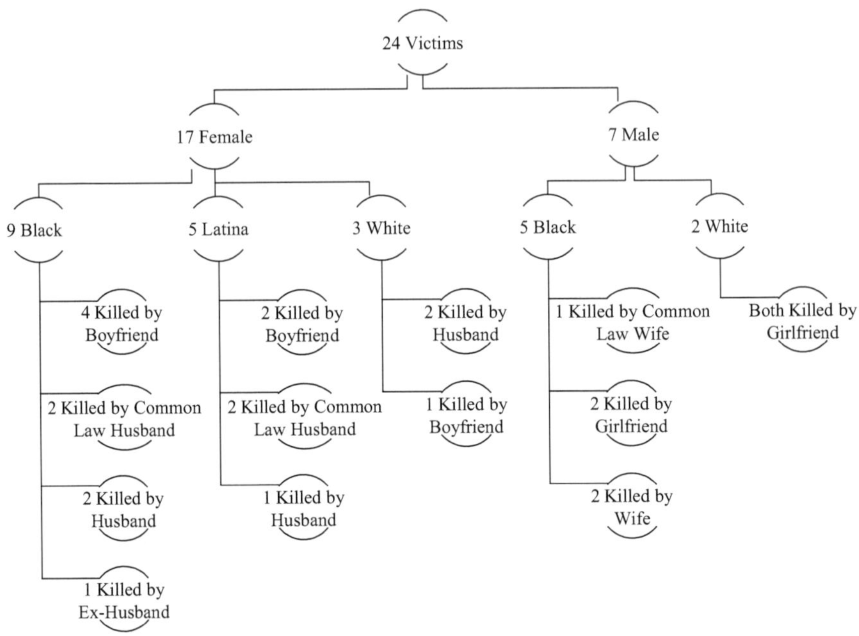

Fig. 2. IP Homicide Victims Characteristics, DPD, 2016–2017.

these murders. In roughly one out of four cases, one or more persons witnessed the homicide.

Finally, Fig. 2 offers a comprehensive, detailed schematic overview of all 24 IP homicides and their characteristics between June 2014 and May 2017. In this three-year period, there were 17 females and seven male victims; proportionately, more than two-thirds of all these victims were females (71%). Of these 17 female IP homicide victims, nine were Black, five were Latina, and three were White; 82% were non-White victims and show an overrepresentation of people of color as DV homicide victims. All 17 of these female homicide victims were killed by a *current* husband, common-law husband, or boyfriend. Of the seven males killed by IPs in the city of Dallas over the three years, five were Black, and two were White.

Prosecution. Two different prosecutorial entities handle prosecution of DV cases in the city of Dallas. The Dallas County DA's office prosecutes defendants charged with any offense that is a Class B misdemeanor or higher. When police are unable to secure sufficient evidence to file at least a Class B misdemeanor, DPD has the option to file a Class C misdemeanor with the Dallas City Attorney's Office. This office handles all lower-level misdemeanors and citations via prosecutions in the Dallas Municipal Court System. From June 2016 to May 2017, 4,023 Class C misdemeanor family violence cases were received by the Municipal Court System, which is roughly the same as the 4,065 cases received the previous year.

Dallas County DA. The Dallas County DA reported receiving 2,986 misdemeanor DV cases during the 2016–2017 program year, an increase of 7% from the previous year. On average, the DA received 241 cases per month from 2014 to 2017. Overall, 392 cases were rejected in 2016–2017, an increase of 84% from the previous year.

For 2016–2017, an average of 247 family violence cases were received monthly. The total number of felony family violence cases received in 2016–2017 was 2,966, which represented a 12% increase over the 2,643 cases received in the previous year. The metric involves only IP violence cases, and excludes other forms of family violence committed by siblings, parents, or other relatives. In 2016–2017, the DA office also rejected 90 family violence cases, compared to 107 in 2015–2016 and 105 in 2014–2015. This represents a reduction of 15% between 2015–2016 and 2016–2017. On average, the DA rejected eight felony family violence cases per month in 2016–2017, compared to nine in both of the previous two years of annual reporting. Of the total number of felony family violence cases received by the Dallas County DA's office, attorneys presented 92% of these cases to the grand jury. As a result, 2,196 (74% or roughly three-quarters) were indicted, while the grand jury returned no-true bill for 528 cases (18%). The outstanding percentage of these cases (a) were received as felony but reduced to misdemeanors, (b) were rejected by the DA's office, or (c) were returned to the originating law enforcement agency for more investigation. These figures reflect a gradual increase in indictments and a gradual decrease in no bills.

The DA's office also reported data regarding orders of protection, including the number of order petitions that were granted, withdrawn, dismissed, and denied. In 2016–2017, Dallas County judges granted 544 orders of protection, dismissed 56 requests, and denied 25. A total of 70 defendants withdrew their petition before hearing. This figure represents a 36% increase in the number of orders granted over the previous year and a 37% decrease in dismissals. In an effort to make protective services more accessible to victims in need, the office has recently expanded services to 11 satellite offices throughout the county. This expansion may be a driver of the increase in granted orders of protection and decrease in dismissals and is a significant form of community outreach, especially to victims with limited financial resources and transportation.

Dallas Courts. The courts continue to play a critical role in Dallas's systemic response to DV. In 2014, Judge Rick Magnis (now retired) established the Dallas County Felony Domestic Violence Court (FDVC) to promote victim and community safety by increasing the court's monitoring of offenders assessed to be of high risk of lethal violence, who have been placed on probation due to felony offenses against domestic partners. Overall, the FDVC program aims to increase accountability for these offenders while also providing opportunities for prosocial change through cognitive behavioral intervention in areas of need. Between June 1, 2016 and May 31, 2017, the FDVC program conducted 313 forensic DV assessments and recommended 137 participants to presiding Judge Brandon Birmingham's FDVC program from the court of original jurisdiction. A total of 36 new participants joined the court during this period and 27 offenders successfully graduated. A total of 24 FDVC participants were revoked in 2016–2017, with sentencing sanctions ranging from 6 months to 20 years in prison.

Additionally, County Court 10 Judge Roberto Cañas continues to oversee and coordinate the Dallas County Gun Surrender Program. Formally established in

May 2015, the program seeks to collect guns from convicted DV offenders; these offenders are ineligible per federal law for life from owning a firearm, while Texas law prohibits offenders from possessing them for five years. As of May 2016, the Gun Surrender Program has collected roughly 60 guns in coordination with the Dallas County Sheriff's Office over the two years of the program (see Choi, Elkin, Harasim, & Nanasi, 2017, for more information).

POLICY IMPLICATIONS AND CONCLUSION

The members of the DDVTF offered qualitative data on the annual survey regarding policy implications and suggested changes that would advance their work in preventing and ameliorating DV. Of particular importance to respondents were vulnerable populations and transportation. Current immigration laws and pervasive anti-immigrant sentiments have left immigrant women, who are in abusive relationships, more fearful than ever of seeking and receiving services. Respondents also suggested providing culturally relevant resources in multiple languages and increasing education campaigns that reinforce protection for victims regardless of victims' legal status. Similarly, the sector continues to struggle in meeting the needs of lesbian, gay, bisexual, transgender, queer (LGBTQ) victims. Task force members have suggested targeted recruitment within the LGBTQ community to encourage engagement of allies within this population; such an effort might help identify the particular needs facing LGBTQ victims. Agencies also reported barriers to victims who are pressing charges and/or participating in the legal process, with still more need for transportation services and resources to fund victims getting to court. Solutions offered included increasing access to low-to-no cost public transportation by providing victims with a verbal password to which public transportation operators were trained to respond, or alternatively by creating a database of transportation resources to assist victims.

Overall, respondents cited specific needs to strengthen and expand programs that support victim safety and assist in healing survivors after trauma. As many offenders continue to perpetuate their abuse on victims, identifying these offenders and protecting the safety of DV survivors is a top issue. With regard to the FDVC and the Dallas County Gun Surrender Program, Dallas continues to promote and support progressive programs and initiatives and be a national leader in the fight against DV. As noted previously, the Gun Surrender Program seeks to confiscate guns per statutory requirements from persons convicted of DV charges; it is the first of its kind in Dallas and one of the few in existence nationally. Yet, this program needs more active participation and referrals from judges to ensure victim safety. Promoting healing and healthy families after surviving abuse is also a top priority. Some shelters have placed increased emphasis on rules reduction and trauma-informed care training and practices toward this end. As has been reported in previous reports, there is not enough transitional housing available to support all victims and children requesting this level of long-term support. While needs change often, making it difficult to anticipate the beds and rooms needed, partners clearly voiced an ongoing and serious shortage of beds. There is also a need to reprioritize DV transitional housing in funding allocations. Finally, several partners pointed toward the need for policies and practices that have more survivor-centered versus program-centered goals and outcomes.

In conclusion, the DDVTF partners serve in differing capacities and with varying missions, yet share a joint goal of helping victims to heal and holding abusers accountable. The annual report continues to grow each year in size, content, and value due to the joint efforts of these members. The DDVTF Annual Report is one of the most comprehensive DV reports in the nation and reflects the significant and ongoing contributions of this dedicated CCR team.

ACKNOWLEDGMENTS

The authors wish to thank the generous donors who made this report possible: the Communities Foundation of Texas the Dallas Women's Foundation, Mary Kay, Verizon Corporation, and the Embrey Family Foundation.

REFERENCES

Alhabib, S., Nur, U., & Jones, R. (2010). DV against women: Systematic review of prevalence studies. *Journal of Family Violence*, *25*(4), 369–382.

Allen, N. E., Todd, N. R., Anderson, C. J., Davis, S. M., Javdani, S., Bruehler, V., & Dorsey, H. (2013). Council-based approaches to intimate partner violence: Evidence for distal change in the system response. *American Journal of Community Psychology*, *52*(1–2), 1–12.

Anderson, D. K., Saunders, D. G., Yoshihama, M., Bybee, D. I., & Sullivan, C. M. (2003). Long-term trends in depression among women separated from abusive partners. *Violence against Women*, *9*(7), 807–838.

Bacchus, L. J., Colombini, M., Contreras Urbina, M., Howarth, E., Gardner, F., Annan, J., & Watts, C. (2017). Exploring opportunities for coordinated responses to intimate partner violence and child maltreatment in low and middle income countries: A scoping review. *Psychology, Health, and Medicine*, *22*(1), 135–165.

Black, M. C., Basile, K. C., Breiding, M. J., Smith, S. G., Walters, M. L., Merrick, M. T., … Stevens, M. R. (2011). *The National Intimate Partner and Sexual Violence Survey (NIPSVS): 2010 summary report*. National Center for Injury Prevention and Control, Centers for Disease Control and Prevention, Atlanta, GA.

Boots, D. P., Bray, T. M., & Galvan, A. (2017). *Dallas Domestic Violence Task Force annual summary report: 2016–2017*. Institute for Urban Policy Research, University of Texas at Dallas, Richardson, TX. Retrieved from http://dallascityhall.com/government/citycouncil/district13/dvtf/Documents/2016-2017%20Annual%20Summary%20Report%20on%20Domestic%20Violence.pdf

Bridges, F. S., Tatum, K. M., & Kunselman, J. C. (2008). DV statutes and rates of intimate partner and family homicide: A research note. *Criminal Justice Policy Review*, *19*(1), 117–130.

Busch-Armendariz, N. B., Heffron, L., & Bohman, T. (2011). *Statewide prevalence of intimate partner violence in Texas*. Institute on Domestic Violence and Sexual Assault, University of Texas at Austin, Austin, TX.

Campbell, J. C., Webster, D., Koziol-McLain, J., Block, C., Campbell, D., Curry, M. A., … Lauphon, K. (2003). Risk factors for femicide in abusive relationships: Results from a multisite case control study. *American Journal of Public Health*, *93*(7), 1089–1097.

Choi, L., Elkin, R., Harasim, M., & Nanasi, N. (2017). *Taking aim at family violence: A report on the Dallas County Gun Surrender Program*. Retrieved from http://law.smu.edu/Media/Clinics/Hunter%20Legal%20Center/2599-GunSurrender-LowRes.pdf

Clarke, A., & Wydall, S. (2013). 'Making Safe': A coordinated community response to empowering victims and tackling perpetrators of domestic violence. *Social Policy and Society*, *12*(3), 393–406.

DePrince, A. P., Belknap, J., Labus, J. S., Buckingham, S. E., & Gover, A. R. (2012). The impact of victim-focused outreach on criminal legal system outcomes following police-reported intimate partner abuse. *Violence Against Women*, *18*(8), 861–881.

Hirschel, D. (2012). The benefits of more "victim focused" coordinated community responses to intimate partner violence: A critique of "The impact of victim-focused outreach on criminal legal system outcomes following police-reported intimate partner abuse," by DePrince, Belknap, Labus, Buckingham, and Gover. *Violence against Women, 18*(8), 893–901.

Kim, M. E. (2012). Challenging the pursuit of criminalization in an era of mass incarceration: The limitations of social work responses to domestic violence in the USA. *British Journal of Social Work*, *43*(7), 1–18.

Klevens, J., Baker, C. K., Shelley, G. A., & Ingram, E. M. (2008). Exploring the links between components of coordinated community responses and their impact on contact with intimate partner violence services. *Violence Against Women*, *14*(3), 346–358.

Lyon, E., Perilla, J., & Menard, A. (2016). Developing outcome measures for domestic violence programs' work with children and youth. *Family Violence Prevention & Services Program,* 1–13.

Maryland Network Against Domestic Violence. (2017). *Lethality assessment program for first responders.* Retrieved from http://www.bwjp.org/resource-center/resource-results/maryland-s-lethality-assessment-programs.html

Nathanson, A. M., Shorey, R. C., Tirone, V., & Rhatigan, D. L. (2012). The prevalence of mental health disorders in a community sample of female victims of intimate partner violence. *Partner Abuse*, *3*(1), 59.

National Center for Injury Prevention and Control. (2010). *National Intimate Partner and Sexual Violence Survey – 2010 summary report.* Retrieved from https://www.cdc.gov/violence prevention/pdf/NISVS_Report2010-a.pdf

National Coalition Against Domestic Violence. (2015a). *Domestic Violence National Statistics.* Retrieved from https://ncadv.org/assets/2497/domestic_violence.pdf

National Coalition Against Domestic Violence. (2015b). *Facts about domestic violence and physical abuse.* Retrieved from https://ncadv.org/assets/2497/domestic_violence_and_ physical _abuse_ncadv.pdf

National Domestic Violence Hotline. (2016). *Texas state report.* Retrieved from http://tcfv.org/resource-center/learn-the-facts/

Rothman, E., Hathaway, J., Stidsen, A., & de Vries, H. (2007). How employment helps female victims of intimate partner abuse: A qualitative study. *Journal of Occupational Health Psychology*, *12*(2), 136–143.

Salazar, L. F., Wingood, G. M., DiClemente, R. J., Lang, D. L., & Harrington, K. (2004). The role of social support in the psychological well-being of African American girls who experience dating violence victimization. *Violence and Victims*, *19*(2), 171–187.

Shorey, R. C., Tirone, V., & Stuart, G. L. (2014). Coordinated community response components for victims of intimate partner violence: A review of the literature. *Aggression and Violent Behavior*, *19*, 363–371.

Sullivan, C. M. (2006). Interventions to address intimate partner violence: The current state of the field. In J. R. Lutzker (Ed.), *Preventing violence: Research and evidence-based intervention strategies* (pp. 195–212). Washington, D.C.: American Psychological Association.

Texas Council on Family Violence (TCFV). (2016). *Learn the facts*. Retrieved from http://tcfv.org/resource-center/learn-the-facts/

Truman, J. L., & Morgan, R. E. (2014). *Nonfatal domestic violence, 2003–2012*. Retrieved from http://www.bjs.gov/content/pub/pdf/ndv0312.pdf

Violence Policy Center. (2015). *When men murder women: An analysis of 2013 homicide data*. Retrieved from http://www.vpc.org/studies/wmmw2015.pdf

Vittes, K. A., & Sorenson, S. B. (2008). Restraining orders among victims of intimate partner homicide. *Injury Prevention*, *14*(1), 191–195.

CHAPTER 3

FEMINIST PATHWAYS AND FEMALE HOMICIDE OFFENDERS

Alesa Liles and Stacy Moak

ABSTRACT

Purpose – *The purpose of this chapter is to highlight recent research addressing theories of female offending and the context of female perpetrated homicides. Women have often been omitted in research and theory development, thus gendered interventions and treatments lag behind. Additionally, female perpetrated homicides are rare, consequently research examining the context of the events and the events leading up to the homicide are inadequate.*

Design/methodology/approach – *The approach is to examine the historical research on female offenders, the context of female violent offenses particularly homicide offenses, and emerging theories of gendered experiences into criminal activities for women.*

Findings – *Findings indicate that gender matters when explaining theories of female offending and when examining the context of female perpetrated homicides.*

Originality/value – *Females have different life events from males, and these life events create distinct pathways into criminal offending, including the ultimate offense of homicide. Based on these differences, theory development as well as intervention and prevention strategies must be designed that are gender specific.*

Keywords: Female offenders; homicide; feminist theory; pathways to criminality; gender; life events

Homicide and Violent Crime
Sociology of Crime, Law and Deviance, Volume 23, 43–60

ISSN: 1521-6136/doi:10.1108/S1521-613620180000023004

INTRODUCTION

Criminological research has historically given low priority to the role of gender and the experiences created by gender as a source of criminality (Belknap & Holsinger, 2006). Although research on female perpetrated offenses has grown in the past few decades, the criminal justice system has remained inadequate in addressing and responding to the needs of these women once introduced into the system (Holsinger, 2000). With most research in criminology focused on males, female offenders are often disregarded completely or treated as a footnote in criminological research (Klein, 1973; Sondheimer, 2001). These gender-blind strategies of female offending fail "to capture the full nature of delinquency in America; and, more to the point, are woefully inadequate when it comes to explaining female misbehavior and official reactions" (Chesney-Lind, 1989, p. 6).

Traditionally, female offenders were viewed as immoral or indecent and offenses were only committed by women who were evil or "wicked" (Lombroso & Ferrero, 1909, p. 125). These women were perceived as conniving and depicted as deliberately committing offenses because they lacked the social controls of "normal" women (Lombroso & Ferrero, 1909, p. 125). These women were said to have more in common with males than "her normal sister" (p. 125). The assumptions attributed female criminal behavior to an "inherent nature" and disregarded any other explanation, such as social or environmental factors (Klein, 1973, p. 4).

As criminological research with women progressed, social and environmental factors began to emerge as contributing influences on female criminal behavior (Bonger, 1916; Glueck & Glueck, 1934). Bonger (1916) argued that women were often protected from lives of crime because their role in society was primarily limited to the domestic context. When Glueck and Glueck (1934), analyzed the lives of women, they found that the women's backgrounds were significantly related to their criminal behavior and could produce situations amenable to criminality. This led some to predict that the changing social climate advancing the status of women in society between the 1940s and the 1960s would have a profound effect on the nature of female offending (Alder & Simon, 1979; Pollak, 1961).

As criminologists studied the types of crimes in which women were involved, and the life circumstances of women, it was found that their offending patterns did not simply mimic those of male offenders (Shover, Norland, James, & Thornton, 1979). Their life experiences shape both the proclivity to deviate from the norm, as well as the types of crimes in which women may become involved. Scholars began to specifically examine these gendered experiences of women to better understand the extent to which they contribute to patterns of female offending (Daly, 1992; Simpson, 1989; Simpson, Yahner, & Dugan, 2008). These works have continued to build a body of research focused on the specific life circumstances of women as it relates to female criminality. Additionally, many of the early theories of female criminality have been abandoned in favor of more comprehensive theories that are not based on males as the base measure, but instead elaborate on the female condition (Broidy & Cauffman, 2006; Simpson et al., 2008).

HISTORICAL VIEWS OF FEMALE CRIMINALITY

Early criminological research limited female criminality to witchcraft, adultery, and other similar moral or decency crimes, most of which were specifically related to gender stereotypes of the time (Klein, 1973). As society progressed, female criminal behavior became synonymous with prostitution, shoplifting, and homicide of intimate partners, particularly husbands or boyfriends. Because women were expected to uphold socially accepted roles of the wife and mother:

> [...] it has been the traditional opinion of criminologists that women commit relatively few crimes and that when they do so they somehow betray their womanhood by venturing out into a reserve of men. (Pollak, 1961, p. 149)

This idea was perpetuated by the research of Cesare Lombroso in the 1800s.

Lombroso became one of the first criminologists to study female criminality. With Ferrero (1920), he physically analyzed the post-mortem bodies of female offenders. They concluded that these "fallen women" had small cranial capacities, larger jaws, "hollowed out noses," with protruding cheek bones and ears (p. 21). They stated these women were more similar to criminal and noncriminal males than other women and alleged that criminal women deliberately committed crimes out of vengeance. These women premeditated longer than their male counterparts and their offenses were so cold and calculated that the crime was "executed with an ability and a gloating which in the deed of pure passion are psychologically impossible" (Lombroso & Ferrero, 1920, p. 308).

By 1916, Bonger began to study female perpetrated offenses and he stated that the levels of female criminality could be explained by her place in society. Bonger alleged that women were typically protected from negative influences due to the sheltered nature of their lives, particularly women in higher social classes. His findings were one of the first to allege women's criminal behavior could be attributed to their social environment, rather than inherent or physical qualities.

When the Gluecks began an inquiry into the lives of females incarcerated in Massachusetts, they followed Bonger's notion that female criminality may be based on social factors rather than physical characteristics (Glueck & Glueck, 1934). They analyzed the social environment of women convicted of offenses such as larceny, breaking and entering, adultery, prostitution, and murder. The sociological factors included family background, socioeconomic status, mental health, education, employment, marital history, arrest history, and recreational activities (Glueck & Glueck, 1934). These data were among the first of their kind regarding the background of female offenders and the nature of female criminality. They found the women's social environments were significantly related to their criminal behavior. Although the study was groundbreaking, it was not until years later when the incidences of female crime increased and crossed the bounds of gender norms that female offending began to pique the interest of the scientific community and the media.

Many began to predict that with increased societal change, female criminality would rise (Adler & Simon, 1979; Pollak, 1961). By the 1940s, American women had moved into the jobs vacated by men during World War II. This workforce transition coincided with an increase in criminal behavior. Adler and Simon (1979) found that crime rates for women during the 1940s almost doubled, but after the war was over, crime rates for women declined. When the 1960s arrived, another time of societal change, there was again an increase in female criminality. Widespread movements for social justice, not only afforded women legitimate opportunities, but also increased the availability of illegitimate opportunities in the criminal arena. During this time, research directed at female criminality emerged, thus a feminist perspective of criminology was developed (Proctor, 2004). This new research sought to incorporate females in study designs and developed gender-specific theories to bring female offending to the forefront of criminology.

Out of the feminist perspective, four theories were developed to understand female criminal behavior: masculinity theory, opportunity theory, economic marginalization theory, and chivalry theory (Small, 2000). First, the masculinity theory was associated with the women's liberation movement and stated that the liberation of women created a masculinization in their behavior and offending patterns. Adler, Adler, and Levins (1975) hypothesized that when feminine roles become relaxed, females with less feminine role expectations had more opportunities to participate in delinquent activities (Shover et al., 1979). Those who examined female criminality from this perspective found that data may not necessarily support women becoming more masculine as the cause of increased criminal activity; however, those with less feminine traits may be more aggressive and have a higher likelihood of committing crime (Cullen et al., 1979; Shover et al., 1979).

Opportunity theory, developed by Simon (1975), stated that the increase in social and economic opportunities also increased opportunities for criminal behavior. The traditional male masculine gender roles had allowed men to engage in crime because society did not force as many social controls on them, unlike the gender role expectations of girls (Shover et al., 1979). When a change in those roles occurred, however slight, crime committed by females was expected to increase. In particular, research has shown that opportunity theory specifically explains higher rates of female involvement in property and financial crimes as opposed to violent offenses, due to the increased opportunity in traditionally male careers (Shover et al., 1979).

The third theory, economic marginalization theory or gender inequality theory, largely attributed to Steffensmeier (1978), hypothesized that the majority of female crime was due to the lower socioeconomic status of women (Small, 2000). "As patriarchy restricts the power of women, gender inequality and economic disadvantage are byproducts of male oppression and dominance" and "contribute to female offending" (Reckdenwald & Parker, 2008, p. 211). This meant that women were committing offenses as a result of poverty and economic necessity. Research supporting this theory has shown many women had children in their care prior to arrest and had little or no regular employment history, resulting in their dependence on government assistance (Daly, 1992; Gilfus, 2002). This finding led Reckdenwald and Parker (2008) to state that economic marginalization and gender inequalities in education and employment may result in women committing some crime out of necessity or strain resulting from limited resources, options, and support.

The fourth theory, the chivalry theory (Thomas, 1923), stated that the traditionally low rates of female offending was due to the lenient treatment of female offenders by the male-dominated criminal justice system. Therefore, when female crime rates increased, many believed the increase was actually due to changing policies and practices directed at women by the criminal justice system (Small, 2000). Anderson (1976) found that though anecdotal evidence tends to support this theory, data analyzing the differential treatment of offenders depending on gender does not. When age, race, and offense type are considered, girls and women often received harsher punishment than boys and men. According to Klein and Kress (2014) chivalry is typically afforded to affluent White women and is thus a reinforcer of class, race, and gender stereotypes.

Although the development of these theories sought to increase the understanding of women, most focused on the gender roles or gender stratification in society. Hoyt and Scherer (1998) argued that theories emphasizing female sexuality and gender roles alone have not been accurate and do not account for the lifestyles of modern females. Acknowledging the different pathways of men and women into and out of crime may allow for a more appropriate explanation of criminal behavior and end stereotypical thinking (Chesney-Lind, 1989; Taylor & Blanchette, 2009). Furthermore, "the ramifications of the traditionally male-centered approaches to understanding" female criminality "not only involve[s] ignorance about the causes of crime but prevent appropriate criminal justice system responses, interventions and treatment efforts" (Belknap & Holsinger, 2006, p. 48). Understanding the varying life experiences and circumstances involved in the lives of females is necessary to explain their criminal behavior (Broidy & Agnew, 1997).

WOMEN'S PATHWAYS TO CRIME

More contemporary criminological research posits that women acquire their criminal behavior through gender-specific processes, socializations, and experiences unlike those experienced by males (Hoyt & Scherer, 1998). Qualitative methodologies, grounded in feminist criminology, have produced biographies and case narratives of women offenders that were not addressed by previous quantitative methods. Specifically, they have identified key psychosocial risks and needs of female offenders that are substantially different from male offenders (Daly, 1992; Owen, 1998). Additionally, they have also proposed several typified pathways to crime among females including (1) childhood victimization path that was linked to abuse and a pattern of mental illness, substance abuse, depression/anxiety, and other consequences (Chesney-Lind, 1997; Daly, 1992); (2) a pathway of extreme poverty, homelessness, and education/vocational problems that is found in many female offenders (Holtfreter et al., 2004; Reisig, Holtfreter, & Morash, 2006). This research highlights the complex intersection of gender, race, and class with extreme marginalization (Bloom & Owen, 2003); and (3) a relational pathway has been identified that links dysfunctional abusive intimate relationships to an erosion of the female's self-efficacy with on-going victimization, depression/anxiety, and substance abuse.

Some of the most influential research defining the variety of pathways for female offenders comes from Kathleen Daly (1992). Findings are based on qualitatively developed research involving 34 women offenders. The research identified five distinct pathways: (1) Street women engage in criminal behavior either to escape or to survive. This involves women or girls fleeing abuse and violence and entering street life, where they may become addicted to drugs and/or rely on prostitution, drug dealing, or theft to survive. (2) Drug-connected women become users, or traffickers, in collaboration with intimate partners or family members. (3) Harmed and harming women become involved in criminal activity after suffering serious child abuse (physical and sexual) and neglect, leading to adolescent school and family problems, delinquency, a hostile aggressive or a withdrawn suspicious demeanor, and, ultimately, chronic adult criminality. (4) Battered women are situational offenders who have suffered violent abuse from intimate partners. Criminal behavior by these woman is seen as unlikely except for her involvement in the relationship. She may escape and/or exhibit violence in retaliation to her circumstances. Her subsequent criminal behavior is linked to basic coping and survival. (5) Finally, the economic offender pathway reflects economic crimes such as fraud, theft, and embezzlement. Women in this pathway are poor women coping with poverty and women motivated by greed or social aspiration who themselves are marginalized or have a history of abuse, addiction, or violence.

Daly's study is important because it suggests that multiple pathways are present to explain criminal behavior in females and that although some of the pathways overlap for men and women, gender plays a significant role in defining criminal pathways. Additional information concerning pathways was identified by Richie (1994, 1996) indicating that race also plays a role in pathways to offending. Using biographical information to compare a group of sentenced African-American and White women at Rikers Island, New York, Richie (1996, p. 4) identified "gender entrapment" to illustrate how battered Black women are compelled to crime. She highlights how a young girl's childhood experiences reflect race and gender intersections, which affect her construction of identity and interpretation of structural and institutional events such as employment and education. Richie identified three distinct groups of female offenders: battered African-American women, African-American women who were not battered, and abused White women. Richie found that many of the women identified as battered African-Americans were protected, privileged, and insulated as children, which led to positive self-concept and optimism for their futures. Later, however, racial discrimination in the public and violence in their private lives challenged this optimism and these women eventually became fearful of dying from life's challenges. This fear propelled them into criminal activity (Richie, 1994). In contrast, the nonbattered African-American women were less privileged as children, with a more realistic sense of the social world. These women blamed the system for their socioeconomic plight and did not define themselves as criminals. Their pathways to jail were generally through drug-related offenses, robbery, or burglary. The White battered women were different from both groups of Black women because they had grown up in traditional patriarchal homes and believed themselves inferior to males. Once the battering began in their relationships, they were more likely to seek help. Their pathways into criminal activity were more likely to be through sex crimes, drugs, and assaults (Richie, 1994). Richie's work is important because it suggests that women's racial/ethnic and social class background can affect perspectives of responses to life circumstances.

Another significant contribution to the discussion of female offenders comes from Terri Moffitt's developmental taxonomy. Her work stems from the field of developmental psychology and describes two pathways that apply to both men and women offending (Moffitt, 1993; Moffitt & Caspi, 2001). She identified the adolescent limited pathway to offending in which adolescent girls react to parental constraints and limits and begin to respond in delinquent ways. Most of this delinquency is an attempt to obtain more autonomy and freedom, and the delinquency is temporary and typically dissipates by late teens and early adulthood (Moffitt, 1993). On the other hand, the life-course persistent pathway is defined by a complex biosocial etiology characterized by a fearless risk-taking personality with a callous temperament. This pathway emerges in early childhood with sustained problems and persistent delinquency that continues into adulthood (Moffitt, 1993). Moffitt left open the question of whether the life-course persistent pathway existed for female offenders, any discussion of the characteristics of these offenders, and whether this dichotomous taxonomy is sufficient to cover all offending patterns.

Although instrumental in developing the concept of pathways to offending, previous studies relied on small sample sizes, which made generalizability difficult. To overcome this barrier, Simpson et al. (2008) conducted research on 351 female offenders held in the Baltimore City Detention Center using a computerized life-event calendar. Their research involved extensive in-person interviews incorporating both closed-ended questions and qualitative descriptions of violent incidents in which the women participated. Their research supported Daly's initial explanation of female pathways to offending (Simpson et al., 2008). Simpson et al. (2008) included age of onset variables in their study to contribute to the life-course and developmental literature. Findings indicated that more than half (54%) of the women in their sample committed their first offense as adults. Another third (35%) began offending in adolescence and only 10% began offending in childhood. Adolescent onset offenders were more apt to have used violence than adult or childhood onset offenders. Results indicated that women who were sexually abused as children were more likely to have begun offending in childhood. Further, women who first offended in childhood were more heavily involved in drug dealing, property crime, and offensive violence as adults than were later onset offenders. Neither childhood physical abuse nor sexual abuse had significant association with adolescent onset offending. Women who first offended as adults were less likely to have used violence offensively, but more likely to experience violent victimization in adulthood than were earlier onset offenders (Simpson et al., 2008).

Brennan, Breitenbach, and Dieterick (2010) again tested feminist pathways paradigms on a sample of 718 female inmates from two California prisons. Cases were randomly selected from the total roster of women who were eligible to be released from confinement. Each of the women selected for the study was interviewed by trained facility staff and the research team prior to release. Their study confirmed the prior work of Daly and Moffitt while extending the concept of pathways through greater explanation. Their study revealed a total of 8 pathways to offending that were gender specific. Pathways 1–3 and 5 consist mainly of marginalized drug offenders with few instances of abuse and other unique variations such as age and motherhood.

Pathway 4 reflects the prototypical lifelong victim pathway. It incorporates the basic elements of Daly's (1992) battered women, drug connected, and relational pathways. Many have antisocial partners who influence their antisocial behaviors, personal drug abuse, and drug trafficking. Pathway 4 includes lifelong victims, stressed depressed single mothers in abusive relationships, addiction, and relative violence. These single mothers reflect a pattern of lifelong victimization and extreme child sexual and physical abuse that extends into current abusive adult relationships. This pathway is atypical in high percentage of current violent felonies, for being angry at the time of the current offense, and for having domestic violence convictions.

Pathways 6 and 7 appear to match Moffitt's life-course persistent and Daly's harmed and harming pathway. Pathway 6 is chronic serious and noncompliant offenders with antisocial personality and hostility, mental health issues, lifelong abuse, battered, marginalized, and are often homeless. This pathway comprises mostly single mothers, have the highest criminal history with high numbers of prior arrests (15), many revocations, returns to prison, and arrests while on probation. Pathway 7 contains chronic serious noncompliant offenders with extreme mental health problems and violent hostility, lifelong abuse, marginalization, and high parenting stress. These pathways include childhood and adult abuse, educational and vocational failure and poverty, as well an antisocial personality patterns. They have atypically high scores for violent offenses, prior weapon offenses, fights with other inmates, and prison misconducts (Brennan et al., 2010).

Finally, Pathway 8 represents lifelong victims, older addicted women in abusive relationships, nonparenting women, and chaotic lives with relative violence. Many of the women have a history of extreme lifelong abuse. These women see their violent relationships as increasing their criminal involvement. They describe their lives as one crisis after another. This category reflects anger/hostility, above average levels of hitting/hurting someone, and atypically high proportion of violent felony arrests.

Brennan et al.'s (2010) findings support the existence of "gendered" pathways showing that gender-responsive factors are major constituents of six out of eight identified pathways to female offending. Their findings support past research into gendered pathways to violence. Overall, this study confirmed that women's pathways into criminal behavior are different from those of men and involve a complex range of experiences with motherhood, violence, and abuse histories (Brennan et al., 2010).

From these studies, it is clear that researchers have identified a link between negative life experiences and criminality (Daly, 1992; Giordano, Cernkovich, & Rudolph, 2002; Moult, 2008). Many of these life experiences consisted of abuse, drug use, family instability, and mental health issues (Daly, 1992; Gilfus, 2002; Proctor, 2004; Reckdenwald & Parker, 2008; Rossegger et al., 2009). Familial relationships have a significant impact on women, particularly parental conflicts, absence, unavailability, and drug use. For women, trauma, including emotional, physical, and sexual abuse, is a key risk factor for criminal behavior. Early experiences with trauma and relational issues can lead to running away, unhealthy sexual practices, and substance abuse issues (Bloom, 2003). To conclude, the common pathways into criminality for women include the following:

- A woman who has been abused as a child, has run to the streets to escape, ends up supporting her drug habit by selling drugs, prostituting, and stealing (Daly, 1992; Richie, 1996; Simpson et al., 2008).
- Women who seriously harm or kill their abusive partners in response to chronic domestic violence toward them or their children (Daly, 1992; Richie, 1996).
- A woman who is in an abusive relationship and is persuaded/forced into criminal behavior (Richie, 1994).
- Women who commit economically motivated crimes (Daly, 1992; Brennan et al., 2010).
- Women who engage in crime as a result of addiction, marginalization, or mental illness (Bloom, Owen, & Covington, 2004; Covington & Bloom, 2007; Bloom & Covington, 2008).

Age of Onset Relative to Pathways to Crime

Following the line of developmental theorists, "Feminist research implicitly suggests that pathways to crime are age graded," meaning that experiences at different ages during the lifetime produce unique pathways into criminality for girls and women (Simpson et al., 2008, p. 88). Life experiences at varying ages including sexual abuse, domestic violence, drug and alcohol abuse, and mental disorders were found to be important risk factors in accounts of female offending (Byrne & Trew, 2008). Examining the risk factors and the age of onset of criminal behavior can refine the pathways toward criminality (Simpson et al., 2008).

The classifications of onset have been previously divided into three categories: childhood onset, adolescent onset, and adult onset. Simpson et al. (2008) sampled 355 adult female inmates, convicted of various crimes, in Baltimore to create life-event calendars to differentiate the three types of onsets. Other researchers have looked at cohorts of offenders to establish what factors correlate with offending while similarly addressing the time of life in which the experience occurred (Byrne & Trew, 2008; Proctor, 2004; Siegel & Williams, 2003; Zara & Farrington, 2009).

Early onset, also known as childhood onset (before age 13), is the first category used to define women's pathways to crime (Leve & Chamberlain, 2004; Simpson et al., 2008). Simpson et al. (2008) found that childhood onset offenders were more likely to have been sexually abused as children, typically before the sixth grade. "The notion that exposure to sexual victimization, particularly prior to adulthood, predisposes women to becoming engaged in criminality was corroborated" in a study by Proctor (2004, p. 78). Offenders who were asked to recall early memories of sexual abuse identified past and present feelings of rage linked to that specific childhood experience (Flemke, 2009, p. 129). They were also found to more likely be arrested for violent offenses rather than property crimes (Siegel & Williams, 2003). Furthermore, Leve and Chamberlain (2004) stated individuals in the early onset category typically engage in more risky behaviors that increase the likelihood of long-term problems.

Similar to early sexual abuse, women classified as early onset or childhood onset, also engaged in consensual intercourse at a young age (Moffitt, 1993; Simpson et al., 2008). Additionally, these women began offending at a younger age than the other offenders in the study, thus accumulating more lifetime arrests. These women were also found to have several criminally involved friends, deal drugs, and participate in property crime (Simpson et al., 2008). Their history of involvement in crime led them to be more offensive (made the first attack) adult offenders than the other ages of onset (Simpson et al., 2008).

The second category of onset identified was adolescent onset (ages 13–17). Though criminal behavior tends to soar as a whole in adolescence (Moffitt, 1993), according to Simpson et al. (2008) women in this category had fewer criminal friends, less exposure to drugs, and fewer arrests compared to the childhood onset group. Additionally, they were "no more likely to have been sexually or physically abused as children," but they tend to engage in risky behaviors with little family influence (Moffitt, 1993; Simpson et al., 2008, p. 103). Adolescent onset female offenders were more likely to use defensive violence (attack second) and less likely to use offensive violence than childhood onset offenders (Simpson et al., 2008).

The last category of onset was adult onset (Simpson et al., 2008). As stated by Zara and Farrington (2009, p. 278), most research has focused on early onset factors and very few have looked at the "mechanisms involved in delayed criminal manifestations and in late criminal onset." As stated by Eggleston and Laub (2002), some researchers believe adult-onset criminal behavior is rare because it is under-researched. The little available research has shown that adult onset offending can comprise between 23% and 55% of offenses in official records (McGee & Farrington, 2010).

Unlike the other two categories of onsets, these women were more likely to be older, married, had fewer criminal friends, and a less extensive criminal past (Simpson et al., 2008). Furthermore, Eggleston and Laub (2002) found that adult onset offending cannot be predicted using variables predictive of adolescent criminal behavior; however, drug use, exposure to criminal peers and employment problems in adulthood were predictive of adult onset offending. According to Simpson et al. (2008, p. 102), female adult onset offenders were less likely of all three onsets to use offensive violence and reported more extensive histories of violent victimizations and are "involved in fewer incidents of violence overall." These women experienced a more stable lifestyle;

however, it was their high exposure to violent victimizations such as rapes and assaults by partners that distinguished them from the other categories of onsets (Simpson et al., 2008). This was corroborated by Flemke (2009, p. 132) who found that a majority of women "specifically discussed types of emotional pain and/or abuse that occur within their adult intimate relationships that elicit rage" due to past abuse and victimizations.

The experiences of young girls and women at different ages lead to different pathways toward criminality; yet, little is known about which experiences and pathways may lead to violent offenses, such as homicide (Simpson et al., 2008). Research has found that "female homicide offenders experience higher levels of stress earlier in life than do male murders, or nonviolent offenders of either sex" (Humphrey & Palmer, 1986, p. 304). These women have had similar experiences as those described for the general female offending population; yet, possibly to a higher extent as noted by some researchers (Humphrey & Palmer, 1986). They are more likely to have experienced greater losses throughout their lives, including death of parents, separation from parents by divorce, abandonment, or institutionalization, employment difficulties, multiple residence changes, and marital discord (Humphrey & Palmer, 1986). The few studies examining the lives of female homicide offenders have corroborated these findings.

CONTEXTS OF FEMALE PERPETRATED HOMICIDES

Early examination of female offenders led to the conclusion that the context of female offending, particularly homicide offending, was distinctly different from that of males (Ward, Jackson, & Ward, 1969). This difference was often attributed to gender roles ascribed to males and females, which shaped both the frequency and the nature of violent crimes by men and women. Yet, even when the same offense is charged, the circumstances of the offense are often dramatically different for females and males (Daly, 1992; Steffensmeier, 1983). "Context" refers to the circumstances and characteristics of a particular criminal act (Triplett & Myers, 1995), such as the setting, presence of other offender, the relationship between offender and victim, the offender's role in initiating and committing the offense, and purpose of the offense.

Background

Female homicide offenders were less likely than other offenders to have a prior criminal record or a family history of criminality (Mann, 1996; Ward et al., 1969). Additionally, female homicide offenders have been found to have below average to average intelligence, with underemployment and a reliance on public assistance (Mann, 1996; Ward et al., 1969; Weisheit, 1984). Overall, these women tend to have a low degree of education severely limiting their employment opportunities (Shipley & Arrigo, 2004).

Furthermore, research has found many of these women to have serious drinking problems with alcohol being present in a majority of homicides (Mann, 1996; Ward et al., 1969; Weisheit, 1984). Many were also reported to have been "sexually promiscuous or prostitutes" often attributed to early childhood sexual violence and abuse (Field et al., 2017; Mann, 1996; Ward et al., 1969, p. 903). Moreover, some were even diagnosed with some type of psychological disorder, particularly those accused of infanticide (Shipley & Arrigo, 2004; Ward et al., 1969).

Through the few studies examining female homicide offenders, it has emerged that violence by women is deeply rooted in a system of social and economic inequalities between men and women in society (Klein, 1981). Female homicide offenders are responding to past victimization and the fear of continued abuse so that violence becomes a type of self-help when other means are unavailable. Within this perspective, women's homicidal response can be described as a kind of extra legal social control directed against someone else's deviant behavior (Black, 1983). Additionally, it is suggested that economic marginalization creates an environment of elevated stress contributing to the increased likelihood of the commission of a homicide on the part of a woman (Mann, 1996; Shipley & Arrigo, 2004).

Role and Motive

In a study on violent female offenses, Ward et al. (1969) found that when a woman commits a homicide, she may play one of four roles: the conspirator, accessory, partner, or the sole perpetrator. The conspirator instigates the crime but does not participate in the offense. The accessory usually plays a minor secondary role, such as driving the car or carrying weapons. The partner is an accessory of sorts; however, she participates fully in the commission of the offense. The sole perpetrator is a woman who wholly commits the offense herself. They found that women who committed a homicide typically acted as a sole perpetrator and offended against a husband or lover 51% of the time and against a friend or acquaintance 49% of the time. This was later corroborated by Weisheit (1984) and Mann (1996). Ward et al. (1969) stated that for female homicide offenders, 13% claimed innocence, 24% claimed their actions were justifiable, 34% claimed extenuating circumstances such as an accident or intoxication, and 8% and 21% claimed other reasons or there was no information, respectively.

Many of the motives identified by female-perpetrated homicides are often tied to men or seen as the solution to a problem (Shipley & Arrigo, 2004). As noted by Weisheit (1984), anger, revenge, and psychological reasons are the most common explanations of motive. Frequently, these women commit the offense after violence precipitated by the male victim. However, when the victim is female, there is often no evidence of victim precipitation (Goetting, 1988). Still, others have stated there is often a complexity to the offense involving more than one explanation to a motive (Shipley & Arrigo, 2004).

Age and Race

Research has shown the majority of women who kill are Black (Mann, 1996). As most female-perpetrated homicides are intraracial, the majority of victims also tend to be Black (Puzzanchera & Kang, 2014; Mann, 1996; Weisheit, 1984). When compared to their male counterparts, female homicide offenders tend to be older (Mann, 1996; Wilbanks, 1983). Offenders range from late twenties to early thirties in most studies; yet, the victims range in age from early thirties to late thirties, with the only exception being when the victim is a child (Hanke, 1995; Mann, 1996; Weisheit, 1984).

Victims

Additionally, when a woman commits a homicide, the offense tends to be the result of a relational conflict and against a family member, intimate partner, or friend (Mann, 1996; Sondheimer, 2001; Ward et al., 1969; Weisheit, 1984; Wilbanks, 1983). Women most often kill husbands, ex-husbands, and lovers followed by children and then other relatives (Ward et al., 1969; Zimring, Mukherjee, & VanWinkle, 1983). Women seldom kill other women (Wilbanks, 1983). This is considered a rare phenomenon, outside the homicide of a female child. Additionally, women are far less likely to kill a stranger than are their male counterparts. When women kill with the involvement of others, they tend to play secondary roles; their co-defendants tend to be male romantic partners. Overall, female-perpetrated homicides are known to be intragender and intraracial, with few exceptions.

The most dramatic differences between homicides by men and women are found in the relationship histories and situational dynamics leading to the victim's death. Women typically kill intimate partners after suffering long periods of abuse (Chimbos, 1978; Daniel & Harris, 1982). Wives are far more likely to have been victims and turn to murder only when in mortal fear, after exhausting other alternatives. They have often made numerous attempts to obtain outside intervention before resorting to violence (Police Foundation, 1976; Sherman & Berk, 1984). Husbands who murder wives, however, have rarely been in fear for their lives. Rather, they are more likely to be motivated by rage at suspected infidelity, and the murder often culminates a period of prolonged abuse of their wives (Police Foundation, 1976; Sherman & Berk, 1984). It has also been found that many of the victims were incapacitated or precipitated the offense in some way. Ward et al. (1969, p. 852) stated 61% of the victims were either drunk, ill, asleep, caught off-guard, or a "helpless" child. Additionally, Wilbanks (1983) and Mann (1996) also found that many of the victims precipitated the offense during a prior altercation and were also drinking.

Circumstances

More contemporary studies continue to find significant differences between the homicide patterns of men and women (Wilbanks, 1983). The social areas (e.g., living room, family room, etc.) of the residence of the offender appear to be the most common place for a female perpetrated homicide (Mann, 1996). Homicides by women typically take place in the residence of the offender, which is usually also the residence of the victim, while higher percentages of homicides perpetrated by males occur in bars and taverns. According to Ward et al. (1969), 60% of the offenses were committed in the home of the offender. Mann (1996) further elaborated by saying that a majority of the offenses took place on a weekend, after midnight, and in the living room of the offender's or victim's place of residence, in which they most likely cohabitated.

Weapons

Differences also exist in the mode of killing. There has been a popular, though somewhat misguided, belief that women kill in more cruel ways, such as with poison or knives. Though these may have been more common place in the past, firearms are the number one choice of weapon by female homicide offenders (Wilbanks, 1983). For example, Ward et al. (1969) found that the weapon of choice in 35% of the cases was a knife or household item combined, but in 34% of the cases a gun was used. Weisheit (1984) found that 44% of the offenses were committed with a gun and 40% were committed with a knife. This was similar to Mann's (1996) findings that 46.6% used a gun and 37.8% used a knife. Though women are more likely to use a knife than a male to commit a homicide offense, guns are, however, the usual weapon of choice (Weisheit, 1984). This is likely attributed to the rise in availability of guns among the overall population.

INTERVENTIONS SPECIFIC TO WOMEN

Female offending originates from different pathways than that of men, and so interventions should be specifically designed to address their unique histories. From research, it has been ascertained that a significant majority of women who commit violent offenses, such as homicide, enter the correctional system with significant histories of both trauma and addiction. Understanding why and how these experiences shaped the lives of these women is crucial to the implementation of services and policies for treatment, recidivism, and the prevention of future incarceration of others affected, such as the children of these women. Some of these women have a chance of gaining release from the correctional system at some point in their lives. It is evident that these women will need a multitude of services to positively re-enter society.

Accordingly, treatment services must be trauma-informed. Trauma-informed services take into account the prior trauma experienced by the women. By doing this, they avoid triggering trauma reactions and retraumatization of the offender. Trauma-informed services adjust the behavior of counselors, staff, and the organization to support the individual's coping capacity and allow survivors to manage their trauma symptoms successfully so that they are able to access, retain, and benefit from the interventions (Bloom et al., 2004; Covington & Bloom, 2007; Bloom & Covington, 2008).

Since women's psychological growth and health is often tied to a sense of connection, group treatment is often an effective strategy with women offenders (Bloom et al., 2004; Covington & Bloom, 2007; Bloom & Covington, 2008). They provide a forum for problem solving and meet women's relational needs. Further, groups provide immediate feedback, combat negative interpersonal patterns, and allow women to practice pro-social skills (Bloom et al., 2004).

Overall, a specific need exists for gender-responsive services for women in the criminal justice system. Women and men have different histories and different pathways into criminality. These differences must be addressed in the treatment interventions available within correctional facilities. As indicated by prior research (Richie, 2001), comprehensive wrap-around services including substance abuse treatment, mental health treatment, individual therapy for past trauma and victimizations, family therapy, and occupational and educational services are all necessary for the individual and the criminal justice system to successfully reintegrate these women back into society. Programs should be empirically based and address the specific needs of women, integrating services for mental health and substance abuse.

To do this, they must first acknowledge that gender makes a difference (Bloom et al., 2004). Correctional programing must create an environment that focuses on competencies and strengths of women offenders and create an environment based on safety, respect, and dignity. Successful programing for women must also develop policies, practices, and programs that are relational and promote healthy connections to children, family, and significant people within the community. They must also provide a path for women to develop opportunities to improve their socioeconomic conditions, as histories of poverty and survival mechanism contribute significantly to women's pathways into criminality. Finally, programming must address substance abuse, trauma, and mental health that continues through the re-entry process and into the community (Covington & Bloom, 2007; Bloom & Covington, 2008.

CONCLUSION

Research addressing female criminality remains underserved. Original theories attributed female criminality to gender stereotyped behaviors and biological traits (Lombroso & Ferrero, 1920). As research progressed, feminist perspectives have begun to address the social and environmental factors that are specific to the lives of women and how those may attribute to criminal behavior (Daly, 1992; Simpson et al. 2008).

It was found that women who engage in criminal behavior have often experienced abuse, addiction, chaotic familial problems, and chronic economic instability. These experiences create avenues into antisocial subcultures, chronic trauma and victimizations, severe marginalization, and increased criminal involvement (Brennan et al., 2010; Daly, 1992; Owen, 1998; Salisbury & Van Voorhis, 2009). Furthermore, it has been found that women who eventually perpetrate a homicide offense have experienced many of these factors, but often at a higher rate with greater amounts of trauma and losses throughout their lives (Humphrey & Palmer, 1986; Mann, 1996).

Despite some media hype, most available measures of women's violence have failed to show an increase in the commission of offenses. Yet, the arrest and incarceration rate for violent offenses has increased, therefore amplifying the need for evidence-based gender responsive treatment and services focused on each woman's life experiences (Chesney-Lind & Irwin, 2008). Due to the significant amount of trauma incurred through gender, the criminal justice system must become gender-responsive when providing prevention services, treatment, and re-entry processing. The acknowledgement that gender is a contributing factor to criminal behavior, including homicide, is crucial to the success of women encountering the criminal justice system.

REFERENCES

Adler, F., Adler, H. M., & Levins, H. (1975). *Sisters in crime: The rise of the new female criminal*. New York, NY: McGraw-Hill.

Adler, F., & Simon, R. J. (1979). *The criminology of deviant women*. Boston, MA: Houghton Mifflin.

Anderson, E. A. (1976). The "chivalrous" treatment of the female offender in the arms of the criminal justice system: A review of the literature. *Social Problems*, *23*(3), 350–357.

Belknap, J., & Holsinger, K. (2006). The gendered nature of risk factors for delinquency. *Feminist Criminology*, *1*(1), 48–71.

Black, D. (1983). Crime as social control. American sociological review, 34–45.

Bloom, B., Owen, B. A., & Covington, S. (2003). Gender-responsive strategies: Research, practice, and guiding principles for women offenders. Washington, DC: US Department of Justice, National Institute of Corrections.

Bloom, B., Owen, B., & Covington, S. (2004). Women offenders and the gendered effects of public policy. *Review of Policy Research*, *21*(1), 31–48.

Bloom, B. E. (2003). Gendered justice: Addressing female offenders. Carolina Academic Pr.

Bloom, B. E., & Covington, S. (2008). Addressing the mental health needs of women offenders. Women's mental health issues across the criminal justice system, 160–176.

Bonger, W. A. (1916). *Criminality and economic conditions*. Boston, MA: Little, Brown.

Brennan, T., Breitenbash, M., & Dieterich, W. (2010). Unraveling women's pathways to serious crime: New findings and links to prior feminist pathways. *American Probation and Parole Association*, *4*(2), 35–47.

Broidy, L., & Agnew, R. (1997). Gender and crime: A general strain theory perspective. *Journal of Research in Crime and Delinquency*, *34*(3), 275–306.

Broidy, L., & Cauffman, L. (2006). *Understanding the female offender*. Washington, DC: U.S. Department of Justice.

Byrne, C. F., & Trew, K. J. (2008). Pathways through crime: The development of crime and desistance in the accounts of men and women offenders. *The Howard Journal of Criminal Justice*, *47*(3), 238–258.

Chesney-Lind, M. The female offender: Girls, women, and crime. Sage Publications, CA, 1997.

Chesney-Lind, M. (1989). Girls' crime and woman's place: Toward a feminist model of female delinquency. *Crime and Delinquency*, *35*(1), 5–29.

Chimbos, P. D. (1978). *Marital violence: A study of interspouse homicide*. San Francisco, CA: R & E Research Associates.

Covington, S. S., & Bloom, B. E. (2007). Gender responsive treatment and services in correctional settings. *Women & Therapy*, *29*(3–4), 9–33.

Cullen, F. T., Golden, K. M., & Cullen, J. B. (1979). Sex and delinquency: A partial test of the masculinity hypothesis. *Criminology*, *17*(3), 301–310.

Daly, K. (1992). Women's pathways to felony court: Feminist theories of lawbreaking and problems of representation. *Southern California Review of Law and Women's Studies*, *2*, 11–52.

Daniel, A. E., & Harris, P. W. (1982). Female homicide offenders referred for pre-trial psychiatric examination: a descriptive study. *The Bulletin of the American Academy of Psychiatry and the Law*, *10*(4), 261.

Eggleston, E. P., & Laub, J. H. (2002). The onset of adult offending: A neglected dimension of the criminal career. *Journal of Criminal Justice*, *30*(6), 603–622.

Field, C., Cherukuri, S., Kimuna, S., & Berg, Dee. (2017). Women accused of homicide: The impact of race, relationship to victim, and prior physical abuse. *Advances in Applied Sociology*, 7, 281–304.

Flemke, K. (2009). Triggering rage: Unresolved trauma in women's lives. *Contemporary Family Therapy, 31*(2), 123–139.

Gilfus, M. E. (2002). *Women's experiences of abuse as a risk factor for incarceration.* Harrisburg, PA: Pennsylvania Coalition Against Domestic Violence.

Giordano, P. C., Cernkovich, S. A., & Rudolph, J. L. (2002). Gender, crime, and desistance: Toward a theory of cognitive transformation1. *American Journal of Sociology, 107*(4), 990–1064.

Glueck, S., & Glueck, E. T. (1934). *Five hundred delinquent women.* Oxford: Knopf.

Goetting, A. (1988). Patterns of homicide among women. *Journal of Interpersonal Violence, 3*(1), 3–19.

Hanke, P. J. (1995). Sentencing disparities by race of offender and victim: Women homicide offenders in Alabama, 1929–1985. *Sociological Spectrum,15*(3), 277–297.

Holsinger, K. (2000). Feminist perspectives on female offending: Examining real girls' lives. *Women and Criminal Justice, 12*(1), 23–52.

Holtfreter, K., Reisig, M. D., & Morash, M. (2004). Poverty, state capital, and recidivism among women offenders. *Criminology & Public Policy, 3*(2), 185–208.

Hoyt, S., & Scherer, D. G. (1998). Female juvenile delinquency: Misunderstood by the juvenile justice system, neglected by social science. *Law and Human Behavior, 22*(1), 81.

Humphrey, J. A., & Palmer, S. (1986). Stressful life events and criminal homicide. *OMEGA –Journal of Death and Dying, 17*(4), 299–308.

Irwin, K., & Chesney-Lind, M. (2008). Girls' violence: Beyond dangerous masculinity. *Sociology compass, 2*(3), 837–855.

Klein, D. (1981). Violence against women: Some considerations regarding its causes and its elimination. Crime & Delinquency, 27(1), 64–80.

Klein, D. (1973). The etiology of female crime: A review of the literature. *Issues in Criminology, 8*(2), 3–30.

Klein, D., & Kress, J. (2014). Any woman's blues: A critical overview of women, crime, and the criminal justice system. *Social Justice, 40*(1), 162–191.

Leve, L. D., & Chamberlain, P. (2004). Female juvenile offenders: Defining an early-onset pathway for delinquency. *Journal of Child and Family Studies, 13*(4), 439–452.

Lombroso, C., & Ferrero, G. (1920). *The female offender* (Vol. 1). New York, NY: D. Appleton and Company.

Mann, C. R. (1996). *When women kill.* New York, NY: Suny Press.

McGee, T. R., & Farrington, D. P. (2010). Are there any true adult-onset offenders? *British Journal of Criminology, 50*(3), 530–549.

Moffitt, T. E. (1993). Adolescence-limited and life-course-persistent antisocial behavior: A developmental taxonomy. *Psychological Review, 100*(4), 674.

Moffitt, T. E., & Caspi, A. (2001). Childhood predictors differentiate life-course persistent and adolescence-limited antisocial pathways among males and females. *Development and psychopathology, 13*(2), 355–375.

Moult, K. (2008). Gender and the life course theory of crime: Developing a model to explain women's desistance from delinquency. *The Public Purpose, 6*(1), 7–37.

Owen, B. (1998). In the mix: Struggle and survival in a woman's prison. New York: State University of New York Press.

Police Foundation. (1976). *Domestic Violence and the Police: Studies in Detroit and Kansas City.* Washington, D.C.: The Police Foundation.

Pollak, O. (1961). *The criminality of women.* New York, NY: AS Barnes.

Proctor, J. (2004). Understanding the range of female criminality: A prison-based test of three traditional theories. *Women's Studies Quarterly, 32*(3/4), 61–85.

Puzzanchera, C., & Kang, W. (2014). Easy access to FBI arrest statistics. Online. Available: http://www.ojjdp.gov/ojstatbb/ezaucr

Reckdenwald, A., & Parker, K. F. (2008). The influence of gender inequality and marginalization on types of female offending. *Homicide Studies, 12*(2), 208–226.

Reisig, M. D., Holtfreter, K., & Morash, M. (2006). Assessing recidivism risk across female pathways to crime. *Justice Quarterly, 23*(3), 384–405.

Richie, B. (1996). *Compelled to crime: The gender entrapment of battered Black women.* Psychology Press.

Richie, B. E. (1994). Gender entrapment: An exploratory study. *Reframing Women's Health*, 219–232.

Richie, B. E. (2001). Challenges incarcerated women face as they return to their communities: Findings from life history interviews. *Crime and Delinquency*, *47*(3), 368–389.

Rossegger, A., Wetli, N., Urbaniok, F., Elbert, T., Cortoni, F., & Endrass, J. (2009). Women convicted for violent offenses: Adverse childhood experiences, low level of education and poor mental health. BMC psychiatry, 9(1), 81–88.

Salisbury, E. J., & Van Voorhis, P. (2009). Gendered pathways: A quantitative investigation of women probationers' paths to incarceration. Criminal justice and behavior, 36(6), 541–566.

Sherman, L. W., & Berk, R. A. (1984). The specific deterrent effects of arrest for domestic assault. American sociological review, 261–272.

Shipley, S, & Arrigo, B. (2004). The female homicide offender. New Jersey: Pearson.

Shover, N., Norland, S., James, J., & Thornton, W. E. (1979). Gender roles and delinquency. *Social Forces*, *58*(1), 162–175.

Siegel, J. A., & Williams, L. M. (2003). The relationship between child sexual abuse and female delinquency and crime: A prospective study. *Journal of Research in Crime and Delinquency*, *40*(1), 71–94.

Simon, R. J. (1975). *Women and crime*. Lexington, MA: Lexington Books.

Simpson, S. S. (1989). Feminist theory, crime, and justice. *Criminology*, *27*(4), 605–632.

Simpson, S. S., Yahner, J. L., & Dugan, L. (2008). Understanding women's pathways to jail: Analysing the lives of incarcerated women. *Australian and New Zealand Journal of Criminology*, *41*(1), 84–108.

Small, K. (2000). Female crime in the United States, 1963–1998: An update. *Gender Issues*, *18*(3), 75–90.

Sondheimer, D. L. (2001). Young female offenders: Increasingly visible yet poorly understood. *Gender Issues*, *19*(1), 79–90.

Steffensmeier, D. J. (1978). Crime and the contemporary woman: An analysis of changing levels of female property crime, 1960–75. *Social Forces*, *57*(2), 566–584.

Taylor, K. N., & Blanchette, K. (2009). The women are not wrong: It is the approach that is debatable. *Criminology and Public Policy*, *8*(1), 221–229.

Thomas, W. I. (1923). *The unadjusted girl: With cases and standpoint for behavior analysis*. Criminal Science Monographs (pp. 1–257). England: Oxford.

Triplett, R., & Myers, L. B. (1995). Evaluating contextual patterns of delinquency: Gender-based differences. Justice Quarterly, 12(1), 59–84.

Ward, D. A., Jackson, M., & Ward, R. E. (1969). Crimes of violence by women. *Crimes of Violence*, *13*, 843–909.

Weisheit, R. A. (1984). Female homicide offenders: Trends over time in an institutionalized population. *Justice Quarterly*, *1*(4), 471–489.

Wilbanks, W. (1983). Female homicide offender in Dade County, Florida, *The Criminal Justice Review*, *8* (2), 9–14.

Zara, G., & Farrington, D. P. (2009). Childhood and adolescent predictors of late onset criminal careers. *Journal of Youth and Adolescence*, *38*(3), 287–300.

Zimring, F. E., Mukherjee, S. K., & Van Winkle, B. (1983). Intimate violence: A study of intersexual homicide in Chicago. *The University of Chicago Law Review, 50*(2), 910–930.

PART II

INSTITUTIONS AND IDENTITY

CHAPTER 4

DURKHEIM, TOTEMISM, AND THE MANSON FAMILY: THEORIZING ON THE RELATIONSHIP BETWEEN RELIGION AND VIOLENCE

Danielle Sutton

ABSTRACT

Purpose – *To explain the unswerving loyalty given to Charles Manson by his followers from a religious perspective by drawing on Durkheim's (1912/1976) theory of religion and Hall's (2003, 2013) theory of religion and violence.*

Design/methodology/approach – *A qualitative analysis of archived multimedia either quoting, or written by, members of the Manson Family. Specifically, a theoretical thematic analysis is used to draw inferences on how members explained their participation in the 1969 murders.*

Findings – *The Manson Family display a unified belief system premised on the sacredness ascribed to Helter Skelter, forming a moral community at Spahn Ranch. Manson was conceived as the clan's God, thereby meeting most of Durkheim's requirements for a religious formation. A main component of their belief system was the inevitability of Helter Skelter, or the upcoming racial revolution; the ultimate war and end of the world. This belief provides one explanation for the Manson murders; that they were carried out as a religious duty to initiate Helter Skelter.*

Originality/value – *Despite the continued public fascination with the Manson murders, only a few studies have applied a sociotheoretical*

Homicide and Violent Crime
Sociology of Crime, Law and Deviance, Volume 23, 63–79

ISSN: 1521-6136/doi:10.1108/S1521-613620180000023005

framework to explain this event and none have used a religious account from the perspective of those involved. By introducing religion as one plausible framework, this research is not only an extension of Durkheim's work but also contributes to existing literature on the relationship between religion and violence.

Keywords: Charles Manson; religion; homicide; violence; Manson Family

INTRODUCTION

Although the Manson Family murders were committed more than 40 years ago, they continue to spark public discussion and fascination as to how one man could exert such power over a group of individuals leading them to engage in behaviors that would have unlikely occurred without his influence (McKie, 2009). Therefore, the primary focus of this chapter is on explaining the unswerving loyalty given to Charles Manson by analyzing the Tate-LaBianca murders from a religious perspective. It will begin with an overview of the mass murders of 1969, followed by a more in-depth analysis of the wider context in which these murders were committed. Durkheim's (1912/1976) theory of religious formations will then be explored with an emphasis on totemism, drawing explicit connections between his perspective and the Manson Family. Thus, it will be demonstrated how Helter Skelter became the clan's totem and through totemism the Manson Family became a (pseudo)religion with Manson as their God. However, it is insufficient to conclude that the murders were committed because a religion was formed, hence attention will be given to John Hall's (2003, 2013) theory of religion and violence. A brief overview will be provided on Hall's theory with an emphasis on pre-apocalyptic warring sects. It will be demonstrated how the family's religious beliefs legitimated violent behavior and the murders were committed on the basis of social reconstruction.

These arguments were developed by collecting and analyzing primary documents that had a central focus on the family's perspective. By analyzing materials that were written by the family allows for the acquisition of deeper insight regarding the thought processes of those involved in the events leading up to, and surrounding, the weekend of the murders. The importance of this research lies in its ability to fill a gap in existing literature. Despite continued public fascination with the Manson murders, few studies (Atchinson & Heide, 2010; Fine, 1982; Geis & Huston, 1970) have been published attempting to apply sociological theory to explain this event. Atchinson and Heide's (2010) study applies strain theory, social learning theory, and labeling theory to explain the murders and thus has a criminological focus. Geis and Huston (1970) recognize the importance of Durkheim's work in the murders but their primary focus is on media portrayals and their influence on public perceptions. Fine (1982) adopts a more sociocultural approach in understanding the murders through traditions of folklore groups. Second, the importance of this research lies in the ability to reframe how the Manson murders are perceived. Currently, the dominant public perception attributes the murders as resulting from drug-induced actions perpetuated under the influence of a charismatic, manipulative leader who was skilled in the art of brainwashing (Emmons, 1986; Linder, 2014; Stanley, 2004). By introducing religion as one plausible framework for understanding these murders, this research is not only an extension of Durkheim's work but also contributes to existing literature on the relationship between religion and violence.

Overview of Tate-LaBianca Murders

On August 9, 1969, acting on the orders given by Charles Manson, three members of the "Family" – Charles Tex Watson, Patricia Krenwinkle, and Susan Atkins – brutally murdered actress Sharon Tate and her unborn baby, three of her houseguests as well as a friend of her caretaker (Emmons, 1986). Collectively, they were stabbed over 100 times while one victim was shot four times at close range (Linder, 2014). The word "PIG" was written in blood on the front door of the posh Bel-Air home (Emmons, 1986). The following night, Leslie Van Houten and Charles Manson accompanied Watson, Krenwinkle, and Atkins to a residence in the Los Feliz district of Los Angeles. Manson entered the home, bound and gagged Leno and Rosemary LaBianca, then left. He instructed the others to not be as "messy" as they were the previous night and also not to let on that they were going to kill the LaBiancas (Emmons, 1986). The Family members obliged and Leno was stabbed 26 times, some of the wounds inflicted with a carving fork, while Rosemary sustained 41 stab wounds (Emmons, 1986, pp. 8–9). Moreover, the word "war" was carved into Leno LaBianca's stomach post mortem. Similar to the Tate murders, "death to pigs" and "rise" were written in blood on the walls and "Helter Skelter" on the refrigerator (Emmons, 1986).

These were neither the first, nor the last, murders committed by members of the Manson Family. On July 31, 1969, Robert Beausoleil and Susan Atkins stabbed Gary Hinman repeatedly and then inscribed the words "political piggy" in blood on the wall alongside smudges of a panther paw print (Emmons, 1986, p. 8). The ninth victim, Donald (Shorty) Shea was an employee at Spahn Ranch and often expressed disagreement with Manson's philosophy. Shortly after the Tate-LaBianca murders, the police raided the Ranch and Manson believed this was due to Shea snitching (Emmons, 1986). Rumors emerged that Shea was completely dismembered and buried; however, when the body was finally discovered all limbs were intact (Bugliosi & Gentry, 1974; Emmons, 1986).

Manson and the previously mentioned co-defendants were all indicted on first-degree murder charges and convicted on January 25, 1971 (Bugliosi & Gentry, 1974). Prior to sentencing, the three women confessed their role in the murders, testifying they acted on their own accord and Manson was not aware of the murders until after they occurred (Caldwell, 1971). Despite these confessions, Manson and his co-defendants were sentenced to death but this was substituted with life imprisonment when California abolished the death penalty (Linder, 2014).

Context

The context in which these murders occurred cannot be ignored. In the 1960s there was a strong counterculture forming, especially in San Francisco, emphasizing an overall disengagement from capitalist culture, the outlaw persona, exoticism, the new age of sexuality, spirituality, "escaping to the now," and the natural persona (Zimmerman, 2008). The outlaw persona was fundamental in establishing the counterculture primarily due to its potential for disregarding or breaking the law (Zimmerman, 2008). Any laws that restricted individual freedom and did not conform comfortably within the countercultural movement were disregarded in their entirety (Zimmerman, 2008).

Arguably, one of the better-known tenets of the 1960s counterculture was an overarching emphasis on the exotic – immersing oneself in a radically different lifestyle than was endorsed by the mainstream culture (Zimmerman, 2008). "Everyday activities, such as drug taking, listening to music, dancing, and sex, were transformed into 'mystical' quests, secular experiences into sacred adventures" (Zimmerman, 2008, p. 58). A related element of the counterculture was an emphasis on the new age persona valuing spirituality, non-Western philosophies, and sexual freedom (Zimmerman, 2008). These components were intensely interrelated – sexual freedom could produce or increase one's spirituality or spiritual and philosophical ideologies could be used in pursuit of sexual hedonism (Zimmerman, 2008). This persona can be summarized as an ideology promoting "free love" (Zimmerman, 2008).

Finally, the natural persona was associated with having the freedom to be whatever you want to be (Zimmerman, 2008). Similar to the mainstream, a number of items were found in the counterculture – sex, food, drugs, clothing, shelter, etc. – but the difference was in how these items were used, regarded, and evaluated (Zimmerman, 2008). "What was important for the counterculture was to distinguish itself and its brand of freedom from that of the mainstream. Nature was the key to making that distinction" (Zimmerman, 2008, p. 93). Therefore, importance was placed on "natural" materials – handcrafted items, noncommercial ideas, and home-grown music and musicians (Zimmerman, 2008). It should, therefore, be kept in mind that the natural persona did not explicitly require a literal return to nature; rather it involved a consumption of "natural signifiers in its attempts to appear free of that which seemed commercial" (Zimmerman, 2008, p. 95). All of these elements of the counterculture were embedded within wider sociopolitical movements emphasizing antiwar protests, liberation of the suppressed, and skepticism surrounding consumer capitalism (McKay, 2005; Zimmerman, 2008).

DURKHEIM'S THEORY OF RELIGION: TOTEMISM

In an attempt to explain the unswerving loyalty given to Manson by his followers, Durkheim's (1912/1976) theory on the origins of religion will be used to show how a religion formed among the family. This section will begin by reviewing Durkheim's theory, with an emphasis on totemism, followed by a subsection making explicit connections between his theory and the Manson Family.

The bulk of Durkheim's work is centered on the analysis of nonmaterial social facts, emphasizing the importance of morality, collective conscience, collective representations, and social currents (Ritzer, 1992). Religion has been conceived as the ultimate nonmaterial social fact and has a "dynamogenic" quality, which is the capacity to not only inhibit the actions of individuals but also to elevate them above their conventional powers and capabilities (Jones, 1986; Ritzer, 1992). As follows, the ultimate goal for Durkheim was to decipher the origins of religion in modern society. He concludes that society is the source of religion through designating certain things as sacred – things set apart and forbidden – and others as profane (Durkheim, 1912/1976). There is nothing inherently religious or sacred about these "things" but their power is determined by the opinion conferred on them by members of society (Durkheim, 1912/1976). Differentiating between the sacred and profane is a necessary, but not sufficient, condition in the formation of religion. There must also be three other conditions: (1) development of religious beliefs as an expression of the nature of sacred things relative to the profane; (2) a collection of religious rites outlining how one should conduct oneself in the presence of the sacred; and (3) the presence of a Church, or an overarching moral community (Durkheim, 1912/1976).

Based on the sacred profane dichotomy, Durkheim defined religion as "a unified system of beliefs and practices relative to sacred things – things set apart and forbidden – beliefs and practices which unite into one single moral community called a Church" (Durkheim, 1912/1976, p. 47). He conceptualized the sacred through totems, which are merely symbols, a tangible expression of something else (Durkheim, 1912/1976). A totem is recognized as either the outward and visible form of the totemic principle or the symbol of a particular society, also known as a clan (Durkheim, 1912/1976). Oftentimes the totem of a clan is either an animal or plant, yet a totem can also be an object or individual (Durkheim, 1912/1976). Durkheim (1912/1976) identified a clan as a composition of individuals who are united by a bond of kinship. The clan is recognized as a single family, regardless of whether they are blood relatives, because they have achieved unity through a collective endorsement of the sacred totem (Durkheim, 1912/1976). Therefore, the clan has ascribed sacredness to a totem, giving it a symbolic representation that is meaningful to them. In this way, the totem has a religious character and becomes inseparable from the clan itself (Durkheim, 1912/1976). This argument alludes to society being the source of religion. Accordingly:

> [...] the god of the clan, the totemic principle, can be none other than the clan itself, but the clan transfigured and imagined in the physical form of the plant or animal that serves as totem. (Durkheim, 1912/1976, p. 206)

Totemism, or religion more generally, therefore emerges from a collective morality of beliefs. For the clan to successfully unite into a religion, however, there must be collective effervescence, which occurs when "a collectivity is able to achieve a new and heightened level of collective exaltation that in turn can lead to great changes in the structure of society" (Ritzer, 1992, p. 199). This implies that one clan's symbolic representation of a totem has been institutionalized and endorsed within the wider society.

Subsequent to defining religion and carefully outlining the primacy of totems in religion, Durkheim (1912/1976, p. 206) defined a God as:

> [...] a being that man conceives of as superior to himself in some respects and one on whom he believes he depends [...] the faithful believe they are bound to certain ways of acting that the nature of the sacred principle they are dealing with has imposed upon them.

This ties back to the dynamogenic quality of religion. According to Durkheim (1912/1976, p. 207):

> When we obey someone out of respect for the moral authority we have accorded to him, we do not follow his instructions because they seem wise but because a certain psychic energy intrinsic to the idea we have of that person [which] bends our will and turns it in the direction indicated [...] We are then moved not by the advantages or disadvantages of the conduct that is recommended to us or demanded of us but by the way we conceive of the one who recommends or demands that conduct.

Therefore, the totemic principle, or god of the clan, can inhibit an individual's behavior as the faithful are subject to "restraints, privations, and sacrifices determined by the sacred principle" (Durkheim, 1912/1976, p. 206). The faithful can also be elevated beyond their routine actions and behaviors in pursuit of the sacred.

This behavior can also be connected to what Durkheim calls the demon of oratorical inspiration. When one is speaking to a group and has achieved spiritual union with them, their language becomes ostentatious, which would be considered unacceptable in regular circumstances. Their gestures take on a dominating quality, and their thought "becomes impatient of limits and slips easily into every kind of extreme" (Durkheim, 1912/1976, p. 210). The hallmark of the demon of oratorical inspiration is a feeling of being influenced by a moral force greater than oneself, of which they are the sole interpreter (Durkheim, 1912/1976). In this way, the speaker may be deified by the group and perceived of as greater than oneself.

In sum, religion is a product of a unified system of beliefs regarding what is deemed sacred to a moral community. Sacredness is determined by the meaning ascribed to totems, which is inseparable from the clan itself. A god, or totemic principle, is a being conceived of as superior to the clan, upon which the clan depends. Actions or behaviors are carried out by faithful members in the name of the totemic principle regardless of the potential consequences of engaging in that conduct. Based on these definitions, it will be argued that Helter Skelter was constructed as the clan's totem and through totemism the Manson Family evolved into a religious sect. Due to the opinion conferred on Manson by his followers, it will then be argued that he was virtually deified. The following section provides a brief overview of the methodological approach taken.

METHODOLOGICAL APPROACH

In mapping out connections between Durkheim's theory of religion and the details of the Manson Family murders, multimedia files were collected and analyzed qualitatively. Media files were not selected randomly, rather, the inclusion criteria required that the documents quoted members of the family or were written by them. This selection strategy, although not entirely free of media construction biases, allows for inferences to be drawn based on statements made by the Family, rather than perceptions about them.

In selecting primary documents, two search engines were used: ProQuest and Google. The former is powered through the University of Guelph library and provides archived newspapers dating back to the 19th century; two historical newspaper databases are included within: *New York Times* and the *Globe and Mail*. These two news sources were relied upon exclusively in collecting newspaper articles that covered the criminal trials. Using the search term "Charles Manson," 2,163 results were generated from the *New York Times* and 1,105 from the *Globe and Mail*. Of these, 83 news articles were selected for analysis (30 published in the *Globe and Mail* and 53 from the *New York Times*). In addition to news articles, two books were included in the analysis: *Manson in His Own Words* (Emmons, 1986) and *Child of Satan, Child of God* (Atkins & Slosser, 2005). Finally, *Google* was used to find videotaped interviews with any member of the Manson Family, resulting in the collection of 33 YouTube videos. These videos were then transcribed prior to data analysis.

A theoretical thematic analysis was executed on the sample of media files, following a step-wise process outlined by Braun and Clarke (2006). Accordingly, based on Durkheim's theory of religion, a number of codes were developed a priori (i.e., perceptions of Manson as a deity, messiah, god, or Jesus Christ, perceptions of sacredness, the belief system of the Family, etc.). These initial codes were subsequently collated to identify broader themes – the sacredness ascribed to Helter Skelter, the unified belief system, rites of conduct, Manson as the totemic principle, and the presence of a moral community – each of which are discussed, in turn, below.

CHARLES MANSON AND THE FAMILY

Sacredness Ascribed to Helter Skelter

To reiterate Durkheim's position, a necessary condition in the formation of a religion is the clan's designation of an object, animal, or individual as sacred. Within the Manson Family, sacredness was ascribed to The Beatles *White Album,* more specifically, the song titled *Helter Skelter.* Manson was infatuated with the songs of this album and their "messages" to the point where he repeatedly played the album (Atkins & Slosser, 2005; Waldron, 1970b). Manson believed the Beatles were speaking to him, that he had some sort of apocalyptic connection with them (Atkins & Slosser, 2005). Aligned with his philosophy of an impending revolution, Helter Skelter became the code name for it and witnesses have testified that Manson became obsessed with lecturing his followers on the immediacy of *Helter Skelter* (Waldron, 1970a, 1970b). There was nothing inherently sacred about this album but it was given a symbolic representation. Manson perceived the lyrics as instructions for his Family on how to prepare for the upcoming racial revolution. Most of his followers believed in

Helter Skelter, which was conceived as the end of the world, and they believed it was "coming down fast" (Atkins & Slosser, 2005). This viewpoint was not questioned. According to Susan Atkins, "the whole thing was done to instil fear in the establishment and cause paranoia. Also to show the black man how to take over the white man. This would be the start of 'Helter Skelter,'" which was conceptualized as the last war on the face of the earth (Bugliosi & Gentry, 1974, p. 217). "It would instil fear into the 'pigs' and to bring on judgment day which is here now for all" (Bugliosi & Gentry, 1974, pp. 217–218). The symbolic representation accorded to Helter Skelter is unique to the Manson clan and is reflective of their belief system at the time.

It will now be demonstrated how the ascription of sacredness to Helter Skelter solidified the belief system of the Family and also influenced how they behaved in relation to it.

Unified Belief System and Rites of Conduct

Although the Manson Family membership shifted constantly, it generally consisted of 12 permanent female members and six males who lived communally, partaking in heavy drug use and sexual promiscuity (Roberts, 1969). Charles Manson slowly recruited members into the Family; these recruits were typically from middle-class backgrounds who desired to break free from the conventional establishment (Roberts, 1970).

> Once Manson succeeded in making recruits, he tried to eradicate their "hang-ups" about conventional society. By "hang-ups" he essentially meant anything he did not like, and their removal was not a very difficult process. He was dealing with lonely, insecure people in need of a father figure. What he did, in effect, was to tear down that ego and substitute himself, thus achieving enormous control over his followers. They became empty vessels for whatever he poured in. As Susan Atkins said bleakly: '*I never questioned what Charlie said. I just did it*' [Emphasis added]. (Roberts, 1970, p. 180)

Through eradicating their "hang-ups" Manson was fundamentally reprogramming his followers. He believed that everyone had been "programmed" by societal institutions and it was his job to reprogram them to give up individual egos in pursuit of his philosophy (IRF4905, 2014; MichaelsBackporch, 2011c). In doing so, the beliefs held by Manson became unified and widely endorsed by the Family.

Originally, Manson's philosophy was premised on not recognizing good or evil, right or wrong, death, time or pain, and prioritized living in the "now"; he embraced the natural while condemning the evils of urban life and corrupt power structures (Roberts, 1970; Waldron, 1970b). Since Manson believed man constructed time, none of the family members wore watches nor did they talk about their past or celebrate birthdays (Helter Skelter Forum, 2010a). All the activities at the ranch were designed so that Manson's followers would take on his will, he preached oneness to his followers and would say, "each man is a god. I am god, and you are god" (Roberts, 1969, p. 84). To further foster this sense of oneness, according to Krenwinkle, Manson would stop members at any point throughout the day and begin a mirroring exercise, where they would repeat his gestures and expressions (Helter Skelter Forum, 2010a). To illustrate the unified belief system, many of Manson's followers were quoted saying, "I am Charlie and Charlie is me" (Roberts, 1970, p. 180). Another member of the Family, Sandra Good, stated in an interview, "He's whatever a person wants to make of him. He's a mirror… a reflection of yourself" (The Manson Family Today, 2006a). To provide another example, during the trial a few of Manson's followers were outside the courthouse in support of him, their heads shaved the same as his, and claimed, "whenever we move, we move together. We are one thought" (MichaelsBackporch, 2011a). Similarly, when Manson carved an "X" in his forehead, so too did many of his devoted followers (IRF4905, 2014; MichaelsBackporch, 2011b).

In the months preceding the murders, however, his philosophy began to revolve around the idea of an impending revolution, or a racial holocaust, where Black people would emerge triumphant (Kneeland, 1970). Manson would continually talk about how Helter Skelter was the basis of what they wanted to do in terms of chaos (MichaelsBackporch, 2011d). To quote Leslie Van Houten:

> [Manson] said that it was the blacks turn, that the white had been on top for too long, and all they did was put harm on other people, that we're not like them. (The Manson Family Today, 2008a)

As a collective, the Family endorsed and inherently believed Manson's philosophy to be true; many believed that "Helter Skelter" was "coming down fast" (Atkins & Slosser, 2005). Tex Watson admitted to believing that the world was going to come to an end the very next day, and to him, that provided enough justification to carry out the murders at Manson's command (The Manson Family Today, 2006b). According to Atkins, Manson would consistently preach about the impending Helter Skelter and upon its arrival they would need to flee into the desert, to the bottomless pit, where they would eventually emerge once the Blacks realized they need help in running the world (Atkins & Slosser, 2005). When Manson said they needed supplies for their retreat into the desert, some of his followers were arrested for stealing cars which were converted into dune buggies to increase operating efficiency in the desert terrain (Atkins & Slosser, 2005).

With respect to Durkheim's conditions in forming a religion, there must also be a collection of rites outlining how members of a clan are to conduct themselves in the presence of the sacred. This was evident among the Family. They did not question the sacredness ascribed to Helter Skelter. Rather, they exhibited a concerted effort to prepare for it; the Family collected guns, cars, and other material possessions and would regularly search the desert looking for a hole that would lead to the bottomless pit (Atkins & Slosser, 2005). The aforementioned quotes provide evidence of a unified belief system and also rules for conducting themselves in the presence of the sacred, however, it should also be noted that it was Manson's beliefs that became unified and endorsed among the Family. With this in mind, it will now be illustrated that Manson's philosophy was accepted unquestionably due to the opinion conferred onto him by his followers.

Manson as the Totemic Principle of the Clan

According to Durkheim (1912/1976, p. 206), a God is:

> a being that man conceives of as superior to himself in some respects and one on whom he believes he depends [...] the faithful believe they are bound to certain ways of acting that the nature of the sacred principle they are dealing with has imposed upon them.

Based on this definition, it will be illustrated in this section that Manson was conferred with a god-like grandeur by the clan. His deification was not immediate, but rather attributable to a number of social processes. Subsequent to recruiting Family members, Manson would usually begin by having sex with the female members, simultaneously convincing the plain that they were beautiful (Bugliosi & Gentry, 1974). Male members would be taken on an LSD trip:

> [...] ostensibly "to open his mind." Then, while he was in a highly suggestible state, he would talk about love, how you had to surrender yourself to it, how only by ceasing to exist as an individual ego could you become one with all things. (Bugliosi & Gentry, 1974, p. 235)

Once the recruit was under the influence, Manson would offer any of his girls to pleasure him and once they accepted they were obligated to him in some way, shape, or form (Bugliosi & Gentry, 1974).

Oftentimes, Manson would compare himself to Jesus Christ and other times, when the group was high on LSD, he would re-enact the crucifixion, with his followers pretending to nail him on a cross (IRF4905, 2014). Aligned with this display, there would often be bizarre tests of devotion. Manson would ask his followers to stand against a tree and he would throw a hatchet at them, asking, "Do you trust me? Will you die for me? Will you be me?" (Helter Skelter Forum, 2010b; IRF4905, 2014). Members obliged without hesitation (Helter Skelter Forum, 2010b). This is illustrative of the dynamogenic quality of religion. Manson was obeyed out of the moral authority that was accorded to him; his instructions followed due to the opinion conferred onto him by his followers. According to Krenwinkle, when questioned on why she committed the Tate-LaBianca slayings, she replied "I was following Charlie's orders because they were Charlie's orders" (Helter Skelter Forum, 2010b). Moreover, Manson would exert power displays with the group by preaching to them atop a large rock; no other members ever sat or stood on that rock, but rather circled it embracing his words (Bugliosi & Gentry, 1974). He would preach that each member was independent but in reality they were dependent upon him.

> He said that he couldn't tell anyone else what to do, that they should "do what love tells you," but he also told them, "I am your love," and his wants became theirs. (Bugliosi & Gentry, 1974, p. 225)

In a documentary (1991), Van Houten admitted that in 1971 she felt that Manson was Jesus Christ and Helter Skelter was necessary (The Manson Family Today, 2008a). Atkins and Slosser (2005) also acknowledged that when Manson grew out his hair and beard he looked like Jesus and she felt that he very well could be. Similarly, another of Manson's girls was quoted, "I felt he was the messiah come again: you know, the second coming of Christ, I thought he was another Jesus Christ" (Robinson, 1970, p. 21).

These perceptions can also be connected to what Durkheim calls the demon of oratorical inspiration. Manson genuinely felt tuned in with God and messages were relayed to him through the Beatles music; he was the sole interpreter. One night, while listening to the *White Album*, Manson proclaimed, "They're speaking to me" (Atkins & Slosser, 2005). This furthered the groups belief that he was godly – they felt as if they were tuned into God through Charlie and the primary message was survival above all else (Atkins & Slosser, 2005). Other family members testified to this: Manson believed he was the vehicle chosen to bring about Helter Skelter (Waldron, 1970a). In sum, the opinion conferred onto Manson by his followers resulted in him being virtually deified and placed in a position of superiority relative to his Family.

Presence of an Overarching Moral Community

The final condition necessary in the formation of a religion is the presence of a Church, or an overarching moral community (Durkheim, 1912/1976). This is necessary to renew the clan's common faith through public demonstrations of their beliefs. Durkheim (1912/1976) believed that without this, emotional ties to the religion would dissipate. Although there was no "Church" attendance within the Family, because they lived communally on Spahn's Ranch there was a constant demonstration of their faith. As mentioned previously, activities at the Ranch were centered upon taking on Manson's will and preparing for Helter Skelter. Emotions were continuously strengthened through regular exposure to Manson's philosophy. It initially appears as though the Manson clan had achieved collective effervescence from their attempts to develop an internally coherent religious narrative. However, their symbolic representation of Helter Skelter did not become institutionalized or embraced by the wider culture, leading to its demise.

In summary, connections were drawn between the Manson Family and Durkheim's theory of religious formation. According to this theory, in order for a religion to form, a clan must ascribe sacredness to an object, animal, or individual, which subsequently determines the conduct of its members. There must also be a unified system of beliefs and rules of conduct within the group as well as the presence of a church or overarching moral community. Within this section, it has been demonstrated that the Family ascribed sacredness to The Beatles *White Album*, more specifically, the song titled *Helter Skelter*. Devoted members of the family never questioned this totem and their beliefs were reflective of Manson's, resulting in a unified belief system. Moreover, it has been shown how Manson was virtually deified by members of the clan and there was a definite presence of an overarching moral community. Since collective effervescence was not attained, however, it can only be inferred that a pseudo-religion formed among the Family. Their symbolic representation of Helter Skelter was not widely endorsed yet they were still able to form an internally coherent narrative among themselves, resulting in a religious formation.

Hall's Theory of Religion and Violence

It has been shown how a pseudoreligion formed among the Manson Family, the remainder of this chapter will be dedicated to demonstrating a connection between religious affiliation and violence using John Hall's theory (2003, 2013). In speculating on religion and violence, Hall (2013, p. 7) proposes "a phenomenological and cultural approach that theorizes multiple kinds of relationships between religion and violence according to structural situations." In some circumstances, religion itself structures the sacred meaning of action, "thereby not only legitimating violence but also actually shaping its character as well as the patterns of social organization and the processes in which violence occurs" (Hall, 2013, p. 7). Building off of Durkheim's *Elementary Forms of Religious Life,* Hall (2013) notes that the sacred and profane are socially and culturally constructed and based on these constructions lies the possibility of violence occurring as a sacred duty. Hall (2013, p. 7) concludes that it is "not religious traditions but religious formations and their contextual circumstances [that] shape their potential instantiations with violence." This statement initially appears contradictory to Durkheim's theory; however, it can be argued that it merely compliments his work, adding insight into the associative link between religion and violence.

One kind of relationship between religion and violence concerns utopian "apocalyptic" movements where a sacred course of action is developed in preparation of "the end of the world as we know it" (Hall, 2013, p. 6). Within the apocalyptic orientation, Hall further differentiated between pre-apocalyptic and post-apocalyptic counterhegemonic conflicts. The former involves sects preparing for the apocalypse, whereas the latter involves sects who believe they have somehow escaped or survived it (Hall, 2003). These sects can either be peaceful or violent depending upon group orientation. Of relevance to this chapter is pre-apocalyptic warring sects who view "themselves as agents of apocalyptic history battling to defeat the forces of evil" (Hall, 2003, p. 372). Hall (2003, p. 372) has described this group as:

> A band of true believers, who become certified as charismatic warriors through a process of rebirth, acts alone or in concert with a wider underground network of sympathizers and similar bands. These warriors engage in the moment-to-moment coordination of guerilla-style action in pursuit of strategic, symbolic, and terrorist missions [...] [T]he successful execution of actions related to missions and contingency plans depends on interpersonal trust, the development of high proficiency at various technical and strategic skills, and acts of commitment and bravery which place mission ahead of personal survival.

These warring sects arise within the context of a wider countercultural movement, frequently in relation to social conditions perceived as a threat to the existing social order (Hall, 2003). Violence is thus pursued as the basis for social reconstruction (Hall, 2003). A religious component is always evident within these sects but is often confounded with broader "nationalist, anticolonial, and revolutionary class movements" (Hall, 2003, p. 372).

In the remaining section of this chapter it will be argued that the Manson Family originally came together as a countercultural group who evolved into an apocalyptic movement. The religion that formed legitimized violent behavior and also structured "the 'sacred' meaning of action" (Hall, 2013, p. 374). It should first be mentioned, however, that this argument alludes to motive. Throughout the criminal proceedings, prosecutor Vincent Bugliosi was striving to develop a motive for the murders (Bugliosi & Gentry, 1974). He decided that they were motivated by the group's belief in Helter Skelter. From this point of view, Bugliosi was merely interested in the defendants' mens rea. From a sociological perspective, however:

> [...] motive acquires its analytic character as a public product rather than as a private "state," and must be understood grammatically (as part of the meaning of an action) rather than as a factual report on some contingent, antecedent event. (Blum & McHugh, 1971, p. 101)

Grammar of motives is used whenever an event is to be interpreted within a collection of owned experiences, what Blum and McHugh (1971) call a biography. Actors conceive themselves as having particular pasts, which routinely inform the observer about behavioral possibilities (Blum & McHugh, 1971). In other words, motive is a sociological procedure for describing how individuals show themselves as persons. Therefore, the murderous event should be interpreted against Manson's collection of owned experiences and this will give you the motive. Helter Skelter was aligned with his past experiences of distrust with institutions and racist tendencies while providing the means to accomplish an organized and concerted cure to what he (and others around him) perceived as a problem.

The Manson Family as a Warring Sect

The primary tenet of Hall's (2003, 2013) argument is that religious violence is situational and how the resulting violence is structured depends on contextual circumstances unique to the religious group. Within this section it will be demonstrated that the Manson Family came together as a countercultural movement yet evolved into a warring sect. The religion that formed legitimized violent behavior and also structured "the 'sacred' meaning of action" (Hall, 2013, p. 374). To contextualize the Tate-LaBianca murders, reference must be made to the broader social forces permeating the group in the late 1960s.

The Manson Family originally came together as a countercultural group – they believed in the notion of "dropping out" or disengaging from the mainstream and they adopted many of the previously mentioned personas (i.e., the outlaw, the new age, and the natural persona). Additionally, the 1960s were marked by a period of civic activism in an effort to liberate the suppressed; Black people, homosexuals, and women were demanding equality (McKay, 2005). This furthered Manson's paranoia of a racial revolution. While listening to the *White Album*, Manson would make connections between the lyrics and Revelations 9 from the Bible. From this he argued that Armageddon was at hand and news reporting on Black riots and Black militancy groups, such as the Black Panthers, furthered this belief (Helter Skelter Forum, 2010b). As previously demonstrated, the Family believed that "Helter Skelter was coming down fast" and eventually realized they would have to be the ones to initiate the revolution (Atkins & Slosser, 2005). Given that *Helter Skelter* was conceived as sacred, the ensuing murders were legitimized as a necessary religious duty. The brutality of the murders can also be understood within this framework. In order to spark a war between races, the murders had to be "witchy" and "memorable" to capture the attention of society (Helter Skelter Forum, 2010c, 2010d). In so doing, they were made to look like the Blacks had committed them, the "establishment" would then come down on their race and, in retaliation, Black people would rise and the revolution would begin (Bugliosi & Gentry, 1974; Helter Skelter Forum, 2010c, 2010d).

It will now be argued that the Manson Family evolved into a pre-apocalyptic warring sect. According to Hall (2003), a warring sect is composed of agents who have experienced rebirth in pursuit of a symbolic mission. The success of these sects is dependent upon interpersonal trust, the development of strategies and skills that foster commitment, resulting in a pursuit of the mission at the expense of personal survival (Hall, 2003). The emergence of these groups is often a response to a perceived external threat and violence is pursued as a basis for social reconstruction (Hall, 2003). Each of the Family members had experienced a process of rebirth from their original identities through Manson eradicating their "hang-ups," essentially replacing individual egos with his philosophy (Roberts, 1970). In the development of a unified belief system, a strong sense of interpersonal trust was fostered among group members. When Manson's philosophy became centered upon the immediacy of Helter Skelter, he began to focus his energy on preparing the group for the revolution. They began collecting supplies for their survival and were taught how to use guns (Atkins & Slosser, 2005). They were continually asked if they were willing to die for him; whether they were willing to die in pursuit of heaven on earth (Helter Skelter Forum, 2010c). Leslie Van Houten provides support for these inferences:

> I felt that because [Krenwinkle] had gone [to the Tate murders the previous night], I felt that what *we were doing was a mission that needed to be done*. I felt that if they went again, I wanted to go, *I wanted to be a soldier and surrender myself for what I believed in* [Emphasis added] (MichaelsBackporch, 2012)

CONCLUSION

In conclusion, it has been demonstrated that a pseudoreligion formed among the Manson Family through (1) ascribing sacredness to *Helter Skelter*, (2) by developing a unified system of beliefs and corresponding rules of conduct, and (3) the presence of an overarching moral community. Charles Manson had become the clan's totemic principle, or god, by the opinion conferred onto him by his followers. Once this religion developed and solidified it then structured the subsequent violence committed by the Family. By giving their unswerving loyalty to Manson, he was conferred with the power to give orders that would be obeyed out of a respect for his moral authority. His instructions to kill were not questioned and the consequences of his orders were not considered. The religion that formed among the Family also structured the course of subsequent violence. Embedded within the group's orientation, the sacredness ascribed to *Helter Skelter* allowed for the creation of a warring sect whose mission was to combat the evil forces of the establishment and prevent the demise of the White race.

ACKNOWLEDGMENT

I would like to thank Dr Mervyn Horgan for providing a strong foundation in sociological theory and all his assistance and feedback in writing this chapter.

REFERENCES

Atchinson, A., & Heide, K. (2010). Charles Manson and the family: The application of sociological theories to multiple murder. *International Journal of Offender Therapy and Comparative Criminology*, *55*(5), 771–798.

Atkins, S., & Slosser, B. (2005). *Child of Satan, child of God.* CA: Menelorelin Dorenay.

Blum, A., & McHugh, P. (1971). The social ascription of motives. *American Sociological Review*, *36*(1), 98–109.

Braun, V., & Clarke, V. (2006). Using thematic analysis in psychology. *Qualitative Research in Psychology*, *3*(2), 77–101.

Bugliosi, V., & Gentry, C. (1974). *Helter Skelter: The true story of the Manson murders.* New York, NY: Bantam Books.

Caldwell, E. (1971). 'Robot theory' cited in defense of Manson's 3 co-defendants. *New York Times,* January 13, 1971. Retrieved from http://www.nytimes.com/1971/01/13/archives/-robot-theory-cited-in-defense-of-mansons-3-codefendants.html. Accessed on November 11, 2014.

Durkheim, E. (1912/1976). *The elementary forms of the religious life*. London: Allen & Unwin.

Emmons, N. (1986). *Manson in his own words as told to Nuel Emmons.* New York, NY: Grove Press.

Fine, G. (1982). The Manson Family: The folklore traditions of a small group. *Journal of the Folklore Institute*, *19*(1), 47–60.

Geis, G., & Huston, T. (1970). Charles Manson and his girls: Notes on a Durkheimian theme. *Criminology*, *9*, 342–353.

Hall, J. (2003). Religion and violence: Social processes in comparative perspective. In M. Dillon (Ed.), *Handbook of the sociology of religion* (pp. 359–381). New York, NY: Cambridge University Press.

Hall, J. (2013). Religion and violence from a sociological perspective. In M. Jerryson, M. Juergensmeyer, & M. Kitts (Eds.), *The Oxford handbook of religion and violence* (pp. 363–374). New York, NY: Oxford University Press.

Helter Skelter Forum. (2010a). Diane Sawyer meets Manson, Krenwinkle and Van Houten – Part 1. *YouTube*. Retrieved from https://www.youtube.com/watch?v=uHQTulrAS5Y. Accessed on November 11, 2014.

Helter Skelter Forum. (2010b). Diane Sawyer meets Manson, Krenwinkle and Van Houten – Part 2. *YouTube*. Retrieved from https://www.youtube.com/watch?v=Zn2zULFwB_w. Accessed on November 11, 2014.

Helter Skelter Forum. (2010c). Diane Sawyer meets Manson, Krenwinkle and Van Houten – Part 3. *YouTube*. Retrieved from https://www.youtube.com/watch?v=LBlDOE_pNPo. Accessed on November 11, 2014.

Helter Skelter Forum. (2010d). Diane Sawyer meets Manson, Krenwinkle and Van Houten – Part 4. *YouTube*. Retrieved from https://www.youtube.com/watch?v=8PX7O3r3VyY. Accessed on November 11, 2014.

IRF4905. (2014). The Manson women documentary. *YouTube*. Retrieved from https://www.youtube.com/watch?v=yTabHM5ieQg. Accessed on November 30, 2014.

Jones, R. (1986). Durkheim, Frazer, and Smith: The role of analogies and exemplars in the development of Durkheim's sociology of religion. *American Journal of Sociology*, *92*, 596–627.

Kneeland, D. (1970). Witness says Manson gives off "vibrations" in the courtroom. *New York Times,* August 14, 1970. Retrieved from http://www.nytimes.com/1970/08/14/archives/witness-says-manson-gives-off-vibrations-in-the-courtroom.html. Accessed on November 11, 2014.

Linder, D. (2014). The Charles Manson (Tate-LaBianca) murder trial. *Famous Trials.* Retrieved from http://law2.umkc.edu/faculty/projects/ftrials/manson/mansonaccount.html. Accessed on November 30, 2014.

The Manson Family Today. (2006a). Sandra Good 1989 current affair interview part 1. *YouTube.* Retrieved from https://www.youtube.com/watch?v=XR_k6NG6qRE&list=PL9FC046F17949422C&index=4. Accessed on November 30, 2014.

The Manson Family Today. (2006b). Manson Family – special report part 2. *YouTube.* Retrieved from https://www.youtube.com/watch?v=4Nfy7MAy1_I. Accessed on November 30, 2014.

The Manson Family Today. (2008). Excerpt from Leslie Van Houten documentary, 1991. *YouTube.* Retrieved from https://www.youtube.com/watch?v=n6CepHzjlJw. Accessed on November 30, 2014.

MichaelsBackporch. (2011a). Charlie Manson's girls threaten to pour gas on herself blue backporch tapes collections. *YouTube.* Retrieved from https://www.youtube.com/watch?v=QDJffCi1FHM&index=35&list=PLE06A570739A752FB. Accessed on November 30, 2014.

MichaelsBackporch. (2011b). Charles Manson Family girls singing on the corner courthouse Helter Skelter backporch tapes. *YouTube.* Retrieved from https://www.youtube.com/watch?v=TbQMXJwuqeI&index=65&list=PLE06A570739A752FB&spfreload=1. Accessed on November 30, 2014.

MichaelsBackporch. (2011c). The Charles Manson family trial Los Angeles 1969 sounds pictures backporch tapes collections. *YouTube.* Retrieved from https://www.youtube.com/watch?v=A-RhY3xzKoE&list=PLE06A570739A752FB&index=111. Accessed on November 30, 2014.

MichaelsBackporch. (2011d). Charles Manson Family Helter Skelter murder/ trials time machine lookback VH1 backporch tapes. *YouTube.* Retrieved from https://www.youtube.com/watch?v=K-GvO30H9hI&index=64&list=PLE06A570739A752FB. Accessed on November 30, 2014.

MichaelsBackporch. (2012). Killer Leslie Van Houten speaks about Helter Skelter and the Charles Manson Family. *YouTube.* Retrieved from https://www.youtube.com/watch?v=qgj3_7MAWOg. Accessed on November 30, 2014.

McKay, G. (2005). The social and (counter)cultural 1960s in the USA, transatlantically. In C. Grunenberg & J. Harris (Eds.), *Summer of love: Psychedelic art, social crisis and counterculture in the 1960s* (pp. 35–62). Liverpool: Liverpool University Press.

McKie, R. (2009). Charles Manson follower ends her silence 40 years after night of slaughter. *The Guardian,* August 2, 2009. Retrieved from http://www.theguardian.com/world/2009/aug/02/charles-manson-linda-kasabian-polanski. Accessed on November 11, 2014.

Ritzer, G. (1992). *Classical sociological theory.* United States: McGraw-Hill.

Roberts, S. (1969). Charlie Manson, nomadic guru, flirted with crime in a turbulent childhood. *New York Times,* December 7, 1969. Retrieved from http://query.nytimes.com/gst/abstract.html?res=9504E5D61E3AEF3BBC4F53DFB4678382679EDE&legacy=true. Accessed on November 11, 2014.

Roberts, S. (1970). Charlie Manson: One man's family. *New York Times,* January 4, 1970. Retrieved from http://www.nytimes.com/1970/01/04/archives/charlie-manson-one-mans-family-charlie-manson-one-mans-family.html. Accessed on November 11, 2014.

Robinson, D. (1970). Key witness says that she once regarded Manson as a 'Messiah.' *New York Times,* August 1, 1970. Retrieved from http://query.nytimes.com/gst/abstract.html?res=9400EFDB1F3EEE34BC4953DFBE66838B669EDE&legacy=true. Accessed on November 11, 2014.

Stanley, A. (2004). Manson Family's summer of death: Helter Skelter. *New York Times,* May 14, 2004. Retrieved from http://www.nytimes.com/2004/05/14/movies/tv-weekend-manson-family-s-summer-of-death.html. Accessed on November 11, 2014.

Waldron, M. (1970a). Cyclist describes 'family'. *New York Times,* September 12, 1970. Retrieved from http://www.nytimes.com/1970/09/12/archives/cyclist-describes-family.html. Accessed on November 11, 2014.

Waldron, M. (1970b). A Manson motive is heard at trial: Witness links Beatles and the Bible to slayings. *New York Times,* October 18, 1970. Retrieved from http://www.nytimes.com/1970/10/18/archives/a-manson-motive-is-heard-at-trial-witness-links-beatles-and-the.html. Accessed on November 11, 2014.

Zimmerman, N. (2008). *Counterculture kaleidoscope: Musical and cultural perspectives on late sixties San Francisco*. Ann Arbor, MI: University of Michigan Press.

CHAPTER 5

A DECADE AFTER VIRGINIA TECH: CONSIDERATIONS OF CAMPUS SAFETY AND SECURITY FOR HIGHER EDUCATION INSTITUTIONS

Daniel Adrian Doss

ABSTRACT

Purpose – *A decade after the heinous act of moral turpitude at Virginia Tech, this chapter examines considerations of deterrence and mitigation for campus violence, and discusses the arming of campus police.*

Design/methodology/approach – *This chapter incorporates campus violence from a phenomenological perspective.*

Findings – *This chapter highlights the notion that no universal panacea exists toward abating violence among higher education settings. However, various preventive and control strategies may be employed to support the long-term campus safety initiatives of higher education institutions.*

Originality/value – *This chapter provides a commentary regarding preventive strategies, control strategies, and policy considerations for higher education institutions. It emphasizes the notion that all higher educations are unique, and must craft their own individual policies that satisfy the requirements of their specific situations.*

Keywords: Campus safety; campus security; campus shooting; violence; Virginia Tech

Homicide and Violent Crime
Sociology of Crime, Law and Deviance, Volume 23, 81–99

ISSN: 1521-6136/doi:10.1108/S1521-613620180000023006

INTRODUCTION

At the time of this authorship, a decade had passed since the 2007 tragic shooting at Virginia Tech. The incident demonstrated the necessity of implementing violence prevention, control, and response strategies among higher education environments. The insidious nature of the incident was demonstrated through the quantity of killings amassed during the rampage. The quantity of casualties almost doubled the quantity of murdered individuals that resulted from the 1966 University of Texas shooting (Fein, Carlisle, & Isaacson, 2008). Jenson (2007) and Davies (2008) indicate that a total of 33 individuals perished (including the suicide of the perpetrator), and 17 individuals suffered gunshot wounds.

Although infrequent, campus shootings are a realistic consideration of modern higher education administrators and leaders. Anyone may be the perpetrator, victim, or witness of such crime (McElreath et al., 2013). For instance, during 2017, at Texas Tech University, Floyd East, a campus police officer, while in the performance of his duties, was shot and killed by a student (Dobuzinskis, 2017). The Texas Tech police department discovered "evidence of drugs and drug paraphernalia" when they entered the student's room while checking upon the student's welfare (Dobuzinskis, 2017, p. 1). Hollis Daniels, the student who confessed to the killing, indicated that he had done "something illogical" during the ensuing investigation (Dobuzinskis, 2017, p. 1).

Another 2017 incident occurred at the Georgia Institute of Technology (Georgia Tech). Scout Schultz, an undergraduate engineering student, was shot and killed by campus police during an altercation occurring within a dormitory (Newlin, 2017). Campus police were called to the dormitory to respond to reports of an armed perpetrator (Newlin, 2017). When interacting with Schultz, he became uncompliant and uncooperative with police personnel (Newlin, 2017). Despite being told to disarm himself, Schultz approached the responding officers wielding a knife thereby prompting a fatal shot from police personnel (Newlin, 2017).

These incidents show the extremes of criminality that may result in death within the academic setting. Although such incidents are primarily uncommon, the risk of lethal danger exists within the confines of any institution. As a means of enhancing the safety levels of both the campus community and police personnel, numerous academic institutions have opted toward employing armed police personnel among their respective campuses.

Among higher education institutions, preparedness is a primary aspect of fielding an effective response to active shooter incidents (LaBanc & Hemphill, 2015). Institutions that fail to sponsor any type of security or police organization may experience increased dangerousness (LaBanc & Hemphill, 2015). Higher education institutions that rely solely upon external law enforcement organizations as safety and security resources may not experience immediate responses to incidents. Incident response times may increase with respect to the distance traveled by responding entities and the availability of resources (Doss, Sumrall, McElreath, & Jones, 2013). Thus, regarding decisions concerning the type of resource sponsored by the academic institution, some may deem it wise to possess an armed police force.

Regardless of armed police entities among campus settings, although it is assumed that colleges and universities are presumably and relatively safe areas for studying, working, living, and visiting, several threats exist within the contemporary educational setting. With respect to Clery reports, examples include assault (Coker, 2016), arson (Chekwa, Thomas, & Jones, 2013), burglary (Chekwa et al., 2013), homicide (Rao et al., 2016), robbery (Sheffield, Gregg, & Lee, 2016), and both theft and motor vehicle theft (McGrath, Perumean-Chaney, & Sloan, 2014). Given these examples, in addition to shootings, colleges and universities exhibit an array of dangers.

These incidents show the extremes of criminality that may result in death within the academic setting. Although such incidents are primarily uncommon, the risk of danger exists within the confines of any higher education institution. As a means of enhancing the safety levels of both the campus community and police personnel, numerous schools, colleges, and universities have opted toward employing armed police personnel among their respective campuses. Given these notions, this chapter examines various facets of institutional policies, methods, and modern endangerments existing within the American educational domain.

FRAMEWORK

Decisions rendered by campus administration must be toward the overall benefit of students. Thus, administrators should take efforts to render decisions that contribute to the well-being and the best development of students. In order to accomplish these goals, administrators must provide safe locations wherein learning may occur within the academic setting throughout the duration of the experience. Given these notions, the conceptual framework herein is derived from three primary areas: (1) student personnel theory, which emphasizes decisions toward crafting environments that are supportive of student development (Barrett, 2014); (2) emergency management cycle (EMC), which accommodates preparedness, mitigation, response, and recovery (McElreath et al., 2014a); and (3) Maslow's hierarchy (safety and security human needs) (Van Blerkom, 2013).

CAMPUS VIOLENCE

Olujuwon (2007, p. 39) defined violence as "any unjust or unwarranted exertion of force or power against a person, which could be physical, psychological, or sexual." Academic settings are not immune to acts of violence. Violence affects both secondary campuses and the environments of higher education institutions. Although recent activities of violence are prevalent among news reports involving school shootings, this type of violence is not the sole manifestation of violent activity among educational settings. Despite incidents that result in homicide and suicide, violence is also demonstrated through the acts of stalking, rape, and assault.

Secondary school violence represented "less than one percent of all homicides and suicides that occur among school-ages children," and demonstrated an increase among American campuses since the 1990s (Logue, 2008, p. 58). Logue (2008, p. 59) indicated that the quantity of these homicides ranged annually from "28 to 34" during the 1990s, ranged between "13 and 11" between 1999 and

2001, and had "steadily increased" to a quantity of 21 after the year of 2001. Logue (2008) indicated that firearms were a leading contributor among deaths attributed to violence.

Another example of such violence involved the West Nickel Amish School in Pennsylvania during 2006 (Logue, 2008). This event represented a loss of five lives among the student populace, and resulted in the suicide of the perpetrator (Logue, 2008). This incident represented the nineteenth Pennsylvania event that resulted in deaths (after 1992), and was the ninth homicidal event of the twenty-first century among Pennsylvania schools (Logue, 2008).

The settings of higher education are also susceptible to violence. Similar to the increases of violent events among secondary environments, Jenson (2007) indicated that violence among higher education settings was increasing. According to Jenson (2007), homicidal acts of violence may be traced historically to the Kent State University shootings that occurred during 1970. After the Kent State incident, Jenson (2007) indicated that 12 other such incidents occurred, and continue to affect contemporary settings among American higher education institutions. With respect to these twelve incidents, Jenson (2007) indicated that seven occurred after the year 1991, and four occurred after the year 2000. Historically, other deadly shootings to which deadly violence is traceable occurred at Jackson State University (1970) and the University of Texas (1966) (Doss et al., 2017).

Not all forms of violence among educational settings involved shooting as the primary basis of the offense. Stalking among campuses is a criminal offense that often results in violence and death (Maxey, 2003). With respect to such violence, Maxey (2003) described the 1996 stalking incident of San Diego State University, in which three professors were stalked and killed by a graduate student prior to a thesis defense, and the 2002 stalking incident, which occurred at the University of Arizona, in which three professors and the perpetrator died. According to Maxey (2003, p. 30), such stalking events were unique because they involved a pattern, a threat, and reasonable fears among the intended victims. However, Maxey (2003) indicated that such events were not always necessarily uncommon among the American populace. Therefore, based on these considerations and descriptions, stalking represents a dangerous form of violence among American educational settings.

Another form of campus violence is sexual violence, and both males and females may be the perpetrators or the victims of this crime. Similar to the increases of incidents involving campus shootings and campus stalking, McMahon (2008) indicated that incidents of campus rape were increasing within the educational domain. Quantitative characteristics of such violence demonstrated that about one in five "college women reported experiencing a sexual assault during their college years" (McMahon, 2008, p. 361). According to McMahon (2008, p. 361), campus rape contributes to an atmosphere of "fear after the assault" because both the victim and perpetrator may have resided together among living residences or shared enrollments within the same courses. Further, McMahon (2008) indicated that succeeding victimizations may have occurred because the offender(s) may have learned that victims opted to pursue legal actions within the justice via local or campus police entities. Given such considerations, sexual violence has represented a form of criminal activity that endangers academic settings.

Campus assaults are another form of violence that impact educational settings. According to Cass (2007, p. 351), approximately "80% of victimizations committed against students" were committed by peer students. Cass (2007) indicated that the risk of exposure to violence may have occurred because of an increased amount of time expended within the academic setting on campus and amount of exposure to potential offenders thereby exacerbating the possibility of risk victimization. According to Cass (2007), additional factors that contributed toward campus assaults resulted from the activities of Greek organizations (i.e., fraternities and sororities) and various forms of substance abuse among students. Further, Cass (2007) indicated that increases of such violent activity may have been related to the sizes and enrollment demographics of educational institutions. Therefore, as evidenced in the writings of Cass (2007), anyone has the potential to become a victim of violent crime among campus settings.

Based on the preceding discussions, campus violence may be manifested among a variety of fashions that results in death, physical suffering, or emotional and psychological distress. Although the discussed examples consider American institutions, the scope and magnitude of such campus violence is not domestically limited. Olujuwon (2007) confirmed this notion, and considered the worldwide perspective of violence as a threat among the academic communities of the United States, Russia, Germany, and Nigeria. Violence has the potential of impacting any institution, any personnel, or any students regardless of nationality or geographic location.

CAUSES OF VIOLENT ABERRANCE

A brief review of literature indicates that various causes contribute toward the manifestation of violence among the institutions of secondary and higher education. Antisocial behaviors (Farmer, Farmer, Estell, & Hutchins, 2007), abusive upbringing (Kang, 2007), attributes of terrorism (Stevens, 2005), individual irresponsibility (Williams, 1999; Young, Morales, McCabe, Boyd, & D'Arcy, 2005), and a myriad of cultural and ethical characteristics (Olujuwon, 2007) all contribute toward violence among campus settings within higher education.

Antisocial behaviors provide a basis for the manifestation of violence (Farmer et al., 2007). The arguments of Farmer et al. (2007) explore antisocial behavior as a form of bullying that continues into the years of adulthood. From the perspective of school shootings concerning antisocial behavior, Farmer et al. (2007, p. 199) indicate that perpetrators:

> [...] indicated that their motives were to obtain justice against peers or adults who they believed had wronged them and to obtain a higher status or greater importance among their peers.

Such aggression may be generated through a history of multiple individual, social, and family risks, including academic problems, attention problems, hyperactivity, social information processing difficulties, peer rejection, associations with deviant peers, coercive family systems, and poor parental monitoring (Farmer et al., 2007). Based on the writings of Farmer et al. (2007), the expression of such antisocial behavior, stemming from these characteristics, often resulted in death, physical harm, or mental distress within the academic community.

Kang (2007) suggested that childhood neglect and abusive rearing also contributed to future acts of violence. According to Kang (2007, p. 15), an expert consensus existed that "pathological family behavior bears primary responsibility for the development of pathological individual behavior." Kang (2007, p. 15) indicated that childhood exposure to violence presented identical "psychological distress symptoms as those who are actually abused," and argued that future acts of violence may have resulted from such childhood exposures to violence within home settings. Further, Olujuwon (2007) indicated that exposure to violent video games, during formative years, may have contributed to future violence. Therefore, the writings of Kang (2007) and Olujuwon (2007) suggested that an exposure to violence during the formative years of childhood may cause future acts of violence during adulthood.

The effects of terrorism must be considered, with respect to violence, among academic settings. Stevens (2005) indicated that various terror movements and ideologies, such as the *Movimiento Revolucionario Tupac Amaru*, have origins within the academic community. Such organizations manifest acts of violence through the instigation of terror attacks and extortion (Stevens, 2005). Given that terrorist organizations exist globally, incite atmospheres of control and fear, and espouse a variety of ideologies, academic settings are not immune to acts of terrorism. This susceptibility is confirmed by Stearns (2008) with respect to campus violence from the perspective of school shootings.

The characteristics of the individual must be considered when contemplating violence. Young et al. (2005) indicated that personal conduct and behavior (e.g., excessive drinking and drunkenness) of the individual may contribute to the potential of violence among academic settings because of the impairment of senses and diminished ability to render sound personal judgments. This notion was corroborated by Williams (1999) with respect to the use of alcohol among college populations and instances of rape. Given these arguments, personal behavior and a diminished capacity of the individual to render sound judgments contributed to instances of violence.

Cultural and ethical influences cannot be ignored when considering their potential to affect school settings. According to Olujuwon (2007, p. 42), students among academic settings may "rebel against the values and beliefs of their parents and those in authority and act out their dissatisfaction by assaulting those in authority." Social and moral components of such rebellion were deemed as attributes that facilitated campus violence (Olujuwon, 2007). Moral components consisted of "offences which are considered reprehensible on the ground that offenders lack moral conscience," and social components were:

> [...] offences which are disruptive to social harmony or to the attainment of desirable social objectives and which are viewed as indicator of an absence of social conscience of the part of the offender. (Olujuwon, 2007, p. 43)

Based on these descriptions, differing moral and ethical values among familial, student, employee, and faculty populations impact the potential of violence.

Violence affects academic communities both domestically and internationally. Examples of such events include assault, rape, homicide, suicide, and various forms of terrorism. Contributing factors that increase the risk of violence include antisocial behaviors (Farmer et al., 2007), abusive upbringing and neglect (Kang, 2007), attributes of terrorism (Stevens, 2005), individual irresponsibility (Williams, 1999; Young et al., 2005), and a variety of cultural and ethical characteristics (Olujuwon, 2007). Despite decreases in violence and criminal offenses among the non-academic sector, increases among criminal incidents occur within academic settings (McMahon, 2008).

Hence, it may be ascertained that violence originates from many sources, and no single cause may be identified as the cause of violence. Further, based on the preceding writings, no solution exists for violence given the imperfections of human nature and differences of societal morals and ethics among academic settings. However, based on the preceding writings, preventive and control strategies may be implemented to diminish the occurrences of violence.

PREVENTION STRATEGIES

An array of preventive strategies may be implemented with respect to the various causes of violence. With respect to the cause of antisocial behavior, Farmer et al. (2007) advocates preventive strategies that are classified as universal, selective, and indicated. Universal strategies are targeted toward the study body and the public, selective strategies are targeted toward people who exhibit above-average risk for problem development, and indicated strategies are targeted toward those who are "symptomatic of a disorder" (Farmer et al., 2007). Universal strategies provided academic support and social contexts, selective strategies provided positive limitations for at-risk youth, and strategies provided service coordination during the stages of youth development (Farmer et al., 2007). Within these categories, examples of activities designed to reduce antisocial behavior included peer tutoring, development of social skills, student monitoring, and development of emotional and behavioral adaptations (Farmer et al., 2007).

Preventive strategies also exist with respect to instances of neglect and abusive upbringings. Among such situations, Kang (2007, p. 17) indicated that the typical parent spent around four hours each week with "his or her child(ren)." According to Kang (2007), increased parental involvement within the lives of such children provided a preventive basis for diminishing the potential of future violence. Further, Kang (2007) suggested that strong levels of family stability, improved visitations of non-custodial parents, and improvements within the educational infrastructure were possibly preventive approaches (Kang, 2007).

The potential of terrorism must be considered with respect to preventive strategies. Stevens (2005) indicated that various counterterrorism strategies exist to prevent terrorist acts from occurring within academic environments. Based on the writings of Stevens (2005), the use of screening methods and profiling behavior were forms of violence prevention. Stevens (2005) advocated the teaching of anger management, critical thinking, and conflict resolution as methods of terrorism deterrence. The teaching of tolerance occurred as a strategy for preventing violence.

Crepeau-Hobson, Filaccio, and Gottfried (2005) advocated violence prevention as a strategy. According to Crepeau-Hobson et al. (2005, p. 158), components of such strategy included "developing individual skills and competencies, improving the social climate of the school, improving parent effectiveness, and changing type and level of involvement in peer groups." Additional components of this strategy included the use of physical mechanisms (e.g., metal detectors, etc.) to indicate the presence of weapons among student belongings (Crepeau-Hobson et al., 2005). However, such tools are not perfect – many weapons enter academic settings despite their use.

Additional strategies for preventing violence included religious and spiritual programs (Windham, Hooper, & Hudson, 2005), the use of school policies designed to provide preventive and punitive measures (Gerler, 2005; Philpott, 2008), the use of information technologies (Harris, 2008), behavior modification and bully prevention (Safran, 2007), and a variety of intervention strategies (Logue, 2008; Pittaro, 2007). Cheurprakobkit and Bartsch (2005, p. 236) also advocated the use of school "surveillance cameras, alarms, metal detectors, and the development of closed campuses," and the use of school uniforms. Regardless of the selected violence prevention strategy, any method implemented to curtail violence involved imaginative and creative approaches (Gerler, 2005).

CONTROL STRATEGIES

Control strategies may complement preventive strategies with respect to instances of violence. Examples of control strategies represented police responses (Cheurprakobkit & Bartsch, 2005; Grinberg & Wade, 2007; Maxey, 2003), court responses (Davies, 2008; McMahon, 2008), correction system responses (McCarthy & Butler, 2003), and community responses (McCarthy & Butler, 2003; Peterson & Skiba, 2001). Cheurprakobkit and Bartsch (2005) advocated the use and cooperation of police and security guards among school settings.

Grinberg and Wade (2007) examined the Virginia Tech police response with respect to the 2007 shooting incident. Based on the writings of Grinberg and Wade (2007), criticism of the Virginia Tech police occurred because of the lack of notification among the campus community immediately after the commencement of violence. As a result, Virginia Tech developed an alert system that warns the campus residents and personnel during periods of emergencies (Grinberg & Wade, 2007).

Legal responses, derived from various incidents within systems of courts and corrections, must also be considered from the perspective of legislation that resulted from acts of violence. McMahon (2008) indicated that such responses include the initial Clery Act, the Student Right to Know and Campus Security Act of 1990, and the revised Jeanne Clery Disclosure of Campus Security Policy and Campus Crime Statistics Act of 1998. McMahon (2008) emphasized the necessity of punitive requirements for offenders, and indicates the necessity of protecting the rights of the accused perpetrator and the victim. Additionally, McMahon (2008, p. 363) indicated that responses to violence must consider appropriately the jurisdictions between any external law enforcement and the academic institution, and the punitive outcomes for violent offenders.

Responses of the community may be considered. Based on the writings of McCarthy and Butler (2003), various stress considerations (e.g., anxiety, irritableness, etc.) decreased during the annual period succeeding tragic events. Further, according to McCarthy and Butler (2003), responses considered various facets of contingency planning. This observation was commensurate with the observations of Grinberg and Wade (2007) with respect to criticisms of the police response involving the Virginia Tech scenario and the necessity of planned responses.

The use of control strategies provides a mechanism through which preventive strategies may be complemented. Control strategies facilitate a variety of responses to violence. Although such responses may be legal, involve community actions, and involve interactions of law enforcement agencies, they must provide both administrative and punitive functions that are designed to deter acts of violence among school campuses.

THE VIRGINIA TECH INCIDENT

The Virginia Tech killings were commensurate with the writings of Olujuwon (2007) and Grinberg and Wade (2007) because the incident demonstrated that any campus is subject to violence. The psychological profile of the offender, Sueng Hui Cho, was commensurate with the writings of Jenson (2007) as the shooter did not demonstrate a prior history of such violence, but did possess mental illness before the killings. Given the history of mental illness of the shooter, Ward (2008) indicated that various warning indicators were present that warranted serious consideration of the dangerousness of the offender. Such warnings included unwanted advances toward females, suicidal tendencies, content of English class essays, and a ruling that Cho endangered himself because of his mental illness (Ward, 2008). Such warning signs were commensurate with the writings of Windham et al. (2005, p. 209) as they demonstrated expressions of "despair, frustration, anguish, and anger." Based on the writings of Holmes and Holmes (2002) and Farmer et al. (2007) regarding causation, the Virginia Tech murders were the physical manifestation of such emotions, and may have been motivated by emotions associated with revenge.

Davies (2008) indicated that the Virginia mental health system was inadequate for the provision of necessary services for preventing similar types of happenings. Davies (2008) also indicated that Cho was not prevented from purchasing a firearm despite his diagnosis of mental illness and classification as a hazard to himself or others. Because of privacy considerations associated with the Family Educational and Record Privacy Act (FERPA) and the Health Insurance Portability and Accountability Act (HIPAA), pertinent information was unshared with the counseling services of Virginia Tech regarding the counseling and specificity of assistance that may have prevented Cho from implementing the attack (Davies, 2008).

Similar observations regarding FERPA and HIPPA were noted by Ward (2008) with respect to the Virginia Tech shootings. Despite an English professor alerting the institution concerning the content of Cho's writings and behaviors before the shooting incident, the institution inadequately investigated or assisted Cho (Davies, 2008). Based on these observations, the attack was unpreventable given the shortcomings manifested among the Virginia mental health system, State of Virginia, and Virginia Tech infrastructure.

According to Grinberg and Wade (2007) and Davies (2008), the strategies of violence control were not optimal during the Virginia Tech shooting incident. Davies (2008) indicated that the institute reacted slowly to the shootings to avoid panic, and disseminated incomplete warning information nearly a couple of hours following the initial shootings. Failures also occurred as the Virginia Tech Chief of Police was unable to act in a unilateral fashion to implement emergency notifications, and also because the institution did not implement an emergency operations center to manage control of the event (Davies, 2008). Davies (2008) also attributed control shortcomings to poor leadership, uncoordinated interaction among services, and untrained personnel. With respect to support from the State of Virginia, Davies (2008) indicated that assistance arrived anywhere from mere hours to days after the shooting incident. Based on the arguments of Davies (2008), control strategies were inadequate and inefficient.

The consequences of the shootings were severe with respect to the offender, victims, community, and criminal justice system. The offender committed suicide after slaying 32 individuals and wounding 17 others (Jenson, 2007). The Virginia Tech scenario resulted in pronounced, definitive changes that affected the community and criminal justice system. According to Jenson (2007), greater awareness and attention were considered for individuals, whose risk for performing such crimes is manifested because of mental illness, with respect to the prevention of violence. Such awareness and attention must be integrated among policy endeavors (Jenson, 2007). Jenson (2007) also indicated that stronger legislation, concerning the purchase and ownership of firearms by mentally ill individuals, was approved as a result of the Virginia Tech scenario.

Ward (2008) indicated that an evaluation of FERPA and HIPAA privacy concerns facilitated safety and security improvements. Davies (2008) indicated that greater communications and coordination among responding agencies, the development of an emergency services plan, the implementation of emergency scenario drills, and an improved timeliness of responses to emergencies were recommended among higher education settings as a result of the Virginia Tech scenario. Based on such arguments regarding the societal, community, and criminal justice system impacts, an array of improvements may be witnessed nationally among higher education settings with respect to violence prevention, response, and control strategies.

Each organization must craft its own unique strategy commensurate with its vision, goals, objectives, and values regarding campus safety and security. The Virginia Tech incident served as a mass shooting catalyst for campus law enforcement organizations throughout the nation to examine whether their personnel should be armed. Increasingly, as a preventive method and influential deterrence, many campuses opted to employ full-time, state-certified law enforcement personnel instead of unarmed security guards. For instance, the University of Rhode Island now possesses an armed, state-certified police force instead of unarmed security personnel.

THE DECISION TO ARM CAMPUS POLICE

A variety of campus police organizations are now armed and trained concerning an array of possible endangerments that may affect the academic setting. Decisions regarding whether to facilitate armed personnel are common among higher education institutions (LaBanc & Hemphill, 2015). During recent years, an increasing number of higher education institutions have opted toward permitting weapons within campus boundaries involving varying constraints and different situations (Somers, Fry, & Fong, 2017). For instance, during active shooter situations, police response necessitates a sense of immediacy toward neutralizing the situation (Texas A&M University, 2017). Thus, some trend exists toward implementing campus safety and security paradigms that involve certain facets of defensive weaponry.

Arming the University of Rhode Island Police Force

During 2015, the University of Rhode Island generated much conflict and debate regarding its decision to arm campus police (Arditi, 2015). The decision to arm its police force was attributed to the need to provide additional means of enhancing public protection, and was commensurate with similar decisions rendered among colleges and universities throughout the nation (Arditi, 2015). For instance, between 2005 and 2011, armed campus police forces among higher education settings increased from 68% to approximately 75% (Arditi, 2015). Thus, the decision to arm its police force was commensurate with trend exhibited nationally, wherein higher education campuses integrated firearms among their respective police organizations (Arditi, 2015).

Training and arming police forces necessitates some consideration of financial resources (Doss, Guo, & Lee, 2012). Criteria selection methods may be considered quantitatively within the contexts of various financial management principles (Brigham & Ehrhardt, 2008). For instance, Dalton-Noblitt (2012) and Sheffield et al. (2016) advocated cost-benefit analysis and capital budgeting approaches as methods of financially justifying potential investment opportunities among higher education institutions. Among higher education institutions, an array of possible campus safety investments may be evaluated using such methods (Sheffield, 2016).

An additional paradigm includes analyzing the return on investment (ROI) value of potential investments toward campus safety and security (Dalton-Noblitt, 2012). For instance, at the University of California (2017), Davis, a 1.25 to 1 expected ROI was determined regarding the hiring of investigative personnel. The anticipated benefit involved expectations that cumulative claim costs would be decreased (University of California, 2017).

From the perspective of capital budgeting, Rasmussen and Johnson (2008, p. 25) indicate that selection involves rendering decisions "according to the relative rate of return expected from different investments in hardware, equipment, and personnel." Derived from Lasher (2017), when considering rates of return, the selection rules are expressed as follows: (1) accept the investment opportunity if the expected rate of return surpasses the cost of capital and (2) reject the investment opportunity if the expected rate of return fails to exceed the cost of capital. If the organization considers multiple projects with respect to the influences of mutual exclusion, then it is appropriate to accept the investment opportunity that exhibits the highest expected rate of return (Lasher, 2017).

Rasmussen and Johnson (2008) indicated that resource investment decisions may involve cost-benefit analysis. This analytical method represents a ratio of the potential benefits gleaned from an investment versus its respective costs through time. Regarding selection criteria, investment opportunities whose resulting cost-benefit ratio value exceeds the value of 1.0 are generally deemed to be acceptable endeavors (Doss, Sumrall et al., 2013). If the value of the cost-benefit ratio is less than the value of 1.0, then the investment is rejected (Doss, Sumrall et al., 2013).

Strengths and Weaknesses

Examining the Rhode Island decision to arm campus police may be contemplated from the perspectives of strengths and weaknesses. From a human resources perspective, strengths involve the presence of trained personnel who are capable of responding to a variety of hazards and threats. This notion is commensurate with the use of police personnel as first-responders to a variety of incidents arising from both human and natural origins (McElreath et al., 2013). For instance, trained personnel would be available as response resources for immediate countermeasures for incidents involving active shooters, as measures toward regaining normalcy during the aftermath of calamities, and for supporting any corresponding civic events (e.g., campus vigils) (LaBanc & Hemphill, 2015).

Money is a limited resource for any academic institution, including Rhode Island. Higher education operations all involve some monetary requirements – including policing. Given this notion, the availability and accessibility of financial resources may be a weakness for implementing an armed campus police force. Financial management is a chief concern of any organizational administration (Lasher, 2017). Legislatures and administrators contemplate various methods of allocating scare tax monies to satisfy the unlimited wants and needs of society. In other words, public institutions compete with other entities, such as the prison system, for funding resources and opportunities (Doss, Sumrall et al., 2013). Essentially, public colleges and universities must compete with an array of competitors for scare monies, ranging from roadway infrastructure to the justice system. Thus, for any public institution seeking to arm its campus police, funding constraints and allocations may be substantial weaknesses.

Opportunities and Threats

Implementing armed campus police may pose a variety of opportunities. One opportunistic perspective involves financial management. Financial outcomes involve cost savings and meaningful investment returns over time. For instance, at the University of California, Davis, its campus safety endeavors yielded expected positive ROI outcomes for a variety of projects (University of California, 2017). Within the context of policing, examples included hiring investigative personnel (ROI 1.25:1) and theft outreach (ROI 2:1).

Any environment poses some amount of risk and corresponding threat (Thompson, Peteraf, Gamble, & Strickland, 2016). No panacea exists whereby campus safety and security paradigms may be implemented among collegiate settings. Essentially, some compromise must exist given the economic considerations of resource allocation. In other words, funding is a scarce, limited resource whose use must be judicious toward the maximizing of campus safety. For instance, in Illinois, an example of these notions involved the case of McHenry County College. By replacing its security force with a police department, the institution reduced its personnel quantities from 22 security force personnel to 10 sworn, full-time police personnel (LaBanc & Hemphill, 2015). Some risk trade-offs occurred from incorporating armed police within the academic setting (LaBanc & Hemphill, 2015). Examples included questionable use of force issues, discharging weapons accidentally, increased weapons use, and collateral damages (LaBanc & Hemphill, 2015). Similarly, trade offs for institutions that employed unarmed security personnel included exacerbating possible dangerousness for personnel, students, and faculty (LaBanc & Hemphill, 2015).

POLICY ISSUES

Policies represent forms of organizational guidance for influencing behavior and conduct throughout the academic setting. Within the context of the EMC, policies may exist for preparedness, mitigation, response, and recovery regarding calamities. Policies may accommodate the arming of campus police to perform throughout the entirety of the EMC. However, the presences of armed police and the allowance of weapons within campus settings are subjects of debate nationally. Through legislation, an array of laws may be crafted that illegalize certain activities and items within the campus boundaries. For instance, among some campuses, weapons possession is disallowed thereby fueling numerous debates concerning firearms and knives (Kopel, Cramer, & Olson, 2013). Certainly, some individuals advocate weapons as a method of enhancing campus safety whereas others decry the use of weaponry as an exacerbating factor regarding threat levels within the higher education setting. Thus, little agreement exists universally within the educational domain concerning the presence of weapons among campus settings (Birnbaum, 2012).

Somers et al. (2017) indicated that higher education institutions may craft their respective policies that uniquely permit or disallow weapons within the campus setting with the intention of bolstering campus safety. For instance, given recent legislation and court proceedings, several states allow some types of concealed weaponry within campus boundaries (Somers et al., 2017). These states consist of Arkansas, Colorado, Georgia, Idaho, Kansas, Mississippi, Oregon, Tennessee (faculty possession only), Texas, Utah, and Wisconsin (Somers et al., 2017).

Some institutions may exercise certain cooperative agreements with external law enforcement organizations or may provide law enforcement services to external entities during emergencies. For instance, near the University of West Alabama, in 2010, a deadly shooting occurred at a high school that was directly adjacent to the higher education institution and which shared resources with the university (Doss et al., 2017). The event involved a domestic dispute between estranged spouses in which the wife, a school teacher, was shot and killed in front of the school by her husband (Doss et al., 2017). After committing murder in broad daylight in front of 15 witnesses, the perpetrator fled thereby necessitating law enforcement responses from multiple organizations (Doss et al., 2017). One of the responding organizations was the police department at the University of West Alabama (Doss et al., 2017). Thus, the university's police resources were used as a cooperative response entity to a murder that occurred off campus.

No universal policing paradigm exists for implementing campus safety and security organizationally throughout the higher education domain. Some institutions may incorporate armed campus police, others may sponsor unarmed security forces, and certain others may opt for no police or security personnel whatsoever with reliance solely upon external law enforcement organizations (LaBanc & Hemphill, 2015). Although a lack of universal policy exists, many campus police forces have increasingly armed their respective personnel over the last decade. Arming law enforcement personnel among educational settings provides much fuel for contention and debate. Regardless, such decisions are intended to contribute toward the overall enhancement of campus safety and security.

Policy Alternatives

Two distinctive views of weapons possession exist among collegiate settings: complete disallowance and allowance with some restrictions. Thus, two potential courses of action exist when contemplating decisions and organizational structures whereby campus safety activities are implemented. For the sake of brevity, this chapter considers these alternatives within the contexts of armed campus police forces, unarmed campus security entities, and a complete absence of any campus police or security organization with reliance upon external police entities.

Because of the potential of different scenarios to exist among higher education institutions, alternatives may be examined according to risk and probability of some event occurring. Typically, from economic and financial perspectives, such risk considerations and their corresponding alternatives may be examined quantitatively through a variety of methods, such as capital budgeting, cost-benefit analysis, sensitivity analysis, and scenario analysis (Brigham & Ehrhardt, 2008; Samonas, 2015). The costs associated with facilitating campus safety involve a variety of considerations. Examples include personnel, training, insurance, and obligations (Powell, 1981). Alternatives should not be crafted haphazardly. Instead, they must accommodate some realistic consideration of financial constraints with respect to the anticipated return and expected safety level (Rasmussen & Johnson, 2008).

GOVERNANCE

Campus safety and security are primary concerns of higher education administrations. Executive decisions regarding policing affect the entirety of the organization, ranging from patrol shifts to chains-of-command organizationally (McElreath et al., 2013). Within the context of institutional governance, administrative and executive decisions involving campus safety and security often incorporate some facets of policing. Incorporating armed police forces among collegiate settings may enhance campus safety and security in a variety of fashions. For instance, regarding the case of McHenry County College, financial savings were incurred by implementing an armed police force. Specifically, because of the personnel changes, the institutional budget decreased from the 2009–2010 amount of $598,909 to the 2013–2014 amount of $512,565 (LaBanc & Hemphill, 2015). Thus, in the terms of campus safety and security expenditures, the institution exhibited a savings of $86,344 across the four academic years. Such savings present potential investment resources. Any saved, excess amount may be reinvested toward the original purpose, or it may be implemented elsewhere depending upon organizational need and direction (Lasher, 2017). Additionally, campus police chiefs and executives must exhibit proper credentials, satisfactory training, relevant experience, and commitment to policing (McElreath et al., 2013). Campus executives and administrators must decide how much influence and power may reside with their respective police entities. Thus, some legitimacy and accountability must be attributed to campus police with respect to governance issues.

TECHNOLOGY

From the perspectives of Western society and philosophical instrumentalism, technology is nothing more than a neutral tool used toward accomplishing human goals and objectives (Liu, Yang, He, Li, & Doss, 2016). Law enforcement training requirements often incorporate some aspects of technologies, ranging from computer systems for mapping crime hot spots to mobile radio systems (McElreath et al., 2013). Law enforcement officer training for campus police is analogous to the requirements necessary for entering the policing vocation within external society (Anderson, 2015). Thus, law enforcement officers among higher education institutions must satisfy training requirements necessary for mastering proficiency with multiple weapons, including firearms, tasers, sprays, and batons (Joyner, 2011; Winfree, Mays, & Alarid, 2015). Additional training may involve communication systems and electronic resources (Doss, Glover, Goza, & Wigginton, 2015). Such mastery and acumen are necessary for bolstering officer safety and protecting others against a variety of threats, many of which may be lethal. The aforementioned incidents at Virginia Tech, Texas Tech, and Georgia Tech show the potential dangerousness among modern campus settings. Thus, campus law enforcement personnel must be equipped technologically to address a variety of incidents defensively.

CLOSING COMMENTARY

An examination of Virginia Tech tragedy provides a variety of lessons that may be learned from the performances of the institution and law enforcement agencies. Based on the writings of Jenson (2007), concerning the unexpected nature of violence, criminal acts of violence may occur anytime regardless of the higher education setting. Institutions are not immune to acts of violence. Based on the writings of Davies (2008), Jenson (2007), and Ward (2008), various shortcomings and failures within the institutional setting and State of Virginia contributed toward the instigation of the criminal act and impeded an efficiently coordinated response.

Maintaining order and deterring crime represent the common missions of all law enforcement organizations, including campus police (McElreath et al., 2013). Although organizations may make every effort to identify threats and assess the chances of endangerment, it is impossible to predict with full certainty and accuracy which events may or may not occur in time. Similarly, it is impossible to imagine every combination of threats that may pose danger (McElreath et al., 2014a, 2014b). Despite their best efforts, academic institutions cannot guarantee invincibility with respect to potential endangerments (Rasmussen & Johnson, 2008).

Academic institutions must not be reactionary with respect to potential endangerments. Instead, they must exhibit efforts proactively toward preventing incidents as best as is possible. Thus, academic entities must consider a long-term perspective through which criminality may be prevented or abated. Essentially, within the context of long-term, strategic planning, higher education organizations may consider the arming of their respective law enforcement organizations for the purposes of deterring and controlling violence.

Despite the senselessness of the Virginia Tech massacre, the act of moral turpitude incited change among other higher education institutions throughout the nation (Rasmussen & Johnson, 2008). For instance, higher education institutions enacted "awareness campaigns" for the purpose of helping students recognize aberrant behaviors (Rasmussen & Johnson, 2008, p. 24). Such change is commensurate with the reviewed literature. Based on the writings of Davies (2008), Jenson (2007), and Ward (2008), numerous improvements may be recommended to diminish the potential of such criminal acts from occurring among higher education settings. Campuses should maintain an emergency services plan and enforce emergency scenario practice drills frequently as methods of ensuring adequate and effective reactions and responses to emergency situations. Administrators must seriously consider and investigate faculty alerts and warnings regarding any potential threats posed within the academic setting. Further, all members of the academic community must remain aware of the potential of violence within the academic setting, and prepare themselves accordingly. Although such recommendations may facilitate a safer environment among academic settings, they will not completely eliminate campus violence.

Although infrequent, society cannot discount the violence of campus homicide. Certainly, any form of campus violence must not be taken lightly. The Virginia Tech massacre garnered national spotlights and remained the subject of discussion for years afterward. The incident drew blatant attention among news media outlets. Given these notions, future studies may question whether reported incidents of campus violence affect institutional enrollment across the enterprise or among its academic programs. Similarly, future studies may also explore whether violence originating external to a campus affects its enrollments either among programs or across the enterprise.

Motivations for crime among virtual environments often mimic motivational factors of criminality within physical reality (Doss, Henley, & McElreath, 2013a, 2013b). The advent and proliferation of electronic technologies within modern society provide ample opportunities for committing some type of crime in the virtual domain or using technology as a tool of crime to facilitate criminality in physical reality. Future studies may explore the potential role of virtual technologies in homicide events. For instance, for premeditated incidents, does a killer use technology to better understand the surroundings in which a planned crime occurs? Does a killer use technology when planning incidents to better the chance of successful homicide? Possible scenarios could include using mapping software and imagery visualization to gain an understanding of potential obstacles, structures, entry points, escape routes, roadways, traffic flows and congestions, potential hideaways, expected weather conditions, and so forth. Thus, does modern mapping software, available freely via the Internet, provide potential perpetrators with tools for performing virtual reconnaissance of a potential incident location?

In any case, all higher education institutions are unique. Regardless, all are susceptible to violence, including homicide. Thus, leaders and administrators must craft policies that uniquely fit their respective situations. Not all possible scenarios may be envisioned. However, the identified possibilities exhibiting high risk must be acknowledged as potential happenings for which some preparations are considerable. Not all policy decisions will be popular or accepted completely within the organizational setting. Some may herald decisions as positive directions toward abating the possibility of incidents whereas others may laud them as transgressions against the well-being of campuses, students, and employees. In any case, leaders and administrators are responsible for providing campus safety and security. Regardless of the popularity of decisions, they must accommodate a common notion: enhance the safety and security of campus settings whereby the chances of violent events are diminished.

REFERENCES

Arditi, L. (2015). After much debate, URI campus police now carry firearms. *South Coast Today*, May 10. Retrieved from http://www.southcoasttoday.com/article/20150510/NEWS/150519908. Accessed on August 5, 2017.

Barrett, L. A. (2014). *The college union and a sense of community for students in public higher education: Is there a relationship?* Rochester, NY: St. John Fisher College.

Birnbaum, R. (2012, November). *Ready, fire, aim: The college campus gun fight*. Paper presented to the annual meeting of the Association for the Study of Higher Education, Las Vegas, NV.

Brigham, E., & Ehrhardt, M. (2008). *Financial management: Theory and practice* (12th ed.). Mason, OH: Thomson.

Cass, A. (2007). Routine activities and sexual assault: An analysis of individual- and school-level factors. *Violence and Victims*, *22*(3), 350–366.

Chekwa, C., Thomas, E., & Jones, V. J. (2013). What are college students' perceptions about campus safety? *Contemporary Issues in Education Research*, *6*(3), 325–332.

Cheurprakobkit, S., & Bartsch, R. (2005). Security measures on school crime in Texas middle and high schools. *Educational Research*, *47*(2), 235–250.

Coker, D. (2016). Crime logic, campus sexual assault, and restorative justice. *Texas Tech Law Review*, *49*, 147–209.

Crepeau-Hobson, M., Filaccio, M., & Gottfried, L. (2005). Violence prevention after columbine: A survey of high school mental health professionals. *Children and Schools*, *27*(3), 157–165.

Dalton-Noblitt, A. (2012). Cost of ownership and getting ROI you feel good about. *Allegion*, September 1. Retrieved from https://us.allegion.com/content/dam/allegion-us-2/web-documents-2/Article/Campus_Cost_of_Ownership_and_Getting_ROI_109083.pdf. Accessed on August 22, 2017.

Davies, D. K. (2008). Connecting the dots: Lessons from the Virginia Tech shootings. *Change*, *40*(1), 8–15.

Dobuzinskis, A. (2017). Student confesses in fatal shooting of police officer at Texas college: Warrant. *Reuters*, October 9. Retrieved from https://www.reuters.com/article/us-texas-shooting/student-confesses-in-fatal-shooting-of-police-officer-at-texas-college-warrant-idUSKBN1CF04Y. Accessed on November 22, 2017.

Doss, D., Guo, C., & Lee, J. (2012). *The business of criminal justice: A guide for theory and practice*. Boca Raton, FL: CRC Press.

Doss, D., Henley, R., & McElreath, D. (2013a). The Arizona border with Mexico: A Pearson correlation coefficient analysis of US border crossing data versus US reported cybercrime incidents for the period of 2001–2011. *International Journal of Social Science Research*, *1*(2013), 17–26.

Doss, D., Henley, R., & McElreath, D. (2013b). The California–Mexican border: Investigating Pearson correlation coefficient outcomes representing U.S. border crossing data versus U.S. reported cybercrime incidents during 2001–2011. *Mustang Journal of Law and Legal Studies*, *4*, 17–27.

Doss, D., Jones, D., & Sumrall, W. (2010, September). A quantitative analysis of Animal Liberation Front incidents versus Earth Liberation Front incidents. Presented to the annual meeting of the Southern Criminal Justice Association. Clearwater Beach, FL.

Doss, D., Lackey, H., McElreath, D., Jones, D., Goza, R., & Sheffield, J. (2017). Revisiting violence in rural academic settings: A school killing impacting Livingston High School and considerations of policy and programs. *Journal of Studies in Social Sciences*, *16*(2), 156–191.

Doss, D., Sumrall, W., McElreath, D., & Jones, D. (2013). *Economic and financial analysis for criminal justice organizations*. Boca Raton, FL: CRC Press.

Farmer, T. W., Farmer, E. Z., Estell, D. B., & Hutchins, B. C. (2007). The developmental dynamics of aggression and the prevention of school violence. *Journal of Emotional and Behavioral Disorders*, *15*(4), 197–208.

Flannery, D., & Quinn-Leering, K. (2000). Violence on college campuses: Understanding its impact on student well-being. *Community College Journal of Research & Practice*, *24*(10), 839–855.

Gerler, E. (2005). Creative acts of school violence: Rational thinking required. *Journal of School Violence*, *4*(2), 1–2.

Grinberg, M., & Wade, J. (2007). In the wake of Virginia Tech. *Risk Management*, *54*(12), 24–28.

Harris, M. (2008). Technology review: Waiting for "ubiquitous technology" when it's already here. *Community College Enterprise*, *14*(2), 113–114.

Holmes, R., & Holmes, S. (2002). *Profiling violent crimes: An investigative tool* (3rd ed.). Thousand Oaks, CA: Sage.

Kang, M. (2007). Parents as scapegoats. *Journal of Contemporary Legal Issues*, *16*(1), 15–21.

Jenson, J. (2007). Aggression and violence in the united states: Reflections on the Virginia Tech shootings. *Social Work Research*, *31*(3), 131–134.

Kopel, D. B., Cramer, C. E., & Olson, J. E. (2013). Knives and the Second Amendment. *University of Michigan Journal of Law Reform*, *47*(1), 167–215.

LaBanc, B. H., & Hemphill, B. O. (2015). *College in the crosshairs: Administrative perspective of prevention of gun violence*. Sterling, VA: Stylus.

Lasher, W. R. (2017). *Practical financial management* (8th ed.). Boston, MA: Cengage.

Logue, J. N. (2008). Violent death in American schools in the 21st century: Reflections following the 2006 Amish school shootings. *Journal of School Health*, *78*(1), 58–61.

Maxey, W. (2003). Storming the ivory towers: A look at violence and stalking on campus. *Journal of Psychosocial Nursing and Mental Health Services*, *41*(4), 26–31.

McCarthy, M., & Butler, L. (2003). Responding to traumatic events on college campuses: A case study and assessment of student postdisaster anxiety. *Journal of College Counseling*, *6*(1), 90.

McElreath, D., Doss, D., Jensen, C., Wigginton, M., Kennedy, R., Winter, K., … Estis-Sumerel, J. (2013). *Introduction to law enforcement*. Boca Raton, FL: CRC Press.

McElreath, D., Doss, D., Jensen, C., Wigginton, M., Nations, R., Van Slyke, J., & Nations, J. (2014a). *Foundations of emergency management*. Dubuque, IA: Kendall Hunt.

McElreath, D., Jensen, C., Wigginton, M., Doss, D., Nations, R., & Van Slyke, J. (2014b). *Introduction to homeland security* (2nd ed.). Boca Raton, FL: CRC Press.

McGrath, S. A., Perumean-Chaney, S. E., & Sloan, J. J. (2014). Property crime on college campuses: A case study using GIS and related tools. *Security Journal*, *37*(3), 263–283.

McMahon, P. (2008). Sexual violence on the college campus: A template for compliance with federal policy. *Journal of American College Health*, *57*(3), 361–366.

Newlin, B. (2017). Knife-wielding Georgia Tech student killed by campus police; shooting captured on cellphone video. *Local 4 News*, September 18. Retrieved from https://www.clickondetroit.com/news/national/disturbing-video-shows-fatal-police-shooting-of-knife-weiding-georgia-tech-student. Accessed September 20, 2017.

Olujuwon, T. (2007). The schools' violence and learning. *International Journal of Learning*, *14*(7), 39–47.

Peterson, R., & Skiba, R. (2001). Creating school climates that prevent school violence. *Clearing House*, *74*(3), 155–164.

Philpott, D. (2008). Learning lessons about school security. *Homeland Defense Journal*, *6*(4), 44–47.

Pittaro, M. L. (2007). School violence and social control theory: An evaluation of the Columbine massacre. *International Journal of Criminal Justice Sciences*, *2*(1), 1–12.

Powell, J. W. (1981). *Campus security and law enforcement*. Woburn, MA: Butterworth-Heinemann.

Rao, A. L., Poon, S., Drezner, J. A., Zigman, M., Asif, I. M., & Harmon, K. G. (2016). Death by homicide in national collegiate athletic association athletes between 2003 and 2013. *British Journal of Sports Medicine*, *50*, 172–175.

Rasmussen, C., & Johnson, G. (2008). *The ripple effect of Virginia Tech: Assessing the nationwide impact on campus safety and security policy and practice*. Minneapolis, MN: Midwestern Higher Education Compact.

Safran, E. (2007). Bullying behavior, bully prevention programs, and gender. *Journal of Emotional Abuse*, *7*(4), 43–67.

Samonas, M. (2015). *Financial forecasting, analysis, and modeling: A framework for long-term forecasting*. Hoboken, NJ: Wiley.

Sheffield, J. (2016). *The quality of life and the financial burden of living on campus versus living off campus at the University of West Alabama: A cost versus benefit analysis of renovating Selden Hall*. Livingston, AL: University of West Alabama.

Somers, P., Fry, J., & Fong, C. J. (2017). Duck and cover, little lady: Women and campus carry. *Thought and Action, 2017*, 37–50.

Stearns, P. (2008). Texas and Virginia: A bloodied window into changes in American public life. *Journal of Social History* (Winter), 299–318.

Stevens, M. (2005). What is terrorism and can psychology do anything to prevent it? *Behavioral Sciences and the Law*, *23*(4), 507–526.

Thompson, A., Peteraf, M., Gamble, J., & Strickland, A. (2016). *Crafting and executing strategy: The quest for competitive advantage* (20th ed.). New York, NY: McGraw-Hill.

University of California. (2017). *UC Davis analysis of return on investment for loss prevention programs*. University of California, Davis. Retrieved from http://www.ucop.edu/risk-services/_files/bsas/roi_ucd.pdf. Accessed on August 29, 2017.

Van Blerkom, D. (2013). *Orientation to college learning* (7th ed.). Boston, MA: Wadsworth.

Ward, M. A. (2008). Reexamining student privacy laws in response to the Virginia Tech tragedy. *Journal of Health Care Law and Policy*, *11*(2), 407–435.

Williams, L. B. (1999). The wrong rap on rape. *About Campus*, *4*(5), 26–26.

Windham, R., Hooper, L., & Hudson, P. (2005). Selected spiritual religious, and family factors in the prevention of school violence. *Counseling and Values*, *49*(3), 208–216.

Young, A. M., Morales, M., McCabe, S. E., Boyd, C. J., & D'Arcy, H. (2005). Drinking like a guy: Frequent binge drinking among undergraduate women. *Substance Use and Misuse*, *40*(2), 239–265.

CHAPTER 6

THE RELEVANCE OF BIAS VIOLENCE IN THE 21ST CENTURY

Kayla Allison

ABSTRACT

Purpose – *The overall purpose of this chapter is to discuss what is known about serious forms of bias violence, obstacles to studying bias violence, and how alternative theoretical and methodological approaches can advance our understanding of bias violence in the twenty-first century.*

Design/methodology/approach – *Following a review of the literature, the applicability of identity fusion theory for explaining bias violence is considered and applied to the anti-racial mass shooting at an historically Black church in Charleston, South Carolina. Data come from an innovative open-source project known as the United States Extremist Crime Database.*

Findings – *Drawing from identity fusion theory, information from open-source data on the Charleston church shooting suggests that the perpetrator was a highly fused individual who perceived African Americans as a threat toward his social identity group and committed an act of extreme behavior (i.e., bias homicide) as a means for stabilizing his self-views.*

Originality/value – *This chapter builds upon prior studies of bias violence by demonstrating how (1) publicly available open sources (e.g., court documents and media reports) may be systematically compiled and used as reliable data for studying serious forms of bias violence, and (2) the use of social psychological theories, specifically identity fusion theory, can help to explain the role of personal and group identities in discriminatory violence.*

Keywords: Bias crime; hate crime; violence; identity fusion; online radicalization; social psychology

Homicide and Violent Crime
Sociology of Crime, Law and Deviance, Volume 23, 101–117

ISSN: 1521-6136/doi:10.1108/S1521-613620180000023007

INTRODUCTION

Scholars have studied different forms of violence such as homicide for more than a century (Redfield, 1880/2000; Wolfgang, 1958), resulting in an expansive literature on violence typologies, theories, and methodologies (Smith & Zahn, 1999). However, one form of violence in particular, hate- or bias-motivated violence that targets people based on their social status or identity, has to date received much less attention by scholars. This lack of consideration is a subject of concern given that researchers find that bias violence can be especially harmful to victims and their respective communities (Cogan, 2002; Green, McFalls, & Smith, 2001; Herek, Gillis, & Cogan, 1999; Levin & McDevitt, 1993; McDevitt, Balboni, Garcia, & Gu, 2001; Noelle, 2002). There are several possible explanations for why there has been considerably less research on bias violence in comparison to other forms of crime, including noted challenges of applying traditional criminological theories to bias crime (Perry, 2001) and gaps in relevant and reliable official bias crime data (Bell, 2002; Berk, Boyd, & Hamner, 1992; Boyd, Berk, & Hamner, 1996; Green et al., 2001; Haider-Markel, 2002; Levin & McDevitt, 1993, 2002; McDevitt, Balboni, & Bennett, 2002; Nolan & Akiyama, 1999).

Bias violence occurrences are relatively rare, but the seriousness of these crimes has in the past been evidenced by the passage of federal bias crime legislation. The first federal hate crime legislation is arguably the Civil Rights Act of 1964, a monumental set of laws passed in the United States to protect minority groups following widespread violence and discrimination specifically targeting African Americans. More associated with the modern understanding of bias crime is the passage of the Hate Crime Statistics Act of 1990, a piece of federal legislation that required the United States Attorney General to collect national data on crimes specifically targeting persons based on their race, religion, disability, sexual orientation, or ethnicity. In addition, the most recent manifestation of federal hate crime law is the Matthew Shepard and James Byrd Hate Crimes Prevention Act passed in 2009 and is named after the victims of two acts of deadly bias violence. This law required the Attorney General to also collect information on anti-gender and gender identity crimes. In 2018, most states have followed the federal government's lead by passing their own hate crime laws, though South Carolina, Arkansas, Wyoming, Indiana, and Georgia still have not. Concern about bias violence continues to be fueled by high-profile bias homicides, recurrently making the issue of bias crime more salient, albeit usually only temporarily, for the public and policymakers. Over the last several years, numerous cases of bias violence have become sensationalized, intersecting with fears about mass shootings becoming more frequent and lethal and homegrown terrorists carrying out ideologically motivated attacks.

The overall purpose of this chapter is to discuss what is known about serious forms of bias violence, obstacles to studying bias violence, and how alternative theoretical and methodological approaches can advance our understanding of bias violence in the twenty-first century. First, I review the existing scholarly literature on bias violence and follow it with a discussion of the theoretical and methodological challenges to studying this type of violence. Second, I move outside traditional criminological theories to offer insights into how social psychology can help us to understand how personal identities can become fused with social group identifies in such visceral ways as to fuel acts of bias violence. Third, I suggest that the increasing use of open-source data for studying some forms of serious bias offending is one way to overcome some of the methodological challenges facing bias crime researchers. Finally, and fourth, I discuss the deadly bias shooting at the Charleston Emanuel African Methodist Episcopal (AME) Church as an illustrative example of how identity fusion theory and open-source data can be used to advance our understanding of serious forms of bias violence.

LITERATURE REVIEW

How are Bias Offenders Unique from Traditional Violent Offenders?

In the past, researchers have suggested that bias violence is more harmful than other traditional forms of violence by deleteriously affecting immediate victims and those close to them, while increasing feelings of vulnerability and tearing at the social cohesion of communities more broadly (Green et al., 2001; Levin & McDevitt, 1993, 2002). Studies have also found dissimilarities in the demographics of bias crime participants and offenders of more routine forms of violence. For instance, bias offenders are comparatively more likely to be young, White, and male than traditional offenders (Berrill, 1990; Comstock, 1991; Garofalo, 1991; Garofalo & Martin, 1993; Gruenewald, 2012; Harry, 1992; Herek, Cogan, & Gillis, 2002; Martin, 1996; Maxwell & Maxwell, 1995; Messner, McHugh, & Felson, 2004; Strom, 2001; Tomsen, 2009; Van Der Meer, 2003), while victims of bias violence are more likely to be male (Garofalo, 1991; Garofalo & Martin, 1993; Gruenewald, 2013; Gruenewald & Kelley, 2014; Martin, 1996; Messner et al., 2004) and a racial minority in comparison to victims of routine violence (Garofalo & Martin, 1993; Klein & Allison, 2017; Levin & McDevitt, 1993; Martin, 1996; Messner et al., 2004). Studies have also shown that victims of bias-motivated violence tend to be younger than victims of traditional violence (Garofalo, 1991; Garofalo & Martin, 1993; Martin, 1996).

Prior research has also examined the situational characteristics of bias violence in relation to routine criminality. These studies have generally found that, relative to parallel offenses, bias offenders are more likely to commit acts of violence in small, loosely organized groups consisting of multiple perpetrators (Berrill, 1990; Comstock, 1991; Garofalo, 1991; Garofalo & Martin, 1993; Gruenewald, 2012; Herek et al., 2002; Klein & Allison, 2017; Martin, 1996; Tomsen, 2009; Van Der Meer, 2003) who target multiple victims (Comstock, 1991; Garofalo, 1991; Klein & Allison, 2017; Levin & McDevitt, 1993; Martin, 1996) often unknown to them prior to the incident (Garofalo, 1991; Garofalo & Martin, 1993; Herek & Berrill, 1992; Klein & Allison, 2017; Levin & McDevitt, 1993; Martin, 1996; Messner et al., 2004; Stacey, 2011; Tomsen, 2009). Compared to more routine types of crime, bias violence is more likely to occur in public spaces (Garofalo, 1991; Garofalo & Martin, 1993; Martin, 1996) outside of the home (Messner et al., 2004), and is less likely to rely on the use of weapons (Comstock, 1991). In regard to lethal violence, bias homicide is less likely to involve the use of firearms relative to routine types of homicide that are overwhelmingly committed with firearms. Some forms of bias homicide, such as fatal anti-sexual orientation and gender identity attacks, are most often committed with knives, blunt objects, and bodily weapons (Gruenewald, 2012; Gruenewald & Kelley, 2014; Levin & McDevitt, 1993; Tomsen, 2009).

Although several prior comparative studies of bias crime have identified demographic and situational differences, there has been less attention on theoretical explanations for how and why bias offending occurs. Barbara Perry (2001) has argued that most traditional criminological approaches are not applicable to bias crime. For instance, while Social Control Theory (Hirschi, 1969) suggests that strong, tightly held social bonds prevent individuals from committing crime, Perry suggests that it is these social bonds that may in some cases actually lead offenders to committing bias violence. As another example, Strain Theory (Merton, 1938) suggests that individuals commit crime out of frustration stemming from lack of opportunities and resources to achieve culturally prescribed goals. This would suggest that those maintaining lower social status (e.g., African Americans and immigrants), would most often be the perpetrators of bias violence. However, it is individuals who are the most economically and socially disadvantaged who are ordinarily the targets of violent discriminatory acts (Perry, 2001). In light of these theoretical challenges, other scholars have begun to use macro-level sociological theories for predicting where bias crime is most likely to occur, and interactional-level theories to understand the underlying processes that result in bias crime.

Applying Criminological Theory to Bias Offenders

Bias crime researchers have relied on several prominent macro-level theoretical frameworks to explain this form of crime, including social disorganization theory, group threat theory, and the defended neighborhood perspective, which seek to explain how broader social structural forces are related to where bias crimes are more likely to occur (see Gale, Heath, & Ressler, 2002; Grattet, 2009; Green, Glaser, & Rich, 1998; Green, Strolovitch, & Wong, 1998; Lyons, 2007; Medoff, 1999; Pinderhughes, 1993). Findings on what ecological correlates are most associated with bias crime are mixed, depending in large part on the geographic scope and methodological approaches utilized in studies. In some instances, variability in findings may be due to issues of underreporting by victims and law enforcement officials responsible for investigating bias crime (this issue has been extensively covered by Bell, 2002; Berk et al., 1992; Boyd et al., 1996; Green et al., 2001; Haider-Markel, 2002; Levin & McDevitt, 1993, 2002; McDevitt et al., 2002; Nolan & Akiyama, 1999). Some scholars have attempted to circumvent problems with official bias crime data by relying on units of analysis such as states and single cities. The result has been a set of diverse findings about what contextual factors are associated with where bias crime is most likely to occur.

At the state-level, research has shown poverty and other measures of social disorganization to be positively associated with the occurrence of bias crime (Gale et al., 2002; Medoff, 1999). Community-level scholars, however, have found no such evidence that bias crimes are more likely to occur in impoverished areas (Green, Glaser et al., 1998). In fact, some scholars have found that bias crimes are more likely to occur in more organized and affluent communities (Green, Strolovitch et al., 1998; Lyons, 2007). While macro-level studies shed light on the ecological correlates associated with bias crime, often overlooked are processes operating at the micro-level that increase the likelihood for this type of crime to occur.

Researchers have more recently advocated for exploring the interactional dynamics underlying bias violence. Bufkin (1999) and Perry (2001), for instance, have highlighted the importance of understanding the situational dynamics of bias crime offending. According to both scholars, bias crime can, under certain circumstances, be utilized as a resource for "doing difference," or outwardly expressing one's social identity status (e.g., race and gender) and as a means for policing perceived boundaries between offenders, victims, and their communities.

Kelley and Gruenewald (2015), for instance, demonstrated how offenders may use acts of fatal violence against lesbian, gay, bisexual, and transgender (LGBT) persons as a means for "doing gender," especially in situations where an offender's gender was being challenged. Relying on theories of "doing difference" (Perry, 2001; West & Fenstermaker, 1995), Klein and Allison (2017) found that racial bias homicides may be viewed as a resource for Whites to reaffirm their hegemonic social positions in society and restore racial and ethnic boundaries when a threat to traditional norms have been perceived.

In another study focused on the contexts in which bias crime offenders situationally accomplish race and ethnicity, sexual orientation and gender identity, and class through bias homicide, Gruenewald and Allison (2018) examined the situational dynamics of various bias victim groups. Findings from their study suggested that bias offenders achieve difference in distinct ways based on the types of victims they select. For example, opportunities to achieve difference may, in some instances, be situationally shaped by an offender's accessibility to weapons. This was demonstrated by Gruenewald and Allison (2018) when they found that while anti-racial/ethnic homicide offenders relied heavily on firearms, anti-LGBT and anti-homeless homicide offenders achieved difference through homicidal acts using knives, blunt objects, and bodily weapons.

Similar to more traditional theories of criminal behavior, interactional explanations of bias violence are not without their limitations. In particular, while prior interactional research suggests that it may be a lack of resources for accomplishing difference that is a key motivating factor behind bias offending, such perspectives do not explain why all, or more, individuals who lack the resources to accomplish difference through legitimate channels are also not committing bias violence.

THEORETICAL FRAMEWORK

It is possible that what is missing from prior explanations of bias violence are deeper considerations of how group identity may factor into bias offending. Such theories as social identity theory (Tajfel & Turner, 1986) have been suggested by scholars as a possible framework for studying specific types of bias violence (see Hamner, 1992). Social identity theory views both personal and social identities as distinct from one another (Tajfel & Turner, 1986). The personal self refers to the way in which one defines oneself according to idiosyncratic characteristics (e.g., intelligent and outgoing), but the social self refers to the ways in which one defines oneself in terms of group memberships (e.g., White and American) (Swann, Jetten, Gomez, Whitehouse, & Bastian, 2012). According to social identity theory, when one's social identity is salient, their personal identity fades from awareness and vice versa. Therefore, at the heart of social identity theory is the idea that intergroup behavior rests solely on relevant social identities (Hopkins et al., 2007; Levine & Crowther, 2008). Moreover, social identity theorists have suggested that as group members define themselves in relation to their social identity they go through a process of "depersonalization" in which they view themselves and their group members as one in the same (Swann et al., 2012). In other words, rather than viewing other group members in terms of personal relationships, their perceptions of others are based on their membership in a group. Social identity theorists have also suggested that the attractiveness of group members is largely based on the degree to which they embody ideal characteristics of the group. In this way, "membership-based" attraction is different from "unique-based" attraction in which the attractiveness of a person is based on personal characteristics (Swann et al., 2012, p. 443). Also relevant, social context is thought to play an important role in shaping one's identification as a group member, such that group membership identification fluctuates based on contextual changes (Turner, 1999; Turner, Oakes, Haslam, & McGarty, 1994).

Glaser, Dixit, and Green (2002) have laid the groundwork for exploring group identity as a motivating factor in advocating for prejudicial forms of violence. Based on interviews with persons who participate in racist online chat rooms, the authors found that respondents were more likely to advocate for acts of violence when the topic concerned interracial marriage. Many of the observed statements advocating for violence referenced the "purity" of their group as a justification, suggesting that group identity can serve as a driving factor behind bias violence, as opposed to other more common explanations, such as perceiving racial minorities to be economic threats.

Relying on Tajfel and Turner's (1986) social identity theory is a step in the right direction, but the use of such a theory is problematic for two reasons. First, fatal acts of bias violence are committed by individuals emboldened by their own beliefs (i.e., personal self) while also being validated with rationales supplied by their group (i.e., social self). Therefore, the use of social identity creates issues in understanding whether bias crime offenders are acting on behalf of their group (a social identity motive) or on behalf of themselves as individuals (a personal identity motive) when committing bias attacks. Second, social identity theory suggests that it is the desire of perceived superior in-groups to differentiate themselves from perceived lesser outgroups that drives people to commit bias attacks against members of other groups. However, if it were only for the "othering" of various social groups or a lack of resources according to interactional and situational theories, would we not expect to see more individuals committing bias violence?

While these theoretical frameworks provide us with some insight into why some people might engage in acts of bias violence, they do not explain why most people do not engage in this specific act of extreme behavior. Therefore, I propose the use of identity fusion theory (Swann et al., 2012) as an alternative explanation for bias crime occurrences. Identity fusion suggests that one's personal identity is fused with the group's identity and thus, the enactment of one identity activates the other. Moreover, it is those highly fused individuals who share a visceral oneness with a social identity status (e.g., White and heterosexual) who use extreme behaviors like bias violence to simultaneously compensate for a perceived threat to both their social and personal identities.

Identity Fusion Theory

Identity fusion theory expands upon social identity theory while also suggesting that personal and social identities of group members may be more closely aligned than previously conceived. Indeed, identity fusion theorists contend that, while distinguishable boundaries between personal and social identities do exist for most people, such boundaries are much more pervious for persons highly fused with a group. Swann et al. (2012) claim that identity fusion occurs when "people experience a visceral feeling of oneness with a group" (p. 442). Boundaries that ordinarily distinguish personal from social identities become exceedingly porous when an individual's unification with a group is especially strong, allowing for personal and social identities to fuse.

Highly fused persons experience a reciprocally influencing process, perceiving their group through the personal self while perceiving the self through the lens of group membership (Swann et al., 2012). Therefore, the saliency of one identity does not necessarily require the diminishment of the other identity. In fact, the permeability of the borders between personal and social identities for highly fused persons allows group members to simultaneously feel intensely connected to their group and individual group members. This produces opportunities for building stronger relational ties to other group members, and creates an obligation to dutifully defend in-group members (Swann et al., 2012; see also Swann, Gomez, Seyle, Morales, & Huici, 2009). Moreover, highly fused persons tend to believe that fellow group members are similarly committed to their protection. Such thinking exacerbates the perceived strength and invulnerability of the in-group for highly fused persons.

Four unique principles of identity fusion warrant further elaboration. First, according to Swann et al. (2012), the agentic-personal-self principle suggests when persons fuse to groups, their personal identities do not diminish. Rather, social and personal identities affect a highly fused person's behavior when engaging in pro-group activity. Second, the identity synergy principle states that pro-group activities are motivated by the synergistic interaction between social and personal identities for highly fused individuals (Swann et al., 2012, p. 442). The permeability of personal and social identities means that activating one identity will necessarily activate the other, providing increased motivation to engage in pro-group actions. Third, the relational ties principle maintains that highly fused persons not only evaluate the attractiveness of fellow group members based on the degree to which they embody ideal group characteristics, but also on their personal qualities. In effect, the combination of these evaluative processes fosters strong relational ties among group members. Since contact with all members of a group is not always possible, Swann et al. (2012) note that the relational ties that highly fused persons develop with in-group members "are metaphorical rather than literal" (p. 443). The exceptional strength of these ties is notable, as they have the ability to encourage highly fused individuals to engage in extreme behavior for the sake of the group (Swann et al., 2012).

The fourth, and final, principle is the irrevocability principle. Unlike social identity theory, which suggests that identification with a group fluctuates with social context, a highly fused person will remain steadfast in their group identification regardless of contextual changes (Swann et al., 2012). This is due in part to the exceptional strength of the relational ties of highly fused persons and their commitment to the group, which reinforce fusion. Moreover, the permeability of boundaries between the personal and social identities of highly fused persons allows for feelings of support and commitment, by both identities, to the group. As such, when a highly fused individual perceives a threat to either identity (i.e., personal or social), there is a need for a stabilization of self-views. In order to compensate, highly fused persons are impelled to engage in self-verifying actions under certain conditions (Swann, 2011), which can provide an avenue for reaffirming threatened identities as well as reinforcing feelings of fusion.

IDENTITY FUSION AND BIAS VIOLENCE

Identity fusion theory would suggest that violent bias offenders are highly fused individuals, and unique from others maintaining discriminatory or prejudicial beliefs, who share a visceral oneness with their dominant social identity statuses (e.g., White, heterosexual, Christian, and male). These individuals feel an intensified sense of duty to defend their in-group and police existing boundaries between their membership groups and those labeled "others." Pro-group activities enacted by highly fused individuals reflect both their personal and social identities, and are triggered by perceived threats to either (or both) of them. Such perceived challenges may come from various directions, such as beliefs that African Americans commit an excess of violence against Whites, immigrants take jobs and resources from Americans, homosexuals threaten traditional ways of life, or all Muslims are at war with Western civilization. Under certain circumstances where highly fused individuals perceive such threats, their need for stability in their self-views may prompt self-verifying, compensatory actions. Importantly, when perceived to be under siege, acts of self-verification also serve as verification of the social group. In response to perceived threats to both their social and personal identities, offenders may resort to extreme violence against other social groups, including racial, ethnic, religious, sexual orientation, and gender identity groups.

While some prior research on identity fusion and extreme behavior has focused on identity with a literal group, whether it be ISIS (Wilson, 2017), or radicalization with other Jihadi terrorist groups (Knapton, 2014), there has been little empirical research focusing on social identity groups defined by race, gender, and class, and the consequences of individuals fusing themselves to these social identity groups. I contend that theories, such as identity fusion, can be applied to the study of bias violence in order to explain how extreme actions are committed by highly fused individuals on behalf of groups with which they identify.

METHODOLOGICAL ISSUES AND ADVANTAGES OF STUDYING BIAS VIOLENCE IN THE DIGITAL AGE

Before applying identity fusion theory to bias violence, it is important to (1) acknowledge the methodological issues scholars face in studying this type of crime and (2) suggest an alternative method to overcome these issues. One of the major concerns crime scholars face in their search for a better understanding of bias offending is a scarcity of official bias crime data. Many scholars rely on available official crime data to study bias crime, but these data tend to suffer from reporting and consistency issues across jurisdictions. Due to limited resources and minimal training in bias crime identification, underreporting by law enforcement continues to be an issue. Moreover, officer prejudices as well as a general reluctance to record offenses as bias-motivated further undermine the reliability and validity of such data (Bell, 2002; Berk et al., 1992; Boyd et al., 1996; Green et al., 2001; Haider-Markel, 2002; Levin & McDevitt, 1993, 2002; McDevitt et al., 2002; Nolan & Akiyama, 1999).

Some scholars have avoided concerns of official bias crime data by utilizing surveys and interviews with victims of bias crime (Herek, 2009; Herek, Gillis, Cogan, & Glunt, 1997; Iganski, 2001; McDevitt et al., 2001; Rose & Mechanic, 2002) and bias crime offenders (Van Der Meer, 2003) to gain a better understanding of this type of crime. As discussed previously, others studying bias crime have found ways to narrow the scope of their study to specific law enforcement jurisdictions (e.g., Baltimore, Chicago, Sacramento, and New York City) where bias crime reporting is considered more reliable (Grattet, 2009; Green, Glaser et al., 1998; Green, Strolovitch et al., 1998; Lyons, 2007; Martin, 1996; Pinderhughes, 1993) or aggregating data to larger geographic units (e.g., state-level), while overlooking heterogeneity in bias violence (Gale et al., 2002, Medoff, 1999). Scholars using official bias crime data have examined general trends and patterns based on available event-level measures, as opposed to overall numbers of reported offenses. Nonetheless, studies relying on official data still must contend with limitations in the number of variables available and issues of data representativeness and the generalizability of findings (Messner et al., 2004; Stacey, 2011).

Open-Source Data

An alternative to relying on official bias crime data and more resource-intensive surveys and interviews is the use of publicly available open sources. The expansion of the Internet has ushered in a digital era where an abundance of information exists and can be culled from websites. Open-source data consist of publicly available documents available on the Internet, such as news articles, legal documents, and scholarly works, all of which may be systematically collected, organized, and coded into functional databases on a particular topic. Information from open-source web-based content is available for many types of crimes, but may be especially useful for rare forms of serious crime that are likely to result in media and criminal justice responses.

While the usefulness of open-source data for studying crime may still be novel, a study by Parkin and Gruenewald (2017) examined the validity and reliability of open-source homicide data by comparing them with official homicide data over a one-year period in a single jurisdiction. Their results indicated that open-source data not only replicated the population of homicides found in official data, but open-source measures were consistent with those found in official crime data. In some cases, open-source data provided more information on variables than those found in official data. Moreover, the authors argued that while several variables that are commonly used to test criminological theory cannot be found in official data, the use of open-sources allowed for their identification. Thus, Parkin and Gruenewald (2017) concluded that open-source data are just as reliable as official data for studying homicide, whether it be at the macro-, individual-, or situational-level.

Open-source data have been used in empirical research to study topics that are often covered to a much higher degree by media sources due to their sensational and unusual nature, including terrorism and extremism (Cothren, Smith, Roberts, & Damphousse, 2008; Gruenewald, Chermak, & Freilich, 2012; LaFree, Dugan, Xie, & Singh, 2012; Parkin, Freilich, & Chermak, 2015; Sageman, 2004) and bias violence (Gruenewald, 2012, 2013; Gruenewald & Allison, 2018; Kelley & Gruenewald, 2015; Klein & Allison, 2017; Levin & Reichelmann, 2015). In the following section, I illustrate the usefulness of open-source data in reconstructing an account of a fatal act of bias violence, including case details and indicators of personal and social identity to demonstrate the application of identity fusion theory to bias violence.

ILLUSTRATIVE EXAMPLE

Over 800 pages of open-source documents containing relevant information to the Charleston church shooting were collected from systematic searches of over 30 online search engines and stored in the United States Extremist Crime repository (see Freilich, Chermak, Belli, Gruenewald, & Parkin, 2014 for a thorough discussion of the process for collecting and coding open-source data). Open-source materials for this case include court and other legal documents, scholarly articles, news, and other online media reports. Based on a close reading of all collected materials I present a brief summary of the tragic bias homicide that took place and draw from identity fusion theory to explain how this particular fatal act of bias violence was perpetrated by a highly fused individual acting in response to a perceived threat to his social group identity (i.e., Whites).

Incident Summary

On June 17, 2015, 21-year-old Dylann Storm Roof walked into the Emanuel AME Church in Charleston, South Carolina, a church that played a very important role during the Civil Rights Movement. After quietly entering the building, he was welcomed by the group as he sat down to join an 8.00 p.m. Bible study. That day the slight young man wore a fanny pack and long-sleeved grey shirt with a Border Patrol logo on the sleeve. At approximately 9.00 p.m., Roof pulled out his .45-caliber handgun, a gun he had purchased with money gifted to him on his birthday. He proceeded to tell the group, "I have to do it. You are raping our women and taking over our country. You have to go," (Zavadski, 2015, para. 29) before firing at them. After Roof fired and reloaded the weapon approximately five times, nine of the African American parishioners were dead. Three members of the Bible study survived the attack, including a woman who Roof intentionally spared so she could recount for others what had happened that night. After enduring a 12-hour manhunt, Roof was eventually captured during a traffic stop in Shelby, North Carolina, and arrested wearing a bullet-proof vest. A local resident spotted a man fitting Roof's description driving along the highway near Shelby, a town 250 miles north of the Charleston AME church. Roof later confessed to the murders and stated to investigators that he had intended for it to start a race war. When probed by reporters, the Charleston police chief stated that he believed this incident was in fact a hate crime.

Offender Background

Roof, who grew up in a rural town outside of Columbia, South Carolina, had a deviant past and criminal record. Before dropping out of high school in the tenth grade, he was known for abusing drugs and making racist remarks and jokes to classmates. Acquaintances of Roof told of his hatred of African Americans, his pro-segregation beliefs, and his hopes of inciting a race war (Bell, 2015). In the years directly preceding the incident, Roof began to withdraw from family and friends. It was not until February 28, 2015, however, that he was first arrested and criminally charged with a serious crime. While visiting a mall in Columbia, South Carolina, employees phoned the police to complain about Roof, who they described as dressed in all black, acting unusual, and asking questions about store hours and the number of store employees (Robles, 2015). A search of Roof's person turned up strips of Suboxone, a drug commonly prescribed for pain and as a treatment for opiate addiction (Robles, 2015). Since he did not have a prescription for the drug, police arrested Roof for drug possession. In addition to the felony drug charge, Roof was banned from the mall for one year. However, two months later, while out on bond, Roof showed up at the mall again and was charged with trespassing (Ortiz, 2015).

In the weeks leading up to the attack, Roof became increasingly agitated. He reached out to an old friend whom he had not seen in several years to rant about the controversial Trayvon Martin and Freddie Gray cases in which unarmed Black men were killed. He believed that "blacks were taking over the world" and that "someone needed to do something about it for the white race" (Weiss, Kinnard, & Jordan, 2015, para. 6). However, it was primarily through online White supremacist websites where he found support for his views from likeminded individuals. Roof suggested that his radical beliefs about race relations in the United States were fueled in part by content he was consuming on the Internet following the high-profile Trayvon Martin case. In his view, the man responsible for the killing was justified in shooting the unarmed teen (Hersher, 2017). The case sparked his interest in "Black on White violence" (Zavadski, 2015, para. 2). While searching for more information on "Black on White" violent offenses, he discovered a website belonging to the South Carolina-based hate group Council of Conservative Citizens, formerly known as the White Citizens' Council (Hersher, 2017). On this website, Roof read through several pages of incidents, many fictitious, where White individuals were the victims of violent acts perpetrated by African Americans. After reading through stories, Roof exclaimed that he was never the same. He bought into the White supremacist propaganda stories, which was evidenced in his Facebook profile picture, where he wore a jacket with the flags of the White-ruled Rhodesia and apartheid-era South Africa, both of which are popular symbols among White supremacists.

Roof's own website, "The Last Rhodesian," included a picture of him holding a Confederate flag and a racist manifesto. In it he stated that he believed "Niggers are stupid and violent" (Zavadski, 2015, para. 5) and questioned America's history of slavery, adding:

> I wish with a passion that niggers were treated terribly throughout history by Whites, that every White person had an ancestor who owned slaves, that segregation was an evil an[d] oppressive institution, and so on [...] but it isn't true. None of it is. (para. 6)

It was Roof's belief that slavery was not as malignant as American history would suggest because not all Southern Whites owned slaves and many slave narratives Roof claimed to have read spoke positively of slave-owners. Furthermore, Roof believed that segregation "existed to protect us from them…integration has done nothing but bring Whites down to [the] level of brute animals" (para. 8).

Roof also discussed his thoughts on other minority groups in his online manifesto. In particular, because he believed that Jews denied their own whiteness, he wanted to "destroy the Jewish identity" (Zavadski, 2015, para. 13).

> The problem is that Jews look White, and in many cases are White, yet they see themselves as minorities. I don't pretend to understand why [J]ews do what they do. They are [an] enigma. (para. 14)

Regarding Hispanics, Roof believed there were both good ones and bad ones. However, he believed that the most powerful among them were generally White and have a "respect for White beauty" (para. 15). Despite believing that "there is good White blood worth saving in Uruguay, Argentina, Chile, and even Brasil [*sic.*]," he felt that "they are still our enemies" (para. 16).

At the end of his manifesto, Roof begins to provide an explanation for his mass shooting that would take the lives of nine African Americans.

> To take a saying from my favorite film, "Even if my life is worth less than a speck of dirt, I want to use it for the good of society,"…I have no choice. I am not in the position to, alone, go into the ghetto and fight. I chose Charleston because it is [the] most historic city in my state, and at one time had the highest ratio of blacks to whites in the country. We have no skinheads, no real KKK, no one doing anything but talking on the internet. Well someone has to have the bravery to take it to the real world, and I guess that has to be me. (Zavadski, 2015, para. 21)

As a bewildering conclusion to his online manifesto, he ends with "Please forgive any typos, I didnt [*sic.*] have time to check it" (para. 22).

Applying Identity Fusion

Through the use of data from publicly available online sources, it is evident that Roof viewed himself as a White individual, thereby making Whiteness an integral part of his personal identity. Moreover, Roof believed that he was an important part of a White social group and acted on behalf of the White race for what he believed was the "good of society" (Zavadski, 2015, para. 21). In his online explanation for his attack on the AME Church, he acknowledged that his act of violence would be a lone mission. He suggested that as no other frustrated White person had the bravery to take the hatred they spewed on the Internet "to the real world" (para. 21), the responsibility for protecting the White race fell on him. He believed that as a member and defender of the purity of the White race, he had no other choice.

Evidence of fusion to the White social identity group is found in Roof's online manifesto. Much of his discourse included an us (White social identity group) versus them (Black social identity group) perspective. When Roof wrote about segregation, he stated that its purpose was "to protect *us* from *them*" and that "integration has done nothing but bring Whites down to [the] level of brute animals" (Zavadski, 2015, para. 8, emphasis added), suggesting that *they* (i.e., African Americans) have a bad influence on *us* (i.e., Whites). We can also see how closely he identities with the White race as a social group when he writes negatively about other groups, who he suggests, deny their whiteness (i.e., Jews). Roof insinuates that Jews should identify more with their White social group, but because they do not, they should be destroyed. He also believed that despite the fact that several Hispanics have a "respect for White beauty…*they* are still *our* enemies" (para. 15, emphasis added).

Roof found affirmation in his beliefs about White superiority with other like-minded people through Internet-hate sites. His interest in the Trayvon Martin case lead him down a spiral of misinformation found online concerning the supposed "Black on White violence" epidemic spurred on by White supremacist websites, further fusing his personal identity as a White individual with the social identity of White people as a whole (Zavadski, 2015, para. 2). The "Black on White violence" literature he was reading likely triggered a perception of threat toward his White social identity group, thus creating a need for stabilization of self-views. Roof relied on bias homicide against those perceived to represent the existential threat as a violent way to reaffirm his threatened (and fused) identities.

CONCLUSION

The purpose of this chapter was to discuss what is known about serious forms of bias violence, obstacles to conducting research on this topic, and how alternative theoretical and methodological approaches can advance our understanding of bias violence in the twenty-first century. An illustrative case was also presented to highlight how (1) publicly available open-source materials (e.g., court documents and media reports) can be systematically compiled and used as reliable data for studying serious forms of bias violence and (2) the use of social psychological theories, specifically identity fusion theory, can help to explain the role that personal and group identities may have in fueling prejudicial violence. Additionally, the combination of information provided through open-source data as well as the use of identity fusion provides direction for future research to untangle complex issues of bias violence and the blurred boundaries of this form of violence with mass shootings and domestic extremism.

Official data will continue to provide valuable insights into the nature of bias crime, despite the limitations of these data discussed in this chapter. Official crime data, however, cannot be the only source of information we rely upon to further our understanding of bias violence. Instead, it is imperative that bias crime researchers supplement official crime data and make use of alternative data collection methods to explore macro-, meso-, and micro-level explanations of bias violence. Doing so, will lead to new insights on the dynamic nature of bias violence that have yet to be considered.

As bias crime as a topic of research continues to gain traction, scholars must also be open to applying new theoretical approaches to explain how and why these crimes occur. There remain many issues with relying on traditional criminological theory for explaining bias violence (Perry, 2001), so it will be necessary to draw from alternative theoretical perspectives and disciplines. In the past, sociological theories have offered an avenue for exploring the situational and interactional dynamics of bias violence, but questions still remain about social processes leading some individuals to commit this rare form of violence against others because of their social group status. It will be by integrating new concepts like identity fusion that we can begin to expand our understanding of the role that personal and social identities play in motivating offenders to commit acts of bias violence.

REFERENCES

Bell, J. (2002). *Policing hatred: Law enforcement, civil rights, and hate crime*. New York, NY: New York University Press.

Bell, J. (2015). There are no racists here: The rise of racial extremism, when no one is racist. *Michigan Journal of Race and Law*, *20*(2), 349–376.

Berk, R. A., Boyd, E. A., & Hamner, K. M. (1992). Thinking more clearly about hate-motivated crimes. In G. M. Herek & K. T. Berrill (Eds.), *Hate crimes: Confronting violence against lesbians and gay men* (pp. 123–138). Newbury Park, CA: SAGE.

Berrill, K. T. (1990). Anti-gay violence and victimization in the United States. *Journal of Interpersonal Violence*, *5*, 274–294.

Boyd, E., Berk, R., & Hamner, K. (1996). Motivated by hatred or prejudice: Categorization of hate-motivated crimes in two police divisions. *Law and Society Review*, *30*(4), 819–850.

Bufkin, J. L. (1999). Bias crime as gendered behavior. *Social Justice*, *26*, 155–176.

Cogan, J. C. (2002). Hate crime as a crime category worthy of policy attention. *American Behavioral Scientist*, *46*(1), 173–185.

Comstock, G. D. (1991). *Violence against lesbians and gay men*. New York, NY: Columbia University Press.

Cothren, J., Smith, B. L., Roberts, P., & Damphousse, K. R. (2008). Geospatial and temporal patterns of preparatory conduct among American terrorists. *International Journal of Comparative and Applied Criminal Justice*, *32*, 23–41.

Freilich, J. D., Chermak, S. M., Belli, R., Gruenewald, J., & Parkin, W. (2014). Introducing the United States Extremist Crime Database (ECDB). *Terrorism and Political Violence*, *26*(2), 372–384.

Gale, L. R., Heath, W. C., & Ressler, R. W. (2002). An economic analysis of hate crime. *Eastern Economic Journal*, *28*, 203–215.

Garofalo, J. (1991). Racially motivated crimes in New York City. In M. J. Lynch & E. B. Patterson (Eds.), *Race and criminal justice* (pp. 161–173). Albany, NY: Harrow & Heston.

Garofalo, J., & Martin, S. E. (1993). *Bias-motivated crimes: Their characteristics and law enforcement response*. Carbondale, IL: Southern Illinois University, Center for the Study of Crime, Delinquency, and Corrections.

Glaser, J., Dixit, J., & Green, D. P. (2002). Studying hate crime with the Internet: What makes racists advocate racial violence? *Journal of Social Issues*, *58*(1), 177–193.

Grattet, R. (2009). The urban ecology of bias crime: A study of disorganization and defended neighborhoods. *Social Problems*, *56*(1), 132–150.

Green, D. P., Glaser, J., & Rich, A. (1998). From lynching to gay bashing: The elusive connection between economic conditions and hate crime. *Journal of Personality and Psychology*, *75*(1), 82–92.

Green, D. P., McFalls, L. H., & Smith, J. K. (2001). Hate crime: An emergent research agenda. *Annual Review of Sociology*, *27*, 479–504.

Green, D. P., Strolovitch, D. Z., & Wong, J. S. (1998). Defended neighborhoods, integration, and racially motivated crime. *The American Journal of Sociology*, *104*(2), 372–403.

Gruenewald, J. (2012). Are anti-LGBT homicides in the United States unique? *Journal of Interpersonal Violence*, *27*, 3601–3623.

Gruenewald, J. A. (2013). Using open-source data to study bias homicide against homeless persons. *International Journal of Criminology and Sociology*, *2*, 538–549.

Gruenewald, J., & Allison, K. (2018). Examining differences in bias homicide across victim groups. *Crime and Delinquency*, *64*(3), 316–341.

Gruenewald, J., Chermak, S. M., & Freilich, J. D. (2012). Distinguishing "loner" attacks from other domestic extremist violence. *Criminology and Public Policy*, *12*, 65–91.

Gruenewald, J., & Kelley, K. (2014). Typifying anti-LGBT homicide events by mode of victim selection. *Criminal Justice and Behavior*, *41*(9), 1130–1142.

Haider-Markel, D. P. (2002). Regulating hate: State and local influences on law enforcement actions related to hate crime. *State Politics and Policy Quarterly*, *2*(2), 126–160.

Hamner, K. M. (1992). Gay-bashing: A social identity analysis of violence against lesbians and gay men. In G. M. Herek & K. T. Berrill (Eds.), *Hate crimes: Confronting violence against lesbians and gay men* (pp. 179–190). Thousand Oaks, CA: SAGE.

Harry, J. (1992). Conceptualizing anti-gay violence. In G. M. Herek & K. T. Berrill (Eds.), *Hate crimes: Confronting violence against lesbians and gay men* (pp. 113–122). Newbury Park, CA: Sage.

Herek, G. M. (2009). Hate crimes and stigma-related experiences among sexual minority adults in the United States. *Journal of Interpersonal Violence*, *24*(1), 54–74.

Herek, G. M., & Berrill, K. (1992). *Hate crimes: Confronting violence against lesbians and gay men*. Thousand Oaks, CA: SAGE.

Herek, G. M., Cogan, J. C., & Gillis, J. R. (2002). Victim experiences in hate crimes based on sexual orientation. *Journal of Social Issues*, *58*, 319–339.

Herek, G. M., Gillis, J. R., & Cogan, J. C. (1999). Psychological sequelae of hate-crime victimization among lesbian, gay, and bisexual adults. *Journal of Consulting and Clinical Psychology*, *67*, 945–951.

Herek, G. M., Gillis, J. R., Cogan, J. C., & Glunt, E. K. (1997). Hate crime victimization among lesbian, gay, and bisexual adults: Prevalence, psychological correlates, and methodological issues. *Journal of Interpersonal Violence*, *12*(2), 195–215.

Hersher, R. (2017). What happened when Dylann Roof asked google for information about race? *National Public Radio*, January 10, 2017. Retrieved from https://www.npr.org/sections/thetwo-way/2017/01/10/508363607/what-happened-when-dylann-roof-asked-google-for-information-about-race. Accessed on January 6, 2018.

Hirschi, T. (1969). *Causes of delinquency*. Berkeley, CA: University of California Press.

Hopkins, N., Reicher, S., Harrison, K., Cassidy, C., Bull, R., & Levine, M. (2007). Helping to improve the group stereotype: On the strategic dimension of pro-social behavior. *Personality and Social Psychology Bulletin*, *33*, 776–788.

Iganski, P. (2001). Hate crimes hurt more. *American Behavioral Scientist*, *45*, 626–638.

Kelley, K., & Gruenewald, J. (2015). Accomplishing masculinity through anti-lesbian, gay, bisexual, and transgender homicide. *Men and Masculinities*, *18*, 3–29.

Klein, B. R., & Allison, K. (2017). Accomplishing difference: How do anti-race/ethnicity bias homicides compare to average homicides in the United States? *Justice Quarterly*. Published online, doi: 10.1080/07418825.2017.1351576

Knapton, H. M. (2014). The recruitment and radicalisation of western citizens: Does ostracism have a role in homegrown terrorism? *Journal of European Psychology Students*, *5*(1), 38–48.

LaFree, G., Dugan, L., Xie, M., & Singh, P. (2012). Spatial and temporal patterns of terrorist attacks by ETA 1970 to 2007. *Journal of Quantitative Criminology*, *28*, 7–29.

Levin, J., & McDevitt, J. (1993). *Hate crimes: The rising tide of bigotry and bloodshed.* New York, NY: Plenum Press.

Levin, J., & McDevitt, J. (2002). *Hate crimes revisited: America's war on those who are different.* Boulder, CO: Westview Press.

Levin, J., & Reichelmann, A. (2015). From thrill to defensive motivation: The role of group threat in the changing nature of hate-motivated assaults. *American Behavioral Scientist, 59*, 1–16.

Levine, M., & Crowther, S. (2008). The responsive bystander: How social group membership and group size can encourage as well as inhibit bystander intervention. *Journal of Personality and Social Psychology*, *95*, 1429–1439.

Lyons, C. J. (2007). Community (dis)organization and racially motivated crime. *American Journal of Sociology*, *113*(3), 815–863.

Martin, S. E. (1996). Investigating hate crimes: Case characteristics and law enforcement responses. *Justice Quarterly*, *13*, 455–480.

Maxwell, C., & Maxwell, S. R. (1995). *Youth participation in hate-motivated crimes: Research and policy implications.* Boulder, CO: Center for the Study and Prevention of Violence.

McDevitt, J., Balboni, J. M., & Bennett, S. (2002). *Improving the quality and accuracy of bias crime statistics nationally: An assessment of the first ten years of bias crime data collection*. Washington, DC: U.S. Department of Justice.

McDevitt, J., Balboni, J., Garcia, L., & Gu, J. (2001). Consequences for victims: A comparison of bias- and non-bias-motivated assaults. *The American Behavioral Scientist*, *45*(4), 697–713.

Medoff, M. (1999). Allocation of time and hateful behavior: A theoretical analysis of hate and hate crimes. *American Journal of Economics and Sociology, 58*, 959–973.

Merton, R. K. (1938). Social structure and anomie. *American Sociological Review*, *3*, 672–682.

Messner, S., McHugh, S., & Felson, R. (2004). Distinctive characteristics of assaults motivated by bias. *Criminology, 42*(3), 585–618.

Noelle, M. (2002). The ripple effect of the Matthew Shepard murder: Impact on the assumptive worlds of members of the targeted group. *American Behavioral Scientist*, *46*, 27–50.

Nolan, J., & Akiyama, Y. (1999). An analysis of factors that affect law enforcement participation in hate crime reporting. *Journal of Contemporary Criminal Justice*, *15*(1), 111–127.

Ortiz, E. (2015). Dylann Roof, suspected Charleston church shooting gunman has troubled past. *NBC News*, June 18, 2015. Retrieved from https://www.nbcnews.com/storyline/charleston-church-shooting/dylann-roof-suspected-charleston-church-shooting-gunman-has-troubled-past-n377686. Accessed on January 6, 2018.

Parkin, W. S., Freilich, J. D., & Chermak, S. M. (2015). Ideological victimization: Homicides perpetrated by far-right extremists. *Homicide Studies*, *19*, 211–236.

Parkin, W. S., & Gruenewald, J. (2017). Open-source data and the study of homicide. *Journal of Interpersonal Violence*, *32*(18), 2693–2723.

Perry, B. (2001). *In the name of hate: Understanding hate crimes.* New York, NY: Routledge.

Pinderhughes, H. (1993). The anatomy of racially motivated violence in New York City: A case study of youth in southern Brooklyn. *Social Problems, 40*(4), 478–492.

Redfield, H. V. (1880/2000). *Homicide, North and South: Being a comparative view of crime against the person in several parts of the United States.* Columbus, OH: The Ohio State University Press (Originally published by J. B. Lippincott).

Robles, F. (2015). Dylann Roof had AR-15 parts during police stop in March, record shows. *The New York Times*, June 26, 2015. Retrieved from https://www.nytimes.com/2015/06/27/us/dylann-roof-was-questioned-by-police-in-march-record-shows.html. Accessed on January 6, 2018.

Rose, S. M., & Mechanic, M. B. (2002). Psychological distress, crime features, and help-seeking behaviors related to homophobic bias incidents. *The American Behavioral Scientist*, *46*(1), 14–26.
Sageman, M. (2004). *Understanding terror networks.* Philadelphia, PA: University of Pennsylvania Press.
Smith, M. D., & Zahn, M. (1999). *Homicide: A sourcebook of social research.* Thousand Oaks, CA: SAGE.
Stacey, M. (2011). Distinctive characteristics of sexual orientation bias crimes. *Journal of Interpersonal Violence, 26*(15), 3013–3032.
Strom, K. I. (2001). *Hate crimes reported in NIBRS, 1997–99.* Washington, DC: Bureau of Justice Statistics.
Swann, W. B., Jr. (2011). Self-verification theory. In P. Van Lang, A. Kruglanski, & E. T. Higgins (Eds.), *Handbook of theories of social psychology* (pp. 23–42). London: SAGE.
Swann, W. B., Jr, Gomez, A., Seyle, C. D., Morales, J. F., & Huici, C. (2009). Identity fusion: The interplay of personal and social identities in extreme group behavior. *Journal of Personality and Social Psychology, 96*, 995–1011.
Swann, W. B., Jetten, J., Gomez, A., Whitehouse, H., & Bastian, B. (2012). When group membership gets personal: A theory of identity fusion. *Psychological Review*, *119*(3), 441–456.
Tajfel, H., & Turner, J. C. (1986). The social identity theory of inter-group behavior. In S. Worchel & L. W. Austin (Eds.), *Psychology of intergroup relations* (pp. 7–24). Chicago, IL: Nelson-Hall.
Tomsen, S. (2009). *Violence, prejudice, and sexuality*. New York, NY: Routledge.
Turner, J. C. (1999). Some current issues in research on social identity and self-categorization theories. In N. Ellemers, R. Spears, & B. Doosje (Eds.), *Social identity* (pp. 6–34). Oxford: Blackwell.
Turner, J. C., Oakes, P. J., Haslam, S. A., & McGarty, C. (1994). Self and collective: Cognition and social context. *Personality and Social Psychology Bulletin*, *20*, 454–463.
Van Der Meer, T. (2003). Gay bashing – A rite of passage? *Culture, Health, and Sexuality*, *5*(2), 153–165.
Weiss, M., Kinnard, M., & Jordan, J. (2015, June 19). *Friend says church shooting suspect ranted about race*. New York, NY: The Associated Press. Retrieved from https://apnews.com/a60d4bab-877c428ca9ed296e7ec6bd67/suspect-church-shooting-had-apartheid-era-patches. Accessed on January 6, 2018.
West, C., & Fenstermaker, S. (1995). Doing difference. *Gender & Society*, *9*, 8–37.
Wilson, L. (2017). Understanding the appeal of ISIS. *New England Journal of Public Policy*, *29*(1), 1–10.
Wolfgang, M. (1958). *Patterns of criminal homicide*. Philadelphia, PA: University of Pennsylvania Press.
Zavadski, K. (2015). Dylann Roof's racist manifesto is chilling. *The Daily Beast,* June 20, 2015. Retrieved from https://www.thedailybeast.com/dylann-roofs-racist-manifesto-is-chilling. Accessed on January 6, 2018.

PART III

POLICE AND STATE POWER

CHAPTER 7

SOLVING HOMICIDES: UNDERSTANDING TRENDS AND PATTERNS IN POLICE CLEARANCES OF LETHAL VIOLENCE

Wendy C. Regoeczi

ABSTRACT

Purpose – *The goal of this chapter is to assess the state of evidence examining and explaining trends and patterns in homicide clearances.*

Design/methodology/approach – *After reviewing the varying bodies of literature on homicide investigations and clearances, the author assesses the degree of support for the prevailing explanations of why some homicides are more likely to be solved than others. The author also use national data to evaluate several reasons for declining clearances.*

Findings – *Changes in the nature of homicide and deteriorating police–community relations are likely major contributors to declining clearance rates. The most consistent findings regarding patterns are the greater likelihood of clearance in homicides involving young children, contact weapons, residential locations, and killings not occurring in the course of another crime. Explanations relying on notions of victim devaluing generate the least support. There is considerable support for the legal factors approach and community-level explanations show promise. The findings regarding the role of forensic evidence are mixed. Smaller scale studies are beginning to help identify best practices for homicide investigations.*

Homicide and Violent Crime
Sociology of Crime, Law and Deviance, Volume 23, 121–138

ISSN: 1521-6136/doi:10.1108/S1521-613620180000023008

Originality/value – *This chapter assesses several explanations for declining clearance rates and brings together divergent streams of research to summarize the current state of knowledge on homicide clearances, best practices in homicide investigations, and gaps to be filled by further studies.*

Keywords: Homicide; clearance; investigation; solvability; forensic evidence; arrest

INTRODUCTION

Given the serious nature of the crime, we would expect a great deal of time and resources to be devoted to the investigation and prosecution of homicide cases. And while this is generally true, many homicides today remain unsolved. This chapter examines trends and patterns in solving homicides, including the role of forensic technology, and assessing the prevailing explanations behind them.

The term that law enforcement uses for solving homicides is clearances. A case can be cleared in one of two ways. A homicide can be cleared by the arrest of one or more suspects believed to have committed the murder. These cases are described as cleared by arrest and are the most common form of clearances. It is also possible, however, that the police may know who committed the homicide but for a variety of reasons cannot physically arrest the suspect. For example, the suspect may have committed suicide, been killed in another homicide or died from some other cause, may be serving a prison sentence in another jurisdiction, or have fled to another country. In these circumstances, homicides can be cleared by exceptional means. The Federal Bureau of Investigation (FBI) defines exceptional clearances the following way:

> In certain situations law enforcement is not able to clear offenses known to them. Many times all leads have been exhausted and everything possible has been done in order to clear a case. If the following questions can all be answered "yes," the offense can be cleared "exceptionally" for crime reporting purposes: 1) Has the investigation definitely established the identity of the offender? 2) Is there enough information to support an arrest, charge, and turning over to the court for prosecution; 3) Is the exact location of the offender known so that the subject can be taken into custody now? 4) Is there some reason outside law enforcement control that precludes arresting, charging, and prosecuting the offender? (FBI, 1984, p. 42)

Exceptional clearances are far less common than clearances by arrest. For example, a study examining exceptional clearances among law enforcement agencies submitting data to the National Incident-Based Reporting System (NIBRS) found exceptional clearances comprised approximately 10 percent of US homicide clearances among those agencies (Jarvis & Regoeczi, 2009). A similar percentage was found in Chicago (Riedel & Boulahanis, 2007).

TRENDS IN HOMICIDE CLEARANCES OVER TIME

One very puzzling yet little discussed trend concerns the dramatic decline in the percent of US homicides cleared today compared to the early 1960s. In 1961,

93 percent of homicides resulted in the arrest of a suspect; by 2016 this percent had dropped to 59.4. The dramatic decline in homicide clearances is surprising given other changes occurring during this same period, which may have been expected to help, not hinder, the ability of police to solve cases. These changes include the movement toward community policing (one of the goals of which was to improve police–community relations) and improved technology for scientific investigations.

The significant drop in the percent of murders resulting in the arrest of a suspect is clearly evident from Fig. 1. Much of the theorizing surrounding declining clearance rates has focused exclusively on the crime of murder. However, efforts to explain the downward trend in homicide clearances must recognize that declining clearance rates are not limited to murder. Clearance rates have also declined for other serious violent crimes such as rape, aggravated assault, and robbery during this same time period (Jarvis, Mancik, & Regoeczi, 2017; Riedel, 1995), suggesting the increasing challenges facing law enforcement in solving crimes are not restricted to murder investigations. However, some have argued that murder clearances represent a unique form of violence in the sense the victim typically cannot supply information about the crime (Riedel & Rinehart, 1996).

Furthermore, much of the theorizing concerning the drop in murder clearance rates has focused exclusively on the United States. However, efforts to explain declining murder clearances would benefit from the recognition that murder clearance rates have fallen in other countries as well, including Canada.

Changes in the Nature of Homicide

One of the most commonly cited explanations for declining homicide clearances in the United States points to a change in the nature of homicide. Specifically, the decline in recent decades in the proportion of homicides involving intimates

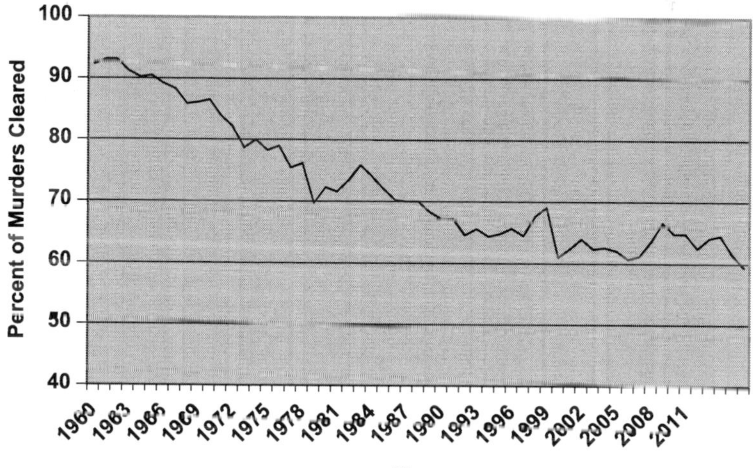

Fig. 1. Murder Clearance Rates in the United States, 1960–2016.

and family members (which pose fewer obstacles to clearing the case) may explain the corresponding decline in homicide clearances (Corwin, 1997; Riedel & Jarvis, 1998). This explanation is difficult to assess empirically, however, due to the difficulty posed by the increasingly large category of "unknown" victim/offender relationships in homicide cases. It could perhaps be indirectly tested by examining trends in felony-related homicides over time (i.e., those homicides committed during the commission of other crimes such as robberies and burglaries), since these infrequently involve intimates and family members (and thus may act as a proxy for types of homicides, which would be more difficult to clear). However, given the lack of availability of information on the circumstances surrounding the homicide prior to 1976, as well as significant reservations regarding the validity of the coding of the circumstance variable in the Supplementary Homicide Reports (SHR) (see Maxfield, 1988), a more straightforward approach is to compare murder arrest clearance rates with robbery rates obtained from the Uniform Crime Reports.

Fig. 2 shows a clear connection between murder clearance rates and robbery rates. Murder clearance rates were high in the early 1960s, a time when robbery rates were in the low 50s per 100,000 population. By the time the murder clearance rate had dropped to approximately 88 percent in 1967, the robbery rate had exceeded 100 and was more than double the 1960 rate. Not until the 1990s does this pattern begin to change; in the early 1990s the robbery rate begins a dramatic decline, while murder clearance rates begin to level off. Generally, however, these patterns support the argument that a shift in the nature of homicide toward more felony-related killings that pose greater obstacles to solving the case contributed to reduced murder clearances.

Another potential change in the nature of homicide concerns shifts in the prevalence of child homicide victims over time. Research on homicide clearance

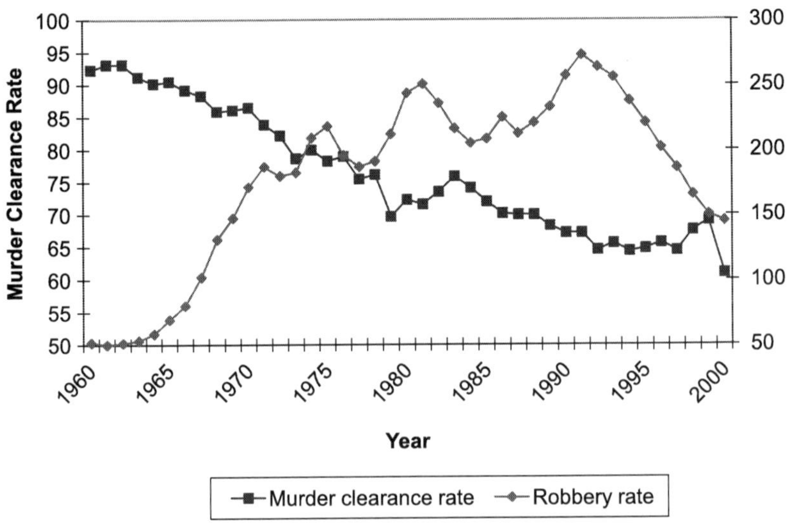

Fig. 2. Murder Clearance and Robbery Rates for US Cities, 1960–2000.

consistently finds a higher likelihood of clearing homicides for cases involving child victims. If the proportion of murders involving child victims has declined over time, clearance rates may subsequently decrease due to smaller proportion of cases, which are most likely to result in arrest.

Fig. 3 compares changes in murder clearance rates to changes in the percent of murder victims under 10 years of age (obtained from the Supplementary Homicide Reports). As with murder clearance rates, the proportion of young murder victims declines for most years between 1962 and 1980, suggesting the initial drop in murder clearance rates may be attributable, at least in part, to a shift in the nature of homicide toward older victims, who would be more likely to be killed by a stranger than victims under 10 years of age.

Police Resources

Given the importance of arrest clearances as a measure of police effectiveness at the individual or departmental level (Cordner, 1989; Corwin, 1997; Riedel & Jarvis, 1998; Waegel, 1981), it is difficult to imagine the dramatic decline in arrest clearances for the most serious and publicly scrutinized offense is the result of a declining interest or motivation to solve these cases on the part of homicide detectives. However, a decline in police resources could increase the obstacles faced by homicide investigators. Heavier caseloads can also affect the quality of investigations (Corwin, 1997). Unfortunately, we lack any reliable annual data on police resources to assess the validity of this explanation.

Declining Trust in the Police

Violence can function as a dispute resolution mechanism. Where individuals feel the law is unavailable to them, or lack faith in the criminal justice system to resolve

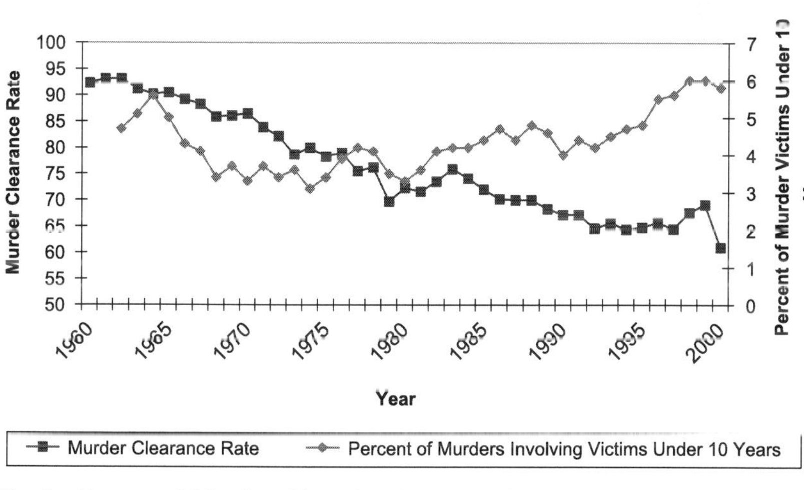

Fig. 3. Percent of Murders Cleared and Percent of Homicides Involving Children in the United States, 1960–2000.

their problems, they may resort to committing violence against those they perceive have wronged them (Anderson, 1999). In this respect, violence functions as a form of self-help (Black, 1983; Cooney, 1997). A number of studies provide evidence supporting this view (see, e.g., Anderson, 1999; Cooney, 1997; Lundsgaarde, 1977).

What compels individuals to take the law into their own hands may also affect their willingness to cooperate with legal officials. In other words, their rejection of the law can be seen in both their unwillingness to invoke the law in settling their own disputes and to provide knowledge of others operating outside of the law. As LaFree (1998, p. 80) argues, "when members of a society begin to doubt the fairness of their political institutions, even if they do not themselves violate laws, they become less enthusiastic agents for the social control of others." Leovy and Smith (1994) report that, "occasionally [investigators] are told flatly: Forget it. We will take our own revenge." The lack of arrests in many homicide cases further undermines trust, which further increases reliance on street justice, creating a vicious circle.

Puckett and Lundman (2003) argue that the lack of trust in the police in African American communities results in less cooperation and information during homicide investigations (see also Corwin, 1997). In contrast, the high levels of public trust characteristic of Japan appear to be linked to the high levels of public cooperation with police and consequently high clearance rates (LaFree, 1998). Because levels of trust in the police in the United States may fluctuate considerably over time, a deterioration in police–community relations in recent decades, especially within minority communities, may be a major contributor to declining clearance rates.

Ousey and Lee (2010) explore variations within cities in homicide clearance rates over the 20-year period between 1980 and 2000. Their findings support the notion that changes in the nature of homicides explain why homicide clearance rates have declined. In particular, they find some support for the idea homicide clearance rates drop where homicides involving firearms and strangers become more prevalent and where argument-driven homicides become less prevalent. Increases in drug markets were associated with higher homicide clearance rates while increased immigration was associated with lower clearance rates.

PATTERNS IN CLEARING HOMICIDE CASES

What types of homicides are most likely to result in the arrest of a suspect and which are most likely to remain unsolved? There are a number of different factors that have been examined, which could influence the likelihood a case will be solved. These can be grouped into the following categories: characteristics of the victim, the incident, the investigators, and the investigation. What we know about how these various types of characteristics influence homicide clearances is described below.

Victim Characteristics

Previous research has examined several characteristics of homicide victims to assess their association with homicide clearance. These characteristics include the victim's age, gender, and race. One of the more consistent findings in the literature on homicide clearances is the high likelihood of clearing cases involving child victims, and the greater difficulty of clearing cases involving the elderly (Addington, 2006; Cardarelli & Cavanagh, 1992; Puckett & Lundman, 2003; Regoeczi, Kennedy, & Silverman, 2000; Riedel & Rinehart, 1996). Both of these patterns are explained best with respect to the victim/offender relationships and circumstances surrounding homicides of children and the elderly. Children are most often killed by parents or other family members. These homicides are frequently the outcome of a pattern of physical abuse gone too far, the inability of caregivers to cope with the stress of parenting, or Shaken Baby Syndrome (Christoffel, 1984; Kajese et al., 2011; Smithey, 1998). Furthermore, young children are frequently under the surveillance of caregivers, reducing their likelihood of being killed by a stranger (Cardarelli & Cavanagh, 1992). Thus, these cases tend to be more easily solved. In contrast, elderly persons are disproportionately involved in robbery-related homicides and killed by strangers (Abrams, Leon, Tardiff, Marzuk, & Sutherland, 2007; Block, 1987; Copeland, 1986; Falzon & Davis, 1998; Fox & Levin, 1991; Kennedy & Silverman, 1990; Nelson & Huff-Corzine, 1998; Titterington & Reyes, 2010; Weaver, Martin, & Petee, 2004), which reduces the likelihood the case will be cleared.

No clear patterns exist with respect to whether homicide cases involving female or male victims are more likely to be solved. A couple of studies report a higher likelihood of clearance for female victim cases (McEwen & Regoeczi, 2015; Regoeczi et al., 2000) while others find no gender differences (Addington, 2006; Mouzos & Muller, 2001) or a greater likelihood of clearance for male victims (Litwin & Xu, 2007). These mixed findings are somewhat surprising given women have a greater likelihood of being killed by an intimate partner and intimate partner homicides are generally more easily solved. However, women are also more likely to be victims than men in some other types of homicides that are generally difficult to solve, such as killings occurring during the commission of a rape (FBI, 2009).

The findings with respect to whether the victim's race impacts the likelihood the case will be solved are mixed. Some research finds cases involving non-White victims are more likely to be solved (Mouzos & Muller, 2001; Regoeczi et al., 2000), while other studies find the opposite (Litwin & Xu, 2007; McEwen & Regoeczi, 2015; Petersen, 2017). The handful of studies examining victim ethnicity find cases involving Hispanic victims are less likely to be cleared (Alderden & Lavery, 2007; Litwin, 2004; Roberts & Lyons, 2011)

Incident Characteristics

Several characteristics of homicide incidents have been linked to the likelihood of solving the case. These incident characteristics include the circumstances surrounding the homicide, weapon use, location, and time of the homicide's occurrence. A number of studies report felony-related homicides such as those committed during the course of a robbery or rape are more difficult to solve than homicides resulting from other circumstances (Cardarelli & Cavanagh, 1992; Lee, 2005; Litwin, 2004; Mouzos & Muller, 2001; Petersen, 2017; Regoeczi et al., 2000;

Riedel & Rinehart, 1996; Rinehart, 1994; Roberts, 2007). Robbery and rape offenses, which have the potential to produce lethal outcomes, are characteristically hit-and-run in nature and therefore are less likely to produce on-scene arrests (Black, 1970). They are also more likely to involve strangers, making it more difficult to identify the perpetrator. Drug- and gang-related homicides also generally have lower clearance rates (Jiao, 2007; Lee, 2005; Pastia, Davies, & Wu, 2017). In contrast, more expressive, argument-driven homicides are more likely to occur among individuals known to one another.

Homicides involving firearms are generally less likely to be cleared (Litwin, 2004; Litwin & Xu, 2007; Mouzos & Muller, 2001; Regoeczi et al., 2000; Rinehart, 1994; Rydberg & Pizarro, 2014). In contrast, killings committed with weapons that bring the victim and offender into contact with each other (such as fists, knives, or blunt instruments) increase the likelihood of clearing the case, possibly by making the transference of evidence between them more likely (Addington, 2006; Mouzos & Muller, 2001; Puckett & Lundman, 2003; Roberts, 2007).

Among the more consistent findings concerning homicide clearance is the greater likelihood of clearance for cases occurring in homes (Addington, 2006; Litwin & Xu, 2007; Mouzos & Muller, 2001; Wellford & Cronin, 1999). There are several possible explanations for this pattern. One is that homicides occurring within residences are more likely to occur between intimate partners, other family members, and individuals known to one another more generally, making it easier to identify the perpetrator. Second, forensic evidence is likely to be better preserved when the incident occurs in a residence than outdoors where it may become contaminated by weather, people, etc. (Addington, 2006; Regoeczi, Jarvis, & Riedel, 2008).

The impact of time of day on homicide clearance has rarely been examined. The two studies located which included measures of time did not find a significant effect (Puckett & Lundman, 2003; Roberts, 2007). This is surprising given one might expect homicides occurring in the late evening and early morning hours to take longer to clear due to delays in interviewing witnesses, collecting and processing physical evidence, and publicizing calls for assistance through the media that can occur when someone is killed in the middle of the night.

Investigators' Work Context

Far fewer studies have examined characteristics of homicide investigators' work context to assess their impact on the likelihood of solving cases. Accessing this type of information requires cooperation from individual law enforcement agencies, which can be difficult to obtain, and researchers must collect it by hand as it is not routinely collected by the agencies themselves. The handful of studies to do this have generally focused on the work context characteristics of manpower and case volume.

All else being equal, one might expect having a larger number of detectives devoted to investigating a homicide case would make it more likely the case would be solved. Consequently, it is somewhat surprising that the findings with respect to the influence of manpower on solving homicides are mixed. Wellford and Cronin (1999) found a case is more likely to be solved if 3, 4, or 11 detectives were assigned to the case, compared to just 1 detective. In contrast, Rinehart's study (1994) finds detective manpower levels did not influence murder clearances in Chicago.

It seems logical to expect that when detectives have large volumes of cases to investigate they will become spread too thin and not able to devote sufficient time to every case they have been assigned. However, based on the handful of studies examining this work context characteristic it is not clear whether having a larger volume of cases to investigate is a major obstacle for detectives trying to solve homicides. One the one hand, a study by Rand found having detectives work on larger numbers of cases is associated with reduced clearance (Greenwood, Chaiken, & Petersilia, 1977). Rinehart's study (1994) of Chicago, in contrast, found workload did not affect the likelihood of murders being cleared. The number of homicides per sworn officer was not a significant predictor of homicide clearances in Los Angeles County (Petersen, 2017).

A more indirect way of assessing the impact of large volumes of cases on the ability of law enforcement to clear them is to examine the relationship between clearance rates and homicide rates across geographical areas. In comparing homicide rates to clearance rates, Borg and Parker (2001) found cities with higher homicide rates had lower clearance rates. However, two other studies found no association between homicide rates and murder clearance rates (Litwin, 2004; Puckett & Lundman, 2003). Thus, the relationship between case volume and clearances remains uncertain. A better test of the potential importance of workload may be to examine changes in case volume over time within one or more departments and assess its impact on the ability of detectives to effectively investigate cases.

The Homicide Investigation

The process of the investigation itself has received the least attention in terms of how it influences the solvability of cases. This is most likely due to the necessity of having a high level of detail about a case in order to examine these aspects. A handful of studies have examined the impact of specific investigative processes on the likelihood of clearing homicide cases. In their study of Manhattan homicides, Schroeder and White (2009) found very large effects on clearance of detectives producing new leads through follow-ups on witness information and running computer checks on suspects (odds ratios = 60.7 and 33.9, respectively). Detectives running computer checks on witnesses and being present at postmortem examinations were negatively associated with case clearance.

A relatively new area of research in homicide investigations concerns the role and use of forensic evidence. Although we often talk of the general category of forensic evidence, there are actually a number of different types of evidence that fall within it (Table 1).

National and regional databases exist for several types of forensic evidence against which evidence in individual homicide cases can be compared. For example, the FBI's Combined DNA Index System program (CODIS) includes a National DNA Index System (NDIS) that contains DNA profiles provided by federal, state, and local forensic labs (FBI). A DNA profile from a homicide

Table 1. Types of Forensic Evidence Collected in Homicide Investigations.

Evidence Type	Description
DNA Evidence	The two most common types of DNA evidence are blood and saliva. Blood evidence comes in the form of wet blood (e.g., a tube of blood from an autopsy) or swabs of bloodstains collected at crime scenes. Buccal swabs are usually collected from a victim or suspect. Other types of biological evidence include seminal stains, and urine. In each case, the aim is to provide sufficient samples of biological evidence to allow DNA profiling.
Weapons/Firearms	Weapons evidence consists of firearms (handguns, rifles, assault weapons, etc.), ammunition (e.g., spent casings, fired projectiles, bullet fragments, and unfired bullets), gunshot residue tests, and knives. Gunshot residue tests are used to determine whether an individual was close to a firearm at the time the firearm was discharged.
Fingerprints	Fingerprint evidence includes complete sets of prints (such as when fingerprints are available for both hands and palms where a victim or suspect has been fingerprinted) and latent prints (where only partial prints of one or more fingers are available, usually through a powdering technique on physical evidence such as a weapon or vehicle).
Drugs	Drug evidence includes drugs (e.g., marijuana, cocaine, methamphetamine etc.), and drug paraphernalia (pipes, spoons, etc.) found at a crime scene.
Impressions	Impressions evidence includes shoeprint impressions, tire tracks, and tool marks.
Trace	Trace evidence is a generic term for small, sometimes microscopic, material. It covers a wide variety of evidence, including fibers, hair, building materials (asbestos, paint, etc.), cigarettes, tobacco, glass, and others.
Natural and Synthetic Materials	Natural and synthetic materials include clothing, bed and bath material, carpet cuttings, metal objects, plastic, and paper.
Electronic and Printed Materials	Electronic and printed materials can include anything from documents to various forms of electronics such as computers and cell phones.

Source: Adapted from McEwen and Regoeczi (2010).

investigation can be compared against the DNA records contained in NDIS to identify a previously unknown perpetrator.

As with DNA, digital images of fingerprints taken from vehicles, weapons, and other objects at the crime scene can be compared with fingerprints in a national database in the hopes of discovering the identity of a homicide suspect. The FBI provides a national database of fingerprints, criminal histories, head shots, photos of tattoos, and descriptions of physical characteristics through their Integrated Automated Fingerprint Identification System (AFIS). Fingerprints and criminal histories are submitted by local, state, and federal law enforcement agencies for inclusion in the database (FBI, N.D.).

The Bureau of Alcohol, Tobacco, Firearms, and Explosives (ATF) maintains a national database containing ballistics information. The program, known as the National Integrated Ballistic Information Network (NIBIN), was originally established in 1999. The program works through the establishment of NIBIN partners, which can be a federal, state, or local law enforcement agency, forensic science agencies, or attorney agencies. According the ATF (2012):

> Partners use Integrated Ballistic Identification Systems (IBIS) to acquire digital images of the markings made on fired ammunition recovered from a crime scene or a crime gun test fire and then compare those images (in a matter of hours) against earlier NIBIN entries via electronic image comparison. If a high-confidence candidate for a match emerges, firearms examiners compare the original evidence with a microscope to confirm the match or NIBIN "hit." A hit is a linkage of two different crime scene investigations by NIBIN participants where previously there had been no known connection between the investigations. A hit is a linkage between cases, not individual pieces of evidence.

The program assists in identifying links between violent crimes committed with firearms. An evaluation of the use of NIBIN across 150 sites reveals that while the program has generated a very large number of hits (more than 50,000), they were seldom used to identify unknown suspects and infrequently contributed to suspect arrests (King, Wells, Katz, Maguire, & Frank, 2013).

According to the small number of studies examining the impact of forensic evidence on investigations, forensic evidence is collected in a majority of homicide cases (McEwen, 2010). In their exploration of the use of DNA evidence by homicide detectives in the New York City Police Department from 1996 to 2003, Schroeder and White (2009) report that the detectives rarely used DNA evidence. Further, they did not find a relationship between DNA evidence and whether the case was cleared. They concluded that investigators used DNA only as a final option, after other investigative measures had been exhausted. However, research by McEwen (2010) indicates the bulk of testing of forensic evidence in homicide cases solved by arrest occurs after the arrest has taken place. In other words, forensic evidence seems to play a bigger role in assisting police and prosecutors with building their cases than in identifying the suspect in the first place. In cases where the investigation has stalled, matches of DNA or fingerprints through the CODIS or AFIS have been shown to be important in rejuvenating the investigation (McEwen, 2010).

An examination of the impact of forensic evidence in homicide investigations and prosecutions in Cleveland, Ohio, found the collection of knives, gunshot residue kits, and clothing at the scene increased the odds of clearance, while DNA and ballistics evidence were associated with lower clearance rates (McEwen & Regoeczi, 2015). In the bulk of cases, probative results were obtained after the suspect's arrest. Cases with probative results from forensic analysis resulted in more severe charges against defendants, a greater likelihood of trials, and higher conviction rates.

A National Institute of Justice study on the impacts of forensic evidence on the investigations and prosecutions of five major offenses including homicide reported no effect of the collection of evidence at homicide scenes or the examination of evidence by the crime laboratory on arrests, referrals to prosecutors, or convictions (Peterson, Sommers, Baskin, & Johnson, 2010). The collection of evidence (but not its examination) was related to the likelihood of pressing charges. Forensic analysis linking the defendant to the crime resulted in longer sentences.

The community context in which homicide investigations take place may also have a significant impact on investigation outcomes. Eye witnesses are present for a significant number of homicides (McEwen, 2009; Regoeczi & Jarvis, 2013) and the presence and/or number of eyewitnesses significantly increase the likelihood of clearing homicides (McEwen & Regoeczi, 2015). Residents may also be privy to information about the murder through informal neighborhood networks. The cooperation of community residents is critical to the success of many homicide investigations. Whether or not they are willing to cooperate with police in their search for suspects may be influenced by a variety of factors. Recent research on homicide investigations in Cleveland neighborhoods reveals the success of investigations is influenced by views of street justice and self-help as well as fear of retaliation (Regoeczi & Jarvis, 2013). This same study also found that while the presence of third party witnesses in general increased the likelihood of clearing the case, this varied by neighborhood. For example, having witnesses to the homicide was less helpful in solving the case if the homicide occurred in a disadvantaged neighborhood (i.e., high levels of poverty, unemployment, and female-headed households with children). In Los Angeles County, California, Petersen (2017) finds homicides are less likely to be cleared in areas with larger Black and Latino populations, but more likely to be cleared in neighborhoods with greater concentrated disadvantage. At the city level, Graham and Ousey (2010) report that cities experiencing increased income, employment, and education boast increased clearance rates.

GENERAL EXPLANATIONS

Why would some types of homicides be more likely to be solved than others? Although some specific explanations exist for the influence of particular victim, incident, and investigative factors on homicide clearance, three general theoretical explanations have been applied to understanding patterns of homicide clearance.

The Behavior of Law

Donald Black's work (1976, 1980) on the law and policing has been used to explain why demographic characteristics like victim race, age, and gender would impact the likelihood of an arrest in a homicide (e.g., Litwin, 2004). According to this perspective, minority victims have lower clearance rates as a result of victim devaluing where police give less attention and effort to solving these crimes. In terms of homicide clearance, this is often expressed as victims from lower social strata receive less law (less clearances) than that of higher social strata (see Borg & Parker, 2001).

Of the three general explanations for differences in homicide clearance, this victim devaluation perspective has received the least support. In fact, the only victim characteristic that has been shown to influence the solvability of the case across a number of studies is victim age. As discussed previously, this finding is most easily explained by the nature of child homicides and is opposite to what Black's theory would predict.

Legal Factors and Seriousness of the Crime

Given the serious nature of the crime and the public attention it receives, an alternative view is that all homicides receive a thorough investigation, regardless of the individual views of particular investigators (Klinger, 1997; Puckett & Lundman, 2003). According to this perspective, it is the nature of the homicide itself that makes it more or less likely to lead to the identification and arrest of a suspect. For example, one of the most consistent findings in this literature is that homicides committed during the course of another felony are much less likely to be solved. This is likely due to the greater involvement of strangers in felony homicides, making it harder to identify a suspect. The high solve rate for cases involving child victims almost certainly reflects the fact that children are most often killed by a parent or other relative, thus increasing the chances the police will identify the perpetrator. The consistent findings in the literature regarding the impacts of the homicide location, weapon, and circumstances lend significant support to this explanation.

Social Disorganization and Community Factors

In their study of urban communities, Shaw and McKay's (1942) find high levels of residential instability and poverty result in socially disorganized communities, in turn generating high rates of juvenile delinquency. More recent versions of the theory elucidate the processes intervening between structural factors and crime rates, emphasizing the ways in which such neighborhood conditions may weaken social institutions, collective efficacy, and the power of residents to exercise informal social control by regulating the behavior of individuals in the neighborhood (e.g., Bursik & Grasmick, 1993; Sampson & Groves, 1989; Sampson, Raudenbush, & Earls, 1997; Warner, 2007).

These same neighborhood conditions that produce high volumes of criminal activity may also hinder suspect identification, apprehension, and prosecution. Lethal violence in communities lacking traditional informal social control mechanisms including parents, neighbors, and community leaders and where residents do not feel invested in the neighborhood may impede the successful apprehension and conviction of homicide suspects. High levels of residential instability and mobility can reduce the likelihood that residents will know the identity of residents involved in lethal violence in their communities. Low commitment to the neighborhood and a lack of motivation to intercede to control residents' behavior in the neighborhood can, in turn, lead to greater unwillingness to invest time and risk safety to cooperate with police conducting investigations. Neighborhood disadvantage can obstruct the formation of constructive relationships with external agencies including law enforcement, in turn reducing confidence in police integrity (Sampson & Jeglum-Bartusch, 1998, Warner, 2007). Residents' lack of faith in the police can encourage them to seek informal means of conflict resolution instead of requesting assistance from formal authorities (Anderson, 1999; Cooney, 2009; Kubrin & Weitzer, 2003). Fear of retaliation may also discourage residents from becoming involved with police investigations. Even among residents who might otherwise wish to cooperate with police and want to see the offender brought to justice, fear of harm from the suspect or the suspect's family and friends for sharing information with law enforcement may keep them from doing so. This is most likely in cases of violence stemming from drugs and/or gangs (Anderson, 1999).

IDENTIFYING BEST PRACTICES IN HOMICIDE INVESTIGATIONS

Even among large urban departments, clearance rates for homicides vary considerably. Some cities maintain high success rates in solving homicides. Philadelphia, for example, routinely boasts a clearance rate above 80 percent. Other cities constantly struggle to solve homicides. Boston, for example, had a clearance rate of 43 percent in 2012 (Carroll, 2013). The variation among law enforcement agencies, as well as fluctuations in clearance rates within individual agencies over time, points to the importance of developing best practices for law enforcement agencies conducting homicide investigations.

Several prior studies on homicide clearances offer suggestions on how to solve more cases. Wellford and Cronin's study on homicide clearances in four cities, for example, generated a series of recommendations on how police could improve clearance rates, including having patrol officers provide swift notification to the homicide unit, medical examiner, and crime lab, having patrol officers try to identify and locate witnesses while also securing the scene, assigning at least three detectives per case, and reducing the time to arrival of detectives at homicide scenes (Wellford & Cronin, 2000). In his study of 55 homicide units across the United States, Keel (2008) concluded that successful homicide units will include computerized case management systems, accessibility to overtime as needed, case review by all involved personnel within the first 24 to 48 hours of the incident, and avoiding a rotation policy for homicide detectives. Carter and Carter (2016) studied homicide investigation practices in seven cities with clearance rates of 80 percent or more and concluded that effective strategies include analytic-based scheduling of investigators, identifying and taking statements from witnesses at the immediate crime scene, patrol officer training on the use of identifying, detaining, and conducting preliminary interviews with potential suspects and witnesses, ready availability of trained and equipped crime scene investigators, collaboration with other specialized investigative units, collaboration with external agencies, the use of a dedicated analyst to support the investigation, strong police–community relations, and readily available investigative tools such as laptops, cameras, digital records, and departmental take-home cars.

The Bureau of Justice Assistance recently published guidelines for law enforcement administrators with respect to improving homicide closure rates (Carter, 2013). One of the most critical findings concern the importance of community trust and creating a solid foundation of cooperation and information sharing with other law enforcement agencies for producing successful homicide investigations. The companion document, *10 Things Law Enforcement Executives Can Do to Positively Impact Homicide Investigation Outcomes*, provides recommendations aimed at high level administrators that include providing the needed support and resources for the homicide unit to successfully investigate cases and considering alternative measures of success beyond clearance rates (Bureau of Justice Assistance, 2013).

CONCLUSION

The dramatic decline in homicide clearances since the 1960s is most likely due to changes in the nature of homicide over time and declining police–community relations.

The most consistent findings in the existing research on homicide clearance patterns are the greater likelihood of clearance in homicides involving young children, contact weapons, residential locations, and those not occurring in the course of another crime. Explanations relying on notions of victim devaluing generate the least support. There is considerable support for the legal factors approach and community-level explanations show promise. The findings regarding the role of forensic evidence are mixed.

While our understanding of homicide investigations and solvability has grown significantly as a result of the studies conducted over the past several decades, additional research is needed. But much of what remains to be learned cannot happen through additional analyses of national public databases like the Supplementary Homicide Reports and the NIBRS. Research involving intensive original data collection of detailed information on case investigations will be necessary to further fill the gaps in our knowledge with respect to departmental, investigator, forensic evidence, and investigative process variables on homicide clearances. Geocoded data will also be important for exploring the influence of community characteristics on homicide solvability. Further research is needed on the role of forensic science generally, and DNA specifically, on homicide investigations and prosecutions. The contributions of future research will depend on the ability of researchers to foster relationships with police departments in order to gain access to the data necessary to explore these more detailed aspects of homicide investigations.

REFERENCES

Abrams, R. C., Leon, A. C., Tardiff, K., Marzuk, P. M., & Sutherland, K. (2007). "Gray murder": Characteristics of elderly compared with nonelderly homicide victims in New York City. *American Journal of Public Health, 97*, 1666–1670.

Addington, L. (2006). Using National Incident-Based Reporting System murder data to evaluate clearance predictors: A research note. *Homicide Studies, 10*, 140–152.

Alderden, M. A., & Lavery, T. A. (2007). Predicting homicide clearances in Chicago: Investigating disparities in predictors across different types of homicide. *Homicide Studies, 11*, 115–132.

Anderson, E. (1999). *The code of the streets: Decency, violence, and the moral life of the inner city*. New York, NY: W. W. Norton.

Black, D. J. (1970). Production of crime rates. *American Sociological Review, 35*, 733–748.

Black, D. J. (1976). *The behavior of law*. New York, NY: Academic Press.

Black, D. J. (1980). *The manners and customs of the police*. New York, NY: Academic Press.

Black, D. J. (1983). Crime as social control. *American Sociological Review, 48*, 34–45.

Block, C. R. (1987). *Homicide in Chicago: Aggregate and time series perspectives on victim, offender and circumstance*. Chicago, IL: Center for Urban Policy, Loyola University Chicago.

Borg, M. J., & Parker, K. F. (2001). Mobilizing law in urban areas: The social structure of homicide clearance rates. *Law and Society Review, 35*(2), 435–466.

Bureau of Alcohol, Tobacco, Firearms, and Explosives (ATF). (2012). *Fact sheet: National Integrated Ballistic Information Network (NIBIN)*. Washington, DC: ATF Public Affairs Division.

Bureau of Justice Assistance. (2013). *10 Things law enforcement executives can do to positively impact homicide investigations*. Washington, DC: U.S. Department of Justice.

Bursik, R. J., Jr, & Grasmick, H. G. (1993). *Neighborhoods and crime*. New York, NY: Lexington Books.

Cardarelli, A. P., & Cavanagh, D. (1992). Uncleared homicides in the United States: An exploratory study of trends and patterns. Paper presented at the annual meeting of the American Society of Criminology, New Orleans, LA.

Carroll, M. (2013, January 1). Homicides decrease in Boston for third straight year. *The Boston Globe*. Retrieved from http://www.bostonglobe.com/metro/2013/01/01/homicides-track-fall-boston-for-third-straight-year/KKOmMsHDQcyS89vrBGtVUO/story.html

Carter, D. (2013). *Homicide process mapping: Best practices for increasing homicide clearances.* Washington, DC: U.S. Department of Justice, Bureau of Justice Assistance.

Carter, D. L., & Carter, J. G. (2016). Effective police homicide investigations: Evidence from seven cities with high clearance rates. *Homicide Studies, 20*, 150–176.

Christoffel, K. K. (1984). Homicide in childhood: A public health problem in need of attention. *American Journal of Public Health, 74*, 68–70.

Cooney, M. (1997). The decline of elite homicide. *Criminology, 35*, 381–407.

Cooney, M. (2009). *Is killing wrong*. Charlottesville, VA: University of Virginia Press.

Copeland, A. R. (1986). Homicide among the elderly: The Metro Dade county experience, 1979–1983. *Medical Science Law, 26*, 259–262.

Cordner, G. W. (1989). Police agency size and investigative effectiveness. *Journal of Criminal Justice, 17*, 145–155.

Corwin, M. (1997). *The killing season: A summer inside an LAPD homicide division*. New York, NY: Fawcett Crest.

Falzon, A. L., & Davis, G. G. (1998). A 15 year retrospective review of homicide in the elderly. *Journal of Forensic Sciences, 43*, 371–374.

Federal Bureau of Investigation (FBI). (1984). *Uniform crime reporting handbook*. Washington, DC: U.S. Government.

Federal Bureau of Investigation (FBI). (2010). *Uniform Crime Reporting program: Supplementary Homicide Reports 2009*. Washington, DC: U.S. Government Printing Office.

Federal Bureau of Investigation. (N.D.a). *Frequently asked questions on the CODIS program and the National DNA Index System*. https://cdaia.org/wp-content/uploads/2015/09/presentations-2015_CODIS-Frequently-Asked-Questions.pdf

Fox, J. A., & Levin, J. (1991). Homicide against the elderly: A research note. *Criminology, 29*, 317–327.

Greenwood, P., Chaiken, J. M., & Petersilia, J. (1977). *The criminal investigation process*. Lexington: The RAND Corporation.

Jarvis, J. P., Mancik, A., & Regoeczi, W. C. (2017). Police responses to violent crime: Reconsidering the mobilization of law. *Criminal Justice Review, 42*, 5–25.

Jarvis, J. P., & Regoeczi, W. C. (2009). Homicide clearances: An analysis of arrest versus exceptional outcomes. *Homicide Studies, 13*, 174–188.

Jiao, A. Y. (2007). Explaining homicide clearance: An analysis of Chicago homicide data 1965–1995. *Criminal Justice Studies,* 20, 3–14.

Kajese, T., Nguyen, L. T., Pham, G. Q., Pham, V. K., Melhorn, K., & Kallail, J. K. (2011). Characteristics of child abuse homicides in the state of Kansas from 1994 to 2007. *Child Abuse and Neglect, 35*, 147–154.

Keel, T. G. (2008). Homicide investigations: Identifying best practices. *FBI Law Enforcement Bulletin, 77*, 1–9.

Kennedy, L. W., & Silverman, R. A. (1990). The elderly victim of homicide: An application of the Routine Activities approach. *The Sociological Quarterly, 31*, 307–319.

King, W. R., Wells, W., Katz, C. M., Maguire, E. R., & Frank, J. (2013). Opening the black box of NIBIN: A descriptive process and outcome evaluation of the use of NIBIN and its effects on criminal investigations. Washington, DC: US Department of Justice, National Institute of Justice.

Klinger, D. A. (1997). Negotiating order in patrol work: An ecological theory of police response to deviance. *Criminology, 35*, 277–306.

Kubrin, C., & Weitzer, R. (2003). Retaliatory homicide: Concentrated disadvantage and neighborhood culture. *Social Problems, 50*, 157–180.

LaFree, G. (1998). *Losing legitimacy*. Boulder: Westview Press.

Lee, C. (2005). The value of life in death: Multiple regression and event history analyses of homicide clearance in Los Angeles County. *Journal of Criminal Justice, 33*, 527–534.

Leovy, J., & Smith, D. (2004). Getting away with murder in South LA's killing zone. Retrieved from http://www.latimes.com/news/loca/la-me-unsolved1jan01.html

Litwin, K. J. (2004). A multilevel multivariate analysis of factors affecting homicide clearances. *Journal of Research in Crime and Delinquency, 41*(4), 327–351.

Litwin, K. J., & Xu, Y. (2007). The dynamic nature of homicide clearances: A multilevel model comparison of three time periods. *Homicide Studies, 11*, 94–114.

Lundsgaarde, H. F. (1977). *Murder in space city: A cultural analysis of Houston homicides*. New York, NY: Oxford University Press.

Maxfield, M. (1988, November). Homicide circumstances, 1976–1985: A taxonomy based on Supplementary Homicide Reports. Paper presented at the annual meeting of the American Society of Criminology, Chicago, IL.

McEwen, T. (2009). *Evaluation of the Phoenix Homicide clearance project*. Washington, DC: National Institute of Justice, U.S. Department of Justice.

McEwen, T. (2010). *The role and impact of forensic evidence in the criminal justice system*. Washington, DC: U.S. Department of Justice, National Institute of Justice.

McEwen, T., & Regoeczi, W. C. (2010). *Forensic evidence in homicide investigations*. Washington, DC: U.S. Department of Justice, National Institute of Justice.

McEwen, T., & Regoeczi. W. C. (2015). Forensic evidence in homicide investigations and prosecutions. *Journal of Forensic Sciences*, *60*, 1188–1198.

Mouzos, J., & Muller, D. (2001). *Solvability factors of homicide in Australia: An exploratory analysis*. Canberra: Australian Institute of Criminology.

Ousey, G., & Lee, M. R. (2010). To know the unknown: The decline in homicide clearance rates, 1980–2000. *Criminal Justice Review*, *35*, 141–158.

Nelson, C., & Huff-Corzine, L. (1998). Strangers in the night: An application of the lifestyle-routine activities approach to elderly homicide victimization. *Homicide Studies*, *2*, 130–159.

Pastia, C., Davies, G., & Wu, E. (2017). Factors influencing the probability of clearance and time to clearance of Canadian homicide cases, 1991–2011. *Homicide Studies*, *21*, 199–218.

Petersen, N. (2017). Neighborhood context and unsolved murders: The sociology ecology of homicide investigations. *Policing and Society*, *27*, 372–392.

Peterson, J. L., Sommers, I., Baskin, D., & Johnson, D. (2010). The role and impact of forensic evidence on the criminal justice process. Washington, DC: U.S. Department of Justice, National Institute of Justice.

Puckett, J. L., & Lundman, R. J. (2003). Factors affecting homicide clearances: Multivariate analysis of a more complete conceptual framework. *Journal of Research in Crime and Delinquency*, *40*(2), 171–193.

Regoeczi, W. C., & Jarvis, J. P. (2013). Beyond on the social production of homicide rates: Extending social disorganization theory to explain homicide case outcomes. *Justice Quarterly*, *30*, 983–1014.

Regoeczi, W. C., Jarvis, J., & Riedel, M. (2008). Clearing murders: Is it about time? *Journal of Research in Crime and Delinquency*, *45*, 142–162.

Regoeczi, W. C., Kennedy, L. W., & Silverman, R. A. (2000). Uncleared homicide: A Canada/United States comparison. *Homicide Studies*, *4*, 135–161.

Riedel, M. (1995). Getting away with murder: An examination of arrest clearances. Proceedings of the annual meeting of the Homicide Research Working Group, Georgia.

Riedel, M., & Boulahanis, J. (2007). Homicides exceptionally cleared and cleared by arrest: An exploratory study of police/prosecutor outcomes. *Homicide Studies*, *11*, 151–164.

Riedel, M., & Jarvis, J. (1998). The decline of arrest clearances for criminal homicide: Causes, correlates, and third parties. *Criminal Justice Policy Review*, *9*, 279–306.

Riedel, M., & Rinehart. T. (1996). Murder clearances and missing data. *Journal of Crime and Justice*, *19*, 83–102.

Rinehart, T. (1994). An analysis of murder clearances in Chicago: 1981–1991. Unpublished M.A. dissertation. Southern Illinois University, Carbondale, IL.

Roberts, A. (2007). Predictors of homicide clearance by arrest: An event history analysis of NIBRS incidents. *Homicide Studies*, *11*, 82–93.

Roberts, A., & Lyons, C. J. (2011). Hispanic victims and homicide clearance by arrest. *Homicide Studies*, *15*, 48–73.

Rydberg, J., & Pizarro, J. M. (2014). Victim lifestyle as a correlate of homicide clearance. *Homicide Studies*, *18*, 342–362.

Sampson, R. J., & Groves, W. B. (1989). Community structure and crime: Testing social-disorganization theory. *American Journal of Sociology*, *94*, 774–802.

Sampson, R. J., & Jeglum-Bartusch, D. (1998). Legal cynicism and (subcultural?) tolerance of deviance: The neighborhood context of racial differences. *Law and Society Review*, *32*, 777–804.

Sampson, R. J., Raudenbush, S. W., & Earls, F. (1997). Neighborhoods and violent crime: A multilevel study of collective efficacy. *Science, 277*(August), 918–924.

Schroeder, D. A., & White, M. D. (2009). Exploring the use of DNA evidence in homicide investigations: Implications for detective work and case clearance. *Police Quarterly, 12*, 319–342.

Shaw, C., & McKay, H. (1942). *Juvenile delinquency and urban areas*. Chicago, IL: University of Chicago Press.

Smithey, M. (1998). Infant homicide: Victim/offender relationship and causes of death. *Journal of Family Violence, 13*, 285–297.

Titterington, V., & Reyes, N. (2010). Elder homicide in urban America: An exploratory analysis of Chicago, Houston, and Miami. *Southwest Journal of Criminal Justice, 6*, 228–249.

Waegel, W. B. (1981). Case routinization in investigative police work. *Social Problems, 28*, 263–275.

Warner, B. D. (2007). Directly intervene or call the authorities? A study of forms of neighborhood social control within a social disorganization framework. *Criminology, 45*, 99–130.

Weaver, G. S., Martin, C. D., & Petee, T. A. (2004). Culture, context, and homicide of the elderly. *Sociological Inquiry, 74*, 2–19.

Wellford, C., & Cronin, J. (1999). *An analysis of variables affecting the clearance of homicides: A multi-state study*. Washington, DC: Justice Research and Statistics Association.

Wellford, C., & Cronin, J. (2000). Homicide: What police can do to improve clearance rates. *National Institute of Justice Journal, 243*, 2–7.

CHAPTER 8

POLICE VIOLENCE ACROSS THE RACIAL–SPATIAL DIVIDE

Malcolm D. Holmes

ABSTRACT

Purpose – *Police violence involving minority citizens is a significant problem in the United States. Efforts to explain the disparate treatment of minorities have often relied on structural-level racial threat hypotheses. However, research framed by this macro-level approach fails to consider meso-level characteristics of spatially specified places within cities. The place hypothesis maintains that police see disadvantaged minority neighborhoods as especially threatening and, therefore, use more violence in them. Reconceptualizing the racial threat model to include meso-level characteristics of place is essential to better explain police violence.*

Design/methodology/approach – *The argument is investigated using literature drawn from quantitative analyses of structural predictors of police violence and qualitative/quantitative studies of the police subculture and police behavior within disadvantaged neighborhoods.*

Findings – *Research on the effects of city-level racial segregation on police violence supports the place hypothesis that the incidence of police violence is higher in segregated minority neighborhoods. City-level segregation is, however, only a proxy for the degree of concentrated minority disadvantage existing at the meso-level. Community-level studies suggest that the police do see disadvantaged places as especially threatening and use more violence in them. Plausibly, meso-level neighborhood characteristics of cities may prove to be better predictors of the incidence of police violence than are structural-level characteristics in cross-city comparisons.*

Homicide and Violent Crime
Sociology of Crime, Law and Deviance, Volume 23, 139–158

ISSN: 1521-6136/doi:10.1108/S1521-613620180000023009

Originality/value – *This analysis builds on structural-level racial threat theories by demonstrating that meso-level characteristics of cities are central to explaining disparities in the use of police violence. A multilevel approach to studying police violence using this analytic framework is proposed.*

Keywords: Racial threat; place; racial-spatial divide; racial segregation; police brutality; police violence

INTRODUCTION

Preserving social order necessitates the use of coercive mechanisms to control violators of law and dissidents who challenge existing social arrangements in a society (Weber, 1968). Complex societies charge the police with the primary responsibility for exercising domestic coercive control. The essence of the role of police in modern democracies is the legitimate authority to use force, including deadly force, to protect citizens and officers from the dangerous people in their midst (Bittner, 1970). Most police use of force falls within the scope of that mandate, but sometimes these actions exceed their authority. While such transgressions usually involve minor infractions that cause little physical harm to suspects, sometimes the violations involve far more egregious acts of violence. Those actions include unnecessary beatings and killings of citizens, which violate departmental regulations and criminal statutes. A major concern about these prohibited practices is whether the police deploy them disproportionately against racial/ethnic minority populations.

The legitimacy of the police rests in large part on the principle that officers will treat citizens fairly and equally. Yet, many Black and Hispanic citizens believe that the police treat them unjustly, and police violence is at the top of their list of grievances (see, e.g., Brunson, 2007; National Association for the Advancement of Colored People and the Criminal Justice Institute at Harvard Law School (NAACP), 1995; Weitzer, 2017). Several controversial police killings of Black citizens during 2014–2016 clearly illustrate citizens' concerns (see, e.g., Austen, 2016; Pérez-Peña, 2015). Far more revealing is a body of research that shows that the racial composition of cities is systematically related to the police use of violence, with relatively large minority populations being at greater risk of victimization (e.g., Holmes, 2000; Jacobs & O'Brien, 1998; Smith & Holmes, 2014).

Explanations of this pattern often rely on the conflict theory of law. That perspective maintains that various forms of coercive crime control, including police violence, are instruments used to protect the interests of powerful groups (e.g., Chambliss, 2001; Holmes, 2000; Turk, 1969). In this view, the economic oppression and legal injustices long experienced by Blacks and Hispanics (particularly those of Mexican origin) make them troublesome populations in the eyes of the dominant group and the police, who perceive them as potential threats to social order and personal safety (Holmes & Smith, 2008). Preservation of the differential structure of racial/ethnic privilege demands the exercise of coercive power to control the threat posed by these disadvantaged groups (Jacobs & O'Brien, 1998).

Racial threat theories are a derivative of the conflict tradition that specify testable relationships between structural indicators of racial threat (e.g., percent Black in a population) and coercive strategies of crime control (e.g., police use of excessive force) at an aggregate level of analysis. This approach postulates that the level of crime control increases as the relative size of populations that threaten the interests of the powerful increase (e.g., Liska, 1992b). White citizens and local police officials are said to exercise their political influence to mobilize coercive crime control against minority citizens in cities with relatively large minority populations. Empirical research in this tradition supports the hypothesis that police violence – excessive force and police-caused homicide – is linked to the racial composition of cities (e.g., Holmes, 2000; Jacobs & O'Brien, 1998; Liska & Yu, 1992; Smith & Holmes, 2014).

Threat theories integrate macro (structural) and micro (individual) approaches to intergroup relations to explain this pattern of discrimination. Blalock's (1967) seminal work on minority threat begins with a discussion of how these approaches might be fruitfully integrated. He maintained that many macro-level variables are summarizing measures of underlying micro-level processes, identifying fear and prejudice as important micro-level factors that may motivate discrimination and result in aggregate patterns of inequality. A more complete conceptualization must also incorporate meso level aspects of urban organization, particularly neighborhood contextual factors, which have received little attention in the racial threat literature on police violence. Police violence against minority citizens is neither deployed uniformly *across* cities, nor is it *within* cities (e.g., Brunson & Miller 2006; Chambliss, 1994; Herbert, 1997; Rios, 2011).

In this chapter, I argue that meso-level characteristics of cities may be fruitfully integrated into racial threat theory to better explain patterns of minority victimization in police violence. In developing the argument, I first outline the historical formation of the police-minority tensions that exist today. I then explicate how minority threat theories explain the use of coercive controls against certain minority groups. Next, I develop the argument that meso-level factors are central to explaining perceived threat of minorities and the disparate use of violence against minority citizens. In the last section, I examine the implications of the argument for empirical research.

POLICING AMERICA'S RACIAL-SPATIAL DIVIDE

Early in the nineteenth century, accelerating industrialization, urbanization, and immigration began fundamentally changing life in US cities. Large waves of immigration from Europe engendered intergroup tensions, which were promoted by historic animosities among ethnic groups and competition over scarce resources in densely populated urban neighborhoods. Large-scale disorder and riots were commonplace during the mid-1800s (Monkkonen, 2002; Walker, 1998). The largely informal systems of social control that existed before then could not adequately respond to the new problems of urban disorder. Increasing concern among business elites and more affluent urban citizens about the "dangerous classes" of the poor, ethnic immigrants, and Blacks led to calls for the creation of a more effective system of social control backed by the coercive power of the state (Silver, 1967). The mobilization of these influential social segments provided the political impetus that culminated in the formation of big-city police departments.

Earlier, police departments were controlled by local political machines and police officer jobs were allocated through patronage (Walker, 1977). Prospective officers were often recruited from the neighborhoods in which they would work. The geographically and administratively decentralized structure of police departments allowed them to become involved in neighborhood affairs and serve the politicians who controlled precinct appointments. Police officer qualifications, training, and supervision were generally minimal, and officers had considerable leeway in carrying out their duties (Walker, 1998). Officers were expected to maintain order on their beats, but their tactics reflected the racial and ethnic composition of neighborhoods. Lack of training and supervision, combined with public hostility and ethnic tensions, forced officers to rely heavily on personal authority to gain compliance and respect from citizens. The police routinely resorted to brute force to establish control in the neighborhoods of the so-called dangerous classes (e.g., Johnson, 2003).

By the early twentieth century, various forms of police brutality and corruption captured public attention and calls for reform arose. In 1931, the National Commission on Law Observance and Enforcement (the Wickersham Commission) harshly censured police brutality in a widely publicized report on *Lawlessness in Law Enforcement* (Walker, 1998). The movement to improve policing was spearheaded by a coalition of political progressives and reform-minded police chiefs. As reform initiatives slowly took hold, the police began to concentrate more on law enforcement and crime control and less on the traditional police role of maintaining order (Fogelson, 1977). The structure of police departments also changed: departments became more centralized; they implemented civil service systems for hiring and promotion; and they developed formal training programs to teach police recruits how to perform their jobs. Greater supervision and accountability measures were also put into place to help ensure that officers carried out their duties professionally. In addition to these changes, technological innovations (e.g., patrol cars, two-way radios) significantly altered policing, including decreasing much of the casual, day-to-day contact between police officers and law-abiding citizens (Walker, 1998).

At the same time that professional policing was emerging, significant changes in racial and ethnic residential patterns were occurring in the United States. Most Blacks lived in the rural South before the twentieth century, after which the harsh tribulations of the Jim Crow system of legalized segregation and the mechanization of southern agricultural production pushed them to northern cities where their labor was increasingly in demand as industrialization escalated (Massey & Denton, 1993). Between 1890 and 1970, Black out-migration from the South resulted in a largely urban Black population living in non-southern cities. Endemic discrimination in labor and real estate markets effectively concentrated many Blacks in impoverished inner-city neighborhoods. Subsequent structural changes in the economy and the exodus of relatively affluent Blacks from urban Black neighborhoods worsened the desolation of the inner-city and eroded the social institutions, such as family and church, upon which social stability is said to be built (Wilson, 1987). Today, poverty is further consolidating geographically within urban areas, a trend that inflicts the greatest disadvantages on groups segregated by race or ethnicity (Massey, 2005). The social and cultural isolation of the inner-city generates crime, social disorder, and hostility toward the larger society (e.g., Massey & Denton, 1993; Peterson & Krivo, 2010 Skogan, 1990; Wilson, 1987).

The Black population is not alone in experiencing geographically concentrated poverty. Many Hispanics, especially those of Mexican origin, have a similar history of segregation and social disadvantage. Although the Mexican-origin population is increasingly dispersing throughout the United States and large enclaves exist in other regions, the majority reside in the Southwest, a region ceded to the United States in 1848 at the conclusion of the United States–Mexico War. Mexicans residing in the Southwest were increasingly displaced from their generations-old land grants and became the backbone of an internal colonial labor system, subordinated to low-paying jobs in agriculture, ranching, mining, and railroad building (e.g., Barrera, 1979). By the early 1920s, the growing industrialization in the Southwest contributed to the urbanization of the Mexican population, which increasingly became concentrated in impoverished barrios (Acuña, 1988). Widespread discrimination in housing, labor, and education created significant poverty and lack of opportunity. While not experiencing the extreme hypersegregation seen in many Black neighborhoods (Massey & Denton, 1989), the Mexican-origin population of the Southwest resides primarily in urban areas and continues to experience significant segregation and economic disadvantage (see Alba & Nee, 2003). The structural disadvantages and isolation of such neighborhoods provide an ecological context that encourages crime (Peterson & Krivo, 2010).

The changing racial/ethnic composition of US cities during the twentieth century established the "racial-spatial divide" that exists today (see Peterson & Krivo, 2010) and created new tensions between minority citizens and police (Holmes & Smith, 2008). Although the movement toward professionalism had significantly changed policing by the late 1950s, events of the 1960s again led to public scrutiny of the police (Uchida, 2010). Widely publicized civil unrest of the era, including civil rights protests and urban riots, brought police into direct conflict especially with Black (but also Mexican American) citizens, and heightened public awareness of police mistreatment of minorities. In their analysis of the urban unrest that occurred in US cities in the late 1960s, the National Advisory Commission on Civil Disorders (1968), better known as the Kerner Commission, identified various problems seen throughout the history of urban policing as the cause of the rioting. These included police violence against Black citizens, which often triggered the unrest, as well as underlying social and economic disadvantages experienced by Blacks residing in inner-city neighborhoods. Clearly, the reforms of the early twentieth century did not eliminate the most pernicious problems of urban life and policing.

In the aftermath of the 1960s, a new reform movement that aimed to ameliorate police-minority tensions took hold. Police agencies implemented various policies toward that end, yet high-profile incidents of police violence involving minority citizens continue to occur. Perhaps the most puzzling question regarding police violence is: Why do highly trained, professional police officers engage in such behavior? The police control the legitimate means of coercion and possess a sophisticated arsenal of nonlethal and lethal weaponry. They need not rely on gratuitous violence to protect themselves from the dangerous people they confront on the job, and they face the possibility of severe punishments when they do. Yet, research testing the minority threat hypothesis suggests that systematic racial bias continues to influence the incidence of police brutality (e.g., Holmes, 2000) and police killings (e.g., Smith, 2003).

RACIAL THREAT AND POLICE VIOLENCE

Racial threat theorists argue that police violence persists in contemporary society because it is deeply rooted in a social structure that separates racial/ethnic groups and produces intergroup conflict. Prevalent stereotypes associate Blacks and Hispanics (particularly those of Mexican origin) with serious criminality and violent proclivities (e.g., Bender, 2003; Quillian & Pager, 2001), and the presence of relatively large minority populations (whether real or perceived) heightens perceptions of criminal threat among Whites (e.g., Chiricos, Hogan, & Gertz, 1997; Wang, 2012). Similarly, police officials may believe that minority groups are inclined to criminality and threaten social order (e.g., Turk, 1969), and thus they may see relatively large minority populations as presenting a substantial problem of social control (e.g., Liska & Yu, 1992). White citizens and police officials may exercise their political influence and legal authority to encourage the strategic use of coercive crime control against minority groups that are perceived as threatening.

Strategies such as the allocation of police resources help preserve existing social arrangements that benefit the dominant group (Holmes & Smith, 2008). Others tactics, however, may primarily serve the interests of police officers on the street, who see certain strategies of coercive control as essential for self-protection from ostensibly dangerous minority citizens (e.g., Holmes, Painter, & Smith, 2018; Jacobs & O'Brien, 1998; Liska & Yu, 1992; Smith & Holmes, 2014). Therefore, an important conceptual concern involves identifying whose interests are served by police violence and how those interests shape the relationship between percent minority population and the incidence of police violence.

The threat hypothesis is generally cast in terms of dominant group interests, with the police being seen as formal agents of social control who guard those interests (e.g., Jacobs & O'Brien, 1998). In his seminal work on minority threat, *Toward a Theory of Minority Group Relations*, Blalock (1967, pp. 166–168) hypothesized that when minority groups are perceived ideologically as posing a greater threat of crime and violence to Whites, social control efforts will increase dramatically. He argued that Whites' political mobilization will escalate at an increasing rate as minority populations become relatively larger, producing an upward curving relationship between percent minority and discrimination (Blalock, 1967, pp. 150–154). Subsequent work suggests, however, that there are limits on the increasing use of social control by the state (e.g., Jackson & Carroll, 1981; Stults & Baumer, 2007).

When a minority group represents a numerical majority, it achieves greater political power and may effectively mobilize resources for collective action on its behalf. In cities with predominantly African American (e.g., Detroit, MI, and Washington, DC) or Hispanic (e.g., El Paso and San Antonio, TX) populations, it is not clear that the majority of citizens would see minorities as threats. Minority citizens' political influence in such cities may reduce the use of coercive crime control strategies by the police, which many minority citizens see as supporting dominant interests (e.g., Brunson, 2007; NAACP, 1995). This modified version of Blalock's original power-threat hypothesis predicts an initially positive relationship between percent minority and the mobilization of coercive crime control strategies, which will turn negative as the size of the minority population reaches a level where it can successfully begin exerting political power (see, e.g., Holmes et al., 2018; Stults & Baumer, 2007). In this view, the distribution of political power in predominantly minority cities would lead to a reduction in the use of police violence.

In contrast to the power-threat model, Liska (1992b) postulated a linear relationship between percent minority and crime control efforts, a hypothesis that has become predominant in research on police violence. He argued that "the greater the number of acts or people threatening to the interests of the powerful, the greater the level of deviance and crime control" (Liska 1992b, p. 18). This approach maintains that the dominant group and police authorities can still effectively marshal coercive crime control where relatively large minority populations exist. While emphasizing the unequal distribution of political power within the total population, this perspective also calls attention to minority threat perceived by police officers on the street (Holmes, 2000; Jacobs & O'Brien, 1998; Liska & Yu, 1992; Smith & Holmes, 2014). The demeanor of some minority citizens may symbolize threat to the officer on the street, irrespective of whether they actually pose any danger (Holmes & Smith, 2008; Skolnick & Fyfe, 1993; Westley, 1970). Insofar as the police see minority citizens as threats to their well-being, the existence of relatively large minority populations may increase the risk officers perceive and, therefore, the likelihood they will employ coercive street-level tactics even in the face of political opposition from minority citizens. Should street-level police behavior reflect primarily the interests of officers, a linear relationship between percent minority and the incidence of police violence would be expected (Holmes et al., 2018; Smith & Holmes, 2014).

The curvilinear power-threat and linear-threat hypotheses both provide potentially fruitful structural explanations of coercive control of minority populations by police, but these insights may apply to specific domains of coercive control. Politically powerful citizens may wield considerable influence over the distribution of resources for policing by state and local government, with studies of police resource allocations (police force size) reporting curvilinear effects of percent Black that are consistent with the modified power-threat hypothesis (Carmichael & Kent, 2014; Stults & Baumer, 2007). At the same time, powerful citizens may exert relatively little influence over the street-level actions of police officers. Yet, police authorities must be cognizant of the resource disadvantages that might befall their agencies should influential citizens become dissatisfied with the operational practices of their departments. Accordingly, rather than observing an official policy of fairly and equally administering justice, police departments may substitute goals and implement policies that accommodate this organizational imperative (Chambliss & Seidman, 1971). Policies and practices that maximize rewards and minimize strains for the organization may thus guide street-level police behavior. Organizational expediency calls for police to refrain from deploying coercive action against more powerful citizens and focus on the powerless instead. In this way, the mobilization of street-level coercive control, especially the use of violence, reflects the organizational imperatives of policing.

Even though often coinciding with dominant-group interests, the day-to-day behavior of police on the street is motivated primarily by the exigencies of their unique position. The perception of minority threat is a key concern. Police stereotypes of minorities conflate race and violent criminality, stereotypes reinforced by selective personal experience and departmental folklore (e.g., Holmes & Smith, 2008; Smith & Alpert, 2007). The attitudes and actions of minority citizens may be perceived as directly threatening to an officer's well-being or challenging to an officer's authority (Skolnick & Fyfe, 1993; Westley, 1970). Moreover, street-level police behavior involves a high degree of discretion and a low degree of visibility, which opens it to the influence of extra-legal factors. Thus, the immediate threats perceived by police during encounters with minority citizens may motivate unnecessary uses of violence (Holmes, 2000; Liska & Yu, 1992). At the same time, these typically clandestine practices of street-level policing do not ordinarily elicit careful scrutiny by dominant group members, who may willfully ignore police "dirty work" that represents their interests (Jacobs & O'Brien, 1998). And minority citizens seeking to file complaints about inappropriate police use of force encounter numerous obstacles that often dissuade them from doing so (see Smith & Holmes, 2014).

Studies testing racial threat hypotheses about police violence have examined the effects of percent Black and percent Hispanic on two outcome variables using aggregated data for large cities. These include the incidence of official complaints alleging police use of excessive force and the incidence of police-caused homicide. Police use of force may be classified as proper or excessive, based on whether its use is necessary and justified to accomplish a legitimate duty. A significant advantage of studying excessive force is that the behavior cannot be justified – it involves actions that violate departmental regulations and criminal statutes (Smith & Holmes, 2014). Research on police-caused homicide usually relies on data that capture what are, presumably, legally justifiable killings of felons. However, police-caused homicides very rarely result in criminal prosecution (see, e.g., Kindy & Kelly, 2015; Stinson, 2017). Many cases involve ambiguous circumstances and limited, if any, independent evidence apart from the statements of officers. Police authorities and prosecutors may try, often successfully, to shield errant officers from public scrutiny and possible sanction. Killings of minority citizens may be ruled justifiable even when they involve questionable circumstances (Holmes et al., 2018). While relatively little research testing threat hypotheses has examined excessive force and police-caused homicide, the results largely support the linear threat hypothesis.

Two studies of excessive force analyzed civil rights criminal complaints alleging police brutality that were investigated by the Federal Bureau of Investigation and reported to the Civil Rights Division of the US Department of Justice (Holmes, 2000; Smith & Holmes, 2003). The first study found that percent Black had a strong positive effect on civil rights criminal complaints in all cities of 150,000 or more population (Holmes 2000). In addition, percent Hispanic was related positively to civil rights criminal complaints, but that effect was restricted to the Southwest. The Mexican-origin population may be perceived as a special threat to dominant interests and the police in that region because of its proximity to the United States–Mexico border and the alleged problem of immigrant criminality that inflames fear of crime (Holmes & Smith, 2008; Holmes, Smith, Freng, & Muñoz, 2008; Wang, 2012).

While providing evidence consistent with the minority threat hypothesis, that study did not consider alternative explanations based on organizational characteristics of police agencies. Certain departmental characteristics (e.g., minority representation) are thought to make the police more accountable to the communities they serve. But after the inclusion of five community accountability measures, the findings for the minority threat variables were virtually identical to the earlier study (Smith & Holmes, 2003). Neither of these studies reported evidence regarding the predictions of the power-threat hypothesis.

Those investigations included only the small number of severe excessive force complaints that came to the attention of federal authorities, whereas most complaints are handled locally by police agencies. Smith and Holmes (2014) analyzed the larger pool of sustained excessive force complaints that were adjudicated departmentally in cities of 100,000 or more population. Both percent Black and percent Hispanic were related positively to the incidence of sustained excessive force complaints, consistent with the linear threat hypothesis. The quadratic terms included to test the predictions of the power-threat hypothesis were not statistically significant. The percent Hispanic effect was not limited to the Southwest in these data, perhaps a reflection of the recent growth of the Hispanic (particularly the Mexican-origin) population outside that region.

Several studies of police-caused homicide report evidence that is consistent with the predictions of the linear-threat hypothesis. Using 1975–1979 Vital Statistics and police records data from 45 cities with populations of 250,000 or more, Liska and Yu (1992) found a positive effect of percent non-White on the total and group-specific (White-non-White) rates of police-caused homicide. Tests for nonlinearity did not support the power-threat hypothesis. Two other studies analyzed Supplemental Homicide Reports (SHR) data on police-caused homicide from the Uniform Crime Reports. Sorensen and colleagues (1993) used data from 1980-–1984. They found that percent Black was positively related to the police homicide rate in cities with populations of 100,000 or more and 250,000 or more. Similarly, Jacobs and O'Brien (1998) used SHR data from 1980–1986 to examine the effects of minority threat on the rate of police killings in cities with populations of 100,000 or more. Their results showed that percent Black was not related to the overall rate of police killings, but it had a positive relationship to police killings in group-specific analyses of Blacks.

More recent studies have considered Hispanics. In two studies analyzing 1994–1998 SHR data for cities with populations of 100,000 or more, Smith (2003, 2004) found that proportion Black had a statistically significant, positive relationship to the incidence of police-caused homicide in cities with populations of 100,000 or more and 250,000 or more. One study included race-specific (Black and White) models, which revealed that proportion Black was a strong predictor of the incidence of police-caused homicides of Blacks (Smith, 2004). Proportion Hispanic was not statistically significant in either study. Another investigation used SHR data for 1999–2001, for large (100,000 or more population) and small (25,000–100,000) cities for which there were no missing data (Willits & Nowacki, 2014). The analyses showed that percent Black had a statistically significant, positive relationship to the incidence of police-caused homicide in the overall dataset, and a positive relationship that approached the conventional level of statistical significance in the sample of larger cities. Percent Hispanic was unrelated to police-caused homicides in all analyses.

Holmes et al. (2018) extended past research by conducting analyses of the overall incidence, Black incidence, and Hispanic incidence of police-caused homicides using SHR data from 2008 to 2013, inclusive. Neither variant of the racial threat hypothesis was supported in the total incidence of police-caused homicide analysis and Black group-specific analysis. The group-specific data for Hispanics generally supported the predictions of the power-threat hypothesis. That finding suggests that, in cities with a very high percentage of Hispanics in the population, Hispanic citizens are able to exert greater influence over the actions of police, at least in respect to these highly visible acts of violence that cannot easily be swept from public view.

A MESO-LEVEL INTERPRETATION OF POLICE VIOLENCE

Structural theories, such as the threat hypothesis, examine disparities in police violence in relation to social forces that comprise enduring, large-scale patterns of social relationships (Liska, 1992a). That research provides important evidence about the extent to which patterns of police violence reflect differences in the racial/ethnic composition of cities. Until recently, however, structural research on police violence has paid little attention to meso-level characteristics of cities that may moderate or mediate the structural-level effects of racial/ethnic composition on police violence.

Meso-level explanations focus on groups, a broad level of aggregation that falls between structural and individual processes. Groups are "characterized by shared place, common identity, collective culture, and social relations, although groups vary in the extent to which [these characteristics] apply" (Fine, 2012, P. 160). Neighborhoods comprise a meso-level of social organization that has considerable relevance to understanding police behavior. In this conceptualization, large-scale structural forces do not directly shape social interaction at the neighborhood level, which is necessarily mediated through contextual forces operating in particular surroundings. These intermediary forces operate above the micro-level phenomena, such as individual characteristics of the actors that influence social interaction. This analytical approach represents a venerable tradition in research on crime causation (e.g., Peterson & Krivo, 2010; Sampson, Raudenbush, & Earls, 1997; Shaw & McKay, 1969) – it also has considerable relevance for understanding police violence.

There are two plausible meso-level explanations of police violence. One longstanding research tradition sees the formal and informal organizational characteristics of police agencies as the primary cause of the problem. The other argues that certain places within cities are subjectively perceived as dangerous by police officers and, therefore, provide a context where police violence is most likely to occur. While approaching the problem from different angles, together these perspectives may prove useful in developing a more comprehensive account of police violence.

The Organizational Perspective on Police Violence

Organizational explanations locate the causes of police violence primarily in the institution of policing. Westley's (1970) pioneering work was highly influential in the development of this approach. Drawing on data collected in 1949–1950, he studied a police department located in a medium-sized industrial city with a large Black population and a large "slum" area. Informal norms of the police subculture involved maintaining authority and respect in a hostile work environment, concerns that shaped their responses to citizens. In particular, the police believed that Blacks are naturally prone to criminality and are a special threat to police authority. Situations eliciting police brutality often involved Blacks who were perceived as being disrespectful to officers. Police felt immune from being punished for relying on gratuitous violence because they saw Blacks as lacking the political power to do anything about it.

The informal subculture of policing has been a prominent focus of subsequent scholarship on the police use of violence in minority communities (e.g., Skolnick & Fyfe, 1993). Rather than improving relationships with citizens, the professionalism movement of the twentieth century appears to have increased the insularity of the police and fostered the occupational subculture that embodies their unique interests (Uchida, 2010). Frequently noted features of the police subculture include solidarity and group loyalty; an "us vs. them" view of the public; suspiciousness and secrecy; intense concern with danger and personal safety; a singular emphasis on crime fighting; and a tendency to stereotype citizens (see, e.g., Crank, 1998; Skolnick, 1975; Skolnick & Fyfe, 1993). The idea that the police perceive minority attitudes and actions as particularly threatening is a common theme in the literature (e.g., Skolnick & Fyfe, 1993). The police have always been concerned primarily with the challenges of their day-to-day work on the streets, and the movement toward professionalism did little to alleviate the problems of policing the "dangerous classes." Many Blacks and Hispanics reside in inner-city neighborhoods characterized by various socioeconomic disadvantages and high crime rates (Massey & Denton, 1993; Peterson & Krivo, 2010), and policing these locales poses many difficulties (Holmes & Smith, 2008).

A characteristic "working personality" is said to develop among police officers in response to such work environments (Skolnick, 1975). They develop a perceptual shorthand that identifies certain kinds of people, those whose demeanor portends the possibility of violence, as "symbolic assailants." This stereotypical imagery generally portrays minority citizens, particularly those encountered in disadvantaged neighborhoods, as criminally inclined and violent (Holmes & Smith, 2008). Given that street-level police behavior involves considerable discretion and low visibility, such conceptions may shape their responses to minority citizens. Police may mete out informal punishments defined as appropriate in the subculture, including gratuitous violence, to those who fit their stereotypes of dangerous people (Skolnick & Fyfe, 1993).

The ability to use force plays a central role in police culture, which encourages the use of violence to resolve problematic situations (Crank, 1998). Learning the appropriate situations for and means of violence pervades the formal training of police recruits. That training highlights the dangers of the occupation and heavily emphasizes self-defense. The use of lethal and nonlethal weapons and techniques consumes a large portion of formal training, and in-service training reinforces that instruction. The informal culture learned on the job accentuates the necessity of physical force in police work and encourages its use, even in situations where it may be legally questionable (Crank, 1998; Hunt, 1985). Unwarranted uses of force may be seen as normal and necessary for handling citizens who are perceived as threats or are otherwise discredited (Hunt, 1985; Skolnick & Fyfe, 1993; Westley, 1970).

While the idea that the subculture of policing is an important determinant of police violence, structural-level research has not directly tested that possibility. However, organizational perspectives maintain that the problem of police violence may be ameliorated by the implementation of policies that break down the subculture of policing and make officers more accountable to the citizens they serve (Smith & Holmes, 2003, 2014). Although the Kerner Commission identified structural disadvantage as the underlying cause of police violence in minority communities, it recommended numerous policies to change police departments in ways that might reduce police-minority tensions (National Advisory Commission on Civil Disorders, 1968). Organizational change ultimately became the priority for dealing with the problem today (see, e.g., President's Task Force on 21st Century Policing, 2015). Police departments have implemented many of the recommendations, such as increasing racial diversity in their ranks, instituting community policing, and creating civilian review boards to investigate complaints. Yet, research consistently shows that these organizational policies and practices do not moderate the effects of racial/ethnic composition of cities on the incidence of police violence (Holmes et al., 2018; Smith, 2003; Smith & Holmes, 2003, 2014).

The Place Perspective on Police Violence

While racial threat hypotheses are frequently framed in terms of the relative size of minority populations, that alone may not be sufficient to explain levels of perceived racial threat within cities. Ecological or spatial characteristics of cities, particularly residential segregation, may exert an important influence. A central part of police organization, both formally and informally, is the division of cities into territories or places where problems of crime and social control are seen as more or less problematic (e.g., Herbert, 1997; Meehan & Ponder, 2002). Police develop conceptions of various geographic locales, or places, which are strongly tied to race and the reputed moral character of people residing in them.

The place hypothesis maintains that the residential segregation of disadvantaged minority populations is central to the deployment of coercive strategies of policing (e.g., Brunson, 2007; Holmes et al., 2018; Meehan & Ponder, 2002; Smith & Holmes, 2014). Whites may believe that minorities living in disadvantaged areas are special threats to social order, and efforts to control and contain citizens in segregated areas may thus serve their interests. Less severe coercive strategies of policing, such as surveillance of minority citizens, may defend White neighborhoods from the intrusion of citizens perceived as threatening (Meehan & Ponder, 2002). More importantly here, the use of violence might protect the interests of police officers on the street who feel threatened when patrolling racially segregated minority areas (Fyfe, 1988; Liska & Yu, 1992; Smith & Holmes, 2014).

The difficult conditions found in disadvantaged minority locales may pose both subjective and objective threats to the police officers patrolling them (Holmes & Smith, 2008). Citizens in disadvantaged communities have a higher risk of contact with the police because coercive crime-control strategies are disproportionately deployed in those areas, which can promote negative attitudes about and tensions with the police (Brunson, 2007; Weitzer, 2017). Minority citizens, particularly young men, fear the police and may attempt to evade or resist them (e.g., Weitzer & Brunson, 2009; Weitzer, 2017). Police may generalize the behavior of some individuals to everyone encountered in disadvantaged locales, subjectively seeing them as potential threats (Holmes & Smith, 2008; Smith, 1986). Thus, officers may be more inclined to employ violence in disadvantaged minority neighborhoods because "segregation may increase the perceived threat for those who work in racially segregated ghettos, while decreasing it for those working outside these ghettos" (Liska & Yu 1992, p. 56). As Fyfe (1980) argued in regard to police shootings, large cities are divided into "free-fire zones" where police violence is prevalent and acceptable, and "sleepy hollows" where it is not. Moreover, officers might face less risk of punishment for the gratuitous use of violence in disadvantaged locales. Police administrators may consider the conditions officers face in those areas when reviewing police violence cases and give the benefit of the doubt to officers who acted under questionable circumstances (Fyfe, 1988).

Simply entering disadvantaged minority neighborhoods may activate mental processes that can trigger gratuitous police violence (Holmes & Smith, 2008). Unconscious and conscious processes for acquiring, storing, and retrieving emotional memories may instill fear and anger in the police officers who patrol those areas. They may learn these emotional responses directly from encounters with citizens perceived as threatening and indirectly from other officers' war stories. In this way, they become conditioned to associate disadvantaged locales and the people who reside in them with danger. Generalized fear and anger toward the citizens of these locales may prime police officers for "defensive" action in the face of subjectively perceived threats that do not have an objective basis (Holmes et al., 2018). Cases of police violence may entail emotional responses to encounters in which officers feel threatened and lack time to consider alternative lines of action.

Cognitive processes involving stereotyping may amplify these emotional responses. Stereotypes consist of collectively shared characterizations of a social group based on essentialist beliefs and illusory (i.e., anecdotal) generalizations (Holmes & Smith, 2008; Smith & Alpert, 2007). While often useful for conserving mental resources and routinizing interactions, stereotyping may also elicit erroneous attributions and inappropriate responses in encounters between police and minority citizens. Mirroring popular imagery of the larger society, police stereotypes of minority groups conflate race and violent criminality and are continually reinforced by selective personal experience and departmental folklore. Situational factors (e.g., time constraints, complex, and competing stimuli) that activate automatic stereotypic responses may be especially prevalent in police encounters with citizens in disadvantaged neighborhoods. Research shows that officers from districts with large populations, high rates of violent crime, and greater concentrations of minorities are particularly prone to stereotypic response biases (Correll et al., 2007). These biases may trigger gratuitous acts of force (Holmes & Smith, 2008). Police officers may also call upon their conscious beliefs about racial inferiority and criminality to justify such actions (e.g., Waegel, 1984).

Structural-level research on racial threat and police violence has paid relatively little attention to the effects of place, and the research that has considered it relies on city-level racial segregation. Segregation and place are necessarily connected, but important distinctions between the concepts exist. Place captures the idea that police officers' behavior is determined by their perceptions of threat in disadvantaged areas. While segregation is a powerful predictor of the existence of disadvantaged minority places (see Peterson & Krivo, 2010), it merely serves as a proxy for a number of conditions in those areas (e.g., dilapidated buildings, incivility, gun ownership) that cannot be adequately captured in a cross-city analysis. It is an imperfect between-city indicator of a within-city characteristic.

Research findings on the effects of segregation on police violence are limited. A single study of excessive force has included segregation measures, but a striking finding for Black-White segregation was observed (Smith & Holmes, 2104). The analysis showed that the level of sustained excessive force complaints was dramatically higher in cities with the highest degree of Black segregation compared with less segregated cities. Plausibly, the difficult conditions of disadvantaged neighborhoods commonly found in highly segregated cities amplifies the strength of the relationship between segregation and police violence. When segregation is extreme, police officers patrolling disadvantaged areas may perceive substantially greater threat and, therefore, become increasingly more likely to employ violence against minority citizens. There was not, however, a significant effect for Hispanic-White segregation, perhaps because it was appreciably less pronounced than Black segregation and may fall below the level required to amplify the minority threat subjectively perceived by police.

A few studies of racial threat and police-caused homicide have considered the effects of segregation. Liska and Yu (1992) found that White-non-White segregation was positively related to police-caused homicide, but it was not statistically significant when the analysis was disaggregated by race. Willits and Nowacki's (2014) study revealed no effect of either Black or Hispanic segregation on police-caused homicide. Holmes et al. (2018) sought to conduct a more comprehensive investigation.

They analyzed the overall incidence, Black incidence, and Hispanic incidence of police-caused homicide. Cities with high levels of Black segregation had an appreciably higher incidence of police-caused homicide compared with less segregated cities. This pattern was more pronounced in the group-specific analysis of Blacks. Very importantly, it is similar to the one observed for sustained excessive force complaints (Smith & Holmes, 2014). The similarity of the findings from the two studies provides compelling evidence that Blacks in highly segregated cities experience greater exposure to police violence. There was no effect of Hispanic segregation in the total incidence model, which mirrors previous findings for excessive force complaints and police-caused homicide. However, it had a linear positive effect in the group-specific analysis: cities with greater Hispanic segregation had a higher incidence of police-caused homicide of Hispanics compared with less segregated cities.

Although the findings of these structural-level studies of police violence are hardly definitive, field research provides evidence of extremely aggressive police tactics (such as highly invasive searches and unnecessary physical force) being used in disadvantaged neighborhoods (e.g., Brunson, 2007; Brunson & Miller, 2006; Chambliss, 1994; Herbert, 1997; Rios, 2011), which further suggests the possibility of a relationship between segregation and police violence. In addition, quantitative studies of neighborhood racial composition reveal that police use more coercive authority (nondangerous encounters involving use of physical force or threat of force, arrest, or surveillance) (Smith, 1986) and deadly force (Klinger et al., 2016) in predominantly Black neighborhoods.

PROSPECTS FOR TESTING MESO-LEVEL THREAT THEORY

Clearly, the meso-level police organization and place approaches to explaining police violence are intricately linked. At the same time, they take distinctive approaches to the problem. The organizational perspective sees police departments as imperfect but malleable. Yet, empirical research provides little evidence that changing police departments in ways thought to reduce police violence in minority communities achieves that end (Holmes et al., 2018; Smith, 2003; Smith & Holmes, 2003, 2014). In many respects, however, past research on the role of organizational characteristics of police departments is limited in its scope. Given the emphasis placed on the subculture of policing as a cause of police violence in minority communities from early on, it is surprising that little research systematically examines how police subculture influences the use of police violence. Although a number of core themes characterize the occupational culture, different aspects of it may be more pronounced in some agencies (Crank 1998). If there are variations in the police subcultural, that could be an important factor influencing the disparate use of police violence across cities. That possibility merits further consideration, but reliably measuring variations in subcultural dimensions – such as the strength of the "us vs them" view of the world or of the code of secrecy – in a sufficient number of agencies to permit aggregate-level multivariate analyses will pose significant challenges for researchers.

Like the threat hypothesis, the place perspective locates the source of disparities in police use of violence in obdurate patterns of social organization, but it focuses on the meso-level characteristics of neighborhoods within cities. It argues that disadvantaged minority neighborhoods are the loci of police violence. Past research on the effects of racial segregation on police violence provides evidence consistent with the place hypothesis, but it does not directly test it. Although the studies discussed above suggest that police violence is most prevalent in disadvantaged minority places within cities, that cannot be inferred from structural-level data with certainty. Even in relatively unsegregated cities, police violence may happen in certain areas perceived as problems by police, but not in others. That meso-level effect may be obscured in analyses of city-level data. Moreover, after neighborhood characteristics are included in statistical analyses, it is quite possible that structural-level measures of the racial-spatial composition of cities will no longer predict the incidence of police violence.

Future studies must examine variations in police-caused homicide within and between cities using both structural and event-based data. Recent analyses of police-caused homicide using structural and event data show that minority citizens are more likely than Whites to be killed by police, but they use crude measures of structural characteristics and do not include within-city neighborhood characteristics (Nix, Campbell, Byers, & Alpert, 2017; Ross, 2015). Event-based analyses conducted within a single or small number of cities can identify the effects of neighborhood characteristics on police violence (e.g., Klinger et al., 2016), but generalizations beyond the geographically limited research site are highly problematic. It cannot be determined whether the findings are unique to the specific research setting or whether they apply to other cities of a similar type.

These considerations indicate the need for multilevel analyses that incorporate city (e.g., percent minority, segregation), neighborhood (e.g., poverty, crime rate), and individual (e.g., race and gender of officers and suspects) characteristics. It seems very unlikely that such analyses can be conducted for the incidence of excessive force in cities, simply because no event-based data exist for a sufficient number of cities to allow multilevel modeling. New national data sources on police-caused homicide may eventually be developed to the point that such analyses become feasible. But currently there are various issues with these datasets that make them very problematic or impossible to use in research that examines patterns of police-caused homicide across large cities (see Holmes et al., 2018, fn. 1). While these problems can be overcome as the datasets are better developed, the difficulties of verifying and merging these event data with city and neighborhood data will require a major initiative. That notwithstanding, it is essential that future research examines how the incidence of police violence is related to meso-level within and structural-level between city characteristics.

CONCLUSION

Research on minority threat and social control has become a venerable tradition in sociology since the publication of Blalock's (1967) seminal book a half-century ago. While his work focused on structural-level patterns of discrimination, he recognized that underlying micro-level processes produce those patterns. He did not, however, explicitly consider the role of intermediary group characteristics, the focus of meso-level analyses. Over time it has become apparent that threat has multiple dimensions, which may involve the unique interests of the larger population and social control agents in a city (Holmes, 2000; Liska & Yu, 1992). Increasingly, neighborhood characteristics of places or territories within cities are being linked conceptually to the interests of police and their use of violence in research that tests racial threat hypotheses (Holmes et al., 2018; Smith & Holmes, 2014). As we have seen, this observation has important implications for understanding disparities in the incidence of police violence across cities.

The structural-level approach of the threat hypothesis focuses on how the size of a minority population shapes the degree of minority threat perceived by powerful groups and, consequently, the amount of discrimination experienced by minority citizens. A large body of structural-level research proffers important evidence that coercive strategies of crime control reflect systematic differences in racial composition of jurisdictions. While that argument is persuasive and well supported in regard to outcomes that involve collective political influence, it remains in question with respect to outcomes that involve the actions of smaller groups within the collectivity. Whereas citizens may sway decisions about how local governments distribute resources, they may have appreciably less influence on the day-to-day practices of government employees. Nowhere is that more apparent than in policing. Police responses to citizens are framed by a powerful subculture and the ecological context of the places in which they work. Certainly, police reactions to a young Black man seen entering a suburban church would be different than when he is seen standing on an inner-city street corner. Ecological context is critical to the elicitation of the emotional and cognitive processes thought to trigger perceptions of threat and violent responses by police. By expanding the conceptualization of threat theory to incorporate within-city ecological contexts, a better understanding of police coercion may become feasible.

ACKNOWLEDGMENT

The author thanks Christopher J. Holmes for insightful comments on a draft of this chapter. The author remains fully responsible for all analyses and interpretations presented herein.

REFERENCES

Acuña, R. (1988). *Occupied America: A history of Chicanos* (3rd ed.). New York, NY: Harper Collins.

Alba, R., & Nee, V. (2003). *Remaking the American mainstream: Assimilation and contemporary Immigration*. Cambridge, MA: Harvard University Press.

Austen, B. (2016). Chicago after Laquan McDonald. *New York Times Magazine*, April 20. Retrieved from http://www.nytimes.com/2016/04/24/magazine/chicago-after-laquan-mcdonald.html

Barrera, M. (1979). *Race and class in the Southwest: A theory of racial inequality*. Notre Dame, IN: University of Notre Dame Press.

Bender, S. W. (2003). *Greasers and Gringos: Latinos, law, and the American imagination*. New York, NY: New York University.

Bittner, E. (1970). *The functions of police in modern society.* Washington, DC: US Government Printing Office.

Blalock, H. M., Jr. (1967). *Toward a theory of minority group relations*. New York, NY: Wiley.

Brunson, R. K. (2007). "Police don't like Black people": African-American young men's accumulated police experience. *Criminology and Public Policy, 6*, 71–102.

Brunson, R. K., & Miller, J. (2006). Young Black men and urban policing in the United States. *British Journal of Criminology, 46,* 613–640.

Carmichael, J. T., & Kent, S. L. (2014). The persistent significance of racial and economic inequality on the size of municipal police forces in the United States, 1980–2010. *Social Problems, 61*(2), 259–282.

Chambliss, W. J. (1994). Policing the ghetto underclass: The politics of law and law enforcement. *Social Problems, 41*, 177–194.

Chambliss, W. J. (2001). *Power, politics and crime.* Boulder, CO: Westview.

Chambliss, W. J., & Seidman, R. B. (1971). *Law, order, and power*. Reading, MA: Addison-Wesley.

Chiricos, T., Hogan, M., & Gertz, M. (1997). Racial composition of neighborhood and fear of crime. *Criminology, 35,* 107–131.

Correll, J., Park, B., Judd, C. M., Wittenbrenk, B., Sadler, M. S., & Keesee, T. (2007). Across the thin blue line: Police officers and racial bias in the decision to shoot. *Journal of Personality and Social Psychology, 92*, 1006–1023.

Crank, J. P. (1998). *Understanding police culture.* Cincinnati, OH: Anderson.

Fine, G. A. (2012). Group culture and the interaction order: Local sociology on the meso-level. *Annual Review of Sociology, 38,* 159–179.

Fogelson, R. M. (1977). *Big-city police.* Cambridge: Harvard University Press.

Fyfe, J. J. (1980). Geographical correlates of police shootings: A microanalysis. *Journal of Research in Crime and Delinquency, 17*, 101–113.

Fyfe, J. J. (1988). Police use of deadly force: Research and reform. *Justice Quarterly, 5*, 165–205.

Herbert, S. (1997). *Policing space: Territoriality and the Los Angeles Police Department*. Minneapolis, MN: University of Minnesota Press.

Holmes, M. D. (2000). Minority threat and police brutality: Determinants of civil rights criminal complaints in U.S. municipalities. *Criminology, 38,* 343–367.

Holmes, M. D., Painter, M. A., II, & Smith, B. W. (2018). Race, place, and police-caused homicide in U.S. municipalities. *Justice Quarterly.* DOI: 10.1080/07418825.2018.1427782

Holmes, M. D., & Smith, B. W. (2008). *Race and police brutality: Roots of an urban dilemma*. Albany, NY: State University of New York Press.

Holmes, M. D., Smith, B. W., Freng, A. B., & Muñoz, E. A. (2008). Minority threat, crime control, and police resource allocation in the southwestern United States. *Crime and Delinquency*, *54*, 128–152.

Hunt, J. (1985). Police accounts of normal force. *Urban Life, 13*, 315–341.

Jackson, P. I., & Carroll, L. (1981). Race and the war on crime: The sociopolitical determinants of municipal police expenditures in 90 non-southern US cities. *American Sociological Review, 46*(3) 290–305.

Jacobs, D., & O'Brien, R. M. (1998). The determinants of deadly force: A structural analysis of police violence. *American Journal of Sociology, 103*, 837–862.

Johnson, M. S. (2003). *Street justice: A history of police violence in New York City.* Boston, MA: Beacon Press.

Kindy, K., & Kelly, K. (2015). Thousands dead, few prosecuted. *The Washington Post*, April 11. Retrieved from http://www.washingtonpost.com/sf/investigative/2015/04/11/thousands-dead-few-prosecuted/

Liska, A. E. (1992a). Conclusion: Developing theoretical issues. In A. Liska (Ed.), *Social threat and social control* (pp. 165–190). Albany, NY: State University of New York Press.

Liska, A. E. (1992b). Introduction to the study of social control. In A. Liska (Ed.), *Social threat and social control* (pp. 1–29). Albany, NY: State University of New York Press.

Liska, A. E., & Yu, J. (1992). Specifying and testing the threat hypothesis: Police use of deadly force. In A. Liska (Ed.), *Social threat and social control* (pp. 53–68). Albany, NY: State University of New York Press.

Massey, D. S., & Denton, N. A. (1989). Residential segregation of Mexicans, Puerto Ricans, and Cubans in selected U.S. metropolitan areas. *Sociology and Social Research, 73*, 73–83.

Massey, D. S., & Denton, N. A. (1993). *American apartheid: Segregation and the making of the underclass*. Cambridge, MA: Harvard University Press.

Meehan, A. J., & Ponder, M. C. (2002). Race and place: The ecology of racial profiling African American motorists. *Justice Quarterly, 19*, 399–430.

Monkkonen, E. H. (2002). *Crime, justice, history*. Columbus, OH: Ohio State University Press.

National Advisory Commission on Civil Disorders. (1968). *Report of the National Advisory Commission Civil Disorders*. New York, NY: Bantam Books.

National Association for the Advancement of Colored People and the Criminal Justice Institute at Harvard Law School (NAACP). (1995). *Beyond the Rodney King story: An investigation of police conduct in minority communities.* Boston, MA: Northeastern University Press.

Nix, J., Campbell, B. A., Byers, E. H., & Alpert, G. P. (2017). A bird's eye view of civilians killed by police in 2015. *Criminology* and *Public Policy*, *16*(1), 309–340.

Pérez-Peña, R. (2015). University of Cincinnati officer indicted in shooting death of Samuel Dubose. *New York Times*, July 29. Retrieved from http://www.nytimes.com/2015/07/30/us/university-of-cincinnati-officer-indicted-in-shooting-death-of-motorist.html

Peterson, R. D., & Krivo, L. J. (2010). *Divergent social worlds: Neighborhood crime and the racial-spatial divide.* New York, NY: Russell Sage Foundation.

President's Task Force on 21st Century Policing. (2015). *Final report of the President's task force on 21st century policing*. Washington, DC: Office of Community Oriented Policing Services.

Quillian, L., & Pager, D. (2001). Black neighbors, higher crime? The role of racial stereotypes in evaluations of neighborhood crime. *American Journal of Sociology, 107*, 717–767.

Rios, V. M. (2011). *Punished: Policing the lives of Black and Latino boys.* New York, NY: New York University Press.

Ross, C. T. (2015). A multi-level Bayesian analysis of racial bias in police shootings at the county-level in the United States, 2011–2014. *PloS One, 10*(11), e0141854.

Sampson, R. J., Raudenbush, S. W., & Earls, F. (1997). Neighborhoods and violent crime: A multilevel study of collective efficacy. *Science*, *277*(5328), 918–924.

Silver, A. (1967). The demand for order in civil society: A review of some themes in the history of urban crime, police, and riot. *The police: Six sociological essays, 1*.

Shaw, C.R., & McKay, H.D. (1969). *Juvenile delinquency and urban areas: A study of rates of delinquency in relation to differential characteristics of local communities in American cities* (revised ed.). Chicago, IL: University of Chicago Press.

Skogan, W. G. (1990). *Disorder and decline: Crime and the spiral of decay in American neighborhoods.* New York, NY: Free Press.

Skolnick, J. H. (1975). *Justice without trial. Law enforcement in a democratic society* (2nd ed.). New York, NY: Wiley.

Skolnick, J. H., & Fyfe, J. J. (1993). *Above the law: Police and the excessive use of force*. New York, NY: Free Press.

Smith, B. (2003). The impact of police officer diversity on police-caused homicides. *The Policy Studies Journal, 31*, 147–162.

Smith, B. W. (2004). Structural and organizational predictors of homicide by police. *Policing: An International Journal of Police Strategies and Management, 27*, 539–557.

Smith, B. W., & Holmes, M. D. (2003). Community accountability, minority threat, and police brutality: An examination of civil rights criminal complaints. *Criminology, 41*, 1035–1063.

Smith, B. W., & Holmes, M. D. (2014). Police use of excessive force in minority communities: A test of the minority threat, place, and community accountability hypotheses. *Social Problems, 61*, 83–104.

Smith, D. A. (1986). The neighborhood context of police behavior. In A. Reiss & M. Tonry (Eds.), *Crime and Justice. A Review of Research*, vol. 8, (pp. 313–341). Chicago, IL: University of Chicago Press.

Smith, M. R., & Alpert, G. P. (2007). Explaining police bias: A theory of social conditioning and illusory correlation. *Criminal Justice and Behavior, 34*, 1262–1283.

Sorensen, J., Marquart, J., & Brock, D. (1993). Factors related to killings of felons by police officers: a test of the community violence and conflict hypotheses. *Justice Quarterly, 10*, 417–440.

Stinson, P. M. (2017). Charging a police officer in fatal shooting case is rare, and a conviction is even rarer. *Criminal Justice Faculty Publications*. 80. http://scholarworks.bgsu.edu/cgi/viewcontent.cgi?article=1079&context=crim_just_pub

Stults, B. J., & Baumer, E. P. (2007). Racial context and police force size: Evaluating the empirical validity of the minority threat perspective. *American Journal of Sociology*, *113*, 507–546.

Turk, A. (1969). *Criminality and the legal order.* Chicago, IL: Rand McNally.

Uchida, C. D. (2010). The development of the American police. In R. G. Dunham & G. P. Alpert (Eds.), *Critical issues in policing: Contemporary readings* (6th ed., pp. 17–36). Prospect Heights, IL: Waveland Press.

Waegel, W. B. (1984). How police justify the use of deadly force. *Social Problems, 32*, 144–155.

Walker, S. E. (1977). *A critical history of police reform: The emergence of professionalism.* Lexington, MA: Lexington Books.

Walker, S. E. (1998). *Popular justice: A history of American criminal justice* (2nd ed.). New York, NY: Oxford University Press.

Wang, X. (2012). Undocumented immigrants as perceived criminal threat: A test of the minority threat perspective. *Criminology, 50*, 743–776.

Weitzer, R. (2017). Theorizing racial discord over policing before and after Ferguson. *Justice Quarterly Review*, *34*, 1129–1153.

Weitzer, R., & Brunson, R. K. (2009). Strategic responses to the police among inner-city youth. *Sociological Quarterly*, *50*, 235–256.

Weber, M. (1968/1922). *Economy and society,* Vols. 3, New York, NY: Bedminster Press.

Westley, W. A. (1970). *Violence and the police: A sociological study of law, custom, and morality.* Cambridge, MA: Massachusetts Institute of Technology.

Willits, D. W., & Nowacki, J. S. (2014). Police organisation and deadly force: An examination of variation across large and small cities. *Policing and Society, 24*, 63–80.

Wilson, W. J. (1987). *The truly disadvantaged: The inner city, the underclass, and public policy.* Chicago, IL: University of Chicago Press.

CHAPTER 9

A MULTI-LEVEL THEORY OF THE STATE'S MONOPOLY ON VIOLENCE: EXPLAINING THE EFFECT OF THE POLICE ON VIOLENCE

Paige Vaughn

ABSTRACT

Purpose – *This chapter uses preventive and responsive policing strategies in tandem to develop a multi-level theory that explains the relationship between the police and violence.*

Design/methodology/approach – *The chapter brings together classical scholarship and more recent sociological research to demonstrate that an effective response to violence is critical in upholding the state's monopoly on violence and that police officers can reduce violence by preventing it and responding to it.*

Findings – *Theoretical and practical evidence support the balanced use of responsive and preventive policing strategies to reduce violence. Findings from the literature are used to argue that (1) when law enforcement officers do not effectively respond to violence and/or crime prevention strategies are nonexistent in a community, neighborhood crime is increased and (2) when citizens do not perceive law enforcement officers as legitimate and effective agents of authority, they become more likely to engage in violent offending (Tonry, 1995; Tyler, 2006).*

Homicide and Violent Crime
Sociology of Crime, Law and Deviance, Volume 23, 159–176

ISSN: 1521-6136/doi:10.1108/S1521-613620180000023010

Originality/value – *Research has supported the effectiveness of "proactive" (Braga, Papachristos, & Hureau, 2014; Weisburd & Telep, 2014) and "reactive" (Nagin, 2013; Paternoster, 2010) policing strategies in reducing violence, but no research has combined strategies of prevention and response to explain the relationship between the police and violence. The theory proposed in this chapter demonstrates the utility of explaining the instrumental and legitimacy functions of the police across various levels and brings under-protection to the forefront of research on policing and violence.*

Keywords: Policing; social control; violent crime; crime control; police legitimacy; deterrence

INTRODUCTION

Disadvantaged African Americans disproportionately suffer from violence (Lauritsen & Heimer, 2010; Leovy, 2015; Miller, 2013; White & Lauritsen, 2012), are less likely to receive effective attention by law enforcement in regard to crime-solving (Black, 1976; Riedel, 2008), and are less likely to view the police as legitimate (Decker, 1981; Tyler, 2006; Tyler & Huo, 2002), but few attempts have been made to explain the relationships underlying these processes (Leovy, 2015; Rios, 2011). One plausible reason for the lack of understanding is a divide in the literature between police prevention and police response and the emphasis on police "proactivity." In this chapter, I argue that an effective response to crime is as critical to controlling violence as crime prevention, and propose a multi-level theory maintaining that a balanced use of responsive and preventive policing strategies is essential to reduce violence. I use instrumental and normative theories to argue that (1) when law enforcement officers do not effectively respond to violence and/or crime prevention strategies are nonexistent in a community, neighborhood crime is increased and (2) when citizens do not perceive law enforcement officers as legitimate and effective agents of authority, they become more likely to engage in violent offending (Tonry, 1995; Tyler, 2006). This theory is useful in explaining the instrumental and legitimacy functions of the police across various levels, brings under-protection to the forefront of research on policing and violence, and explains why policing strategies that combine reaction and prevention will be most effective in lowering violence.

This chapter is organized into five sections. The first section provides a brief history of the divide between "proactive" and "reactive" policing, demonstrating how the meanings of these strategies have changed over time and highlighting the ways in which weak evidence against "reactive" policing has been used to justify the exclusive use of "proactive" policing. The second section details the problematic implications of neglecting key theoretical information in explanations of policing and translating these inadequate explanations into policy. The third section attributes violent crime to the ineffective operation of the state's monopoly on violence and argues that, in order to better understand how the police might broadly affect crime, it is useful – and in fact necessary – to unify knowledge across various sociological subdisciplines and levels of analysis. The fourth section proposes a multi-level theory to demonstrate how effective crime control will require policing strategies that are responsive and preventive. The final section uses the example of focused deterrence to demonstrate support for the proposed theoretical model. It is suggested that in order to accurately explain the mechanisms underpinning police officers' roles in reducing violent crime, detailed individual- and neighborhood-level data must be made available and the concepts and relationships underlying strategies and interventions must be specified.

THE "REACTIVE" AND "PROACTIVE" POLICING DIVIDE

The "reactive" and "proactive" policing dichotomy was introduced into the policing literature during the 1960s in an attempt to more accurately explain police mobilization (Bordua & Reiss, 1967; Reiss, 1971). The original definitions that emerged from Reiss' (1971) systematic observation of police patrol activities have, however, changed over time in important ways. According to Reiss (1971), "reactive" policing was mobilized by citizens and used by law enforcement officers in responding to calls for service or crises. These strategies differed fundamentally from what Reiss termed "proactive" mobilizations in which police officers initiated contact with citizens in an attempt to prevent, detect, and respond to crimes.

"Proactive" policies made their way into policing during the 1980s and 1990s in an attempt to reinstate confidence in the police that had been eroded due to social unrest, rising crime, and the public's dissatisfaction with traditional policing practices (National Academies of Sciences, Engineering, and Medicine (National Academies), 2017). Such strategies immediately gained traction and support by social scientists and police organizations throughout the nation not only because "reactive" strategies, such as rapid response to calls for service and follow-up investigations, had been shown to be ineffective in combating crime (e.g., Eck, 1983; Skogan & Antunes, 1979; Spelman & Brown, 1984), but also because the rhetoric of "proactivity" was politically appealing. Since "proactive" strategies were developed with the intent to prevent crime, were based on empirical data, and could take various forms, they offered ways for law enforcement to demonstrate its control over crime.

The definitions of "proactive" and "reactive" policing changed from Reiss' (1971) original conceptualizations during this time. Scholars began using the term "reactive" policing to describe strategies used by law enforcement officers in responding to criminal events that have already occurred, and "proactive" policing to describe tactics aimed at preventing future crime and disorder. "Proactive" policing strategies thus no longer included responding to crime, and they came to be defined as:

> [...] policing strategies that have as one of their goals the prevention or reduction of crime and disorder and that are *not reactive* [emphasis added] in terms of focusing primarily on uncovering ongoing crime or on investigating or responding to crimes once they have occurred. (National Academies, 2017, p. 112)

It is useful to think of "proactive" and "reactive" policing strategies as making up the "protect" and "serve" functions of the police, where "reactive" policing strategies are intended to "serve" citizens in need of assistance and "proactive" policing strategies are intended to "protect" citizens from potential harms. "Reactive" policing strategies generally involve responding to citizens' calls and requests for service, investigating crimes, and apprehending suspects, and "proactive" strategies are targeted interventions that more broadly utilize place-based (e.g., hot spots), problem-solving (e.g., problem-oriented), person-focused (e.g., stop-question-frisk), and community-based (e.g., broken windows) approaches to crime control (National Academies, 2017).

Research on the effectiveness of various policing strategies has been mixed but, overall, research that has been done on place-based and person-based "proactive" strategies demonstrates that crime can be reduced, perhaps without long-term negative community outcomes (Braga, Papachristos, & Hureau, 2014; Weisburd & Telep, 2014; Kochel & Weisburd, 2017; Weisburd, Hinkle, Fameda, & Ready, 2011). Findings such as these have led scholars to argue for the prioritization of crime prevention over response in research and in practice (Lum & Nagin, 2017; National Academies, 2017). Explanations favoring crime prevention over crime response, however, have been fragmented and incomplete in many respects.

First, and most importantly, proponents of crime prevention have failed to address clear disparities in police effectiveness (e.g., violent crime clearance) that may be creating or contributing to disparities in violence. In a recent article, for instance, Lum and Nagin (2017) continuously note that crime clearance rates have remained unchanged despite large changes in crime rates, but they fail to recognize that clearance is low for some types of crimes (Riedel & Welsh, 2015) and particularly low for certain minority groups (Black, 1976; Litwin, 2004; Taylor, Holleran, & Topalli, 2009). This is problematic because recent literature suggests that ineffective crime solving can negatively affect individuals and communities through the promotion of violence (LaFree, 1998; Leovy, 2015; Natapoff, 2009).

Second, explanations of police prevention and response use biased samples of "reactive" policing strategies and overlook studies that run counter to their claims, undermining the importance of response strategies (NAS, Lum & Nagin, 2017; National Academies, 2017). They are quick to cite, for instance, Spelman and Brown's (1984) examination of rapid response to calls for service, which found weak evidence for crime control, studies showing that follow-up investigations do not reduce crime in expected ways (Eck, 1983; National Research Council (NRC), 2004), and studies highlighting the problematic implications of "reactive" policing on persons, officers, and society more generally. They fail, however, to cite recent arguments that look at the ways in which officers might reduce crime and promote legitimacy through engaging in response strategies (e.g., thorough investigative work) that are deemed legitimate, equitable, and effective (Engel, 2005; Lafree, 1998; Miller, 2008; Tyler, 2006).

Scholars have also tended to disregard various functions and consequences of police response that do not fit into the deterrence and incapacitation doctrines (e.g., influencing legitimacy through procedural and distributive justice) and that have been shown to affect citizens' perceptions of the police and violence

(LaFree,1998; Leovy, 2015; Natapoff, 2009; Rios, 2011; Sunshine & Tyler, 2003; Tyler & Huo, 2002). While proponents of "proactive" strategies acknowledge that arrest plays a role in incapacitating offenders, bringing perpetrators to justice, and reinforcing deterrence by threatening apprehension, they emphasize the costs of arrest for individuals and groups and use these costs to justify the need for "proactive" techniques (Lum &Nagin, 2017; National Academies, 2017). They do not acknowledge research suggesting that the police can use effective methods of response to reduce retaliatory violence, increase witness cooperation, and ultimately reinstate trust in the police (Leovy, 2015; Miller, 2010; Natapoff, 2009; Stuntz, 2011).

Finally, since researchers are encouraged to study "proactive" policing, research on strategies that are primarily responsive remains dated and inadequate. Studies about follow-up investigations, for instance, have not been conducted since the 1970s and 1980s, are limited to explaining burglary and robbery, and fail to examine the role of investigations in enhancing police legitimacy (Chaiken, Greenwood, & Petersilia, 1977; Eck, 1983; Skogan & Antunes, 1979). Though there is evidence that officers provide less attention to follow-up investigations for violent victimizations that occur in Black communities (Nardulli & Stonecash, 1981), research has not been conducted to determine the effects of unequal service distribution.

The argument that "proactive" policing is superior to "reactive" policing seems, therefore, problematic. The next section dives deeper into the theoretical underpinnings of how the police impact crime, and explains why these two policing approaches are in fact compatible and complementary.

THEORETICAL SHORTCOMINGS AND PRACTICAL IMPLICATIONS OF POLICING RESEARCH

Rather than viewing policing strategies as methods of prevention and response that might be used in conjunction with one another, "reactive" and "proactive" policing have been portrayed as incompatible ideal types, and scholars have lost sight of the importance of both in controlling violence. Framing response tactics as incompatible with preventive tactics and irrelevant to the crime control functions of the police has serious theoretical and practical consequences, particularly because "we are only at the beginning stages of finding solutions to some of the toughest problems we face in policing… and police–citizen relations" (Lum & Nagin, 2017, p. 382). Neglecting police response may cause scholars to invest energy in poorly defined and incomplete solutions, may hinder theoretical advancement, and, most importantly, may lead to inadequate policy making.

Theoretically, scholars are isolating what they believe to be effective preventive strategies from what they believe to be ineffective strategies of response and vice versa when, in reality, most policing theories and strategies encompass elements that involve both. By focusing on either "proactive" or "reactive" policing (i.e., ideal types) and excluding responsive concepts from theoretical and practical models, scholars overlook the otherwise clear potential for policing strategies to both react to and prevent future crime. This leads to fragmented and incomplete explanations that cannot locate the effects that police strategies might have on violent crime and various other outcomes.

The Importance of Response and Prevention in Theory

Most of what we do know about the role of the state – and police officers in particular – in combating violent crime comes from the deterrence and legitimacy strands of criminology. By apprehending violent offenders and demonstrating to citizens that violence will be punished, policing can serve as a crime control mechanism and a measure of police officer effectiveness at the individual and aggregate levels. By demonstrating to citizens that police officers are legitimate sources of authority and protection, policing can also serve as a measure of legitimacy and can reduce individual-level violent offending. While emphasizing different aspects of police function, deterrence and legitimacy should be viewed as complementary goals of police organizations.

The Instrumental Perspective: The Crime Control Function of the Police

Although policing can reduce violent crime by removing violent offenders from the community (i.e., incapacitation), it can also prevent crime through the deterrence of would-be offenders (Nagin, 1998; Zimring & Hawkins, 1995). Deterrence theory argues that severity, certainty, and celerity of punishment matter in deterring crime, and proponents of the theory argue that punishment can influence violent offending at the individual level as well as violent crime rates at the aggregate level (Beccaria, 1764; Nagin, 2013). The theory assumes that individuals are rational actors who are capable of weighing the costs and benefits of their actions and says that, when a person perceives the benefits of committing a criminal act as outweighing the costs, he or she will be more likely to resort to crime (Bentham, 1789; Paternoster, 2010). Deterrence research has led to important findings regarding the effect of punishment on crime, and it can be used to explain the crime-control function of the police at both the individual and aggregate levels.

Deterrence scholars assert that, as a measure of both certainty and celerity, effective police response (e.g., clearance) can lead to violence reduction through specific and general deterrence mechanisms (Kennedy, 2009). Sanctions and punishments that result from offending will deter offenders from committing future crime (specific deterrence) and the threat of sanctions and punishments will promote general deterrence by preventing individuals in the community from committing crimes (Meier & Johnson, 1977). In contrast, when violent offenders are granted immunity from punishment and when communities lack effective response mechanisms, violent offenders will remain in their communities and individuals will be shown that violence is tolerated, allowing violence to persist or even increase (Kennedy, 2009).

Stafford and Warr (1993) present a reconceptualized deterrence model that builds off of findings demonstrating that certainty and swiftness tend to matter in deterring future crime (Nagin, 2013) and that deterrence is likely to affect offenders' thoughts and perceptions about punishments and sanctions rather than objective or actual levels of punishment (Paternoster, 1987). Importantly, they define general deterrence as "the deterrent effect of indirect experience with punishment and punishment avoidance" and specific deterrence as "the deterrent effect of direct experience with punishment and punishment avoidance" (Stafford & Warr, 1993, p. 127). Recognizing the importance of observational and vicarious learning as well as experiential learning concepts underlying contemporary learning theories, their reconceptualization is useful in explaining the ways in which strategies such as arrest can operate at the individual level. Consistent with the notion that crime rates depend on both general and specific deterrence mechanisms, Stafford and Warr (1993) assert that individuals with limited experiences of direct punishment or punishment avoidance will be influenced by general deterrence, while those who have either experienced direct punishment or avoided punishment repeatedly will be deterred by specific deterrence.

Stafford and Warr's (1993) reconceptualized deterrence theory can also be useful in explaining the effect of the police on violence at the neighborhood level. Effective police strategies that are characterized by certain and swift apprehension might not only work to prevent violent offenders from future offending, but can also demonstrate to offenders and community members that violence will be punished, ultimately reducing the likelihood of violent offending by would-be offenders.

The normative perspective: The legitimacy function of the police

Legitimacy arguments, such as procedural justice, focus on how perceptions of legitimacy and fairness influence behavioral compliance with the law at the individual level (Tyler, 2006; Tyler & Huo, 2002). According to this argument, individuals who feel supported by law enforcement actors and who receive fair and just treatment will be less likely to turn to crime (Tyler, 2006). Thus, when the police effectively use their authority to respond to and prevent crime and when individuals feel as though they can rely on the criminal justice system to protect them, violent offending can be reduced.

In discussing the direct effects of legitimacy on crime, procedural justice proponents have been quick to discount instrumental perspectives. In his study of procedural justice, legitimacy, and compliance with the law, Tyler (2006) contrasts normative and instrumental approaches, arguing that normative perspectives are concerned with just and moral procedures and the ways in which individuals internalize and value particular norms of justice that then might lead to compliance with the law. He notes that whereas instrumental arguments view actors as being inherently self-interested and as being concerned with the favorability of case outcomes, normative approaches emphasize the importance of commitments to legal authority and the ways in which individuals who view law enforcement actors as legitimate will be likely to obey the law (Tyler, 2006). Thus, although both approaches emphasize the importance of legitimate police–community relationships in controlling crime, procedural justice and deterrence arguments are pitted against one another, preventing the unification of theory and knowledge (Tyler, 2006; Wilson, 1998).

Importantly, Tyler's (2006) procedural justice theory closely resembles the conclusions made by Stafford and Warr (1993) in their deterrence reconceptualization. Both explanations highlight the importance of the police in responding to and preventing future violence, and both recognize the importance of the authorities in deterring violence through particular behaviors, such as crime clearance, which are perceived as legitimate attempts at preserving social control. Deterrence researchers emphasize how law enforcement officers and their behaviors can demonstrate to individuals that violence will not be tolerated, while procedural justice arguments state that when law enforcement officers respond to crimes while also upholding values of fairness and consistency, they will be viewed as a legitimate source of protection and regulation, and compliance with the law will increase. Both also recognize the importance of individuals' direct and indirect experiences with law enforcement officers. In this way, then, instrumental approaches such as deterrence and normative approaches such as procedural justice can be viewed as complementary, rather than competing perspectives on how the police affect crime.

THE IMPORTANCE OF RESPONSE AND PREVENTION IN PRACTICE

If criminologists were to more carefully document the theoretical underpinnings of effective policing strategies, they might in fact find that the best strategies encompass elements that are both preventive and responsive. Take the example of focused deterrence policing strategies that blend law enforcement elements of deterrence with social service elements of procedural justice to deter a small and specific group of high-risk offenders (Braga & Weisburd, 2015; Kennedy, 2009). Such strategies are preventive in the sense that they seek to prevent crime and the underlying conditions that sustain violence through the use of social services opportunities and increased police–community interactions, but they also involve response because they increase the certainty, swiftness, and severity of punishments when targeted offenders do not comply with the law (Braga & Weisburd, 2015). Thus, they can prevent future crime by providing resources, strengthening police–community relations, and increasing the threat of punishment, but they involve responding to crime, too. Rather than labeling focused deterrence as an effective form of "proactive" policing (Lum & Nagin, 2017), theoretical explanations should comprehensively explain the preventive and responsive functions of the police (i.e., protect and serve).

By pitting "proactive" and "reactive" strategies against one another, criminology scholars are unable to accurately and comprehensively describe programs that utilize response and prevention in conjunction, and, as a result, cannot comprehensively explain the mechanisms underlying the relationships between the police and crime. Perhaps more importantly, policy recommendations that emphasize prevention over reaction can limit policymakers and practitioners in their ability to effectively control crime. Fearing the repercussions of implementing strong strategies of response, police departments may focus all of their energies and resources on prevention, which may keep communities from achieving the most effective outcomes.

The preventive and responsive functions of the police can also be demonstrated using the example of arrest, a policing strategy that has been framed as "reactive" and, if over- or under-emphasized by police departments, can have incredibly important consequences for crime prevention. Scholars have recognized that when disadvantaged minorities are policed too heavily for seemingly minor crimes, crime can be increased because the police come to be viewed as illegitimate sources of authority and protection (Alexander, 2010; Fernández-Kelly, 2015; Tyler & Huo, 2002; Western, 2006). However, as noted, minority victims living in impoverished neighborhoods have also been less likely to see criminals punished, and this might increase crime. Failing to apprehend dangerous individuals can encourage suspects, victims, and community residents to view the police as illegitimate and discriminatory actors who use their unwieldy discretion in problematic ways (Miller, 2015; Stuntz, 2011) and can lower perceptions of deterrence (Stafford & Warr, 1993). Thus, though arrest might increase deterrence and legitimacy, proponents of "proactive" policing fail to address victim neglect in their studies and actively encourage prevention over arrest, leaving policymakers scratching their heads and worrying about the consequences of over-policing without addressing the detrimental consequences of not responding to crime.

This point becomes clearer when we try to imagine what the world might look like without police response. What would stop–question–frisk, which has been labeled "proactive," look like if its responsive components were not implemented? Officers would stop, question, and frisk individuals that they deemed suspicious and worthy of attention but would not respond when weapons, drugs, or other illegal paraphernalia were found. This could arguably lower crime control and increase crime among those who perceive the officers as ineffectively responding to illegal behavior.

THE MISSING LINK: SOCIAL CONTROL AND THE STATE'S MONOPOLY ON VIOLENCE

Links between the police and violence have been demonstrated to exist in various contexts, but most studies that emphasize instrumental and normative perspectives, and prevention and response, can be brought together under an overarching theme of social control and the state's monopoly on violence. This section of the chapter relates macro-, neighborhood-, and individual-level research to the state's monopoly on violence and the role of law enforcement in impacting violence.

The Origins of the State's Monopoly on Violence

The notion of an over–under policing paradox and recent controversial police use of force incidents have led scholars to a renewed interest in the examination of the institution of policing and its effectiveness in controlling crime (Leovy,

2015; Rios, 2011; Rosenfeld, 2016). The idea that a state's monopoly on violence might be important in controlling crime, however, is not new. Classical scholars warned long ago that when a state does not have a monopoly on violence, its people will view it as illegitimate and will be forced to take matters into their own hands (Hobbes, 1668; Locke, 1689; Rousseau, 1762; Weber, 1919). During the early 1900s, Max Weber (1919) suggested that members of society will be more likely to comply with laws when the state and its laws are viewed as legitimate sources of authority and protection. When individuals do not view the state as legitimate and when laws are not applied consistently across groups (i.e., distributive justice), societal members will take matters into their own hands and might turn to crime and violence in the process (Weber, 1919). Weber's (1919) work on the state's monopoly on violence is limited to legal institutions and bureaucracies, and the timing of his writings prevented him from being able to adequately explain modern bureaucracies such as the police, but his ideas remain central to the argument that policing strategies might impact crime through the establishment of the state monopoly on violence.

Macro-Level Law and Society Research

At the macro-level, studies have tended to examine the state's obligation to control violence, particularly in high-crime and disadvantaged areas (Forman, 2017; Miller, 2008; Stuntz, 2008). These studies are typically limited to the study of local, state, and federal groups and agencies but can be valuable in explaining the ways in which changes over time have lowered the state's monopoly on violence. Miller (2013), for instance, has critically examined the ways in which American criminal justice systems have on the one hand, criminalized and expanded legal sanctions in Black communities and on the other hand, consistently ignored Black victims of violence, perpetuating a "security gap" in which minority citizens and groups are simultaneously repressed and neglected by the state. Though the state has an obligation to control violence, it has lost its power to do so in disadvantaged African Americans communities (Miller, 2013, 2015). Though law and society research can be valuable in explaining the ways in which policing practices that disproportionately punish minorities have contributed to the state's weakened monopoly on violence, it is limited to explaining macro-level phenomena and does not specify the ways in which police officers on the ground might affect violence through, for instance, the altering of police legitimacy perceptions. These findings do, however, seem to recognize the importance of crime control and legitimacy functions of the state in the sense that low levels of attention to violent crime can weaken police–community relations and result in lack of respect for the law and crime increases.

Cultural and Neighborhood Arguments

At the neighborhood level, scholars have acknowledged the importance of law and social control and the ways in which individuals' perceptions of law enforcement actors might contribute to violence (Anderson, 1999; Black, 1983; Kirk & Papachristos, 2011; Sampson & Bartusch, 1998). In his theory of self-help, Donald Black (1983) argues that, since "[l]ower-status people of all kinds – blacks and other minorities, the poor, the homeless – enjoy less legal protection, especially when they have complaints against their social superiors, but also when conflict erupts among themselves," they will be more likely to engage in self-help because the law is perceived as unavailable to them (p. 41). Similarly, in his ethnography of community residents in Philadelphia, Anderson (1999) finds that a number of structural conditions, such as high poverty concentration and increased segregation, can lead citizens to lack respect for laws and ultimately to adopt a street-code that encourages toughness, manliness, and aggressiveness. Consistent with procedural and distributive justice notions emphasizing the importance of legitimacy, fairness, and equity, when the legal system is viewed as unfair, as favoring particular groups over others, and as neglecting issues of violence, individuals are forced to take matters into their own hands (Anderson, 1999; Black, 1983).

Other studies have recognized how perceptions of the state might influence violent crime. Sampson and Bartusch (1998) find that minorities are in fact less tolerant of deviance but more cynical of the police and legal norms, and that concentrated disadvantage contributes to this cynicism. Similarly, Kirk and Papachristos (2011) find that, while minority community residents do not tolerate deviance and violence, legal cynicism has short- and long-term effects on neighborhood violence regardless of structural factors, collective efficacy, and other social processes. Neighborhood arguments recognize the importance of utilizing policing tactics that are viewed by citizens as procedurally just.

Scholars have also studied the ways in which criminal justice processes work on the ground to negatively influence the lives of disadvantaged citizens. In her analysis of "snitching," Natapoff (2009) demonstrates how the use of informants by police officers and prosecutors can not only exacerbate tensions between police officers and community residents, but can also reward criminals with lenience and place innocent individuals in highly dangerous situations. Importantly, she notes that "when a government permits criminals to continue offending in exchange for information and cooperation, the community in which those crimes are committed suffers in a number of ways" (Natapoff, 2009, p. 207). Consistent with incapacitation and deterrence arguments, not only is crime increased when police officers fail to effectively respond to violent crimes, but also victim, informant, and witness underprotection can couple with increasing danger and demonstrate to community residents that the state's monopoly on violence is not operating effectively (Natapoff, 2009).

The disconnect between community residents and police officers in disadvantaged African Americans communities has large consequences. One consequence that has resulted from increased distrust of police officers by disadvantaged African Americans youth has been the development of a "stop snitching" campaign, and this not only undermines the state's monopoly on violence, but might also further lower the effectiveness of law enforcement in responding to and preventing crime (Natapoff, 2009; Rios, 2011). Increased tensions between police officers and community members can lead to decreased witness cooperation and increased retaliatory violence, both of which might lower crime-solving and increase violence overall (Leovy, 2015).

Explaining Violence across Multiple Levels of Analysis

While explanations of the police and violence do well on their own to explain specific relationships, they fail to adequately address the ways in which policing might influence violence across micro- and macro-levels (Coleman, 1986; Matsueda, 2017). The theory introduced in this chapter recognizes that processes can be interacting at multiple levels of analysis and uses existing literatures to develop a model that can explain violence outcomes across levels. In particular, it utilizes a theoretical approach developed by Coleman (1986, but more recently see Matsueda, 2017) to explain social phenomena moving from the macro-level "down to the level of individual actions and back up again" (Coleman, 1986, p. 1322). In support of Coleman's (1986) argument that theoretical explanations are most useful when they connect the associations between individual- and macro-level phenomena, the theory presented in this chapter explains relationships between police strategies of response and prevention and violent crime at the individual and neighborhood levels.

A MULTI-LEVEL THEORY OF THE STATE'S MONOPOLY ON VIOLENCE

Here, I propose a multi-level approach to the study of policing as it relates to violence. I argue that when police officers use their authority to prevent and respond to violence, individuals and communities will have lower levels of violence. The theory demonstrates the ways in which various preventive and responsive behaviors can be modeled together to explain the legitimacy and crime control functions of the police. The argument is simple: when the police utilize strategies of prevention and response in conjunction, the state's monopoly on violence can be legitimately strengthened to control crime. After explaining the proposed theory's organization, origins, scope, and variables, evaluations of focused deterrence interventions are used to explain how police strategies that embrace preventive and responsive aspects of policing can be especially practical and useful in reducing violence.

The Theory

Crimes can vary and so can response to crimes. The theory developed in this chapter is designed to explain variation in the degree to which police officers are able to control violent crime at the individual and neighborhood levels through police effort and the establishment of the state's monopoly on violence. The state's monopoly is hypothesized to operate through police response to violence and prevention of violence to indirectly affect neighborhood crime levels and to directly affect individual-level crime through increasing perceptions of police legitimacy. Importantly, the theory demonstrates how deterrence and legitimacy arguments can be used in conjunction when explaining the relationship between the police and violence. The theory can be especially useful in explaining why disadvantaged African Americans neighborhoods might have disproportionately high violent crime rates and malfunctioning relationships with the state. Its full scope, however, is meant to be general and can be used to explain why, when violent crimes are given effective attention and preventive tactics are used to compliment responsive police functions, the state can reduce violence. The proposed model can be modified over time once variables are properly operationalized, concepts are measured, and relationships are established with evidence (see Fig. 1).

The primary independent variable of interest is police effort, which is defined as a balanced set of policing tactics aimed at preventing and responding to violence. It is hypothesized that, when police officers consistently and effectively react to violence and use preventive strategies to avert future violence, the state's monopoly on violence is strengthened at both the individual and neighborhood levels, leading to reduced violent offending and violent crime. When communities have effective police effort, individuals perceive the state as legitimate and would-be offenders are deterred by the possibility of punishment, reducing violence at the individual level.

The theory's main dependent variable is violence. When the state's monopoly on violence is established, both individual-level violent offending and neighborhood-level violent crime will be reduced. Consistent with literature demonstrating the importance of capturing and punishing offenders (Nagin, 2013) and the importance of legitimacy and perceptions of deterrence in controlling crime (Kirk & Papachristos, 2011; LaFree, 1998; Sampson & Bartusch, 1998; Stafford & Warr, 1993; Tyler, 2006; Weber, 1919), police responses demonstrate to individuals on a contextual level that the law is legitimate and fair, that violent crime will be punished, and that adherence to the law is vital in maintaining safety and protection from violence. Such strategies can be used in conjunction with targeted strategies that respond to and prevent particular problems (e.g., community policing and/or problem-oriented policing). Put simply, when police officers respond to the commission of violent crimes in effective ways and use empirically supported prevention strategies, suspects, victims, and community residents come to perceive the police as legitimate and become more willing to adhere to the law.

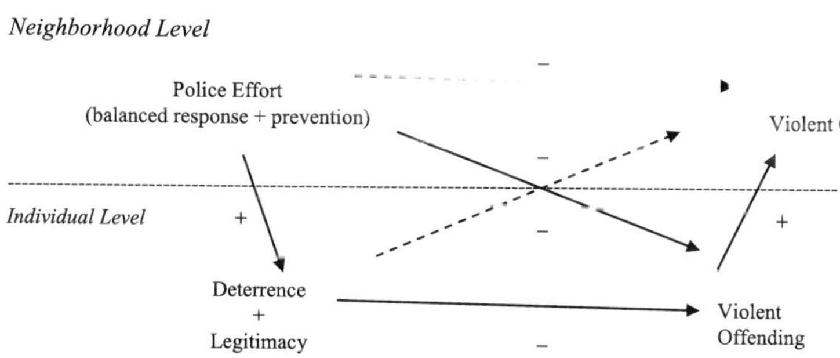

Fig. 1. Micro- and Macro-Level Propositions: A Multi-Level Theory of the State's Monopoly on Violence.

EVIDENCE SUPPORTING THE PROPOSED MODEL

Studies of focused deterrence interventions have recently demonstrated the ways in which prevention and response can lead to reduced levels of violence at the individual and neighborhood levels. Focused deterrence policing strategies combine crime control and legitimacy components, recognizing the importance of offenders' perceptions of the law and the police and seeking to prevent crime and the underlying conditions that sustain violence through the implementation of blended strategies of law enforcement and social services actions (Braga & Weisburd, 2015; Kennedy, 2009). Focused deterrence evaluations suggest that the combination of active law enforcement and notification meetings between officers, community residents, and social service actors might reduce violence at the neighborhood level (Braga & Weisburd, 2015; Kennedy, 2009), and we can use theories about legitimacy to explain the relationship between police effort and violent offending at the individual level.

Focused Deterrence

Arrest is the first stage in the process of punishment, and if a criminal is not arrested, punishment will fail to occur. If swiftness and certainty do in fact promote deterrence, then it can be argued that, in order to combat crime, officers must be able to arrest suspects in a quick and certain manner. One exceptionally promising approach to crime control through clearance is focused deterrence, an intervention strategy that adds components of procedural justice and legitimacy to the deterrence equation (Braga & Weisburd, 2015; Kennedy, 2009).

Focused deterrence strategies typically involve (1) the selection of a crime problem, (2) the formation of an interagency enforcement group, (3) the conduction of research, (4) the framing of enforcement operations, (5) social services provisions, and (6) direct and repeated communication with offenders (Braga & Weisburd, 2015; Kennedy, 2009). During the beginning of focused deterrence interventions, offenders are told that they are being watched and that violence will no longer be tolerated. Focused deterrence methods do not just attempt to increase the certainty, swiftness, and severity of punishments; they also advertise law enforcement strategies and deliver messages to a small and specific group of offenders in order to be rid of a particular problem that has plagued a community, usually through call-ins or notification meetings that occur in public locations and involve interactions between program participants, local and federal law enforcement officers, service providers, and ex-program participants (Braga & Weisburd, 2015). Utilization of response and prevention methods in conjunction is what makes this strategy effective in combating violence. Focused deterrence strategies reduce violence through the swift and certain apprehension of program clients who re-offend and the prevention of future crime through the promotion of deterrence and the development of positive relationships between police officers, individuals, and community members.

Evaluations of focused deterrence programs such as Operation Ceasefire in Boston, MA, and Project Exile in Richmond, VA, have demonstrated that, if we know which areas are impacted by crime as well as the elements involved in offending among high-risk groups, focused deterrence can be used to effectively combat crime (Kennedy, 1997, 2009). Recent meta-analyses provide support for focused deterrence (Braga & Weisburd, 2011, 2015). Most programs have been found to significantly prevent and control gun violence (Braga & Weisburd, 2015), and a recent meta-analysis found that focused deterrence strategies are associated with a significant, medium-sized crime reduction impact (Braga & Weisburd, 2011). To date, however, few evaluations (Hawken & Kleiman, 2009; Hamilton, Rosenfeld, & Levin, 2017) of focused deterrence have implemented randomized controlled designs, evaluations have not been able to tease apart the particular aspects of focused deterrence that are effective (Grunwald & Papachristos, 2017), and few process and outcome evaluations have been conducted to determine whether focused deterrence interventions have been successful in achieving intended outcomes (Boyle, Lanterman, Pascarella, & Cheng, 2010; Braga & Weisburd, 2015; Rosenfeld, Fornago, & Baumer, 2005; Rossi, Lipsey, & Freeman, 2004). Research is thus needed to examine the specific mechanisms underlying focused deterrence in order to determine whether the variables examined in the multi-level model can be used to explain how crime is being controlled at both individual and aggregate levels via strategies that are both responsive and preventive.

CONCLUSION

This chapter integrates findings from various sociological literatures to explain how violence might be related to the ways in which police officers respond to and prevent crime. It suggests that if police officers effectively respond to violent crimes and use preventive strategies to deter future crime, violent offending and neighborhood violence may be reduced.

Thinking about response and prevention together can be useful in demonstrating why we might expect violent crime to be higher in places where responses to crime are simultaneously harsh and dismissive and where preventive strategies overlook reactions to violence. I argue that in communities where the state lacks a monopoly on violence, such as in disadvantaged Black inner-city communities, high crime is inevitable. When strong responsive and preventive strategies are used in tandem to promote crime control, the state's monopoly on violence will be strengthened and violence will be effectively combatted.

The theory proposed in this chapter warrants further development and study. Importantly, the variables and concepts underlying the proposed theory have not been adequately developed, operationalized, or tested. In order to better specify the theory and its components, policing scholars must acknowledge the problems with the reactive/proactive divide and must work collaboratively so that only the most effective and wholesome policies are implemented and thoroughly evaluated. Social scientists can strengthen research on policing and violence by examining comprehensive policing strategies, such as focused deterrence, which enhance police prevention and reaction in ways that can positively affect individuals and communities. If it is the case that strategies of response and prevention are operating in ways that reduce violence, police departments must be willing to implement and provide data regarding policies that emphasize both.

ACKNOWLEDGMENTS

The author thanks Richard Rosenfeld, David Klinger, and Ted Lentz for their insightful comments and constructive feedback on earlier drafts.

REFERENCES

Alexander, M. (2010). *The new Jim Crow: Mass incarceration in the age of colorblindness*. New York, NY: The New Press.

Anderson, E. (1999). *Code of the street: Decency, violence, and the moral life of the inner city*. New York, NY: W. W. Norton.

Beccaria, C. (1764). *An essay on crimes and punishment*. Albany, NY: W. C. Little.

Bentham, J. (1789). *An introduction to the principles of morals and legislation*. London: Athlone.

Black, D. J. (1976). *The behavior of law*. New York, NY: Academic Press.

Black, D. J. (1983). Crime as social control. *American Sociological Review*, *48*, 34–45.

Braga, A. A., & Weisburd, D. L. (2011). The effects of focused deterrence strategies on crime: A systematic review and meta-analysis of the empirical evidence. *Journal of Research in Crime and Delinquency*, *49*(3), 323–358.

Braga, A. A., & Weisburd, D. L. (2015). Focused deterrence and the prevention of violent gun injuries: Practice, theoretical principles, and scientific evidence. *Annual Review of Public Health*, *36*, 55–68.

Braga, A. A., Papachristos, A., & Hureau, D. (2014). The effects of hot spots policing on crime: An updated systematic review and meta-analysis. *Justice Quarterly*, *31*, 633–663.

Bordua, D. J., & Reiss, A. J. (1967). Law enforcement. In P. Lazarsfeld, W. Sewell, & H. Wilensky (Eds.), *The Uses of Sociology*, (pp. 275–303) New York: Basic Books.

Boyle, D. J., Lanterman, J. L., Pascarella, J. E., & Cheng, C. C. (2010). The impact of Newark's Operation Ceasefire on trauma center gunshot wound admissions. *Justice Research and Policy*, *12*(2), 105–123.

Chaiken, J. M., Greenwood, P. W., & Petersilia, J. (1977). The criminal investigation process: A summary report. *Policy Analysis*, *3*(2), 187–217.

Coleman, J. S. (1986). Social theory, social research, and a theory of action. *The American Journal of Sociology*, *91*, 1309–1335.

Decker, S. H. (1981). Citizen attitudes toward the police: A review of past findings and suggestions for future policy. *Journal of Police Science and Administration*, *9*, 81–87.

Eck, J. E. (1983). *Solving crimes: The investigation of burglary and robbery.* Washington, DC: Police Executive Research Forum.

Engel, R. S. (2005). Citizens' perceptions of distributive and procedural justice during traffic stops with police. *Journal of Research in Crime and Delinquency*, *42*, 445–481.

Fernández-Kelly, P. (2015). *The hero's fight: African Americans in West Baltimore and the shadow of the state*. Princeton, NJ: Princeton University Press.

Forman, J., Jr. (2017). *Locking up our own: Crime and punishment in Black America*. New York, NY: Farrar, Straus, and Giroux.

Grunwald, B., & Papachristos, A. V. (2017). Project safe neighborhoods in Chicago: Looking back a decade later. *The Journal of Criminal Law and Criminology*, *107*, 131.

Hamilton, B., Rosenfeld, R., & Levin, A. (2017). Opting out of treatment: Self-selection bias in a randomized controlled study of a focused deterrence notification meeting. *Journal of Experimental Criminology*.

Hawken, A., & Kleiman, M. (2009). *Managing drug involved probationers with swift and certain sanctions: Evaluating Hawaii's HOPE*. Washington, DC: National Institute of Justice.

Hobbes, T. (1668). *Leviathan: Or the matter, form, and power of a commonwealth ecclesiastical and civil*. New York, NY: Macmillan.

Kennedy, D. M. (2009). *Deterrence and crime prevention: Reconsidering the prospect of sanction*. New York, NY: Routledge.

Kennedy, D. M. (1997). *Juvenile gun violence and gun markets in Boston* (pp. 1–4). Research Preview. National Institute of Justice.

Kirk, D. S., & Papachristos, A. V. (2011). Cultural mechanisms and the persistence of neighborhood violence. *American Journal of Sociology*, *116*, 1190–1233.

Kochel, T. R., & Weisburd, D. (2017). Assessing community consequences of implementing hot spots policing in residential areas: Findings from a randomized field trial. *Journal of Experimental Criminology 13*(2),143–170.

LaFree, G. (1998). *Losing legitimacy: Street crime and the decline of social institutions in the United States*. Boulder, CO: Westview.

Lauritsen, J. L., & Heimer, K. (2010). Violent victimization among males and economic conditions: The vulnerability of race and ethnic minorities. *Criminology and Public Policy*, *9*, 665–692.

Leovy, J. (2015). *Ghettoside*. New York, NY: Spiegel & Grau.

Litwin, K. J. (2004). A multilevel multivariate analysis of factors affecting homicide clearance. *Journal of Research in Crime and Delinquency*, *41*, 327–351.

Locke, J. (1689). *Two treatises of government*. London: Awnsham and John Churchill.

Lum, C., & Nagin, D. S. (2017). Reinventing American policing. *Crime and Justice*, *46*, 339–393.

Matsueda, R. L. (2017). Toward an analytical criminology: The micro–macro problem, causal mechanisms, and public policy. *Criminology*, *55*, 493–519.

Meier, R. F., & Johnson, W. T. (1977). Deterrence as social control: The legal and extralegal production of conformity. *American Sociological Review*, *42*, 292–304.

Miller, L. L. (2008). *The Perils of federalism: Race, poverty, and the politics of crime control*. Oxford: Oxford University Press.

Miller, L. L. (2010). The invisible black victim: How American federalism perpetuates racial inequality in criminal justice. *Law and Society Review*, *44*, 805–842.

Miller, L. L. (2013). Power to the people: Violent victimization, inequality and democratic politics. *Theoretical Criminology*, *17*(3), 283–313.

Miller, L. L. (2015). What's violence got to do with it? Inequality, punishment, and state failure in US politics. *Punishment and Society*, *17*, 184–210.

Nagin, D. S. (1998). Deterrence and incapacitation. In M. Tonry (Ed.), *The Handbook of Crime and Punishment* (pp. 345–368). New York, NY: Oxford University Press.

Nagin, D. S. (2013). Deterrence in the twenty-first century. *Crime and Justice*, *42*, 199–263.

Nardulli, P. F., & Stonecash, J. M. (1981). *Politics, professionalism, and urban services: The police*. Cambridge, MA: Oelgeschlager, Gunn & Hain.

Natapoff, A. (2009). *Snitching: Criminal informants and the erosion of American justice*. New York, NY: NYU Press.

National Academies of Sciences, Engineering, and Medicine (National Academies). (2017). *Proactive policing: Effects on crime and communities*. Washington, DC: The National Academies Press.

National Research Council (NRC). (2004). *Fairness and effectiveness in policing: The evidence*. Washington, DC: National Academies Press.

Paternoster, R. (1987). The deterrent effect of the perceived certainty and severity of punishment: A review of the evidence and issues. *Justice Quarterly*, *4*, 173–217.

Paternoster, R. (2010). How much do we really know about criminal deterrence? *The Journal of Criminal Law and Criminology*, *10*(3), 765–824.

Reiss, A. J. (1971). *The police and the public*. New Haven, CT: Yale University Press.

Riedel, M. (2008). Homicide arrest clearances: A review of the literature. *Sociology Compass*, *2*(4), 1145–1164.

Riedel, M., & Welsh, W. N. (2015). *Criminal violence: Patterns, causes, and prevention*. Oxford: Oxford University Press.

Rios, V. M. (2011). *Punished: Policing the lives of Black and Latino boys*. New York, NY: NYU Press.

Rosenfeld, R. (2016). *Documenting and explaining the 2015 homicide rise: Research directions*. NCJ 249895. US Department of Justice, Office of Justice Programs, National Institute of Justice.

Rosenfeld, R., Fornango, R., & Baumer, E. (2005). Did ceasefire, compstat, and exile reduce homicide? *Criminology and Public Policy*, *4*(3), 419–449.

Rossi, P. H., Lipsey, M. W., & Freeman, H. E. (2004). *Evaluation: A systematic approach* (7th ed.). Thousand Oaks, CA: SAGE.

Rousseau, J. J. (1762). *Du contrat social; Ou, Principes du droit politique*. (On the Social Contract; or, Principles of Political Rights). Amsterdam: Chez Marc/Michel Rev)

Sampson, R. J., & Bartusch, D. J. (1998). Legal cynicism and (subcultural?) tolerance of deviance: The neighborhood context of racial differences. *Law and Society Review*, *32*, 777–804.

Skogan, W. G., & Antunes, G. E. (1979). Information, apprehension, and deterrence: Exploring the limits of police productivity. *Journal of Criminal Justice*, *7*(3), 217–241.

Spelman, W., & Brown, D. K. (1984). *Calling the police: Citizen reporting of serious crime*. U.S. Department of Justice, National Institute of Justice.

Stafford, M. C., & Warr, M. (1993). A reconceptualization of general and specific deterrence. *Journal of Research in Crime and Delinquency*, *30*, 123–135.

Stuntz, W. J. (2008). Unequal justice. *Harvard Law Review*, *121*, 1969–2040.

Stuntz, W. J. (2011). *The collapse of American criminal justice*. Cambridge, MA: Harvard University Press.

Sunshine, J., & Tyler, T. (2003). The role of procedural justice and legitimacy in shaping public support for policing. *Law and Society Review*, *37*, 513–548.

Taylor, T. J., Holleran, D., & Topalli, V. (2009). Racial bias in case processing: Does victim race affect police clearance of violent crime incidents? *Justice Quarterly*, *26*, 562–591.

Tonry, M. (1995). *Malign neglect: Race, crime, and punishment in America*. Oxford: Oxford University Press.

Tyler, T. R. (2006). *Why people obey the law*. Princeton, NJ: Princeton University Press.

Tyler, T. R., & Huo, Y. (2002). *Trust in the law: Encouraging public cooperation with the police and courts*. New York, NY: Russell Sage Foundation.

Weber, M. (1919). Politics as a vocation. In H. Gerth & C. Wright Mills (Eds.), *Max Weber: Essays in sociology* (pp. 77–128). New York, NY: Oxford University Press.

Weisburd, D., & Telep, C. W. (2014). Hot spots policing: What we know and what we need to know. *Journal of Contemporary Criminal Justice*, *30*, 200–220.

Weisburd, D., Hinkle, J. C., Fameda, C., & Ready, J. (2011). The possible "backfire" effects of hot spots policing: An experimental assessment of impacts on legitimacy, fear and collective efficacy. *Journal of Experimental Criminology*, *4*, 297–320.

Western, B. (2006). *Punishment and inequality in America*. New York, NY: Russell Sage Foundation.

White, N., & Lauritsen, J. (2012). *Violent crime against youth, 1994–2010*. NJC 240106. Office of Justice Programs, Bureau of Justice Statistics, Department of Justice, Washington, DC.

Wilson, E. O. (1998). *Consilience: The unity of knowledge*. New York, NY: Random House.

Zimring, F., & Hawkins, G. (1995). *Incapacitation*. New York, NY: Oxford University Press.

CHAPTER 10

CONSIDERING AN "ALTERNATIVE CAPACITY TO DESIRE": INSTITUTIONAL ANOMIE THEORY, THE AMERICAN DREAM, AND THE ONTOLOGICAL TURN

James B. Pratt, Jr

ABSTRACT

Purpose – *This chapter problematizes the concept of the "American Dream" – important for Messner and Rosenfeld's Intuitional Anomie Theory (IAT).*

Design/methodology/approach – *The author uses work from political science, specifically Adcock and Collier in conversation with Gerring to consider if the American Dream concept is "good." The author continues by contending that the work on the state, its power and reach, can assist with the reconceptualization of IAT and the American Dream concept theoretically and methodologically.*

Findings – *The author finds that the American Dream concept, while not completely inadequate, significantly departs from Adams' original definition in* The Epic of America *while also being associated with mixed findings as it relates to race and the likelihood of violence. The author concludes that through critical work (e.g., Moten's "The Case for Blackness" and Ahmed's "Phenomenology of Whiteness") that in order to better develop this basis of desire in the American Dream concept there is a need to integrate a growing body of work that critically engages with the legacy of racial violence and racialized social conditioning. The author concludes that by studying the*

Homicide and Violent Crime
Sociology of Crime, Law and Deviance, Volume 23, 177–196

ISSN: 1521-6136/doi:10.1108/S1521-613620180000023011

ontology/phenomenon of race, understandings of cultural desire may be understood in order to inform IAT.

Originality/value – *This chapter provides a framework for evaluating concepts with interdisciplinary conversations with political science. The author's findings also add to a body of work that, through cross-disciplinary conversations, work to tease out the socio-ecological and historical conditions that influence the interaction of structure and culture that lead to anomie and ultimately deviance.*

Keywords: Anomie; race; culture; violence; state power; institutions

INTRODUCTION

> To be a Negro in America is often to hope against hope. It means fighting daily a double battle – a battle against pathology within and a battle against oppression without. (King, 1967/2010, pp. 120–121)

There is duality in the word hope seen in King's quote – in the latter use, an almost neutral expectation and in the prior, a belief in something beyond expectation, that which requires faith. King, writing his final book, recognized that even in the face of the Civil Rights Act of 1964 and the Voting Rights Act of 1965, there was something still beyond, something which to desire and hope for – a dream, a radical version of an "American Dream." The legal creation of a civil status and protections granted post-emancipation in 13th, 14th, and 15th amendments were not sufficient, though they were evidence of change (King, 1968). The second part of King's quote highlights another duality that harkens back to W. E. B. Du Bois's (1903) concept of double consciousness, described as follows:

> [...] a peculiar sensation [...] this sense of always looking at one's self through the eyes of others, of measuring one's soul by the tape of a world that looks on in amused contempt and pity. One ever feels his two-ness, an American, a Negro; two souls, two thoughts, two unreconciled strivings; two warring ideals in one dark body, whose dogged strength alone keeps it from being torn asunder. The history of the American Negro is the history of this strife – this longing to attain self-conscious manhood, to merge his double self into a better and truer self. In this merging he wishes neither of the older selves to be lost. He does not wish to Africanize America, for America has too much to teach the world and Africa. He wouldn't bleach his Negro blood in a flood of white Americanism, for he knows that Negro blood has a message for the world. He simply wishes to make it possible for a man to be both a Negro and an American without being cursed and spit upon by his fellows, without having the doors of opportunity closed roughly in his face. (pp. 2–3)

Moten (2013) asks, in conversation with Dubois and thinking through this concept of double consciousness, "What if blackness is the name that has been given to the social field and social life of an illicit alternative capacity to desire?" and concludes, "Basically, that is precisely what I think blackness is. I want it to be my constant study" (p. 778). Dubois, writing during, of, and in the Jim Crow South, and Moten, writing during, of, and in today's political climate and context along with King, can be put in dialogue with Durkheim and his contemporaries, Messner and Rosenfeld, specifically through his concept of anomie and their Institutional Anomie Theory (IAT). In this chapter, I focus on the theoretical implications of this dialogue: a conversation concerning the subject's aim(s) related to desire – that which is hoped and hoped against – and anomie – normlessness evident through a disruption of means to achieve culturally endorsed social goals (i.e., objects of desire), based on the conception that humans have a natural inclination to perpetually attempt to satiate an endless "capacity for feeling" (Durkheim, 1960, p. 252). Specifically, I highlight the implications of this dialogue for the conceptual development of American Dream concept of IAT and its power in explaining violent crime.

IAT suggests that anomic conditions result in institutional imbalances of power. These imbalances are due, in part, to the cultural impetus of the American Dream as a dominant societally desired goal. In these anomic conditions, individuals develop alternative means to achieve societal goals, including crime. Anomie theories continue to have empirical support and have been refined through critique and consistent study (Applin & Messner, 2015; Muftić, 2006). For IAT, I argue that the discourse on the ontology of blackness and the Black subject is necessary. Through conceptual refinement of the American Dream, IAT can better achieve the goal of understanding the nexus of culture and structure in the quest to explain and predict violence. This American Dream concept has been defined as consisting of four cultural values: achievement, individualism, universalism, and the fetishism of money and has been measured mostly in economic terms or terms of accumulation, with some studies expanding its operationalization to include a greater range of economic measures including career and job positions (Muftić, 2006). While the American Dream concept as traditionally operationalized has been used to test IAT through cross-national empirical analysis, in several studies, this relationship has found limited support for African Americans (Cernkovich, Giordano, & Rudolph, 2000). This reinforces a need for a greater conceptual development and assessment of the ways in which social stratification of race based on Dubois and Moten's conception.

In this chapter, I start by discussing anomie and the Institutional Anomie and its theoretical components. I continue by discussing the project of conceptual development. I rely on insights from work on the conceptual development of state power chiefly from work in political science and argue for how bringing in the state may help with the continued development of IAT. Building on this focus on the state, I consider the ontological turn toward blackness and the insights from the phenomenology of whiteness. While likely insights from this conversation apply to all aspect of IAT, I focus chiefly on the polity/state aspects of IAT and the political nature of race and its relationship to the "American Dream." I go on to consider how the South may be helpful for the continued study of this relationship given what some describe to be a culture of violence that has shaped structure and the meaning, that is, the ontology of blackness. Ultimately, I conclude with a discussion on how interdisciplinary insights on the state and state power, critical insights from race work, and the conceptual assessment of the American Dream concept advance IAT for the study of violence.

INSTITUTIONAL ANOMIE AND THE AMERICAN DREAM

IAT is considered to be a macro-level theory of crime that focuses on social systems. Specifically, IAT gives attention to "the prevailing cultural and social structural patterns that are linked together and manifested in the major social institutions of society" (Applin & Messner, 2015, p. 37). This theory recognizes the pressures of desire and describes the complex relationship between social institutions and culture. Central to this theory is the desire to achieve the American Dream and its role in creating environments that lead to crime. In this section, I highlight the key claims of IAT as an important theory, but with room to grow more refined and studies using it more analytically powerful in the study of violence.

Anomie Theory and the Culture and Structure Nexus

Durkheim (1960) developed anomie based on the view that humans have a natural inclination to perpetually attempt to satiate our endless "capacity for feeling" (p. 252). These feelings, in the form of desires and passions, are to be managed by society, particularly the state, through agreement of "basic values and behavioral norms derived from their cultural heritage and belief systems" including the law (Tenhouten, 2016, p. 468). As societies progress from simple to more complex, the rules guiding individual behavior shift and create a sense of normlessness or anomie – "a condition of inadequate moral norms to guide and control the actions of people and groups in the interests of the total social system" (Olsen, 1965, p. 41). In highly anomic conditions, as passions remain and to satiate their urges, individuals may be more likely to display deviant behaviors perceived as amoral, harmful, and even criminal. Durkheim focused on elevated levels of suicide in highly anomic environments.

Building on Durkheim's work, Robert Merton advanced anomie by specifying how structure interacts with culture to generate deviant behavior (Bernburg, 2002; Messner, 1988). Also building on Durkheim's theory of anomie, and complementary to Merton's use, Messner and Rosenfeld's theory of IAT suggested that when there is a mismatch between the dominant societal goals, considered in their theorization to be "The American Dream," and the means to attain those goals, there is an increased likelihood of crime. The disjuncture between goals and means to obtain them leads to crime because of the pervasiveness of economic-based sociocultural norms in other social institutions thereby weakening their effectiveness for socialization and control (Applin & Messner, 2015).

Hughes, Schaible, and Gibbs (2015, p. 102) advance Messner and Rosenfeld's (2007, p. 67) contribution and highlight the relationship between the American Dream and anomie; they maintain that it is:

> [...] characterized by a "distinctive cultural ethos" with a "value complex [...] conducive to an anomic environment" in which normative restraints lose their efficacy and "anything goes."

As a more grounded concept, The American Dream is a dominant cultural orientation that values individualism, the fetishism of money, achievement, and universalism (Hughes et al., 2015). In anomic conditions, "technical expediency" becomes the focus and deviance may be one expedient way to the American Dream (Applin & Messner, 2015, p. 38).

Messner and Rosenfeld (2001) focus on four institutions and their arrangement which they argue are components of social structures that control human behavior to "meet the basic needs of a society" (p. 65). These institutions are categorized as economic, political, familial, and educational. While they are interdependent, each institution can have their own orientation and obligations. Yet, collectively, these institutions are intended to ensure:

> (1) adaptation to the environment, (2) mobilization and deployment of resources for the achievement of collective goals, and (3) the socialization of members to accept the society's fundamental normative patterns. (Messner & Rosenfeld, 2001, p. 65)

The economy specifically is responsible for providing ways in which society can meet "basic material requirements for human existence" (Messner & Rosenfeld, 2001, p. 65).

In Bernburg's (2002) theoretical assessment of IAT and its relationship with Merton's use of anomie, he argues that:

> Institutional-Anomie theory explains how the anomic culture emerges and how it is sustained and amplified. The strategy of this approach is linking the emergence of this cultural pattern with institutional arrangements, and therefore offering an important link to social change… In contrast, Merton's theory is guided by a notion of people making choices in the context of their socially structured realities (Nee & Brinton, 1998). Merton specifies the objective conditions that translate norms and goals – culture – into crime. Merton's approach is thus more suitable in specifying how anomic culture – given in Merton but explained in Institutional-Anomie theory – creates pressure to innovate because of incompatibility of culture with people's objective conditions. (p. 739)

Bernburg highlights the important integration of culture in criminological theory. Messner and others contending with anomie have worked to mediate the structure versus culture debate with an integration of the culture and its role in shaping the institutional balances of power (Applin & Messner, 2015; Chamlin & Cochran, 1995; Messner, Raffalovich, & Shrock, 2013). With Merton's consideration of culture as a mostly macrosocial construct, building on this work, some cultural psychologists have considered culture as a combination of macro- and micro-level elements, which could expand the reach and scope of IAT. Further, Matsumoto, Kudoh, and Takeuch (1996) distinguish culture as being objective or subjective and dynamic. They consider the objective aspects as factors on the macro-level including "social institutions, physical artifacts, architecture, and the like" (p. 79) while the subjective aspects are "the psychological, introspective aspects of our lives and ourselves that reflect culture. These include our values, attitudes, beliefs, opinions, and the like" (p. 79).

Important for the cultural component of IAT is the recent research on cultural toolkits that helps to better what culture is and how it functions. This shift has been from culture simply as a set of beliefs to culture as a type of Anne Swidler's (1986) "cultural toolkit" model that considers "culture in action". Swidler (1986) brings attention to the fact that power dynamics and social stratification can shape the access to specific cultural toolkits and the specific "pieces" of their cultural repertoires (p. 277). Sampson and Bean (2006) provide a further detailed description of this more advanced conception of culture and outline how in this new model, culture can be understood as: (1) intersubjective versus personal, (2) performative versus authentic, (3) affective-cognitive versus value-rational, (4) relational versus consensual, and (5) worldmaking versus a worldview. Lee and Ousey (2010) and Lee, Becker, and Ousey (2014) use this model to evaluate some of the cultural factors related to violence, specifically honor, related to the Southern culture of violence whereby they consider violence as part of a developed toolkit in the south built to protect honor and one's economic stability.

While not directly using the cultural toolkit model, but still important for the cultural arm of the IAT, Applin and Messner attempt to contend with the power/structure aspects of culture by considering gender and IAT. In the aptly titled *Her American Dream,* they argue that:

> Criminological implications of gender are not ignored in Crime and the American Dream, but they are considered only in the context of compatibility of the arguments advanced therein, with the widely observed gender differential in crime – the lower levels of criminal involvement on the part of females than males for most types of offenses. Gender from this vantage point is implicitly treated simply as a demographic attribute, similar to other demographic attributes such as race that can condition the interpretation of the American Dream and influence the level of participation in different institutional roles.

It is important to note that, in addition to gender, race may operate similarly as a more static demographic factor. Continuing their critique, they now emphasize the American Dream:

> Indeed, a defining characteristic of the American Dream is allegedly its universalistic character. Messner and Rosenfeld (2007) observed that "with few exceptions, everyone is encouraged to aspire to social ascent, and everyone is susceptible to evaluation on the basis of individual achievements. (p. 69)

Yet, despite this assumed universalistic character:

> women allegedly interpret the American Dream differently than do men, and their performance of institutional roles does not conform to the pattern associated with economic dominance in the institutional balance of power. This seems rather curious at first glance. In what sense is it possible or fruitful to speak of a prevailing cultural ethos such as the American Dream and an institutional balance of power tilted toward the economy, if the corresponding characterizations do not apply to more than half of the population? Surely this cannot be dismissed as involving merely a "few exceptions."

With this in mind, the importance of reengaging with the concept of the American Dream is clear when attempting to broadly understand crime, especially as it relates to the few (or many) exceptions of those who ascribe to it.

THE AMERICAN DREAM, CONCEPTUAL DEVELOPMENT, AND THE STUDY OF THE STATE

IAT is a well-developed and sophisticated theory for the study of violence, but as noted in my discussion above, can benefit from continued assessment. Writing from political science, Collier and Adcock along with Gerring provide a helpful discussion that helps to focus on systematic ways to evaluate concepts. I briefly detail their contributions and highlight the American Dream concept as a case for assessment. Continuing with the contributions from the political science discipline, I argue, via Mann and Soifer, how the concept of state power can be beneficial to IAT. I go on to discuss how the study of the state power itself is important for the furtherance of reconceptualizing the American Dream and the material and structural conditions that inform its conceptualization at a subnational level.

Purposive Conceptualization

Adcock and Collier (2001) note that researchers have to "make complex choices about linking concepts to observations, that is, about connecting ideas with facts" basically asking, "Do the observations meaningfully capture the ideas contained in the concepts?" (p. 529). Writing in *American Political Science Review*, they develop a model for a shared method for the evaluation and measurement of concepts for both qualitative and quantitative methodologies. Although an important discussion, their relevant insight here is their model for the stages of developing concepts. They outline four levels of conceptualization and measures that inform the other, I focus on the first two. (1) the background of the concept, "the broad constellation of meaning and understandings associated with a given concept" and (2) systematized concept, "a specific formulation of a concept used by a given scholar or group of scholars; commonly involves an explicit definition." Concerning this background concept, they suggest that while "background concept usually provides a relatively stable matrix" that "It evolves over time, as new understandings are developed and old ones are revised or fall from use." They go on to caution that "scholars should present specific arguments, linked to the goals and context of their research, that justify their particular choices" (Adcock & Collier, 2001, pp. 530–531). Now, while the American Dream has been justified in its use cross-nationally either in more or less economic terms or in broader terms of attainment and success, current theorizations have failed to adequately adopt context sensitive measures of the American Dream. Furthermore, studies of the American Dream in relation to IAT have failed to contend with the material findings related to the proposed relationship between the American Dream and crime and refine the concept in meaningful ways. This failure seems to provide evidence of a need to revisit the core concept of the American Dream, specifically including its background.

In their own work, Messner and Rosenfeld note that James Truslow Adams coined the term, the "American Dream." In his book, *The Epic of America*, Adams (1931), defined it as:

> [...] that dream of a land in which life should be better and richer and fuller for every man, with opportunity for each according to his ability or achievement. It is a difficult dream for the European upper classes to interpret adequately, and too many of ourselves have grown weary and mistrustful of it. It is not a dream of motor cars and high wages merely, but a dream of a social order in which each man and each woman shall be able to attain to the fullest stature of which they are innately capable, and be recognized by others for what they are, regardless of the fortuitous circumstances of birth or position. (p. 317)

This definition, understood in Adcock and Collier's terms as the "background" of the concept, seems opposed to or is not adequately translated in Messner and Rosenfeld's definition, which centers on wealth and financial success. Here, while Adams' and Messner and Rosenfeld's definitions both share the motive to achieve, Adams seems to imagine something beyond the mere material and wealth-based objects of desire. This aspect is important as it undermines the potential reach and theoretical power of the American Dream concept as well as its potential power in the process of socialization.

In discussing these two opposing, but related, conceptualizations of the American Dream, Smith argues that the more contemporary definition used by Messner and Rosenfeld as central to IAT is more related to neoliberalism. She goes on to argue that as Messner and Rosenfeld (2013) define the dream as "the commitment to the goals of monetary success, to be pursued by all members of society, under conditions of open, individual competition" (p. 126), similarly, neoliberalism:

> [...] proposes that human well-being can be best advanced by liberating individual entrepreneurial freedoms and skills within an institutional framework characterized by strong private property rights, free markets, and free trade. (Harvey, 2005, p. 2)

At first review, this conception of the dream, focused on the individual, contradicts the findings that suggest Blacks as opposed to White Americans and to a degree Asian and Latinx American are more likely to hold more collectivist oriented political and social ideologies as opposed to individualist ones (Greenwald, Smith, Sriram, Bar-Anan, & Nosek, 2009; Pratt & Allen, 2015). Given this, one must contend with the claim of the universality of this dream given the material conditions of certain groups, but more pressing, one must consider the missing aspects in this dream given the neoliberal bent of its conceptualization beyond that of Adams. While this chapter doesn't sort out the "proper" Dream, I argue that through revisiting the concept we can get a better understanding of crime. Specifically, later in this chapter, I contend that through an ontological turn that engages with historical contexts and the lived experience and conditions of individuals – people who may recognize the dream differently or imagine it more broadly because of structural, cultural, or systematically oppressive influences – IAT can be more powerful.

Revisiting this the American Dream's background, we begin to contend with this paradox:

> [...] proper concepts are needed to formulate a good theory, but we need a good theory to arrive at the proper concepts [...] The paradox is resolved by a process of approximation: the better our concepts, the better the theory we can formulate with them, and in turn, the better the concepts available for the next, improved theory. (Kaplan, 1964, p. 53)

The American Dream concept is a poor approximation of Adams. This poor approximation is not a sin as this concept has had a great deal of utility, yet, as Adcock and Collier note, a concept can be refined by examining other theories that rely on this concept. One way to better approach the concept is to examine what makes a "good" concept based on this knowledge of the background.

What Makes a Concept "Good"?

The adequacy of a concept is paramount, especially in theories of crime given their focus on behaviors that lead to harm or death. And, as relayed by Adcock and Collier, the research is at the center of the conceptual development decisions. Recognizing the researcher is important given,

> Researchers' lenses are critical to every aspect of a study from defining the problem to interpreting and reporting the findings. A significant component of criminology activism is broadening the diversity of criminologists to provide a lens that more accurately reflects what we study (crime and the responses to it). (Belknap, 2015, p. 5)

In the endeavor to clarify the American Dream, Gerring proves important. He provides eight attributes of a good concept: familiarity, resonance, parsimony, coherence, differentiation, depth, theoretical utility, and field utility. And, when contending with Messner and Rosenfeld in conversation with Adams, the American Dream concept as is could benefit from increased familiarity, resonance, depth, as well as theoretical and field utility. I won't spend time on each of these in the interests of space, yet, tackling each these can be done through an ontological turn, which I discuss later. The American Dream concept can benefit from a re-engagement with the three aspects of concept formation: the extension – the phenomenon to be defined; intention – the properties of the phenomenon; and ultimately, the label or term for the phenomenon and its attributes (Gerring, 2016). The central question here is: "from what vantage point is the concept developed and through which lens are the properties of that concept seen?" In this case, the American Dream concept, as I have shown, has a neoliberal bent, which, given its ahistorical development, obscures the basis of desire – which is central to anomie – within a neoliberal and capitalist political and economic context.

What may be necessary for the advancement of the American Dream concept may be a phenomenological approach as it grips with "the shared meanings that govern discursive practices and social relations situated within a particular time- and space-bound context" (Ahmed & Sil, 2012, p. 942). This necessity is highlighted by the lack of deep qualitative examinations that contend with the subnational variation of the American Dream as used in IAT. Particularly for the subnational variation aspect of the critique, research on the state and state power may be beneficial theory development, particularly for the polity aspect. This body of work may also be methodological beneficial.

Introducing the State and Adam's Conception

Contending with the role of the state is important for several reasons. In one regard, understanding the role of the state in ensuring rights that feed into the polity may more deeply highlight social stratification and power. As it relates to the American Dream, engaging with the state addresses in part Adam's definition of the American Dream. Chiefly understanding the state presents an opportunity to provide historical context. In Collier and Adcock's terms, the state presents an opportunity to re-engage with the background of the concept.

Mann offers a productive definition of the state for the purposes of IAT while Soifer, building on him, extends the definition and provides a methodological insight that anomie theorists have acknowledged but not considered, the subnational variation of the state. The state's power stems, in part, from its legal mandate and in the American context, its contract with its citizens. Mann, using a definition developed by Weber, describes the state as being composed of a: (1) differentiated set of institutions, (2) that have a central orienting point, (3) with a defined territory, (4) in which it has the ability to make rules protected by a threat of physical violence (Mann, 1984).

Yet, Soifer, recognizing the universalistic logic embedded in the study of the state, extends points 3 and 4 of Weber's definition by highlighting the notion of subnational variation. Soifer (2008) refines the concept of the state and offers that "the capabilities of the state vary subnationally: the State is not homogeneously powerful throughout the national territory; its reach is uneven over territory and over societal actors" (p. 242). From this reevaluation, future work can better consider another layer in the matrix of institutions that may be weakened under the American Dream. In essence, the law, a project of the state, influences and is influenced by and radiates into the social problem of violence. Theoretically, the monopoly on violence by the state and the lack of immediate dismantling of the blockages to accessing the state put in place by residents demonstrates the state's complicity and failure in creating unequal conditions for citizens by race as well as class and gender and, in the langue of culture, may shape cultural toolkits, which may include a likelihood to use violence (Lee & Ousey, 2010; Miller, 2010).

Overall, while the American Dream can be viewed as a fixture of Neo-Liberal orientation, by engaging with the background concept given evidence from the measure and systematized development of the concept, a more refined American Dream can be deployed. Along with this, by engaging with the state and state power I have shown both how it is a model and a crucial factor to consider. The depth, theoretical and field utility of the American Dream is broadened and opens a world of research that allows for the exploration of subnational variations of the concept, especially given how Adams features in his definition the maintenance of "a dream of a social order," which arguably implicates the state and other social institutions that maintain order. The state and its law and power seem to be important. In addition, as I will discuss after the next section, a holistic ontological turn may capture the historical aspects and the broader reaching concept of the American Dream that may be useful for future studies using IAT to examine violence.

THE LEGACY OF RACE AND THE ONTOLOGICAL TURN

> Slavery had established a measure of man and a ranking of life and worth that has yet to be undone. If slavery persists as an issue in the political life of black America, it is not because of an antiquarian obsession with bygone days or the burden of a too-long memory, but because black lives are still imperiled and devalued by a racial calculus and a political arithmetic that

> were entrenched centuries ago. This is the afterlife of slavery – skewed life chances, limited access to health and education, premature death, incarceration, and impoverishment.

In the above quote, Saidiyah Hartman connects the past with the present by connecting the legacy of slavery to present-day conditions of Black Americans today. Most poignant about her observation is the notion that the harms of slavery have yet to be undone. The interrogation of this claim and how it functions in shaping desire at a basic level and the American Dream at a theoretical level is at the center of my argument for the advancement of IAT.

In another work, Steven Messner (of Messner and Rosenfeld) and his co-authors, Robert Baller and Matthew Zevenbergen, have attempted to contend with the legacy of slavery by examining the link between lynching and subsequent rates of violent crime. They ultimately find, that their measure of lynching inconsistently related to Black homicide (Messner, Baller, & Zevenbergen, 2005). They consider that these findings may be due to historical conditions where "lynching represented an extraordinary instance of 'lack of access to formal law,' which in turn fostered 'self-help' cultural adaptations conducive to lethal violence" (Messner et al., 2005, p. 649). And, that while they didn't find a significant relationship between lynching and White homicide in general, "when white homicide offending…is disaggregated by race of victim and by homicide circumstance, a positive effect of lynching emerges for white-on-black argument homicides" (Messner et al., 2005, p. 649). Petersen and Ward (2015) build on the work of Messner and colleagues by bridging the gap between lynching and contemporary homicide and find that rates of lynching are significantly related to the co-location of rates of civil rights era assaults and ultimately contemporary rates of homicide. Together, this work indicates the vital role that the legacy of racial violence may play in the colocation of violent crime through socialization.

Geoff Ward (2015), building on this body of work on the legacy of lynching and anti-civil rights era violence argues that criminological theory must "generate knowledge useful to interventions into race- linked (dis-)accumulation and (dis)advantage generations in the making" (p. 308). He continues by highlighting Jerome Miller's (1988) speech in his acceptance of the American Society of Criminology's August Vollmer Award:

> As [criminological] theories have grown more "realistic," and methodology more complicated, criminologists themselves have grown more detached and disconnected from the "stuff" of their studies – offenders, their families, their children, their neighborhoods, their lives. As a result, our prisons and reform schools are filled with *fabricated aliens* made more so by those who should know better, but who *insufficiently understand the subjects of their research* outside narrow methodological parameters, or highly controlled settings which demean and impoverish human experience. (p. 13, emphasis original)

Key here is the subject at the center of the problem. Understanding the subject of study, in particular, the social construction of the subject itself is the overbearing point of my project here, central to the critique of IAT. While Ward argues for a need to consider state organized race crime, which I argue is important here through the inclusion of the state and state power, pressing is the need to examine the objective conditions of the subject and how blackness itself, as a creation of state and culture via colonialization, impact both how we imagine desire and the expanse of its impact. To truly do this, what is necessary is two-pronged: (1) consider the ontology of blackness as a creation that creates meaning and (2) the phenomenon of whiteness, which itself relates to the meaning of blackness as practiced through avoidance or anti-blackness.

Orienting from a Phenomenology of Whiteness and the Ontological Turn: A Case for Blackness

> It is important to remember that blackness is defined here in terms of social relationality rather than identity; thus blackness incorporates subjects normatively defined as black, the relations among blacks, whites, and others, and the practices that produce racial difference. Blackness marks a social relationship of dominance and abjection and potentially one of redress and emancipation; it is a contested figure at the very center of social struggle. (Saidiya Hartman, 1997, pp. 56–57)

Ontology is the study of meaning, in this case, the focus is on the meaning of blackness and the implications for Black people and ultimately all subjects studied as it relates to crime. Here in practice, the ontological turn is one that calls for a looking back at the object/subject of focus in order to rebuild theoretical assumptions related to desire. Some argue that drawing back to the ontology of the object, that is, the ontological turn, is "politically suspect, retrograde move that, in its pursuit of objects and matter, tunes out key questions concerning the social, economics and history" (Thompson, 2017, p. 266). Yet, related to Hartman above, Ahmed (2007) in her project argues that "Whiteness could be described as an ongoing and unfinished history, which orientates bodies in specific directions, affecting how they 'take up' space" (p. 150). She goes on to note the importance of orientations in that they are "…about how we begin, how we proceed from 'here'"(Ahmed, 2007, p. 151). Given this, the objective of this section is not to determine what blackness is, but to highlight what the potential through refocusing and given the theoretical arguments of how both blackness and whiteness in relation to each other may situation desire and specifically the American Dream differently given a body of work that demonstrates the importance of race.

Cernkovich et al. (2000), in their piece where they explore the relationship between the American Dream and orientation to crime by race, found that while Black Americans had a higher commitment to American Dream as conceptualized, doesn't significantly relate to crime rates for the same group. In a more recent study that centers race and racialized experiences and crime where the construct the American Dream concept as measured by economic and career success, they find evidence for racial aggression and strain relates to the likelihood of committing crime (Burt, Lei, & Simons, 2017). They suggest citing a body of evidence, that while:

> Racial disparities in street crime have long been a focus of criminological scholarship…and while differences are vastly magnified by biases in the criminal justice system (Spohn, 2015; Tonry, 1995), evidence from a range of sources indicates that African Americans engage in higher rates of street crime than do Whites. (e.g., Elliott, 1994; Hawkins, Laub, Lauritsen, & Cothern, 2000; Piquero & Brame, 2008)

While I use this finding and study as a point of departure, it is important, given Ward's critique, to problematize the findings. Ward notes that:

> [...] the "Blumstein method" (Blumstein, 1982; Garland, Spohn, & Wodahl, 2008) calculates that around 80 percent of racial disparity in incarceration is explained by legitimate legal factors. This reassuring discovery is rooted in a false binary where "legal factors" (arrest, conviction, and incarceration) are taken to be race-neutral, notwithstanding the contradictions of Clyde Kenard, George Zimmerman, and others. While Blumstein and others stress concern about the unexplained proportion, the remaining 20 percent of the problem, others appear to round up the white-washed statistic of legitimated inequality, such as the criminologist Wilbanks (1987) declaring racial inequality in justice administration an outright myth.

Continuing with Burt et al. (2017) who considered what they title interpersonal racial discrimination (IRD) with violence, they maintain that:

> Over the past decade, more than 15 studies have investigated this topic, and without exception, have shown that IRD increases the risk of offending among racial minority youth (e.g., Burt & Simons, 2015; Martin et al., 2011; Simons et al., 2006; Unnever, Cullen, Mathers, McClure, & Allison, 2009) and, as a pernicious risk factor unique to racial minorities, contributes to racial disparities in offending. Despite compelling evidence that IRD persists and is criminogenic, research has primarily focused on the short-term effects of IRD on offending, invariably among adolescents. Consequently, there is a gap in our understanding of the longer term effects of IRD on offending among African Americans. (p. 939)

Addressing this in part, ultimately, they find that discrimination relates to levels of offending, but what of White offending, the broader cultural context and historical basis for discrimination, and the grounding of discrimination based on race into the more specific, but more damning antiblackness born of slavery itself? While Burt et al. focus on Black perceptions and socialization, missing is a consideration of a larger apparatus of socialization and causal relationships, important, but likely beyond the scope of their study.

In this important, but limited study, the policy suggestions are right:

> [...] that supportive social and institutional relationships are malleable areas where interventions could make a difference. Our model points to the value of designing institutions specifically to address – provide support for – individuals (and groups) who, due to various disadvantages, experience adversities that, for self-protective reasons, have led them to mistrust such institutions and expect to be mistreated. (e.g., Anderson, 1999; Burt et al., 2017, p. 968; Feagin, 2010)

Burt et al. miss the opportunity to engage with this notion, even when discussing the limitations of their project. They recognize the discrimination is perceptually based, subjective, yet, again, over and above the perceptual is the materiality of the historical pain of existing in the hold of a ship, in the brutalizing clutches of the American state supporting slavery, the failure of the 13th, 14th, and 15th amendments, the challenge for their enforcement in the Jim Crow era, and the list continues. Burt's pause can be read as problematic, as a refusal to go further, or inability to. They acknowledge adversity without naming the system that caused the adversities and stop short of calling for redress for this harm. Instead, they offer that what is needed is assistance to come out of disadvantage by those who are disadvantaged and for them to remedy past harm through "institutions" that *still* harm (rather than the sole expectation of harm). The end in mentioning "qualitative studies could be particularly useful in this regard" referencing the need for studies that consider the evolution of African American culture and parental ability to help individuals cope, rather than highlighting the broader political implication, reinvestment in the equalization of Blacks and reckoning with the initial harm.

They conclude with:

> This work points to the stark racist causes and racial consequences of our carceral state, including "civic death" (Gottschalk, 2015) or "social incapacitation [as] a process of dehumanization by which punitive social control becomes an instrument that prevents marginalized populations from *becoming productive citizens who can feel dignity and affirmation from institutions of socialization*." (Rios, 2015, p. 62)

What does it mean to be productive and what affirmation looks like and from whose eyes is this productivity seen and beyond consequences of the carceral state, what lingering role does the abject conditions of slavery have on this outcome? While these are large questions, the function or process of blockage can collectively be understood as anti-blackness. The important relationship they highlight, one of means and goals, one central to the theoretical formulation of anomie – a duality that for some groups is consistent with structural place of their lived experiences – is yet absent in their analysis.

The need to deconstruct and reconsider implicit the assumption of what it means to be productive for society and self is more evident when we approach the work with ontology on the mind as:

> [...] ontologies bear the traces of their historical moment – even when those ontologies "withdraw" from mediation. It is an effect and vehicle of sedimented contextual knowledges, which "constitutes that which it presumes to merely apprehend." (Thompson, 2017, p. 269)

This leads us back to evaluating American Dream's static nature in theory given its continued economic bent that lacks a critical restructuring through a consideration of blockages and the potential feedback loop of intergenerationally shifting dominant desires; further, one must reconsider this dream and the role it has in shaping when violence in an acceptable tool for self-help. The legacy of the dynamic of servitude with all its trauma seems to remain. By understanding the historical comorbidity of types of violence that seem to inform other social processes, in this case lynching impacting identity and status of Blacks, anti-civil rights violence impacting the very law and the attention (or lack) that lead to civil rights "successes" to "inner city" and Black dominated homicide rates shaping perception and political discourse around policing and the law more broadly.

The individual level effect of White supremacy and anti-blackness based on law and property ownership provides a basis for understanding the role of class in further enhancing White supremacy and its influence. White strain taps into race and the way discrimination can lead to crime on an individual level, in criminology, there is a poor construction of the meaning of this supremacy in practice under the law. State failure helps to recognize and highlight this as the failure of the state to specific populations can likely be chiefly boiled down to the racial animus behind achievement. Even with now White groups, the proximity to blackness and anti-blackness has helped to solidify a type of strain felt consistently by certain sectors but moderated by proximity to blackness in phenotype.

Reorienting from Whiteness to Blackness

The critique of what it means to be productive and aspire to the American Dream is neither an argument for the incompleteness of Black people nor their ability to desire. Yet, what remains important here is that blackness as a subject related to Black people and White people and others itself is incomplete. Through the ontological turn and a consideration of the meaning of blackness as Black and as White in relation to each other, one must exhume the repressed memory of America's body politic to be exhumed. The seriousness of Ahmed's claim on whiteness cannot be overstated:

> [...] whiteness is something that does, that reifies and orientates: it is a protocol that produces and orders spatial-temporal relations, and enhances and limits a body's affective capacities in relation to its surroundings. Thus racialization is not simply of "the social" and "the human," but that through which "the human" and "the social" is (re)produced. (Thompson, 2017, p. 269)

In the same vein one must contend with what has been produced through this orientation. At one end, blackness as a pathological effect of being and on the other, a historical negation or basic overassumptive inference of what it is to desire as Black in society.

> In talking about sound and its basic qualities and interpretations of sound as it relates to race, Thompson notes that "ontology requires resituating amongst its co-productive relations with the social world – with culture, materialism, history, politics, science, technology, epistemology, aesthetics, experience and perception. Situating rather than simply dismissing sonic ontologies enables us to ask how "the nature of the sonic" is determined – what grounds the sonic ground – while remaining open to how it might be heard otherwise. (Thompson, 2017, p. 278)

In this case, the same must be done for desire and blackness. One attempt at contending with the ontological turn is the reconsideration of culture. It is through and with culture that comes a determination of what society accepts as real and material, and through cultural practices this acceptance is recreated. Ahmed continues in many respects speaking in line with Swidler's toolkit and highlights how an orientation lead to what could be called a type of cultural toolkit.

> [...] we inherit the reachability of some objects, those that are "given" to us, or at least made available to us, within the "what" that is around. I am not suggesting here that "whiteness" is one such "reachable object," but that whiteness is an orientation that puts certain things within reach. By objects, we would include not just physical objects, but also styles, capacities, aspirations, techniques, habits. Race becomes, in this model, a question of what is within reach, what is available to perceive and to do "things" with.

So, what happens given a White orientation? Moten offers that "blackness, as that which operates 'at the nexus of the social and the ontological, the historical and the essential'", and that

> [...] blackness is paraontological in that lived experiences of blackness both enact and escape the assignment of blackness to social death and non-being [...] it is escaped and it is what escapes. (Ahmed, 2007, p. 154)

So, given the orientation of whiteness and this ontology and description of blackness and its place, if taking these claims seriously, one must explore desire, at least in part, the escape or the moving away from blackness, that is, anti-blackness as an aspect of American Dream's goal. One important insight specifically related to the American Dream and wealth is highlighted best here through Marx (1973):

> Now, wealth is on one side a thing, realized in things, material products, which a human being confronts as subject; on the other side, as value, wealth is merely command over alien labour not with the aim of ruling, but with the aim of private consumption, etc. It appears in all forms in the shape of a thing, be it an object or be it a relation mediated through the object, which is external and accidental to the individual. (p. 487)

Yet, given the history of Black people as objects chasing, in some respect, the ability to be an individual, highlights the core of the American Dream's concept frailty and its lack of attention to the desire and wealth as, in part, moving against blackness as an object. The colonial gaze simultaneously cast blackness as infinitely Other but precisely objectified. In establishing that the constitutive act of civil society is the process of excluding blackness to ward off social death, he indirectly implicates blackness (Hartman, 1997).

CONCLUSION

In this chapter, I start by immediately drawing our attention to the duality that Du Bois and King recognized that Black Americans have had to contend with – (1) a constant internal struggle of existing through the eyes of others while attempting to maintain one's own identity and (2) consistently battling systematic oppression from without (Du Bois, 1903; King, 1967). Moten further fixes our attention to how these conditions reinforce a need for deeper study and critique of race in theory. In introducing IAT, I highlight similarities and points where an adjusted lens can be helpful for its theoretical refinement. I go on to discuss the importance of considering what makes it good and consider the background of the American Dream in Adam's *Epic of America*. Finally, I end with a discussion on where to begin to deconstruct the American Dream by focusing on the ontological turn and insights from work that looks at race as a socializing phenomenon. Overall, my goal here has been to call for a stepping back and reimagine of how the American Dream may be conceived given the already significant body of work on IAT with mixed findings for the race American Dream and crime association.

What is a more integrated IAT? I can't be certain, but at its center, a refined IAT is historically grounded with concepts that accurately reflect the lived experiences and pervasive, pernicious, and piercing dominant social desires that make up the American Dream. One way to do this is through understanding and deconstructing the subjects of study and desires. More immediately, future work should begin to interrogate the conditioning power of the American Dream concept at a subnational level between generations. In addition, future work should highlight the role of the state in shaping access to an individual and collective conceptions of it. Overall, though, entering into the study of violence with a refined lens that directs attention toward the subject and contends with the dynamic nature of the subject and how identity, specifically racial identity along with gender, continues to have legacy effects on desires and crime.

Work that relies on an updated model of culture akin to Swidler's toolkit model will also be helpful for contending with the culture and structure debate. Specifically, recent studies evaluating the Southern Culture of Violence have had promising insights for the ways in which culture shapes perception and reception and how they both relate to the perceived need to use violence to protect affronts against one's honor (Lee & Ousey, 2010). In line with this, in order to engage with the vestiges of slavery, including the ways in which it shapes race and society today, more in-depth studies that use interpretive and grounded ethnographic methods and analysis of the southeast United States are crucial given its particular relationship with slavery. In addition, future work must engage with moments of significant social change, specifically those associated with the law. The mobility of culture through large historical movements from and social movement in the South may be beneficial for understanding the challenges in approaching the American Dream that may impact groups today. While work has begun to engage more intentionally with the intersections of race and gender, theories of crime must be adapted in the face of this work. Finally, as I have attempted to show here, "There is a 'long history of public dishonor and ritualized humiliation of African American by Euro-Americans' that has caused blacks to develop their peerless worldview" (Hagan, Shedd, & Payne, 2005, p. 382; Unnever & Gabbidon, 2011, p. 167) and only through continued study of the dynamics of blackness and its relations can our theories of crime become more refined.

ACKNOWLEDGMENTS

Financial support was provided by National Science Foundation Graduate Research Fellowship Program under Grant No. 13218406, the UC Office of the President HBCU Fellowship, and the University of California, Irvine Eugene Cota-Robles Fellowship. Any opinions, findings, and conclusions or recommendations expressed in this material are those of the author and do not necessarily reflect the views of the National Science Foundation. Additional thanks to James Pratt, Sr. for comments on earlier drafts.

REFERENCES

Adams, J. T. (1931). *The epic of America*. Boston, MA: Little, Brown.

Adcock, R., & Collier, D. (2001). Measurement validity: A shared standard for qualitative and quantitative research. *American Political Science Review*, *95*(3), 529–546. https://doi.org/10.1017/S0003055401003100

Ahmed, A., & Sil, R. (2012). When multi-method research subverts methodological pluralism—Or, why we still need single-method research. *Perspectives on Politics*, *10*(4), 935–953. https://doi.org/doi:10.1017/S1537592712002836

Ahmed, S. (2007). A phenomenology of whiteness. *Feminist Theory*, *8*(2), 149–167. https://doi.org/10.1177/1464700107078139

Anderson, E. (1999). *Code of the street: Decency, violence, and the moral life of the inner city*. New York, NY: Norton.

Applin, S., & Messner, S. F. (2015). Her American dream: Bringing gender into Institutional-Anomie theory. *Feminist Criminology*, *10*(1), 36–59. https://doi.org/10.1177/1557085114525654

Belknap, J. (2015). Activist criminology: Criminologists' responsibility to advocate for social and legal justice. *Criminology*, *53*(1), 1–22. https://doi.org/10.1111/1745-9125.12063

Bernburg, J. G. (2002). Anomie, social change and crime: A theoretical examination of institutional-anomie theory. *British Journal of Criminology*, *42*(4), 729–742. https://doi.org/10.1093/bjc/42.4.729

Blumstein, A. (1982). On the racial disproportionality of United States' prison populations. *Journal of Criminal Law & Criminology, 73*(3), 1259–1281.

Burt, C. H., Lei, M. K., & Simons, R. L. (2017). Racial discrimination, racial socialization, and crime over time: A social schematic theory model. *Criminology*, *55*(4), 938–979. https://doi.org/10.1111/1745-9125.12164

Burt, C. H., & Simons, R. L. (2015). Interpersonal racial discrimination, ethnic–racial socialization, and offending: Risk and resilience among African American females. *Justice Quarterly*, *32*, 532–570.

Cernkovich, S. A., Giordano, P. C., & Rudolph, J. L. (2000). Race, crime, and the American dream. Journal of Research in Crime and Delinquency, *37*(2), 131–170.

Cernkovich, S., Giordano, P., & Rudolph, J. (2000). *Race, crime, and the American dream.*

Chamlin, Mi. B., & Cochran, J. K. (1995). Assessing Messner and Rosenfeld's institutional anomie theory: A partial test. *Criminology*, *33*(3), 411–429. https://doi.org/10.1111/j.1745-9125.1995.tb01184.x

Du Bois, W. E. B. (1903). *The souls of black folk.* New York, NY: Dover.

Durkheim, E. (1960). *Suicide: A study in sociology*. Glencoe, IL: The Free Press.

Elliott, D. S. (1994). Serious violent offenders: Onset, developmental course, and termination. *Criminology, 32*, 1–21.

Feagin, J. R. (2010). *Racist America: Roots, current realities, and future reparations.* New York, NY: Routledge.

Garland, B. E., Spohn, C., & Wodahl, E. J. (2008). Racial disproportionality in the American prison population: Using the Blumstein method to address the critical race and justice issue of the 21st century. *Justice Policy Journal, 5*(2), 1–42.

Gerring, J. (2016). What makes a concept good? A criterial framework for understanding concept formation in the social sciences. *Polity*, *31*(3), 357–393.

Gottschalk, M. (2015). Caught: The Prison State and the Lockdown of American Politics. Princeton, NJ: Princeton University Press.

Greenwald, A. G., Smith, C. T., Sriram, N., Bar-Anan, Y., & Nosek, B. A. (2009). Implicit race attitudes predicted vote in the 2008 U.S. Presidential election. *Analyses of Social Issues and Public Policy*, *9*(1), 241–253. https://doi.org/10.1111/j.1530-2415.2009.01195.x

Hagan, J., Shedd, C., & Payne, M. R. (2005). Race, ethnicity, and youth perceptions of criminal injustice. *American sociological review*, 70(3), 381–407.

Harvey, D. (2005). *A brief history of neoliberalism.* Oxford: Oxford University Press.

Hartman, S. V. (1997). *Scenes of subjection: Terror, slavery, and self-making in nineteenth-century America.* Oxford: Oxford University Press on Demand.

Hartman, S. V. (2007), *Lose your mother: a journey along the Atlantic slave route*. New York, NY: Farrar, Straus and Giroux.

Hawkins, D. F., Laub, J. H., Lauritsen, J. L., & Cothern, L. (2000). *Race, ethnicity, and serious and violent juvenile offending*. Washington, DC: U.S. Department of Justice.

Hughes, L. A., Schaible, L. M., & Gibbs, B. R. (2015). Economic dominance, the "American dream," and homicide: A cross-national test of institutional anomie theory. *Sociological Inquiry*, *85*(1), 100–128. https://doi.org/10.1111/soin.12065

Kaplan, A. (1964). *The conduct of inquiry*. San Francisco, CA: Chandler.

King Jr, M. L. (1967/2010). Where do we go from here: Chaos or community? (Vol. 2). Beacon Press.

King, M. L. (1968). *Where do we go from here: Chaos or community?* Boston, MA: Beacon Press.

Lee, M., & Ousey, G. (2010). Reconsidering the culture and violence connection: Strategies of action in the rural south. *Journal of Interpersonal Violence*, *26*(5), 899–929. https://doi.org/10.1177/0886260510365867

Lee, M. R., Becker, S., & Ousey, G. C. (2014). The transformation of pro-violence norms: An integrative review of the literature. *Aggression and Violent Behavior*, *19*(4), 340–345. https://doi.org/10.1016/j.avb.2014.05.003

Mann, M. (1984). The autonomous power of the state: Its origins, mechanisms and results. *European Journal of Sociology*, *25*(2), 185–213.

Matsumoto, D., Kudoh, T., & Takeuchi, S. (1996). Changing patterns of individualism and collectivism in the United States and Japan. *Culture and Psychology*, *2*, 77–107. https://doi.org/10.1177/1354067X9621005

Messner, S. F. (1988). Merton's "social structure and anomie": The road not taken. *Deviant Behavior*, *9*(1), 33–53. https://doi.org/10.1080/01639625.1988.9967766

Messner, S. F., Baller, R. D., & Zevenbergen, M. P. (2005). The legacy of lynching and southern homicide. *American Sociological Review*, *70*(4), 633–655. https://doi.org/10.1177/000312240507000405

Messner, S. F., Raffalovich, L. E., & Shrock, P. (2013). Reassessing the cross-national relationship between income inequality and homicide rates: Implications of data quality control in the measurement of income distribution quality relationship between of income income inequality and homicide rates. *Implica*, *18*(4), 377–395.

Messner, S. F., & Rosenfeld, R. (2007). *Crime and the American dream* (4th ed.). Belmont, CA: Wadsworth.

Messner, S. F., & Rosenfeld, R. (2013). Crime and the American dream (5th ed.). Belmont, CA: Wadsworth Cengage Learning.

Messner, S. F., & Rosenfeld, R. (2001). Crime and the American Dream (3rd ed.). Belmont, CA: Wadsworth.

Miller, J. (1988) Address given in acceptance of the August Vollmer Award. *The Criminologist*, *13*(1), 7, 13–14, 18.

Miller, L. L. (2010). The invisible black victim: How American federalism perpetuates racial inequality in criminal justice. *Law & Society Review*, *44*(3), 805–842.

Martin, M., McCarthy, B., Conger, R., Gibbons, F., Simons, R., Cutrona, C., & Brody, G. (2011). The enduring significance of racism: Discrimination and delinquency among Black American youth. *Journal of Research on Adolescence*, *21*, 662–676.

Marx, K. (1973). In M. Nicolaus (Trans.), *Grundrisse: Foundation of the critique of political economy*. New York, NY: Vintage Press.

Moten, F. (2013). Blackness and nothingness (mysticism in the flesh). *South Atlantic Quarterly*, *112*(4), 737–780. https://doi.org/10.1215/00382876-2345261

Muftić, L. R. (2006). Advancing institutional anomie theory: A microlevel examination connecting culture, institutions, and deviance. *International Journal of Offender Therapy and Comparative Criminology*, *50*(6), 630–653. https://doi.org/10.1177/0306624X06287284

Nee, V., & Brinton, M. C. (1998), Introduction. In M. C. Brinton & V. Nee, (Eds.), *The New Institutionalism in Sociology*, (pp. xv–xix). New York: Russel Sage Foundation.

Olsen, M. E. (1965). Durkheim's two concepts of anomie. *The Sociological Quarterly*, *6*(1), 37–44.

Petersen, N., & Ward, G. (2015). The transmission of historical racial violence: Lynching, civil rights-era terror and contemporary interracial homicide. *Race and Justice*, *5*(2), 114–143. https://doi.org/10.1177/2153368714567577

Piquero, A. R., & Brame, R. (2008). Assessing the race–crime and ethnicity–crime relationship in a sample of serious adolescent delinquents. *Crime and Delinquency*, *54*, 390–422.

Pratt, J. B., & Allen, W. R. (2015). The pursuit of the public interest: Social and ideological factors influencing career choice of first-year law students. *Journal of Criminal Justice Education*, *1253*(February), 1–19. https://doi.org/10.1080/10511253.2015.1084013

Rios, V. M. (2015). Policed, punished, dehumanized: The reality for young men of color living in America. In D. Johnson, P. Y. Warren & A. Farrell (Eds.), *Deadly injustice* (pp. 59–80). New York, NY: New York University Press.

Sampson, R. J., & Bean, L. (2006). Cultural mechanisms and killing fields: A revised theory of community-level racial inequality. In R. D. Peterson, L. J. Krivo & J. Hagan. *The Many Colors of Crime: Inequalities of Race, Ethnicity and Crime in America* (pp. 8–36). New York: New York University Press.

Simons, R. L., Simons, L., Burt, C. H., Drummund, H., Stewart, E., Brody, G., … Cutrona, C. (2006). Supportive parenting moderates the effect of discrimination upon anger, hostile view of relationships, and violence among African American boys. *Journal of Health and Social Behavior*, *47*, 374–389.

Soifer, H. (2008). State infrastructural power: Approaches to conceptualization and measurement. *Studies in Comparative International Development.*, *43*, 231. Retrieved from http://link.springer.com/article/10.1007/s12116-008-9028-6

Spohn, C. (2015). Race, crime, and punishment in the twentieth and twenty-first centuries. In M. Tonry (Ed.), *Crime and justice: A review of research* (Vol. 44). Chicago, IL: University of Chicago Press.

Swidler, A. (1986). Culture in action: Symbols and strategies. *American Sociological Review*, *51*(2), 273–286. https://doi.org/10.2307/2095521

Tenhouten, W. D. (2016). Normlessness, anomie, and the emotions. *Sociological Forum*, *31*(2), 465–486. https://doi.org/10.1111/socf.12253

Thompson, M. (2017). Whiteness and the ontological turn in sound studies. *Parallax*, *23*(3), 266–282. https://doi.org/10.1080/13534645.2017.1339967

Tonry, M. (1995). Malign neglect: Race, crime, and punishment in America. New York, NY: Oxford University Press.

Unnever, J. D., Cullen, F. T., Mathers, S., McClure, T., & Allison, M. (2009). Racial discrimination and Hirschi's criminological classic: A chapter in the sociology of knowledge. *Justice Quarterly*, *26*, 377–409.

Unnever, J. D., & Gabbidon, S. L. (2011). A theory of African American offending: Race, racism, and crime. Taylor & Francis.

Ward, G. (2015). The slow violence of state organized race crime. *Theoretical Criminology*, *19*(3), 299–314. https://doi.org/10.1177/1362480614550119

Wilbanks, W. (1987). *The myth of a racist criminal justice system*. Monterey, CA: Brooks/Cole.

PART IV

ACROSS THE GLOBE

CHAPTER 11

GLOBAL TRENDS IN HOMICIDE

Mateus Rennó Santos and Alexander Testa

ABSTRACT

Purpose – *This chapter explains what is known about international homicide trends, highlights gaps in existing literature, and proposes avenues for future research that will expand understanding about international homicide.*

Design/methodology/approach – *We review extant literature on international homicide trends, and draw on data from the World Health Organization from 1990 to 2015 to identify patterns in contemporary international homicide trends.*

Findings – *We demonstrate evidence of an international homicide drop across most regions around the world. Nonetheless, the homicide decline is not a global event as several countries – particularly countries with high homicide rates – did not experience reductions in homicide during this period. The key question remains as to what the causes of changes in international homicide rates are and why many countries experience very similar reductions in homicide while a few experienced increasing violence. We propose potential explanations and suggest areas for future research.*

Originality/value – *This chapter documents an international homicide decline occurring between 1990 and 2015. We also demonstrate that homicide trends are likely influenced by factors beyond local phenomena and domestic policies since homicide rates largely track together for regions throughout the world. Accordingly, the chapter suggests potential avenues for future research that can help better explain this trend.*

Keywords: Homicide rates; cross-national; violence; crime trends; Correlates of crime; International homicide decline

Homicide and Violent Crime
Sociology of Crime, Law and Deviance, Volume 23, 199–222

ISSN: 1521-6136/doi:10.1108/S1521-613620180000023012

INTRODUCTION

Homicide is a major global public health issue that results in the death of hundreds of thousands of individuals annually (Krug, Mercy, Dahlberg, & Zwi, 2002). Between 2000 and 2012, homicides were the cause of more deaths than all wars combined, and in 2012 alone approximately half a million individuals lost their lives to homicide worldwide (United Nations Office on Drugs and Crime (UNODC), 2013). While homicide is an issue that affects individuals living in every corner of the globe, homicide rates are very unequal over time and space. According to mortality data from the World Health Organization (WHO), international homicide rates were more than 25% lower in 2015 (10.87 per 100,000 population), than they were in 1990 (14.59 per 100,000 population). Moreover, while the 2015 homicide rate in Latin America was at 20.6 per 100,000 population, it was just at 0.6 in Western Europe. In addition, a high homicide country such as El Salvador has a homicide rate 100-times larger than a low homicide country such as Switzerland (El Salvador: 53.24 vs Switzerland: 0.41 per 100,000) and almost 200-times the rate of Japan (0.28 per 100,000).

Despite being a global issue, contemporary research on international homicide trends lags behind the progress of research on crime trends of individual countries such as the United States. Indeed, extensive efforts have been made to document homicide trends in the United States (see Baumer, Vélez, & Rosenfeld, 2018; Blumstein & Rosenfeld, 1998; Blumstein & Wallman, 2006; Goldberger, Rosenfeld, & Blumstein, 2008; Levitt, 2004; Rosenfeld, Gaston, Spivak, & Irazola, 2017; Zimring, 2007). These studies have thoroughly explored US homicide trends such as the surge in violence in the late 1980s (Blumstein, 1995; Cook & Laub, 1998, 2002), the subsequent decline throughout the 1990s and 2000s (Blumstein & Wallman, 2006), and the recent uptick in homicide in recent years (Rosenfeld et al., 2017). Such research often links these trends to domestic policies that are specific to the United States, such as increasing police presence or growing incarceration rates. However, similar trends in homicide rates also exist in many other countries across the globe, many with vastly different domestic policies and approaches to criminal justice. Indeed, during the 1990s, the rate of violent and property crime decreased by similar amounts in Canada and in other western democracies as it did in the United States, without growth in police force or correctional populations (Paternoster, 2010; Tonry, 2014; Zimring, 2007). Yet, somewhat surprisingly, the existence of parallel homicide trends receives only scant attention among social scientists (see Baumer & Wolff, 2014a; LaFree, Curtis, & McDowall, 2015; Tonry, 2014; Tseloni, Mailley, Farrell, & Tilley, 2010; Weiss, Santos, Testa, & Kumar, 2016).

This chapter aims to take stock of the international homicide trends literature by documenting important patterns in international homicide rates, by exploring potential causes of international homicide trends, and by discussing key ways this literature can be expanded upon. In the following sections, we begin by discussing data sources commonly used to assess homicide across countries including the varying definitions, data collection methods, and quality of these data. Next, we review extant literature, highlighting both what we know and what we do not know about international homicide trends. In doing so, we draw on existing data to demonstrate important patterns in international homicide rates and propose possible explanations for why many countries across the world experienced similar changes in homicide rates over time. Finally, the chapter concludes with promising directions for future research.

INTERNATIONAL HOMICIDE DATA

Historically, homicide data were collected by a multitude of international organizations including the United Nations (UN), WHO, INTERPOL, as well as through independent efforts by academic researchers (see Archer & Gartner, 1984). However, many of these efforts for data collection have been discontinued. At present, there are two ongoing sources of data collection on international homicide: The United Nations Survey on Crime Trends and the Operations of the Criminal Justice System (UN-CTS), and the WHO Mortality Database.

UN Homicide Data

The UNODC has developed its own standardized system of crime classification, the International Classification of Crime for Statistical Purposes (ICCS; UNODC, 2015), which is presented to governments and other organizations as an instrument to define several types of crimes, including homicides. The ICCS defines intentional homicide as "unlawful death inflicted upon a person with the intent to cause death or serious injury." This definition includes all illegal and intentional interpersonal violence that leads to death, including deaths from terrorist activities, and killings by law enforcement or state actors in which excessive force is used. Excluded from this definition are legal killings, such as those resulting from legal intervention by law enforcement, justifiable homicides in self-defense, or homicides committed unintentionally such as involuntary or negligent manslaughter.

The UN data on homicides are primarily sourced from criminal justice statistics requested from governmental organizations. In particular, homicide data are collected through the UN-CTS, an annual survey distributed to country officials globally. Each year, new editions of the survey serve both for the collection of new data, as well as a chance for countries to review data submitted in previous years. In addition, UN staff members review the data prior to its publication in accordance with a validation protocol that considers each data point in relation to the historical trend of the same indicator, as well as to the recording practices of each country. This process involves extensive communication between the UN and member countries in order to ensure that data reported are consistent with the ICCS definition, and to maximize the comparability of the data internationally. Moreover, data are only published if it is considered valid both by UN experts, and approved by member countries (United Nations, 2013).

WHO Homicide Data

The WHO collects annual data on country-level mortality by cause of death since the 1950s. Mortality data are primarily sourced from death certificates recorded by medical professionals (Smit, De Jong, & Bijleveld, 2012). Causes of deaths are defined in accordance to the International Classification of Diseases (ICD), a standardized and international system for the classification of deaths by cause. According to the ICD, a homicide death is defined as "death caused by injuries inflicted by another person with the intent to injure or kill, by any means, excluding injuries due to legal interventions and operations of war."

The WHO data are particularly suitable for long-term longitudinal investigations as data for a few selected countries are available for all decades since the 1950s. In more recent years, the number of countries with available homicide data has expanded. Between 1990 and 2015, the data contain at least one year of data for more than 100 countries. Still, because accurate homicide data are not available for all countries, in recent years the WHO also generates model-based estimates of homicide counts for countries with no data. However, researchers have recently raised potential concerns with estimated cross-national homicide data and users of such data should consult Kanis, Messner, Eisner, and Heitmeyer (2017) to understand the appropriate uses of estimated data. Overall, due to the consistency and objectivity of the ICD, and given the international scale of implementation of the ICD across the world, the WHO mortality data are a key asset for the study of mortality and its causes.

Validity of Data Sources

Traditionally, cross-national homicide research has favored the WHO data over the UN data arguing that WHO provides greater reliability and validity. Studies often contend that the WHO is the best source of international homicide data because the definition focuses on the death of the victim and therefore does not include attempted crimes, because WHO uses a standardized definition of homicide and includes various quality checks, or because it does not rely on police reports, which are potentially subject to bias. To illustrate this point, below are a series of quotes from published research spanning over the course of three decades in which researchers consistently draw upon similar arguments contending WHO data are the most valid and reliable source of cross-national homicide data.

> "In comparing homicide rates of individual countries with that of the United States, WHO is the best source because its data are based on an actual count of deceased persons." (Kalish, 1988, p. 2)

> "WHO's homicide figure can be used as a relatively valid and reliable estimator of the adequacy of indicators of murder used in other series. It can be expected that WHO will report systematically lower rates than other series because its data represent the purest measure of reported murder in a country." (Huang & Welford, 1989, p. 36)

"Nevertheless, Kalish (1988) argues that the WHO data serve as the best source of information on homicide for international comparisons because they are 'based on an actual count of deceased persons' and therefore are not susceptible to biases resulting from intercountry differences in the treatment of 'attempted homicides.'" (Messner & Rosenfeld, 1997, p. 1401)

"Among these three sources of cross-national comparative homicide data, the WHO data are widely believed to be the most valid." (LaFree & Drass, 2002, p. 776)

"Scholars now agree substantially that among the major cross-national homicide data sources, those collected by the World Health Organization are the most valid and reliable." (LaFree & Tseloni, 2006, p. 32)

"Homicide data have been taken from the cause of death statistics reported by the World Health Organization (WHO), which is widely regarded to be the most reliable source of information on homicide for cross-national comparison." (Messner, Raffalovich, & Sutton, 2010, p. 518)

"The WHO data are often considered the most reliable among cross-national criminologists as they use a standardized definition, which includes intentional homicide that does not occur in the context of war or legal intervention." (Nivette & Eisner, 2013, p. 9)

"The WHO homicide data were utilized instead of alternative sources because WHO enforces a uniform definition of homicide. Alternative sources allow for differences in the case definition of homicide, resulting in estimates that may not be comparable across nations due to which violent events are or are not defined as homicide in a given nation." (Rogers & Pridemore, 2013, p. 587)

"Homicide researchers substantially agree that among the major cross-national sources, WHO data are the most valid and reliable." (LaFree et al., 2015, p. 487)

"WHO homicide data is often regarded by researchers as the most valid and reliable source of cross-national homicide data." (Testa, Young, & Mullins, 2017, p. 226)

"While WHO often has homicide data available for fewer nations compared with other sources (e.g. United Nations) they are preferred because they are considered the most valid measure of homicide victimization across nations." (Pridemore & Rogers, 2017, p. 1084)

"As for the quality of the data, homicide data provided by the WHO are established as being of high quality compared to other cross-national homicide data." (Tuttle, 2018, p. 95)

However, despite these claims, relatively little research has empirically compared the validity across data sources and only one study to date has compared the UN and WHO homicide figures using contemporary data. Accordingly, many of the central claims suggesting WHO is the most valid and reliable source of international homicide data are empirically untested.

The seminal study assessing the reliability from various cross-national data sources was conducted by Bennett and Lynch (1990). Using a multi-year average of homicide rates from 1975–1980 the study compared four major sources of cross-national homicide (INTERPOL, UN, WHO, and Comparative Crime Data File) to assess the validity and reliability of homicide data across 31 countries. The findings suggested that while there were some differences across the data sources, analyses using any of the four sources yielded largely similar results.

Moreover, since the 1980s international organizations have made continued efforts to increase the availability and validity of cross-national homicide data

(UNODC, 2013; WHO, 2014). Accordingly, Andersson and Kazemian (2017) updated the Bennett and Lynch (1990) study by comparing contemporary UN and WHO homicide data from 1998 to 2010. Their findings indicated that both data source provided reliable measures of homicide. Specifically, the authors found that while the UN and WHO homicide data differed slightly in magnitude, the two data sources produced similar outcomes in statistical models. Finally, the study found that the UN data produced more robust results with less error in cross-sectional analyses, whereas the WHO data were found to be more reliable for longitudinal analyses.

In short, the claim that WHO is the most reliable and valid source of cross-national homicide data is not supported by empirical research. The definition of homicides used by the UN and the WHO are largely consistent, as are their methods of data collection and validation. Moreover, the major publications on homicides from both the WHO and UN make extensive use of each other's data for validation, and for filling gaps in their own sources (UNODC, 2013; WHO, 2014). Therefore, arguments for ranking one data above the other often overstate the differences between the two sources. Accordingly, we suggest that rather than claiming one source of data as superior, researchers should leverage the strengths from having two largely independent sources of intentional homicides, which can be used to verify and complement one another.

INTERNATIONAL HOMICIDE TRENDS: 1990–2015

In this section, we draw on mortality data from the WHO to document contemporary international homicide trends. Fig. 1 provides the international homicide rate per 100,000 individuals using data from 108 countries from 1990 to 2015.[1] A couple of important patterns are present. First, over this 25-year period the international homicide rate declined by approximately 25% from 14.59 per 100,000 individuals in 1990 to 10.88 per 100,000 in 2015. Second, there was a sizable decline in homicide throughout the 1990s, with the homicide rate declining by 4.7% from 1990 to 2000. However, while the 1990s receives much attention for large declines in violence, an even larger decline occurred after the turn of the century. From 2000 to 2015, the international homicide rate declined by 21.8%. Finally, there have been a few short periods of increasing homicide rates, although these rises in homicide are typically short-lived and followed by sizeable reductions. For instance, between 1999 and 2002 the international homicide rate increased from 13.69 per 100,000 to 14.37 per 100,000 (4.9% increase). Finally, while much has been written about recent increases in homicide in the United States (MacDonald, 2015; Pyrooz, Decker, Wolfe, & Shjarback, 2016; Rosenfeld et al., 2017), there was also a very similar uptick in the international homicide rate from 2012 to 2014, although this has been met with a small decline in 2015. Indeed, many countries and regions of the world such as Western Europe witnessed similar increases in homicide during the same period as homicides increased in the United States (see Fig. 2). Thus, when viewed in a cross-national context it appears that local phenomena limited to the United States such as the

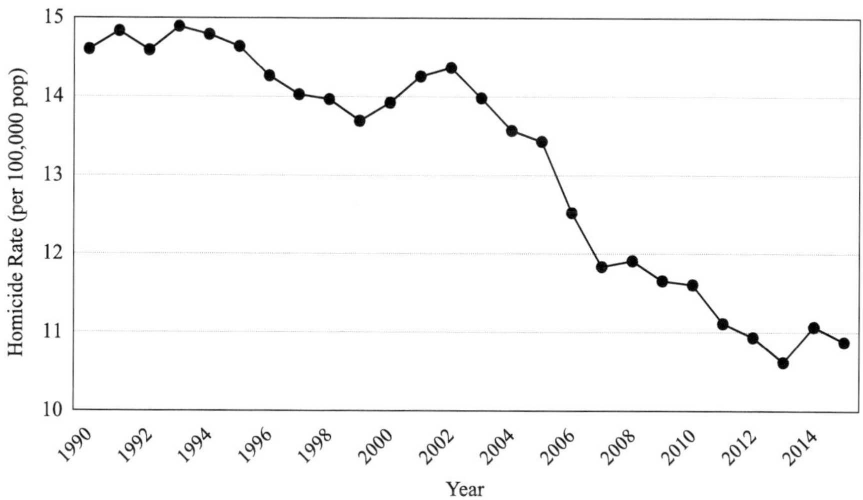

Fig 1 International Homicide Trend – WHO, 1990–2015.

"Ferguson effect" or the spread of the illegal opioid drug markets may not fully explain this trend. While it is unclear what international homicide rates will be in years to come, past trends suggest that this recent increase will be short-lived, and that rates of homicide may stabilize, or continue to decline to new lows in the near future.

Fig. 2 breaks down the percent change in homicide trends by regions of the world.[2] Although the levels of homicide rates vary quite substantially, most regions of the world experienced a homicide decline through the 1990s and during most of the 2000s. Moreover, this figure demonstrates that while most regions experienced a reduction in homicide, the degree of homicide declines were often greatest in the safest regions of the world. Specifically, as Table 1 highlights, the percent reduction over this 25-year period was largest in Oceania and Western Europe, which already had the lowest overall rates of homicide in 1990, whereas regions with higher homicide such as Eastern Europe and Latin America saw smaller homicide declines and slight increases in the homicide rate, respectively. Additionally, homicide trends for Northern America, Eastern Europe, Oceania, and Asia were surprisingly similar over time. Finally, most regions of the world experienced either a flattening or a slight increase of homicide rates since 2013.

Second, although there were fluctuations in homicide rates within regions, there is almost no change in levels of homicide between countries. Regions with high levels of homicide remained high while regions with low levels of homicide remained low. This pattern follows trends documented in past research both at the international level and at the subnational level in the United States. For instance, Weiss et al. (2016) trajectory analysis of homicide rates in 53 countries from 1990 to 2005 found that the reductions in homicide rates were greatest in countries that already had low homicide rates and were smallest in nations within higher levels

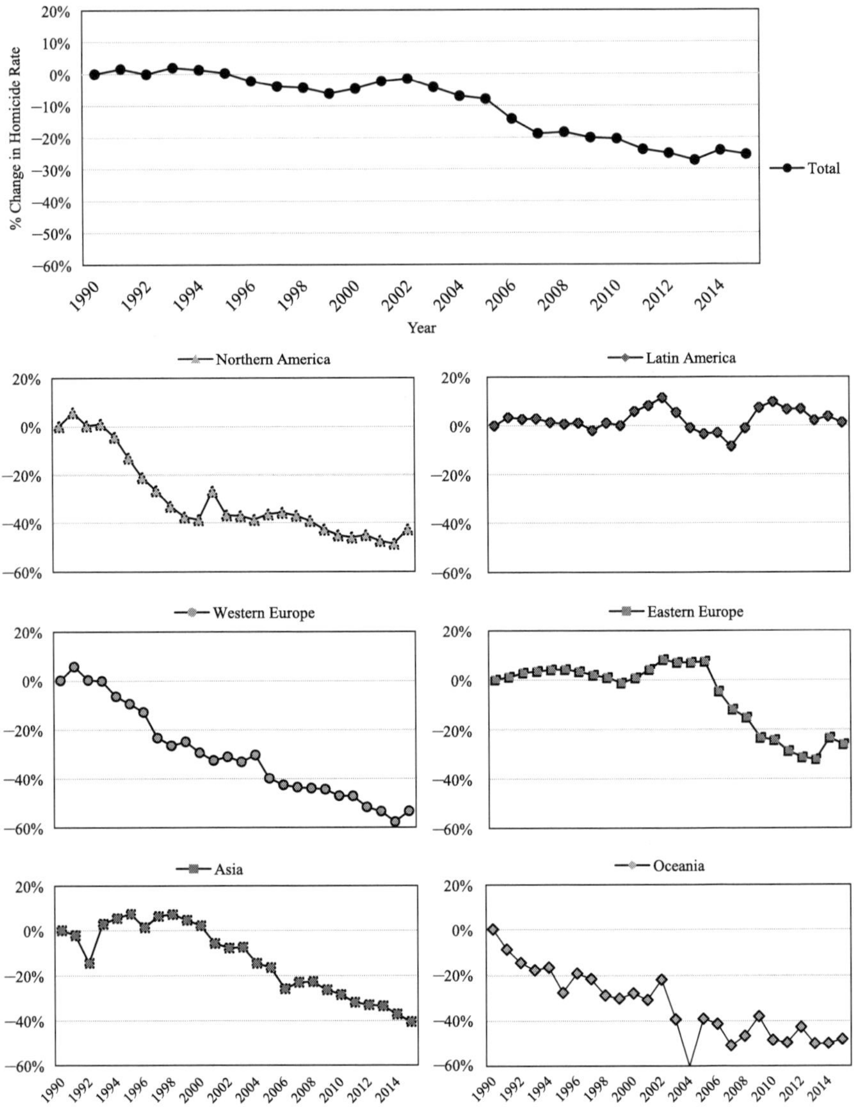

Fig. 2. Homicide Rates Change from 1990 by Region.

of homicide. Similarly, Sampson (2012) notes that, from 1995 to 2006, homicide rates in Chicago declined by 50%, yet when looking across neighborhoods "high violence areas persist and low violence remain so. There is almost no relative change in position, yet violence plummeted and virtually all neighborhoods benefitted" (pp. 110–111).

Next, to illustrate the heterogeneity of homicide trends, we provide an analysis of the percent change in homicide rates from a variety of countries

Table 1. Percent Change in Homicide Rate by Region (1990–2015).

Region	Regional Homicide Rank	1990 Homicide Rate	2015 Homicide Rate	% Change (1990–2015)
Eastern Europe	1	45.0	33.3	−26
Latin America	2	20.4	20.6	1.2
Northern America	3	9.0	5.1	−43
Asia	4	6.6	3.9	−41
Oceania	5	2.2	1.1	−49
Western Europe	6	1.3	0.6	−53
Total	–	*14.6*	*10.9*	*−25*

across the globe that experienced declining homicide rates and those that experienced increases in homicide rates. Fig. 3 provides the change in four countries that experienced decreases in homicide rates (Australia, Italy, Japan, and the United States). As demonstrated, from 1990 to 2015 each of these countries from four separate continents experienced reductions in homicide rate ranging in magnitude from 13% (United States) to 76% (Italy). Thus, developed countries from different corners of the world that had have different domestic policies, homicide rates, and cultural norms shared large homicide reductions over the same period.

Fig. 4 provides an analysis of three countries that experienced homicide increases from 1990 to 2015 (Brazil, Costa Rica, and Guatemala) and one country that experienced both declining and increasing homicide rates during this period (Mexico). As this figure illustrates, the international reduction in homicide rates was not entirely global as there were a number of countries that experienced increased violence during this period. Moreover, most countries experiencing increasing homicide were located in regions of the world with historically high levels of violence such as Latin America. Accordingly, at a time when the entire globe was experiencing approximately 25% reduction in homicide, rates of homicide increased by 89% in Costa Rica, 38% in Guatemala, and 32% in Brazil.

In sum, the analysis above suggests that in the past two and half decades there has been a substantial decline in homicide across much of the world. The internationality of this decline, and the commonalities between homicide trends across regions strongly suggest that the main causes of the decline lie not in domestic policies, but in globalized events shared across many locations. In addition, the homicide decline was largest in the regions of the world that historically have the lowest levels of homicide.

KEY LIMITATIONS IN INTERNATIONAL HOMICIDE TREND RESEARCH

Despite the strides made in recent years in understanding correlates of cross-national homicide (for review see Cole & Gramjo, 2009; LaFree, 1999; Messner &

Rosenfeld, 1999; Nivette, 2011; Trent & Pridemore, 2012), there are several factors that limit our understanding regarding international homicide trends. Two issues are particularly noteworthy.

First, missing homicide data for specific countries and regions of the world remain a key limitation. This is particularly problematic as inconsistent or

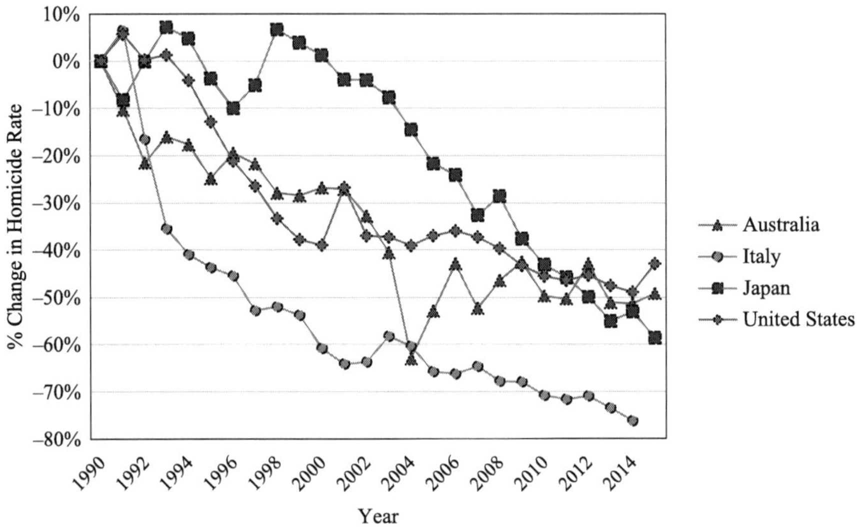

Fig. 3. Homicide Rates Change from 1990 for Countries with Decreasing Rates.

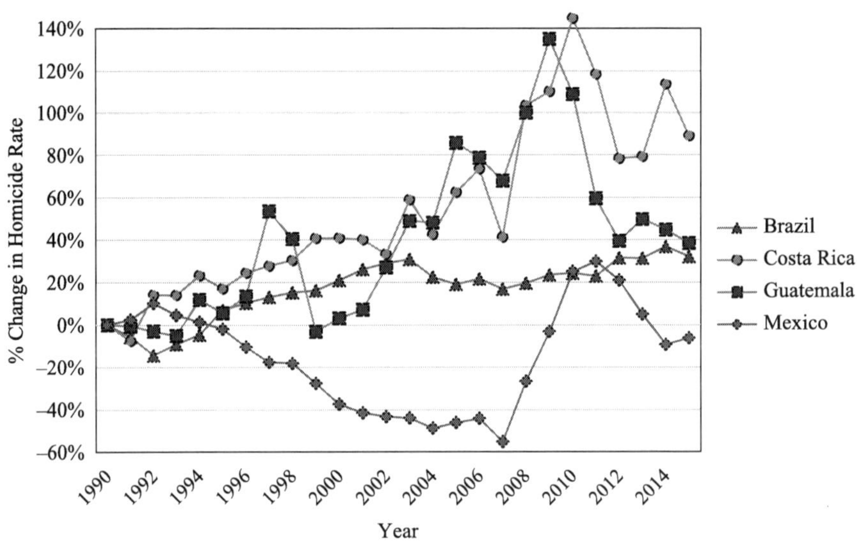

Fig. 4. Homicide Rates Change from 1990 for Countries with Increasing Rates.

nonexistent data reporting in many countries leads analyses of international crime trends to omit portions of the world that likely have some of the highest homicide rates. For example, an analysis by Stamatel (2006) found that the median number of countries included across 81 cross-national studies was of only 39. More recently, a meta-analysis by Nivette (2011) found that, on average, cross-national studies on homicides covered a sample of 44 countries. Consequently, most of what is known about international homicide comes from a small and nonrepresentative portion of the world comprising just one-fifth of all countries (Stamatel, 2006). Such limitation limits the extent to which findings from existing cross-national homicide research can be generalized to the world.

Fig. 5 shows countries with available homicide data versus countries without homicide data for at least one year in the WHO Mortality Database between 1990 and 2015. As the map demonstrates, data on homicide are missing from entire sections of the world including most of Africa and much of Southeast Asia. Moreover, countries with available homicide data have a median gross domestic product per capita of $11,042, compared to $1,171 for countries that do not report homicide data. Similarly, economic inequity as measured by the GINI coefficient, which ranges from 0 (least unequal) to 100 (most unequal), indicates that countries with available homicide data have an average GINI score of 36.83 compared to 41.02 for countries with missing homicide data. Thus, as this pattern demonstrates, data availability is highly uneven and most likely missing for countries with economic issues that are associated with higher homicide rates (Nivette, 2011; Rennó Santos, Testa, & Weiss, 2017; Trent & Pridemore, 2012).

Second, aside from the uneven geographical coverage, another limitation is that robust data over time are unavailable for many countries. Because

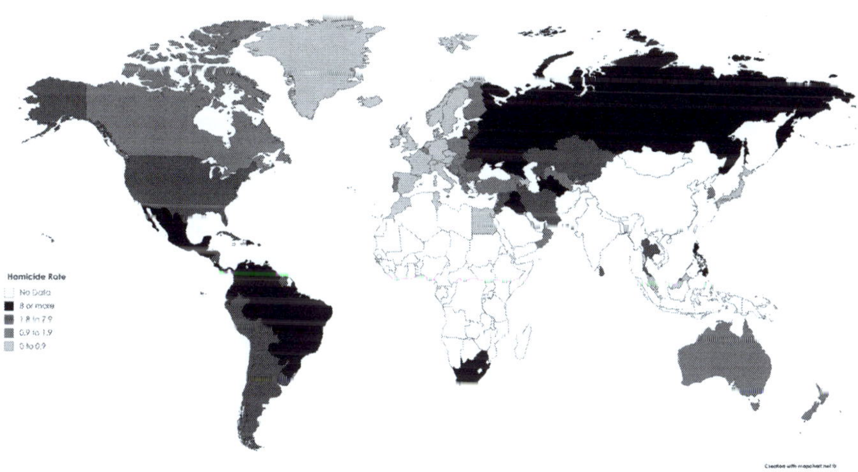

Fig. 5. Homicide Rates by Country According to WHO.

cross-national data are often missing from year to year, many studies rely on a trade-off between more years or more countries. This leads many studies to opt for one year of data or an average of some years of data to perform cross-sectional analyses. While cross-sectional research provides value in determining what factors explain differences between countries at any given time, these studies cannot adequately explore the causes of changes in homicide rates within countries over time.

Continuous efforts by international organizations such as the UN and the WHO have yielded substantial improvements in the amount and quality of available data. Still, it remains somewhat surprising that more attempts have not been made to fill these gaps or to expand existing time series. For instance, Archer and Gartner (1984) independently complied a cross-national data set including crime data for 110 countries and 44 cities from 1900 to 1970. As LaFree (1999, p. 134) points out:

> [...] it is worth noting that by the mid-1970s, two independent researchers with little outside funding, had collected a more extensive data set on cross-national crime than had been collected to date by any international agency.

Perhaps one of the best ways to expand the current state of knowledge regarding international crime trends is to fund partnerships between international agencies and academic researchers with the goal of building more complete and comprehensive international data sets on cross-national homicide.

POTENTIAL CAUSES OF INTERNATIONAL HOMICIDE DECLINES

Because of insufficiencies with data, and because of a lack of attention to the study of crime trends (Baumer et al., 2018), particularly at the cross-national level, a number of potential causes of international homicide trends are yet to be explored in detail. We propose and discuss a few of these potential causes. In doing so, we focus on factors that have been experienced globally, and therefore may hold promise in explaining changes in homicides that were experienced internationally. Due to space limitations, we limit our discussion to four factors: international migration, age-structure, self-control, and routine activities.

International Migration

Over a decade ago, Robert Sampson (2006) suggested that increased immigration could be partly responsible for the crime declines experienced throughout the 1990s in the United States. Since then, a number of empirical studies have shown that areas that absorbed larger amounts of immigrants during this period had greater declines in violent crime than elsewhere in the country (Light, 2017; Ousey & Kubrin, 2009, 2018; Stowell, Messner, McGeever, & Raffalovich, 2009; Wadsworth, 2010).

However, being an international phenomenon, increased immigration may possibly have had an impact on international homicide trends. Specifically, during 1990s and 2000s, while international migration increased substantially across the world, homicide rates declined in many countries (United Nations, 2016). Yet, given the growing interest in the relationship between immigration and crime among both social scientists and policymakers, it is surprising that nearly no research to date has investigated the relationship between international migration and international homicide trends. Indeed, as Ousey and Kubrin (2018, p. 18) recently noted:

> [...] concern about immigration, and its connection to crime and security, is evident in countries around the globe. Examining the nature and magnitude of the immigration–crime relationship within other nations or between countries would serve as an informative comparative lens to aid our overall understanding.

Between 1994 and 2014, 51 studies were published on the immigration–crime relationship in the US context (Ousey & Kubrin, 2018), yet there is nearly no cross-national homicide research that includes a measure of international migration (for an exception see Baumer & Wolff, 2014a).

To illustrate the potential association between cross-national migration rates and homicide over time we draw on international migration data from the UN. The international migrant stock is obtained from the UN Population Division and measures the percent of countries' population who is foreign born (United Nations, 2016). Fig. 6 illustrates the relationship between international migration and homicide for the world and by region. As the figure demonstrates, there is a negative association between migration and homicide internationally. In fact, between 1990 and 2000, the percent change in migration and homicide remained relatively stable. However, beginning in 2000 there was a sizeable increase in the international migrant stock that corresponded with a large reduction in international homicide. Overall, from 1990 to 2015 the international migrant stock increased by about 16%, while the homicide rate declined by nearly 25%.

This relationship is also clear when broken down by region. For instance, Northern America experienced a 55% increase in migration while experiencing a 42% homicide decline and Western Europe experienced a 96% rise in migrant stock along with a 53% reduction in homicide. Moreover, regions that experienced less migration also experienced less homicide declines, with Latin America experiencing a growth in homicide during a period its migrant stock declined nearly 10%. However, these are only correlational and it is possible that a common third factor such as increasing economic opportunities may explain changes in both homicide and international migration stock. Still, given the lack of research on this topic, future studies that assess the link between changes in international migration and international homicide trends would be greatly valuable.

Age-Structure

Age is one of the strongest correlates of criminal activity. In their seminal work, Hirschi and Gottfredson (1983) demonstrated a robust association between age and criminal offending at the individual level, which they argued existed across societies. Accordingly, the association between population age-structure and homicide has been one of the most tested variables in cross-national homicide studies

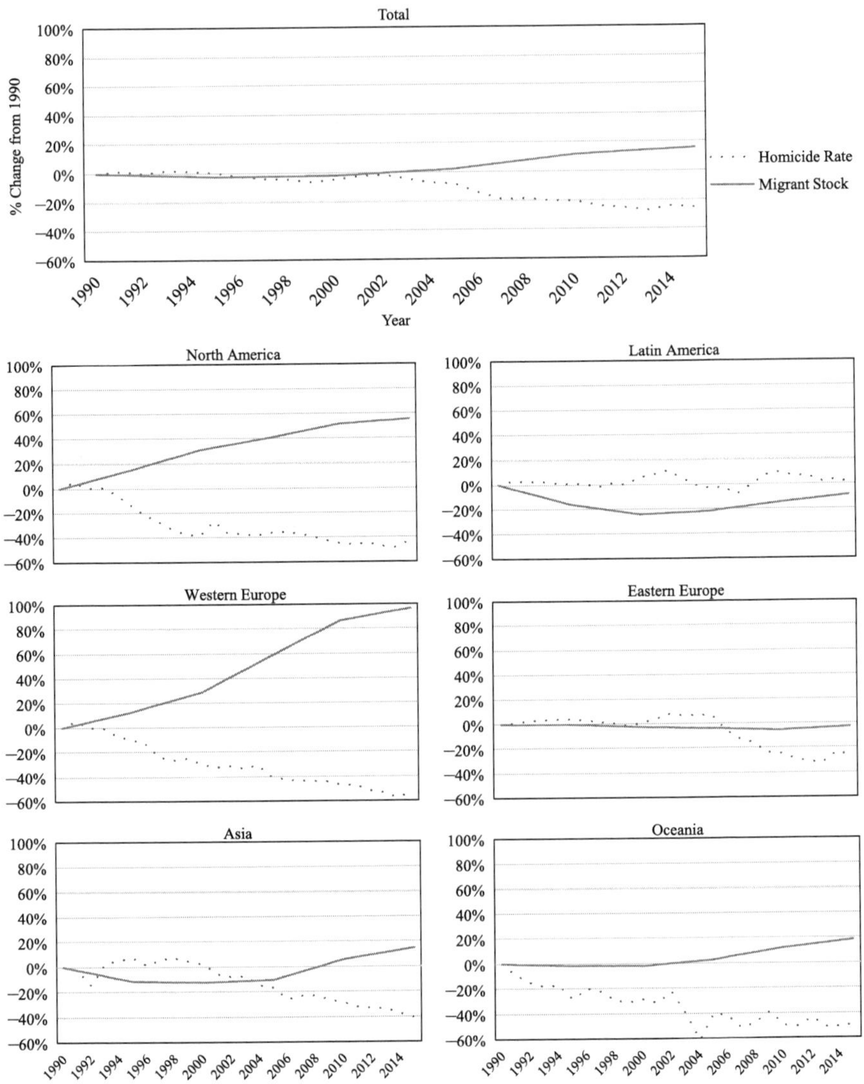

Fig. 6. Homicide Rates and Migrant Stock Change from 1990 to 2015 by Region.

(Nivette, 2011; Rogers, 2014; Rogers & Pridemore, 2016, 2017). Research typically draws on a measure that captures the percentage of the total population that is young (i.e., 15–24 years old). Age-structure may influence homicide rates through two main mechanisms. First, a population with a greater proportion of young people would have higher rates of interpersonal violence due to a larger pool of potential offenders (Bennett, 1991; Rogers & Pridemore, 2017), as well as more potential victims since younger individuals are more likely to live a lifestyle that puts them at a greater risk for interpersonal violence (Hindelang, Gottfredson, & Garofalo, 1978). Second, a smaller ratio of adults per youth may reduce social control by decreasing the amount of supervision youth, and by promoting a youth culture that is more conducive to interpersonal violence (Cook & Laub, 1986, 2002).

To date, a fairly extensive literature has tested the association between age-structure and homicide cross-nationally. Contrary to expectations, however, two recent studies documented a relatively weak association with homicide at the cross-national level. First, Nivette's (2011) meta-analysis of cross-national predictors of homicide found that age-structure has only a modest positive association with cross-national homicide. A second study Rogers and Pridemore (2017) included a comprehensive evaluation of the association between percent young and cross-national homicide rates. First, the study reviewed existing literature finding that 82% of studies did not find a significant association between percent young and homicide rates. Next, their own analysis using the average homicide rate between 1999 and 2004 from 55 countries revealed no significant association between percent young and cross-national homicide rates.

However, each of these studies was limited in specific ways. First, Nivette (2011) study defined youth as all population older than 15 years. Doing so obscures any effects of key age-ranges of interest (i.e., 15–24), which are conflated with a variety of other age groups. Second, Rogers and Pridemore (2017) conducted a cross-sectional analysis using only the average young population between 1999 and 2004. Therefore, their analysis does not explore the longitudinal impact of within-country changes in age-structure on homicide rates. This is a key limitation as variables that explain differences between populations may not be the same variables that explain changes within populations over time. In other words, factors explaining why Japan has less homicides than the United States may not be the same factors that explain why the homicide rate of Japan declined. Thus, it may be that age-structure is better at explaining changes in homicide rates within countries rather than differences in levels of homicide between countries.

Fig. 7 presents the relationship between percent young and change in homicide rates since 1980. As the figure demonstrates, there appears to be an association between the two variables, particularly in certain regions of the world such as Western and Eastern Europe where homicide rates track closely with the size of the youth population. Next, Fig. 8 highlights the strong relationship between age and homicide overtime when focusing on individual countries such as the United States.

Routine Activities

Routine activities theory was developed by Cohen and Felson (1979) to explain the increase in crime rates in the United States following World War II. The theory states that rates of crime (both property and violent) should be highest in ecological areas where motivated offenders are more likely to encounter suitable targets without the presence of some form of guardianship. Moreover, the probability of a situation occurring in which these three factors converge is influenced by the routine activities of a given society (i.e., work, family life, and leisure activities). Thus, in their seminal work on the topic, Cohen and Felson (1979) suggested

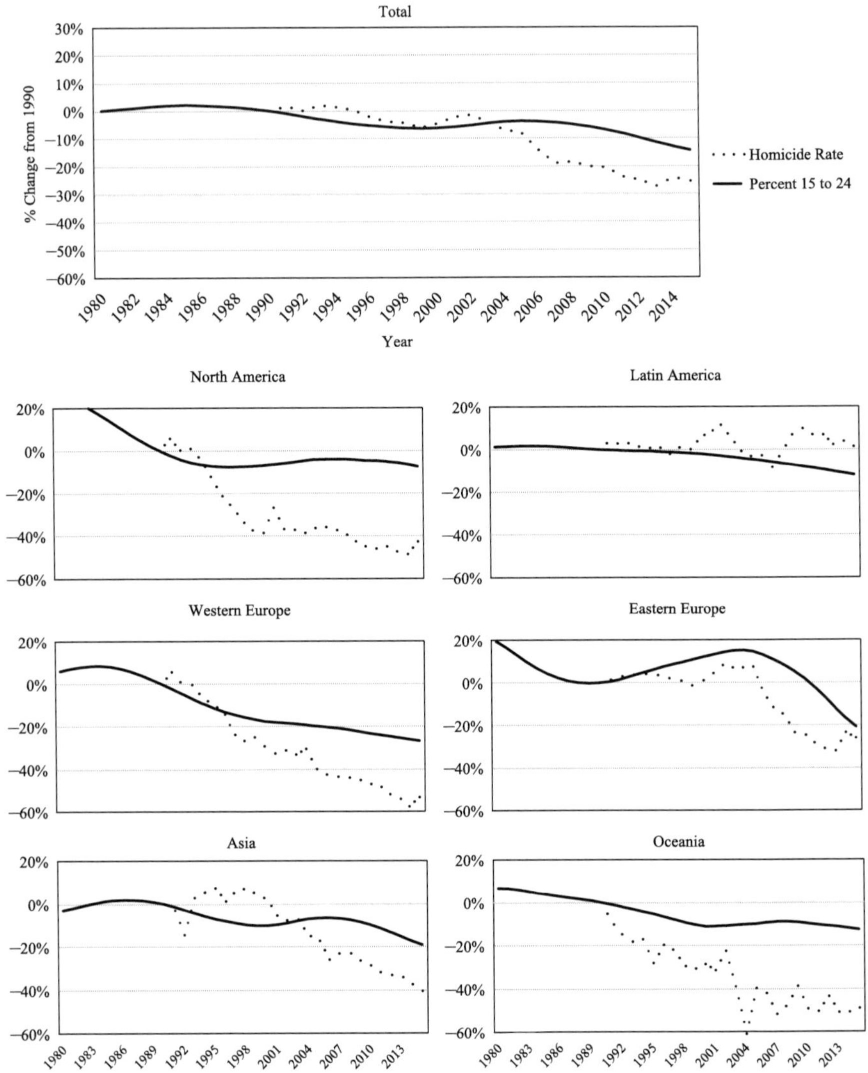

Fig. 7. Homicide Rates and Percent 15–24 Change from 1980 by Region.

that temporal variations in US crime rates could be explained by changes in daily routines among US residents that increased target suitability and/or decreased guardianship. Specifically, factors such as increases in females working in the labor force and individuals spending more time outside the household increase the likelihood of both property and violent crime taking place.

To date, most research on routine activities theory has been limited to the US context (Pratt & Cullen, 2005). Only scant research has applied routine activities theory in a cross-national context and no research to date has tested whether the theory can explain why international crime trends increase in some parts of the world and decrease in others. In this context, Farrell, Tilley, and Tseloni (2014) contend that routine activities theory holds strong promise to explain international crime trends, yet it remains "both under researched and underappreciated" (p. 480). Notably, Bennett (1991) remains one of the only studies to explicitly test routine activities theory in a cross-national perspective. This study assessed the role of routine activities on property crime and homicide for 52 countries from 1960 to 1984. To capture the components of the theory, the study measured target attractiveness using gross domestic product per capita, motivated offenders was measured using the size of the young population, urbanization, and economic inequality, and guardianship was measured using the female labor force participation. The results provided mixed support for the theory as routine activities were found to explain property crime better than homicide.

Although limited research has assessed the routine activities in a cross-national context, the theory may serve as a unifying framework to understand the impact of international shifts in behavior. For instance, the growth of personal computers in homes and the spread of the access to the Internet could be associated with crime drops because they altered the use of time of individuals from public activities to increased time spent inside the home. Similarly, the spread of mobile phones and closed-circuit television have occurred across countries, which may have increased guardianship (Farrell, Tilley, Tseloni, & Mailley 2010). Accordingly, routine activities theory may be an especially prominent factor in explaining international homicide trends as the spread of technology has occurred across countries and has the greatest impact on altering the daily routines of the young population, which is most prone to interpersonal violence.

Self Control

Among criminologist, self-control is one of the most widely discussed and tested correlates of crime. Specifically, Gottfredson and Hirschi (1990) general theory of crime argues that individuals who have higher self-control will be less likely to engage in antisocial behavior across all stages of their life-course, whereas those with low self-control are more likely to engage in various forms of antisocial behavior. Moreover, criminal events are most likely when individuals with low self-control encounter opportunities for offending.

At the individual level, a large body of research has established a strong association between self-control and involvement in crime (Longshore, 1998; Moffitt et al., 2011; Pratt & Cullen, 2000). The link between self control and individual criminality has also been established in countries aside from the United States, including as Russia (Tittle & Botchovar, 2005), Japan (Vazsonyi, Wittekind, Belliston, & Van Loh 2004), Canada (Forde & Kennedy, 1997), and New Zealand (Moffitt et al., 2011). These findings have led some to conclude that association between self-control and crime does not "appear to be unique or culture-specific" (Vazsonyi, Pickering, Junger, & Hessing, 2001, p. 120).

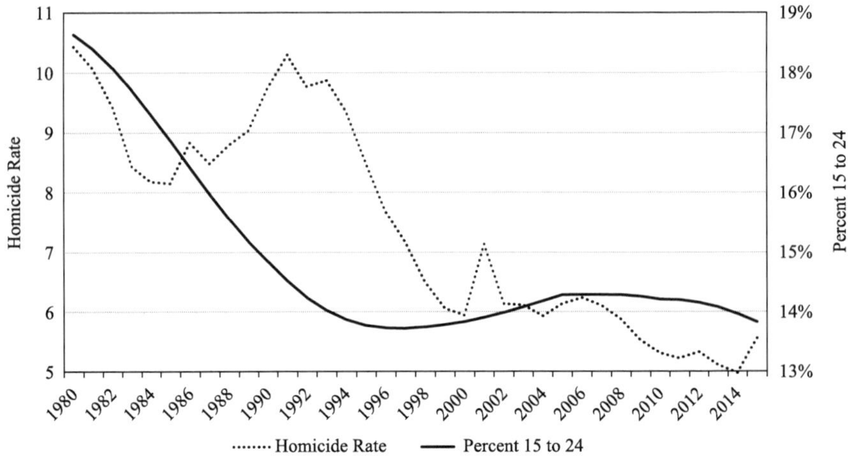

Fig. 8. Homicide Rate and Percent 15–24 – United States, 1980–2015.

Researchers have also suggested that increases in self-control may be linked to international declines in violence. For instance, Pinker (2011, p. 592) notes that self-control has been credited with one of the greatest reductions of violence in history – the thirtyfold drop in homicide between the thirteenth century medieval Europe, and modern Europe from the twentieth century. The contention that self-control can lead to international reductions in homicide rates draws from Elias (2000) civilizing process. In part, the civilizing process proposes that overtime there are psychological changes in which individuals develop greater self-restraint over aggressive tendencies and higher levels of self-control (Elias, 2000; Whitt, 2010). For example, between 1200 and 1900 the homicide rate in London declined from approximately 20, to almost 1 per 100,000 population, a decrease that has been attributed to "a manifestation of cultural change in Western society, especially the growing sensitization to violence and the development of increased internal and external control on aggressive behavior" (Gurr, 1981, p. 295).

However, despite research contending that increased self-control is associated with long-term international declines in homicide, there is little research on whether self-control is associated with contemporary homicide declines. Given the strong association at the individual level between self-control and criminality and the proposed association to centuries of declining violence, increased self-control may be a viable candidate for explaining the crime drop of the past 25 years.

CONCLUSION AND FUTURE DIRECTIONS

This chapter demonstrates that homicide trends throughout much of the world often fluctuate together. This is perhaps best demonstrated by the international homicide decline that occurred throughout the 1990s into the 2000s (see also Weiss et al., 2016). Yet, this chapter also demonstrates that while homicide declined for most of the world over the past couple of decades, regions of the world with historically high levels of violence have experienced little reduction in homicide and some high homicide countries are instead experiencing increasing homicide rates. Unfortunately, very little is known about the drivers of these trends, as international homicide trends remain an understudied area of research. Accordingly, research attempting to understand the underlying causes and correlates of international homicide trends would benefit from a few suggestions.

First, international trends can best be explained by factors occurring on an international level. The main causes of the 1990s homicide decline in the United States probably lie in social forces that occurred concomitantly over large portions of the world, and which are not restricted to domestic policies alone. Homicides also declined in the majority of developed western countries during the turn of the twenty-first century. Therefore, beyond demonstrating the existence of these general trends, future research should focus on the *why* of the international homicide decline. For one, it is important to know what common causes existed throughout the world that may have generated this decline. Possibilities include shared changes in living habits, demographic shifts, changes in attitudes, values and norms related to violence, market forces and changes in the economy, among many others (see also Baumer & Wolff, 2014b). We live in an increasingly connected world, where populations can easily influence one another, and share the same experiences. As this chapter demonstrates, these shared experiences may also include interpersonal violence and crime victimization.

Therefore, future research attempting at explaining homicide trends should also focus on exploring causes that could have been shared across many societies, such as the factors we have suggested above. In addition, equally important is the question of why homicides increased in certain countries, while decreasing more generally in much of the world. It would be useful for researchers to document what features may have driven homicide to increase in some countries and investigate whether common factors across these nations explain their rise in homicide.

Second, future research should not only focus on the causes of homicides, but also on the consequences of violence to the well-being of society and of individuals. A growing body of research is demonstrating that a homicide may carry long-term ripple effects across various actors who are connected to the perpetrator or the victim (Sharkey, 2018). For example, exposure to local violence can negatively affect academic performance (Gershenson & Tekin, 2017; Sharkey, 2010), as well as health and stress levels (Heissel, Sharkey, Torrats-Espinosa, Grant, & Adam, 2017). Accordingly, future research should draw from growing literature on the consequences of exposure to violence to determine whether country level homicide affects the well-being of residents.

Third, while this chapter focused on homicide trends, it would be beneficial for future research to also understand international trends in nonlethal forms of criminal behavior. At present, much cross-national homicide research uses homicide data because it is generally more reliable and more available than data on other types of crime (Aebi, 2010; Baumer, 2011; Lynch & Pridemore, 2011). Consequently, we know very little about the international trends of non-lethal crimes, and about how other types of crimes are related to homicides internationally.

In conclusion, while homicide rates of much of the world have declined substantially over the past two and half decades, little progress has been made on understanding the causes of international homicide trends. For many populations around the world, homicide is still a leading cause of death, particularly among the youth (World Health Organization (WHO), 2014). More resources can be devoted to the collection of detailed data on homicide and on other forms of crime globally. Similarly, social scientists should continue to draw on sociological theories to understand past changes in international homicide rates, and even to forecast future trends. Doing so may guide efforts to reduce homicide, as well as improve overall safety and well-being of countries globally.

NOTES

1. Missing data for each country were interpolated and extrapolated using a moving average (liner weighted, $k = 10$). Together, these countries had 2.7 billion inhabitants in 2015 (United Nations Population Division, 2015), about 36% of the world's total estimated population. India and China, each with about 1.3 billion inhabitants, are missing from the sample.
2. Due to the lack of quality data for Africa, regional trends could not be successfully calculated for the region.

REFERENCES

Aebi, M. F. (2010). Methodological issues in the comparison of police-recorded crime rates. In S. G. Shoham, P. Knepper, & M. Kett (Eds.), *International handbook of criminology* (pp. 221–227). Boca Raton, FL: CRC Press.

Andersson, C., & Kazemian, L. (2017). Reliability and validity of cross-national homicide data: A comparison of UN and WHO data. *International Journal of Comparative and Applied Criminal Justice*, doi:10.1080/01924036.2017.1370676

Archer, D., & Gartner, R. (1984). *Violence and crime in cross-cultural perspective*. New Haven, CT: Yale University Press.

Baumer, E. P. (2011). Describing and explaining crime trends: An assessment of key issues. Current knowledge, and future directions of scientific inquiry. In M. Tonry (Ed.), *Oxford handbook on crime and criminal justice* (pp. 26–59). New York, NY: Oxford University Press.

Baumer, E. P., Vélez, M. B., & Rosenfeld, R. (2018). Bringing crime trends back into criminology: A critical assessment of the literature and a blueprint for future inquiry. *Annual Review of Criminology*, *1*, 39–61. doi.org/10.1146/annurev-criminol-032317-092339

Baumer, E. P., & Wolff, K. T. (2014a). The breadth and causes of contemporary cross-national homicide trends. *Crime and Justice*, *43*(1), 231–287.

Baumer, E. P., & Wolff, K. T. (2014b). Evaluating contemporary crime drop (s) in America, New York City, and many other places. *Justice Quarterly*, *31*(1), 5–38.

Bennett, R. R. (1991). Routine activities: A cross-national assessment of a criminological perspective. *Social Forces*, *70*(1), 147–163.

Bennett, R. R., & Lynch, J. P. (1990). Does a difference make a difference? Comparing cross-national crime indicators. *Criminology*, *28*(1), 153–181.

Blumstein, A. (1995). Youth violence, guns, and the illicit-drug industry. *The Journal of Criminal Law and Criminology*, *86*(1), 10–36.

Blumstein, A., & Rosenfeld, R. (1998). Explaining recent trends in US homicide rates. *The Journal of Criminal Law and Criminology*, *88*(4), 1175–1216.

Blumstein, A., & Wallman, J. (Eds.). (2006). *The crime drop in America*. New York, NY: Cambridge University Press.

Cohen, L. E., & Felson, M. (1979). Social change and crime rate trends: A routine activity approach. *American Sociological Review*, *44*(4), 588–608.

Cole, J. H., & Gramajo, A. M. (2009). Homicide rates in a cross-section of countries: Evidence and interpretations. *Population and Development Review*, *35*(4), 749–776.

Cook, P. J., & Laub, J. H. (1986). The (surprising) stability of youth crime rates. *Journal of Quantitative Criminology*, *2*(3), 265–277.

Cook, P. J., & Laub, J. H. (1998). The unprecedented epidemic in youth violence. *Crime and Justice*, *24*, 27–64.

Cook, P. J., & Laub, J. H. (2002). After the epidemic: Recent trends in youth violence in the United States. *Crime and Justice*, *29*, 1–37.

Elias, N. (2000). *The civilizing process: Sociogenetic and psychogenetic investigations* (Rev. ed.). Oxford: Wiley-Blackwell.

Farrell, G., Tilley, N., & Tseloni, A. (2014). Why the crime drop? *Crime and Justice*, *43*(1), 421–490.

Farrell, G., Tilley, N., Tseloni, A., & Mailley, J. (2010). Explaining and sustaining the crime drop: Clarifying the role of opportunity-related theories. *Crime Prevention and Community Safety*, *12*(1), 24–41.

Forde, D. R., & Kennedy, L. W. (1997). Risky lifestyles, routine activities, and the general theory of crime. *Justice Quarterly*, *14*(2), 265–294.

Gershenson, S., & Tekin, E. (2017). The effect of community traumatic events on student achievement: Evidence from the beltway sniper attacks. *Education Finance and Policy*, 1–54. doi.org/10.1162/EDFP_a_00234

Goldberger, A. S., Rosenfeld, R., & Blumstein, A. (2008). *Understanding crime trends: Workshop report*. Washington, DC: National Academies Press.

Gottfredson, M. R., & Hirschi, T. (1990). *A general theory of crime*. Stanford, CA: Stanford University Press.

Gurr, T. R. (1981). Historical trends in violent crime: A critical review of the evidence. *Crime and Justice*, *3*, 295–353.

Heissel, J. A., Sharkey, P. T., Torrats-Espinosa, G., Grant, K., & Adam, E. K. (2017). Violence and vigilance: The acute effects of community violent crime on sleep and cortisol. *Child Development*. doi.org/10.1111/cdev.12889

Hindelang, M. J., Gottfredson, M. R., & Garofalo, J. (1978). *Victims of personal crime: An empirical foundation for a theory of personal victimization*. Cambridge, MA: Ballinger.

Hirschi, T., & Gottfredson, M. (1983). Age and the explanation of crime. *American Journal of Sociology*, *89*(3), 552–584.

Huang, W. W., & Wellford, C. F. (1989). Assessing indicators of crime among international crime data series. *Criminal Justice Policy Review*, *3*(1), 28–47.

Kalish, C. B. (1988). *International crime rates*. Washington, DC: US Department of Justice, Bureau of Justice Statistics.

Kanis, S., Messner, S. F., Eisner, M. P., & Heitmeyer, W. (2017). A cautionary note about the use of estimated homicide data for cross-national research. *Homicide Studies*, *21*(4), 312–324.

Krug, E. G., Mercy, J. A., Dahlberg, L. L., & Zwi, A. B. (2002). The world report on violence and health. *The Lancet*, *360*(9339), 1083–1088.

LaFree, G. (1999). A summary and review of cross-national comparative studies of homicide. In M. Dwayne Smith & M. A. Zahn (Eds.), *Homicide: A sourcebook of social research* (pp. 125–145). Thousand Oaks, CA: Sage.

LaFree, G., Curtis, K., & McDowall, D. (2015). How effective are our "better angels"? Assessing country-level declines in homicide since 1950. *European Journal of Criminology*, *12*(4), 482–504.

LaFree, G., & Drass, K. A. (2002). Counting crime booms among nations: Evidence for homicide victimization rates, 1956 to 1998. *Criminology*, *40*(4), 769–800.

LaFree, G., & Tseloni, A. (2006). Democracy and crime: A multilevel analysis of homicide trends in forty-four countries, 1950–2000. *The Annals of the American Academy of Political and Social Science*, *605*(1), 25–49.

Levitt, S. D. (2004). Understanding why crime fell in the 1990s: Four factors that explain the decline and six that do not. *The Journal of Economic Perspectives*, *18*(1), 163–190.

Light, M. T. (2017). Re-examining the relationship between Latino immigration and racial/ethnic violence. *Social Science Research*, *65*, 222–239.

Longshore, D. (1998). Self-control and criminal opportunity: A prospective test of the general theory of crime. *Social Problems*, *45*(1), 102–113.

Lynch, J. P., & Pridemore, W. A. (2011). Crime in international perspective. In J.Q. Wilson & J. Petersilia (Eds.), *Crime and public policy*. New York, NY: Oxford University Press.

MacDonald, H. (2015). Trying to hide the rise of violent crime. *Wall Street Journal*. December 25

Messner, S. F., Raffalovich, L. E., & Sutton, G. M. (2010). Poverty, infant mortality, and homicide rates in cross-national perspective: Assessments of criterion and construct validity. *Criminology*, *48*(2), 509–537.

Messner, S. F., & Rosenfeld, R. (1997). Political restraint of the market and levels of criminal homicide: A cross-national application of institutional-anomie theory. *Social Forces*, *75*(4), 1393–1416.

Messner, S. F., & Rosenfeld, R. (1999). Social structure and homicide. In M. Dwayne Smith & M. A. Zahn (Eds.), *Homicide: A sourcebook of social research* (pp. 27–41). Thousand Oaks, CA: SAGE.

Moffitt, T. E., Arseneault, L., Belsky, D., Dickson, N., Hancox, R. J., Harrington, H., … Caspi, A. (2011). A gradient of childhood self-control predicts health, wealth, and public safety. *Proceedings of the National Academy of Sciences*, *108*(7), 2693–2698.

Nivette, A. E. (2011). Cross-national predictors of crime: A meta-analysis. *Homicide Studies*, *15*(2), 103–131.

Nivette, A. E., & Eisner, M. (2013). Do legitimate polities have fewer homicides? A cross-national analysis. *Homicide Studies*, *17*(1), 3–26.

Ousey, G. C., & Kubrin, C. E. (2009). Exploring the connection between immigration and violent crime rates in US cities, 1980–2000. *Social Problems*, *56*(3), 447–473.

Ousey, G. C., & Kubrin, C. E. (2018). Immigration and crime: Assessing a contentious issue. *Annual Review of Criminology*, *1*, 63–84. doi.org/10.1146/annurev-criminol-032317-092026

Paternoster, R. (2010). How much do we really know about criminal deterrence? *The Journal of Criminal Law and Criminology*, *100*(3), 765–824.

Pinker, S. (2011). *The better angels of our nature: The decline of violence in history and its causes*. London: Penguin Books.

Pratt, T. C., & Cullen, F. T. (2000). The empirical status of Gottfredson and Hirschi's general theory of crime: A meta-analysis. *Criminology*, *38*(3), 931–964.

Pratt, T. C., & Cullen, F. T. (2005). Assessing macro-level predictors and theories of crime: A meta-analysis. *Crime and Justice*, *32*, 373–450.

Pyrooz, D. C., Decker, S. H., Wolfe, S. E., & Shjarback, J. A. (2016). Was there a Ferguson effect on crime rates in large US cities? *Journal of Criminal Justice*, *46*, 1–8.

Rennó Santos, M., Testa, A., & Weiss, D. B. (2017). Where poverty matters: Examining the cross-national relationship between economic deprivation and homicide. *British Journal of Criminology*, *58*(2), 372–393. doi.org/10.1093/bjc/azx013

Rogers, M. L. (2014). A descriptive and graphical analysis of the (lack of) association between age and homicide cross-nationally. *International Criminal Justice Review*, *24*(3), 235–253.

Rogers, M. L., & Pridemore, W. A. (2013). The effect of poverty and social protection on national homicide rates: Direct and moderating effects. *Social Science Research*, *42*(3), 584–595.

Rogers, M. L., & Pridemore, W. A. (2016). The (null) effects of percent young on 15 to 24 age-specific and male-and female-specific cross-national homicide rates. *Homicide Studies*, *20*(3), 257–292.

Rogers, M. L., & Pridemore, W. A. (2017). A comprehensive evaluation of the association between percent young and cross-national homicide rates. *British Journal of Criminology, 57*(5), 1080–1100.

Rosenfeld, R., Gaston, S., Spivak, H., & Irazola, S. (2017). *Assessing and responding to the recent homicide rise in the United States*. Washington, DC: National Institute of Justice.

Sampson, R. J. (2006). Open doors don't invite criminals: Is increased immigration behind the drop in crime? *New York Times*. August 18.

Sampson, R. J. (2012). *Great American city: Chicago and the enduring neighborhood effect*. Chicago, IL: University of Chicago Press.

Sharkey, P. (2010). The acute effect of local homicides on children's cognitive performance. *Proceedings of the National Academy of Sciences, 107*(26), 11733–11738.

Sharkey, P. (2018). The long reach of violence: A broader perspective on data, theory, and evidence on the prevalence and consequences of exposure to violence. *Annual Review of Criminology, 1*, 85–102. doi.org/10.1146/annurev-criminol-032317-092316

Smit, P. R., de Jong, R., & Bijleveld, C. (2012). Homicide data in Europe: Definitions, sources and statistics. In M.C. A. Liem & W. A. Pridemore (Eds.), *Handbook of European homicide research: Patterns, explanations, and country studies* (pp. 5–23). New York, NY: Springer.

Stamatel, J. P. (2006). Incorporating socio-historical context into quantitative cross-national criminology. *International Journal of Comparative and Applied Criminal Justice, 30*(2), 177–207.

Stowell, J. I., Messner, S. F., McGeever, K. F., & Raffalovich, L. E. (2009). Immigration and the recent violent crime drop in the United States: A pooled, cross-sectional time-series analysis of metropolitan areas. *Criminology, 47*(3), 889–928.

Testa, A., Young, J. K., & Mullins, C. (2017). Does democracy enhance or reduce lethal violence? Examining the role of the rule of law. *Homicide Studies, 21*(3), 219–239.

Tittle, C. R., & Botchkovar, E. V. (2005). Self-control, criminal motivation and deterrence: An investigation using Russian respondents. *Criminology, 43*(2), 307–354.

Tonry, M. (2014). Why crime rates are falling throughout the Western world. *Crime and Justice, 43*, 1–63.

Trent, C. L., & Pridemore, W. A. (2012). A review of the cross-national empirical literature on social structure and homicide. In M. C. A. Liem & W. A. Pridemore (Eds.), *Handbook of European homicide research: Patterns, explanations, and country studies* (pp. 111–135). New York, NY: Springer.

Tseloni, A., Mailley, J., Farrell, G., & Tilley, N. (2010). Exploring the international decline in crime rates. *European Journal of Criminology, 7*(5), 375–394.

Tuttle, J. (2018). Specifying the effect of social welfare expenditures on homicide and suicide: A cross-national, longitudinal examination of the stream analogy of lethal violence. *Justice Quarterly, 35*(1), 87–113.

United Nations Office on Drugs and Crime (UNODC). (2013). *Global study on homicide 2013: Trends, context, data*. Vienna, Austria: United Nations Office on Drugs and Crime.

United Nations Office on Drugs and Crime (UNODC). (2015). *International classification of crime for statistical purposes (ICCS): Version 1.0*. Vienna, Austria: United Nations Office on Drugs and Crime.

United Nations. (2015). *World population prospects: The 2014 revision*. Vienna, Austria: United Nations.

United Nations. (2016). *Trends in international migrant stock: The 2015 revision*. Vienna, Austria: United Nations.

Vazsonyi, A. T., Pickering, L. E., Junger, M., & Hessing, D. (2001). An empirical test of a general theory of crime: A four-nation comparative study of self-control and the prediction of deviance. *Journal of Research in Crime and Delinquency, 38*(2), 91–131.

Vazsonyi, A. T., Wittekind, J. E. C., Belliston, L. M., & Van Loh, T. D. (2004). Extending the general theory of crime to "The East:" Low self-control in Japanese late adolescents. *Journal of Quantitative Criminology, 20*(3), 189–216.

Wadsworth, T. (2010). Is immigration responsible for the crime drop? An assessment of the influence of immigration on changes in violent crime between 1990 and 2000. *Social Science Quarterly, 91*(2), 531–553

Whitt, H. P. (2010). The civilizing process and its discontents: Suicide and crimes against persons in France, 1825–1830. *American Journal of Sociology, 116*(1), 130–186.

Weiss, D. B., Santos, M. R., Testa, A., & Kumar, S. (2016). The 1990s homicide decline: A western world or international phenomenon? A research note. *Homicide Studies*, *20*(4), 321–334.

World Health Organization (WHO). (2014). *Injuries and violence: The facts*. Geneva, Switzerland: World Health Organization.

Zimring, F. (2007). *The great American crime decline*. New York, NY: Oxford University Press.

CHAPTER 12

IT IS LESS ABOUT WEALTH OR POVERTY THAN WITH EQUALITY AND FORMAL SOCIAL CONTROL: AN ANALYSIS OF THE DETERMINANTS OF THE HOMICIDE RATE IN 145 COUNTRIES OF THE WORLD

Claire Chabot and Marc Ouimet

ABSTRACT

Purpose – *Cross-national comparisons of crime across the world consistently show that homicide rates are higher in more impoverished countries. However, there is a debate on what aspect of poverty is related to violence. Economics aspects have been conceived as wealth, poverty, and inequality. Furthermore, the impact of economic determinants has never been studied against a second potential determinant, which is the quality of the formal social control mechanisms.*

Design/methodology/approach – *In this study, we use official data made available by international agencies as well as new and original data from the World Homicide Survey, based on the responses provided by 1,223 respondents located in 145 countries of the world.*

Homicide and Violent Crime
Sociology of Crime, Law and Deviance, Volume 23, 223–240

ISSN: 1521-6136/doi:10.1108/S1521-613620180000023013

Findings – *Results show that the two main determinants of the homicide rate are economic inequality (Gini) and the quality of the formal social control mechanisms. However, this second dimension is dependent on the wealth of the nation (gross domestic product) and the prevalence of poverty.*

Keywords: Economic inequalities; poverty; wealth; formal social control

INTRODUCTION

The prevalence of homicide varies greatly across the world. Homicide rates are highest in Honduras and Venezuela with more than 50 per 100,000 people, whereas, Japan and Iceland declare a homicide rate of around 0.5 per 100,000 people. These homicide rate variations are well known to researchers and are generally interpreted as evidence that violence is driven by demographic, economic, social, and political factors. This study contributes to knowledge in two ways. First, it compares and contrasts the role of three different economic variables. Second, it tests the possible intervening role that plays criminal justice institutions.

Prior to recent and more extensive studies, including a large number of countries, most publications on cross-national comparisons of homicide rate estimates focused on factors related to small variations in levels of violence among the 40-to-60 most developed nations. Nivette's (2011) meta-analysis of cross-national studies on homicide found only two studies with more than 100 countries (106 and 118), and the average number of countries in the 53 studies published was 46. Studying developed nations is facilitated by the many detailed social indicators available to researchers. However, models interpreting the cause behind, for example, Germany's 0.8 per 100,000 homicide rate, Australia's 1.1 rate, and Canada's 1.7 rate, are not fully satisfactory. The developed countries all have a functional criminal justice system and a lesser violence problem, therefore making them unrepresentative of the world.

In the last few years, international agencies such as the United Nations Office on Drugs and Crime (UNODC) and the World Health Organization (WHO) have researched the issue of homicide prevalence and come up with figures for the prevalence of homicide in almost all countries. Researchers have since published articles on the determinants of the homicide rate variations using available variables such as countries' per-capita gross domestic product (GDP), the Gini coefficient of income inequality, percentage of youths in the population, population growth, and so forth. However, very little attention has been paid to the possible role of more direct factors to crime, such as police efficiency, corruption, or the risks of apprehension and conviction. For that reason, the World Homicide Survey (WHS) project aimed at gathering new data in as many countries as possible and on various aspects of the crime problem, focusing primarily on the functioning of the criminal justice systems.

Pridemore and Trent (2010) conducted a review of all the studies that examined the structural covariates of homicide, using nations as their unit of analysis. They found 65 studies for which the sample of nations ranged from 14 to 106. Among the variables used to explain variations in the homicide rate, they found that the two concepts most frequently taken into consideration by researchers were economic development (either gross national income, GNI, or GDP per capita) and income inequality (Gini coefficient). Their synthesis of the results indicates that relative economic deprivation has a higher likelihood of being significant than measures of economic development. Thus, inequality is considered to be a more consistent predictor of homicide rates at the cross-national level. However, Pridemore (2008) demonstrates that the relationship between inequality and homicide is canceled when a more direct measure of poverty, such as infant mortality, is introduced. Perhaps poverty, not wealth, is responsible for explaining violence. In sum, recent literature leaves us with three different economic concepts that may account for variations in homicide; economic development, income inequality, and poverty.

This study provides a valuable empirical contribution to our knowledge of homicides on two fronts. To begin with, it confronts the three economic dimensions that are currently being debated: wealth or economic development, income inequality, and poverty. Second, it introduces measures of the efficiency of the criminal justice system.

LITERATURE REVIEW

Many factors have been suggested to explain the variations in the homicide rate across nations. A general review of these factors can be found in Pridemore (2000), Lafree and Tseloni (2006), Van Dijk (2008), Pridemore and Trent (2010), and Nivette (2011). When considering the differences in levels of crime across geographic regions, economic dimensions are naturally taken into account. It has consistently been demonstrated that both poverty and wealth are related to the levels of violence between neighborhoods cities, states, and countries. In this section, we individually discuss three separate economic factors, wealth or economic development, income inequality, and poverty. We then present the possible role of criminal justice agencies, which we call formal social control.

Wealth

The majority of cross-national comparisons of homicide utilize a measure of economic development in their study; the most frequently used are either the per capita GDP or GNI. The GNI is the market value of all the goods and services produced by both citizens and corporations of a country for a given year. It is considered a reliable indicator of a country's standard of living. Recent studies that included GDP or GNI to examine homicide across nations found a strong negative relationship (Altheimer, 2008; Antonaccio & Tittle, 2007; Bjerregaard & Cochran, 2008; Fajnzylber, Lederman, & Loayza, 2002; Lafree & Tseloni, 2006; Lin, 2007; Messner, Raffalovich, & Shrock, 2002; Neumayer, 2003).

The general economic development of a country should not be considered a measure of poverty, as the GDP/GNI does not measure the levels of absolute deprivation among citizens (Howard, Newman, & Pridemore, 2000; Pridemore, 2008). For example, due to oil extraction, a country such as Equatorial Guinea has a relatively large GNI (more than 17,000$ annually per citizen), yet a large proportion of its population lives on less than 2$ a day (upwards of 70%). However, it is notable that most cross-national studies who used GDP/GNI to examine homicide rates found a strong relationship, after controlling for other variables. One explanation for this link is that there should be less absolute poverty in richer countries. A second explanation is that wealthier countries have more extensive safety nets, providing impoverished citizens with acceptable, albeit minimal, living conditions. A third explanation is that richer countries have the means to consolidate their criminal justice infrastructure, with well-organized police forces, tribunals, and effective prison systems. Brillon (1985) explained relatively high homicide rates in West Africa by their crumbling justice institutions. According to him, the governments lack the financial resources to maintain a costly criminal justice system. Consequently, clearance rates for homicides in some countries are very low. This finding is also supported by Londono and Guerrero (1999) who reported that only 8% of homicides lead to an arrest in El Salvador, a country with a very high homicide rate.

Economic Inequalities

For many researchers, it is not poverty per se that is criminogenic but rather unequal resource allocation (Chamlin & Cochran, 2006; Fajnzylber et al., 2002; Forde, Kennedy, & Silverman, 1991; Hsieh & Pugh, 1993; Jacobs & Richardson, 2008; Krahn, Hartnagel, & Gatrell, 1986; La Free, 1999; Messner et al., 2002; Neapolitan, 1997; Pratt & Godsey, 2003; Soares, 2002). The most commonly used measurement of inequality by these studies is the Gini coefficient.

For Wilkinson and Pickett (2009), inequality increases tension across all classes of society, not just among the poor. Inequality is also responsible for eroding social cohesion. The link between inequality and homicide can be interpreted by many theories, including the frustration-aggression model, the strain perspective, and the critical perspective (Krahn et al., 1986). Income inequality may also be interpreted using an anomie perspective in which high levels of inequality leads to a weak attachment to the dominant normative system (Messner & Rosenfeld, 1997). Inequality in resource allocation may also fuel tension across social groups, potentially providing crime inducing rationale for the lower classes. According to Daly, Wilson, and Vasdev (2001), much of the variability in homicide between time and space "reflects the variable severity of interpersonal competition for limited material and social resources."

Poverty

Poverty is a different notion than wealth as defined by the general economic development of a nation, which is calculated from national accounts. One nation can be considered relatively wealthy despite a large proportion of the population living in poverty. For Pridemore (2008), it is unclear exactly how levels of absolute deprivation lead to higher homicide rates because several theories (e.g., strain, social disorganization, subcultural theories, and critical theories) claim poverty as one of their central elements. However, it is relatively easy to comprehend that in a country in which a sizeable portion of the population lives in poverty, there will be more homicides. Of course, from an economic perspective, people will tend to be law abiding if the utility of noncriminal behavior exceeds the expected utility of illegal activities (Bourguignon, 1998). When abiding by the rules does not permit minimal living conditions, crime may appear an attractive alternative. A further interpretation is that when people have fewer possessions and are struggling to meet basic survival conditions, a simple theft may more easily escalate into a homicide.

Poverty, as a distinct concept from general wealth, has seldom been considered in studies (Pridemore & Trent, 2010). In fact, measures of poverty are not readily available. Direct measures such as the proportion of people living under the poverty line or the proportion of people living with less than 2$ a day are not without serious limitations (Deaton, 2005). Some researchers, such as Paré (2006) and Pridemore (2008) argue that the infant mortality rate is a measure of poverty (see also Cole & Gramajo, 2009; Conklin & Simpson, 1985; Groves, McCleary, & Newman, 1985; Jacobs & Richardson, 2008; Lee, 2000; Messner, 1989; Neapolitan, 1998). Even if poverty is causally related to infant mortality, poverty and infant mortality remain two distinct concepts. In fact, many other factors, such as the presence of waterborne disease vectors, will influence infant mortality rates independent of poverty. Nevertheless, although infant mortality may not be a direct measure of poverty, it can be considered a good proxy for it. In the current study, we use a wholly new measure of poverty developed by the WHS (Ouimet, 2016; Ouimet, Langlade, & Chabot, forthcoming).

Formal Social Control

Deterrence is the preventive effect that actual or threatened punishment of offenders has upon potential offenders. There are debates about various aspects of deterrence. However, criminologists agree with the idea that the probability of punishment is a more efficient deterrence factor than the severity of punishment (Wright, 2010). Our entire justice system is largely based on the assumption that deterrence works. To quote Thomas Hobbes in his 1651 book *Leviathan*, without negative consequences for theft, rape, and murder, our life would be "solitary, poor, nasty, brutish, and short." Moreover, within the context of a social contract doctrine, Harcourt (2013) believes that the theory of deterrence is the foundation of modern criminal law.

In the current chapter, we are interested in how formal social control is related to crime. At the individual level, many studies show that crimes are the result of decisions made by individuals for which the likelihood of apprehension is an important dimension (Leclerc & Wortley, 2013; Nagin, 1998; Wright, Caspi, Moffitt, & Paternoster, 2004). Of course, there are also other considerations in the decision to commit a crime, such as intoxication or mental illness. And there are people who decide to commit a crime regardless of the risks of apprehension because they have higher motives (religion, justice). Thus, people are believed to adjust their behavior according to their perceived risk of getting caught. Our question then becomes, can we find a relationship at the aggregate level between the probability of arrest and crime levels?

Deterrence research shows that crime increases when police cease to work effectively. For example, Andenaes (1974) revealed that crimes of theft and robbery increased immediately after the German army began arresting Danish police officers during World War II. Other examples have also shown that the number of crimes increase during power blackouts and civil wars. When there is chaos in a region caused by a catastrophic social event such as war, then deterrence ceases to work and plenty of things get stolen, many women are raped, and many people are killed (Kalyvas, 2006). There are examples showing that when the law is weak, violence is frequent. Courtwright (1998) found very large homicide rates in the frontier towns during the American gold rush of the 1870s. Eisner (2003) found that the homicide rate was incredibly high in Medieval London. Similarly, Diamond (1997) demonstrated that, until recently, the homicide rate was also very high among New Guinea tribes. Thus, two major guiding principles seem to explain the increase in violent behaviors, crimes, and homicides when formal social control is weak.

First, in large societies, when the police are absent, incapacitated, or ineffective, certain people will take advantage of others (Haugen & Boutros, 2014). If most people are guided by moral principles and refrain from hurting others, there are some who will if the costs are low. That explains why prostitutes and their clients, drug dealers, the homeless, and to a lesser extent, teenagers and ailing seniors, are more often victimized: individuals from those groups are less likely to call upon the police and therefore make for easy targets for offenders. In an interesting report titled "How to reduce homicide by 50% in the next 30 years," Manuel Eisner (2015) examined possible targets for intervention. He notes that "Without exception societies with high homicide rates suffer from dysfunctional law enforcement and criminal justice systems. This includes high levels of impunity for offenders, corrupt and ineffective policing" (p. 13). Eisner concludes that reform and revitalization of law and order systems should be prioritized in countries with high levels of violence.

The second interpretation of the link between impunity and violence, seldom discussed by scholars, is the justice interpretation. Donald Black (1983) in an article titled "Crime as social control" developed a theory of law and justice, in which he argued that when the State does not act to protect citizens against crime, they will take justice into their own hands. Homicide is sometimes a sanction imposed on an individual as a consequence of his criminal behavior. Here, crime plays the role of both self-help and social control. Based on this perspective, high rates of violence and homicide are expected in countries in which the police and the courts are utterly inefficient, as well as in societies' marginal sub-groups like drug dealers or homeless people.

Research on cross-national variations of the homicide rate, at the conceptual level, suffers from two main problems. First, much of the research lacks a theory linking the predictors to the outcome, especially in terms of operating mechanisms. For example, a researcher may show that poverty is linked to homicide, but there is no real interpretation of the mechanisms involved. The question of why more impoverished countries have more violence is rarely addressed. In her meta-analysis of all cross-national studies on homicides across the last decades, Nivette (2011) shows the results for the most frequent predictors used. They are income inequality, human development index, economic development, social support, urbanism, population density, population total, sex ratio, age structure, female labor force participation, ethnic heterogeneity, and divorce. Those are all higher-order national statistics and fail to measure the criminal justice system's functioning. Very few studies have included any measure of the quality of the functioning of the criminal justice system. Among recent studies we find Albanese (2017) who writes that his results show that "government investment in crime control and intervention in the lives of citizens shown to have measurable impact on crime victimization rates and homicide rates across 40 countries" (p. 9).

We propose a theory of homicide that integrates the concept of formal social control. While there are many agencies that perform formal social control (such as schools, organized religion, government services, and the military), matters of theft, rape, and murder usually are handled by the police, the courts, and corrections. It is hypothesized that weak criminal justice institutions will be linked to higher levels of violence and homicide. A good police force and the application of the rule of law will ensure that homicides are less frequent, and are restricted mostly to cases that are undeterred by the law, such as in cases of mental illness, murder-suicide, or organized-crime related homicides. Unfortunately, there are no readily available measures of the quality of the criminal justice system for all countries of the world. The WHS had produced estimates for 145 countries. The formal social control scale come from four dimensions: Rule of Law, corruption, effectiveness, and satisfaction.

Other Variables

The literature on cross-national variations in homicide has considered a large number of variables. Among others, we find population growth, population density, extent of urbanization, school achievement, health-related measures, gender equality variables, and so on. A preliminary analysis of these variables, studied dimension by dimension, can be found in Ouimet (2011). We decided here to not include other variables and measures because they tend to be highly correlated with GDP, poverty, or inequality. In fact, high multicolinearity plagues cross-national comparisons and make the results unstable and difficult to interpret. By including various variables, the researcher may end up tailoring the results he wants.

DATA AND METHODS

This study uses five variables available for 145 countries of the world. We will first present those that come from international agencies and those that come from the WHS.

Homicide

The dependent variable for this study is the homicide rate. Measuring a valid indicator of the prevalence of homicide across the globe is an intricate and controversial subject matter. Even in developed nations, not all countries define homicide the same way because laws are different. Attempted homicides might legally be considered as homicides in some countries, whereas in others abortions are counted and in still others negligent manslaughter (such as causing death by negligence while driving). For example, if the official homicide rate for Russia is around 11 per 100,000, Lysova and Shchitov (2015) estimate the real rate maybe two times higher. Apparently, there are many homicides not counted by vital and police statistics (missing persons, dead bodies, etc.). We can argue that in every country, there are grey zones on what is counted as a homicide. Yet, researchers are now using the main estimates because they feel that they do provide a valid estimate of the scale of homicide in each country (Lappi-Seppala & Letti, 2014). One could be worried about using the estimates for comparing relatively similar countries, such as comparing Italy (0.9), France (1.0), and Spain (0.8) because small differences in counting rules can make a large difference in the outcome, but the relative imprecision in the homicide estimates worldwide is a lesser problem. No one would dispute that El Salvador has a huge homicide rate (42.6), that Russia has a large homicide rate (11.2), that Canada has a low homicide rate (1.7), and that Japan has a very low homicide rate (0.4). For that reason, analysis will be made with the homicide rate log, therefore, making small differences between countries less influential.

We used two different measures to identify the prevalence of homicide. The first is the official homicide rate published in the United Nations Office on Drugs and Crime (UNODC, 2014) report "Global Study on Homicide: 2013," which proposes the best source of data on homicide for all countries of the world. In certain countries, the best source is the national police, while in others it is the WHO. The second source for homicide rates used is the one produced by the WHO. Since there are important discrepancies for a few countries between the two sources, we used the average homicide rate as a dependent variable. Four countries were discarded because their homicide value seemed improbable (Somalia, Yemen Saint Kitts, and Malawi). We refrained from dropping other countries with values that might seem improbable because we do not want to input our bias into the data by selecting only countries that seems to fit our theory. For analysis purposes, we are using the natural log distribution of the homicide rate.

Wealth and Inequality

All cross-national studies of homicide have some measure of the general wealth of the population as measured by variables such as the per-capita GDP. It is often thought of as a measure of poverty, though this is contested by certain researchers (Ouimet, 2012; Pridemore, 2008). We posit that wealthier countries have less violence because they have better social services offered to the population (education, health, and safety net) and because they can implement a more efficient criminal justice system. Collective poverty is here measured by the log value of the per capita GDP (using the PPP method).

Income inequality has often been linked to violence (Lafree, 1999a, 1999b; Nivette, 2011), presumably because people at the bottom of income distribution feel frustrated, which can motivate some people into lawlessness and violence. However, most cross-national studies of homicide do include a measure of income disparity. We use as a measure of inequality the standard Gini coefficient produced by the World Bank. Countries with larger Gini values have more inequality.

Poverty and Formal Social Control

The current study introduces new data collected through the WHS (for a complete description of the research project, see Ouimet, 2016). Participants in our survey are called "experts." The questionnaire was submitted to people who have a demonstrated expertise in matters of criminal justice, as shown by one of the four following possibilities: (1) published an article on violence, (2) presented a paper at a scientific conference on violence, (3) are in academia and are working on violence, and (4) are working in the criminal justice system.

Respondents were found in a variety of ways. First, we have been to several criminology conferences to distribute our questionnaire to selected participants. Second, we scanned the program of various criminology conferences around the world for people who have presented a paper on violence and homicide in specific countries. We have also looked at university websites for criminology, sociology, or law faculty that seems to have worked on violence in their country. Databases of scientific journals were also examined with keywords such as "Haiti violence," "Argentina homicidio," or "Россия убийство." Once an expert was identified, he was emailed a personalized letter acknowledging his contribution and soliciting his participation. The questionnaire and all correspondence were made using one of the five languages supported by the research (French, English, Spanish, Russian, and Portuguese). For countries with little research infrastructure, we used simple Google searches to find people who have written or commented on the question of violence in this country and wrote to them. It is worth noting that many questionnaires were filled in the context of a parallel research project that we are doing in French-speaking West African countries (a researcher was on site) and by colleagues at the Institut National des Hautes Études de la Sécurité et de la Justice (France).

The response rate from email contacts was relatively low. For example, for the Russian language survey, we contacted approximately 700 individuals from 14 countries where Russian is used and ended up with 60 respondents. We are not able to provide a global response rate because we used several techniques for finding respondents, such as going to conferences or by asking respondents to transfer the questionnaire to other knowledgeable people they know. In all, over the three years of data collection, we contacted many thousands of people. At this point, we have 1,223 workable questionnaires filled out and data points for 145 countries of the world, covering 94% of the planet's population. Only eight countries with more than 10 million residents have no estimates (Ethiopia, Thailand, Iraq, Uzbekistan, North Korea, Angola, Syria, and South Sudan).

Overall, 60% of our respondents declare themselves as working in research and academic fields, 11% are employed by the police force, 9% have judicial and correctional jobs, and 20% work in various other fields (government, journalism, other). Our experts' answers were aggregated at the country level by using the mean value.

For 17 countries, we had only one respondent. In others we had two or three. We could have deleted these countries but we felt that rarely analyzed countries such as Liberia, Bhutan, or Uganda should be part of the study that aims at analyzing violence correlates around the world, not just in developed nations. In each case, the response patterns were closely examined to see whether they made sense given the location of the country, the responses from neighboring countries and its general social condition. Preliminary analyses have shown that response patterns from one expert to another were very congruent in any given country. We decided then to use all countries.

We ran validity checks with outside measures and found our data to co-vary strongly with other data. For example, our measure of the rule of law (explained later) shows a correlation of 0.81 with the rule of law index produced by the World Justice Project (WJP) (2015). The WJP uses data from household surveys and expert surveys to produce indicators for 102 countries on issues such as fundamental rights, corruption, order and security, and constraints of government power. Another example of our data's external validity, our measure of corruption based on expert opinion shows a correlation of 0.77 with the corruption index produced by Transparency International, which comes from polls with business leaders and knowledgeable observers. See our detailed research report (Ouimet, 2016) for the criterion validity tests performed with our measures. These validity tests show that measures gathered from our respondents co-vary strongly with independent measures developed by other agencies using knowledgeable individuals' opinion as their source of data. In sum, we are confident that our original data does represent valid estimates of the various phenomena it measures. It is worth mentioning that we are the first researchers to propose a measure of the quality of the functioning criminal justice system in a very large number of countries.

The WHS produced a brand-new measure of individual poverty. Survey respondents were asked the following two questions: "What would be the proportion of the population living in extreme poverty (having difficulty feeding themselves)?" and "To what extent might the following problems significantly affect the quality of life for a segment of the population: poverty?" These questions were measured using a Likert-type scale from 1 to 5. We computed a factor score using both items (a factor score is a centered scale where countries placed in the middle are given a 0 value, countries with a lower poverty rate are given a negative value, and countries with a higher poverty rate are attributed a positive value).

The WHS also provides an original measure of Formal social control. Respondents were asked questions about four aspects of the criminal justice system. Responses were aggregated into four scales and a factorial analysis was performed with the four scales to produce a global indicator of the quality of the formal social control.

- *Rule of law*. By rule of law we mean a system in which judges are independent, people have access to a fair trial, rights are protected by courts, police officers are not intimidated by criminals, and the police can be called upon (Prillaman, 2002). In the questionnaire, we have several questions pertaining to this dimension: "To what extent do you agree with the following statements: 1) Judges are independent and are not subject to external pressures, 2) Courts have enough resources to deal with most important cases, 3) Civil laws protect property rights (land, goods), 4) People charged before the courts have access to a fair trial, 5) The police are intimidated by criminal organizations."
  We also have one question regarding the availability of the police: "What is the proportion of the population living in sectors or regions where the police are almost absent?" The items were z-scored and the mean value was computed, therefore producing a 0-centered scale.
- *Low corruption.* Corruption is thought to demoralize people; they become cynical of the police and other agencies, and think that criminals are somewhat protected (Gerber & Mendelson, 2008). When the criminal justice agencies are corrupted, they become less efficient in pursuing criminals thereby, lowering their apprehension and condemnation risks. Lappi-Seppala and Lethi (2014) also found that "Homicide is lower under more effective governments in less corrupt environments" (p. 175). When the police and courts do not act, citizens are then more likely to take justice into their own hands. We had two questions measuring corruption: "What would be the proportion of the population that are sometimes required to pay a bribe to police officers?" and "To what extent is the corruption of the criminal justice system a social problem?" Both questions were measured through a Likert-type scale; they were z-scored and averaged. The scale was then reversed (* - 1) to have its direction congruent with other dimensions, producing a low corruption scale as a result.
- *Effectiveness of the criminal justice system.* Our theory presumes that the homicide rate will be relatively high in countries where the police and courts are inefficient (Haugen & Boutros, 2014). In order to measure the effectiveness of the criminal justice system, we asked respondents to provide an estimate of the probability that a given homicide would be solved (clearance rate for five different types of homicide), and the probability that a person accused of a homicide would be found guilty (conviction rate for the five types of homicide). By averaging the probability estimates, we end up with an overall measure of effectiveness based on 10 questions.
- *Satisfaction with criminal justice agencies*. Having an idea of how people perceive the police, the courts, as well as the correctional system is also important. This measure evaluates to which extent people trust people in positions of authority within these institutions (Nivette, 2014). In some countries the police and other agencies are well respected and in certain others these institutions are not well perceived. Hence, we asked respondents to tell us, "What would be the population's level of satisfaction with these agencies: police, criminal courts, civil courts, and prison and correctional services?" They answered using a Likert-type scale from very unsatisfied (1) to very satisfied (5). Our final measure is the mean value for these two items.

RESULTS

A simple analysis of the distribution of homicide rate across the world (see Appendix 1) shows immediately that location and region in which a country is situated is strongly associated with the homicide rate. There are many historical explanations as to why African countries or Central American countries might have more violence. Colonization may have impacted the rise of violence, as well as slavery and resource exploitation. Understanding this would require a historical perspective outside the realm of this chapter. Yet, there is variability in the homicide rate for countries from each region our theory can tackle. Cao and Zhang (2017) have conducted a regionally based analysis of the determinants of the homicide rate. Their findings show that countries from Central America/Caribbean and Sub-Saharan Africa regions present an excess of homicides, which cannot be explained by their theoretical model.

Fig. 1 presents the simple relationship between our four theoretical variables and the log of the homicide rate. On the top-left quadrant, the relationship between wealth (log GDP) and the homicide rate (log) shows a negative correlation. The correlation is −0.50 but, as it can be seen, is not perfectly linear. There is also some degree of heteroscedasticity. Countries with a low GDP have a high homicide rate and countries with a high GDP have a low homicide rate. Countries that are neither wealthy nor poor have various levels of homicide. In fact, one could make the argument that there is no relationship between wealth and homicide below a certain value, around 10 (or around 22,000$ per capita). On the top-right quadrant, we find the relationship between individual poverty and homicide rate. The correlation coefficient is a strong 0.55 and the relationship is linear. Inequality shows an even stronger linear relationship, with a correlation coefficient of 0.65.

The correlations coefficients of the relationship between variables are shown in Fig. 2. All coefficients are statistically significant at $P < 0.01$. The correlations show that richer countries have less poverty, less inequality, and a better system of justice. Countries with more poverty have more inequality and a weak criminal justice system. Countries with more inequality have a lower level of formal social control. All four dimensions are strongly related to the homicide rate.

Although the results clearly show that countries with low, medium, and high homicide rates distinguish themselves across every dimension, it is difficult to pinpoint exactly what causes an increase in homicides. In fact, all the variables are moderately or strongly associated with each other and strongly associated with homicide. Unfortunately, a cross-sectional analysis like ours cannot establish causality. There is also no data on the variations of the formal social control variables across time, rendering impossible the use of a longitudinal research design. What we are left with is the use of techniques that can only suggest whether or not a given conceptual organization of variables appears to be valid.

Table 1 presents the results of three multiple regression analyses produced with the log of the homicide rate as the dependent variable. The first equation presents the results of three social variables on formal social control. Results show that a country's system of formal social control is dependent on wealth (0.28) and

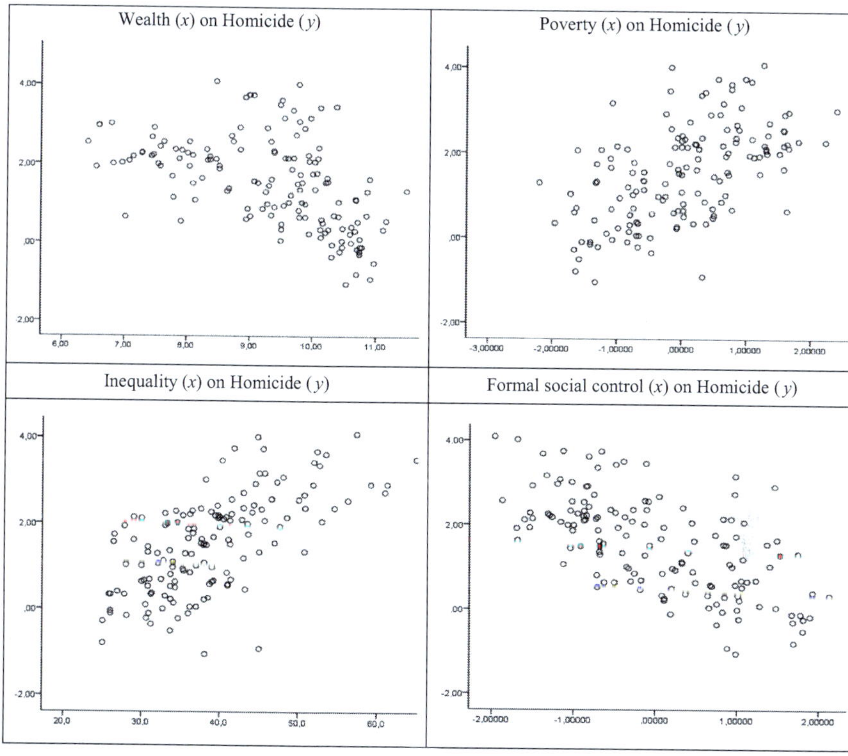

Fig. 1. Scatterplots of the Relationship between Social Factors and the Homicide Rate.

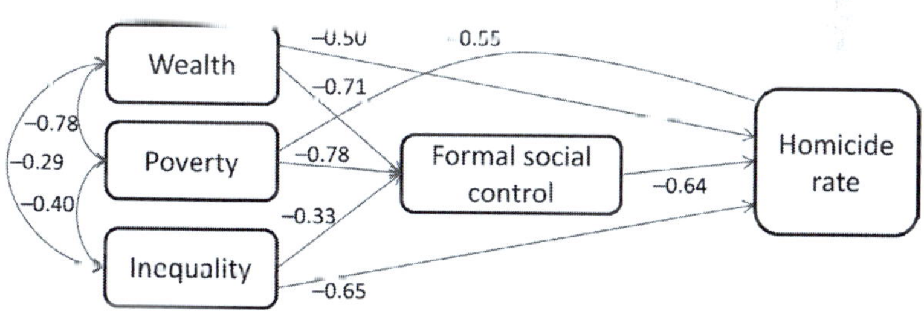

Fig. 2. Correlations between Variables.

poverty (−0.54). Hence, a country with more wealth, as measured by the GDP, and with less poverty have a better criminal justice system (better application of the rule of law, less corruption, better rates of arrests and conviction, and a higher level of public appreciation). Interestingly, inequality plays no part in it.

The second and third regression analyses show the comparative role of wealth, and inequality on the homicide rate. Inequality is the main

Table 1. Multiple Regression Analyses.

	Formal Social Control	Homicide	Homicide	Homicide	Homicide
Wealth	0.28**	−0.04		−0.18*	−0.07
Poverty	−0.54**		−0.02	0.19*	−0.06
Inequality	−0.03	0.50**	0.50**	0.52**	0.50**
Formal social control					−0.47**
R^2 (%)	63	62	62	54	63
Sig. of F	0.0000	0.0000	0.0000	0.0000	0.0000

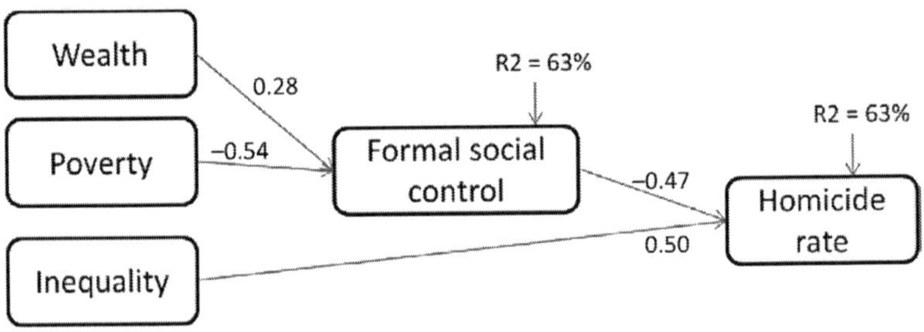

Fig. 3. Determinants of the Homicide Rate across Nations.

determinant; is in fact the only determinant of homicide if either wealth or poverty is included. However, by including both wealth and poverty in the equation, both become significant. Hence, inequality, wealth, and poverty all contribute to explain the variation in the homicide level of countries. The last column considers all three economic measures and the effect of formal social control. When formal social control is considered, only two dimensions are related to homicide; inequality and formal social control. A summary of the results is displayed in Fig. 3.

Our data show that the homicide rate across 145 countries of the world can be determined by two main factors. First, countries with more economic inequality have more violence. Second, countries with a better criminal justice system have less homicide. Yet, it appears that the quality of the formal social control is strongly consequent of the country's wealth and its level of poverty.

CONCLUSION

In the present study, we reviewed the theories and evidence relating to two traditions of research regarding cross-national comparisons on homicide. The first proposes that wealth, poverty, and inequality are the main determinants of violence and homicide. The second, the theory of deterrence, contends that crime flourishes in countries that have weak formal social control mechanisms. The absence of consequence for violating the law will encourage some people to act out on their impulses and influence victims to enact revenge. In this chapter, we have proposed that violence, as measured by the homicide rate, is the product of a combination of negative economic conditions and weak formal social control mechanisms. Our results clearly show that inequality is a more important determinant of violence than wealth or poverty. However, these two variables play in determining the quality of the formal social control mechanisms that is the second determinant of homicide. Countries with more homicides have a weak application of the rule of law, important problems with corruption of justice officials, as well as low levels of effectiveness of the criminal justice system in identifying, charging, and condemning authors of homicide, and have a low level of satisfaction with criminal justice agencies by the population.

There are many limitations to our work. The most important ones are related to the quality and availability of data on most dimensions studied. The dependent variable, the homicide rate, is only an approximation since this information is not gathered in the same way in every country. This is also true for all independent variables, especially those measuring aspects of formal social control. It is our hope that in the future we will be able to extend our survey to more respondents and countries. The second major limitation has to do with causality. Our analysis cannot confirm the existence of causal processes taking place, it only suggests them. The only way to assess causality is to have different data points in time showing, for example, then an increase in the quality of formal social control related to changes in violence levels. We are not there yet.

Haugen and Boutros (2014) propose that violence and homicide, possibly caused by weak criminal justice institutions do, in fact, create poverty. In their book titled *The Locust Effect: Why the End of Poverty Requires the End of Violence*, they show how everyday violence is devastating the developing world and hampering efforts created to more sustainable societies. Hence, violence can be thought as caused by poverty and inequality but also as a cause for poverty and inequality. Some countries located in the most violent regions of the world, such as Costa Rica, have been able to limit violence through a well-functioning criminal justice system. They have benefited from comparatively good standards of living, through multinational corporation investments and tourism, thus creating a virtuous cycle leading to more social programs and a better standard of living. Our results suggest the efforts put into reducing violence and homicide in developing countries should be focused on structuring the criminal justice system, as well as making it less corrupt and more efficient (Albanese, 2017; Haugen & Boutros, 2014).

REFERENCES

Albanese, J. (2017). Crime control measures, individual liberties, and crime rates: An assessment of 40 countries. *International Criminal Justice Review*, *27*(1), 5–18.

Altheimer, I. (2008). Social support, ethnic heterogeneity, and homicide: A cross-national approach. *Journal of Criminal Justice*, *36*, 103–114.

Andenaes, J. (1974). *Punishment and deterrence*. Ann Arbor, MI: University of Michigan Press.

Antonaccio, O., & Tittle, C. R. (2007). A cross-national test of Bonger's theory of criminality and economic conditions. *Criminology*, *45*, 925–958.

Bjerregaard, B., & Cochran, J. K. (2008). A cross-national test of institutional anomie theory: Do the strength of other social institutions mediate or moderate the effects of the economy on the rate of crime? *Western Criminology Review*, *9*, 31–48.

Black, D. (1983). Crime as social control. *American Sociological Review*, *4*(1), 34–45.

Bourguignon, F. (1998). *Crime as a social cost of poverty and inequality: A review focusing on developing countries*. Paris, France: Delta.

Brillon, Y. (1985). *Crime, justice and culture in Black Africa*. Quebec, Canada: Centre International de Criminologie Comparée, Université de Montréal.

Cao, L., & Zhang, Y. (2017). Governance and regional variation of homicide rates: Evidence from cross-national data. *International Journal of Offender Therapy and Comparative Criminology*, *61*(1), 25–45.

Chamlin, M. B., & Cochran, J. K. (2006). Economic inequality, legitimacy, and cross-national homicide rates. *Homicide Studies*, *10*, 231–252.

Cole, J. H., & Gramajo, A. M. (2009). Homicide rates in a cross-section of countries: Evidence and interpretations. *Population and Development Review*, *35*, 749–776.

Conklin, G. H., & Simpson, M. E. (1985). A demographic approach to the cross-national study of homicide. *Comparative Social Research*, *8*, 171–185.

Courtwright, D. T. (1998). *Violent land: Single men and social disorder from the frontier to the inner city*. Cambridge, MA: Harvard University Press.

Daly, M., Wilson, M., & Vasdev, S. (2001). Income inequality and homicide rates in Canada and the United States. *Canadian Journal of Criminology*, *43*, 219–236.

Deaton, A. (2005). Measuring poverty in a growing world. *The Review of Economics and Statistics*, *87*, 1–19.

Diamond, J. M. (1997). *Guns, germs and steel: The fate of human societies*. New York, NY: Norton & Company.

Durkheim, E. (1893). *De la division du travail social*. Paris, France: Presses Universitaires de France.

Eisner, M. (2003). Long term historical trends in violent crime. *Crime and Justice, an Annual Review of Research*, *30*, 83–142.

Eisner, M. (2015). *How to reduce homicide by 50% in the next 30 years*. Technical Report, Igarape Institute, Brazil.

Elias, N. (1939). *The civilizing process*. New York, NY: Blackwell.

Fajnzylber, P., Lederman, D., & Loayza, N. (2002). Inequality and violent crime. *Journal of Law and Economics*, *45*, 1–40.

Forde, D., Kennedy, L., & Silverman, R. (1991). Homicide in urban Canada: Testing the impact of economic inequality and social disorganization. *Canadian Journal of Sociology*, *16*, 397–411.

Gerber, T., & Mendelson, S. (2008). Public experiences of police violence and corruption in contemporary Russia: A case of predatory policing? *Law and Society Review*, *42*(1), 1–44.

Groves, W. B., McCleary, R., & Newman, G. R. (1985). Religion, modernization, and world crime. In R. F. Tomasson (Ed.), *Comparative social research* (Vol. 8, pp. 59–80). London: JAI Press.

Harcourt, B. (2013). *Beccaria's "On Crimes and Punishment": A mirror on the history of the foundations of modern criminal law*. Columbia Law and Economics Working Paper No. 455.

Haugen, G. A., & Boutros, V. (2014). *The locust effect: Why the end of poverty requires the end of violence*. New York, NY: Oxford University Press.

Howard, G., Newman, G., & Pridemore, W. A. (2000). Theory, method and data in comparative criminology. In *Measures and analyses of crime and justice* (Vol. 4). Department of Justice, Office of Justice Programs.

Hsieh, C., & Pugh, M. D. (1993). Poverty, income inequality, and violent crime: A meta-analysis of recent aggregate data studies. *Criminal Justice Review*, *18*, 182–202.

Jacobs, D., & Richardson, A. M. (2008). Economic inequality and homicide in the developed nations from 1975 to 1995. *Homicide Studies*, *12*, 28–45.

Kalyvas, S. (2006). *The logic of violence in civil war*. Cambridge: Cambridge University Press.

Krahn, H., Hartnagel, T. F., & Gartrell, J. W. (1986). Income inequality and homicide rates: Cross-national data and criminological theories. *Criminology*, *24*, 269–295.

LaFree, G. (1999a). A summary and review of cross-national comparative homicide. In M. D. Smith & M. A. Zahn (Eds.), *Homicide: A sourcebook of social research* (pp. 125–145). London: SAGE.

LaFree, G. (1999b). Comparative cross-national studies in homicide. In M. Dwayne Smith & M. A. Zahn (Eds.), *Homicide studies: A source book of social research*. Beverly Hills, CA: SAGE.

LaFree, G., & Tseloni, A. (2006). Democracy and crime: A multilevel analysis of homicide trends in forty-four countries, 1950–2000. *Annals of the American Academy of Political and Social Science*, *605*(1), 25–49.

Lappi-Seppala, T., & Lethi, M. (2014). Cross-comparative perspectives on global homicide trends. In M. Tonry (Ed.), *Crime and justice: A review of research* (Vol. 43). Chicago, IL: University of Chicago Press.

Leclerc, B., & Wortley, R. (2013). *Cognition and crime: Offender decision-making and script analyses*. London: Routledge.

Lee, M. (2000). Community cohesion and violent predatory victimization: A theoretical extension and cross-national test of opportunity theory. *Social Forces*, *79*, 683–706.

Lin, M. (2007). Does democracy increase crime? The evidence from international data. *Journal of Comparative Economics*, *35*, 467–483.

Londono, J. L., & Guerrero, R. (1999). *Violencia en América Latina epidemiología y costos*. Report R-375, Banco Interamericano de Desarrollo.

Lysova, A., & Shchitov, N. (2015). What is Russia's real homicide rate? Statistical reconstruction and the "decivilizing process." *Theoretical Criminology*, *19*(2) 257–277.

Messner, S. F. (1989). Economic discrimination and societal homicide rates: Further evidence on the cost of inequality. *American Sociological Review*, *54*, 597–611.

Messner, S. F., & Rosenfeld, R. (1997). Political restraint of the market and levels of criminal homicide: A cross-national application of institutional anomie theory. *Social Forces*, *75*, 1393–1416.

Messner, S. F., Raffalovich, L. E., & Shrock, P. (2002). Reassessing the cross-national relationship between income inequality and homicide rates: Implications of data quality control in the measurement of income distribution. *Journal of Quantitative Criminology*, *18*, 377–395.

Nagin, D. S. (1998). Criminal deterrence. Research at the outset of the twenty-first century. *Crime and Justice: A Review of Research*, *23*, 1–42.

Neapolitan, J. L. (1997). *Cross-national crime: A research review and sourcebook*. Westport, CT: Greenwood.

Neapolitan, J. L. (1998). Cross-national variation in homicides: Is race a factor? *Criminology*, *36*, 139–156.

Neumayer, E. (2003). Good policy can lower violent crime: Evidence from a cross-national panel of homicide rates, 1980–1997. *Journal of Peace Research*, *40*, 619–640.

Nivette, A. (2011). Cross-national predictors of homicide: A meta-analysis. *Homicide Studies*, *15*(2) 103–131

Nivette, A. (2014). Legitimacy and crime: Theorizing the role of the state in cross-national criminological theory. *Theoretical Criminology*, *18*(1), 93–111.

Ouimet, M. (2011). Un monde d'homicides. *Champ pénal: Nouvelle revue internationale de criminologie*, *8*, 1–30.

Ouimet, M. (2012). A world of homicides: The effect of economic development, income inequality, and excess infant mortality on the homicide rate for 165 countries in 2010. *Homicide Studies*, *16*(3), 238–258.

Ouimet, M. (2016). *World homicide survey global research report*. Research Report, Centre International de Criminologie Comparée, Université de Montréal.

Paré, P. P. (2006). *Income inequality and crime across nations reexamined*. Doctoral Thesis, Pennsylvania State University, University Park.

Pratt, T. C., & Godsey, T. W. (2003). Social support, inequality, and homicide: A cross-national test of an integrated theoretical model. *Criminology*, *41*, 611–643.

Pridemore, W. A. (2000). *Social structure and homicide in Post-Soviet Russia*. Doctoral dissertation, SUNY Albany.

Pridemore, W. A. (2008). A methodological addition to the cross-national empirical literature on social structure and homicide: A first test of the poverty-homicide thesis. *Criminology*, *46*, 133–154.

Pridemore, W. A., & Trent, C. L. S. (2010). Do the invariant findings of Land, McCall, and Cohen generalize to cross-national studies of social structure and homicide? *Homicide Studies*, *14*, 296–335.

Prillaman, W. C. (2002). The judiciary and democratic decay in Latin America: Declining confidence in the rule of law. *Latin American Politics and Society*, *44*(1) 169–174.

Soares, R. (2002). Development, crime and punishment: Accounting for the international differences in crime rates. *Journal of Development Economics*, *73*, 155–184.

United Nations Office on Drugs and Crime (UNODC). (2014). *Global study on homicide: 2013*. Vienna: Office on Drugs and Crime.

Van Dijk, J. (2008). *The world of crime: Breaking the silence on problems of crime, justice and development*. Thousand Oaks, CA: SAGE.

Wilkinson, R., & Pickett, K. (2009). *The spirit level: Why more equal societies almost always do better*. London: Penguin.

Wright, B. R. E., Caspi, A., Moffitt, T. E., & Paternoster, R., (2004). Does the perceived risk of punishment deter criminally prone individuals? *Journal of Research in Crime and Delinquency*, *41*(1), 180–213.

CHAPTER 13

MURDER IN A TWIN ISLAND PARADISE: TRENDS AND STRATEGIES IMPLEMENTED TO ADDRESS CRIMINAL HOMICIDE IN TRINIDAD AND TOBAGO

Ericka B. Adams and Claudio G. Vera Sanchez

ABSTRACT

Purpose – *The purpose of this chapter is to explore homicide trends in Trinidad and Tobago, to describe the factors that impact the risk for homicide perpetration and victimization, and to discuss the effectiveness of strategies implemented by law enforcement agencies to prosecute homicide cases.*

Design/methodology/approach – *The chapter employs a detailed review of relevant literature to explore homicide trends and the strategies instituted to investigate and prosecute this criminal offense.*

Findings – *Our findings suggest that homicide victimization and perpetration is concentrated among young men of African descent, who reside in underprivileged communities with a high population density. Gang violence prompted by a narco-drug economy, coupled with gun violence, accentuates the risk of homicide perpetration and victimization. As homicide rates remained high, law enforcement officials in Trinidad and Tobago were ill equipped to investigate and make arrests in these offenses.*

Homicide and Violent Crime
Sociology of Crime, Law and Deviance, Volume 23, 241–255

ISSN: 1521-6136/doi:10.1108/S1521-613620180000023014

Originality/value – *This chapter adds to the literature on homicide in Trinidad and Tobago by (1) showing that geographic and demographic factors structure homicide victimization and (2) exploring how the political economy of drugs in the Caribbean contributes to murder.*

Keywords: Trinidad and Tobago; homicide; gang violence; Caribbean; urban communities; Neoliberalism

INTRODUCTION

> I witness so much murders already. I see someone who got shot right in front of me. Yeah, and then it had an episode where we hear the gunshots when everybody was like, 'Nah, that was fireworks.' And even when I was walking down the road, nobody else was in the road and I was like 'What is that on the ground?' … When I walk up his brains everything on the ground. In the middle of the road (Lisa, Afro-Trinidadian woman, late twenties).

The above quote, taken from an interview conducted with residents in a high-crime Trinidadian community, illustrates the normality with which some residents in Trinidad and Tobago have come to view homicide. From this quote, we see that Lisa has witnessed many violent incidents during her lifetime. Even more compelling is the fact that homicide is not an oddity for Lisa. Instead of desperately running for her life to seek shelter, Lisa slows down and casually approaches a deceased person in the middle of the street. No crowds formed around the body, first responders were nowhere to be seen, and television crews were conspicuously absent despite such a shockingly horrific event. Instead, the road was empty, uneventful, and the body parts of the slain man lay sprawled across the street abandoned, as if forgotten. Truth be told, residents may have stayed inside their homes as a strategy to disassociate themselves from the crime, but the lack of police presence or acknowledgment by news crews is a testament of how homicide is viewed by various actors. This chapter explores homicide trends in Trinidad and Tobago, possible explanatory factors, and describes law enforcement's response to homicide victimization.

In the last two decades, the homicide rate in Trinidad and Tobago has increased significantly. Between 1999 and 2008, the homicide rate increased by 480 percent from 93 murders in 1999 to 540 in 2008 (Maguire, Armstrong, & Johnson, 2016). In 2008, the murder rate reached a record high of 42 per 100,000 (Pino, 2009). These heightened homicide rates have placed the nation within the top 10 countries with the highest homicide rates in the world (St. Bernard, 2009). Although the homicide rate increased within the last 20 years, homicide perpetration and risk of victimization are not evenly distributed among the nation's economically and racially diverse population. Instead, young men of African descent, residing in poverty stricken urban communities, experience the greatest risk of homicide perpetration and victimization (Maguire, King, Johnson, & Katz, 2010; Miller & Hendricks, 2007; St. Bernard, 2009). This chapter explores homicide trends in Trinidad and Tobago and argues that (1) residents' geographic location and governmental neoliberal policies that accentuate poverty and inequality provide a lens through which to contextualize homicide victimization and perpetration, (2) the increase in gang violence, particularly in economically unstable communities, elevates the risk for homicide, and (3) with a developing criminal justice system, law enforcement agencies in Trinidad and Tobago are often ill equipped to prosecute and combat high caseloads of criminal homicide.

MURDER TRENDS IN TRINIDAD AND TOBAGO

About Trinidad and Tobago

Trinidad and Tobago is an English-speaking nation, located in the southern region of the Caribbean, 7 miles off the Northeast coast of Venezuela (Trotman, 1986). This relatively small republic – 5,128 square kilometers: slightly smaller than the State of Delaware – has a racially diverse population. Of the 1,228,691 inhabitants, 35.4 percent are of Indian descent, 34.2 percent of African descent, 23 percent classify themselves as mixed race, 1.3 percent are another race, and 6 percent are unspecified (Central Intelligence Agency, 2017). The age structure is as follows: 19.29 percent between 0 and 14 years, 11.88 percent between 15 and 24, 45.56 percent between 25 and 54, 12.61 percent between 55 and 64, and 10.65 percent 65 years and older (Central Intelligence Agency, 2017).

Homicide Trends

Urban communities in Trinidad and Tobago, particularly those nestled in hillside of Port-of-Spain, suffer from violence and criminal homicide (Kuhns, Johnson, & King, 2011; Pierce & Kuhns, 2012; Townsend, 2009). Within these poverty-stricken neighborhoods, a murder occurs every 17 hours with most victims dying from gunshot wounds (Townsend, 2009). Other areas in Trinidad, specifically those in the East-West Corridor: Port of-Spain, Northern, North Eastern, and North Western Trinidad, also report high homicide rates (St. Bernard, 2009). Homicide is correlated with population density, low marriage rates, lower social cohesion, and higher school dropouts (Hutchinson, 2005). Large populations of young people, particularly males, within urban areas along with the presence of gang-related activities, constitute the underlying factors for higher homicide rates (St. Bernard, 2009). Given that many homicides are connected with gang activities, an analysis of the time of day and location of these offenses shows that the majority of killings occur in public locations between 8 p.m. and 4 a.m. on both Friday and Saturday nights (Miller & Hendricks, 2007).

Trinidad and Tobago is a tourist destination particularly during carnival, which usually occurs in February or March; however, research shows that residents, and not tourists, are more likely to experience homicide victimization (Mohammed & Sookram, 2015). Young men of African descent are the prime victims of murder; over 81 percent of homicide victims are males between the age group 15–24 and 25–44 years (Maguire et al., 2010; Miller & Hendricks, 2007; St. Bernard, 2009). And, between 1991 and 2000, persons of African descent comprised 68.2 percent of homicide victims; between 2000 and 2006 they represented 72.3 percent of victims (Hutchinson, 2005; St. Bernard, 2009). In the years between 2000 and 2006, of the homicide victims killed by a firearm, 94.6 percent were male, 82.4 percent were of African descent, and 54.6 percent were between 25 and 44 years old (St. Bernard, 2009). The data also reveal that murder victims, or their relatives, were the victims of earlier attacks (Miller & Hendricks, 2007), suggesting a connection between the victim and long-standing violence.

Afro-Trinidadians (Trinidadians of African descent) are more likely to reside in urban areas, which experience higher rates of homicide. Following the abolition of slavery in 1834, many former slaves moved away from the sugar plantations located in the southern region of Trinidad when they experienced full emancipation in an attempt to rid themselves of the painful vestiges of slavery (Green, 1976). They searched for a livelihood in the mountainous region of Trinidad, which later became many of the nation's urban communities. Today, many Afro-Trinidadians still reside in urban areas in the north half of the country.

In terms of weapons, firearms are preferred for murders in this island republic. Death by firearm is associated with the influx of the drug trade, and concomitantly the gang wars, which have infiltrated many Caribbean nations (St. Bernard, 2009; Townsend, 2009). More than half (63 percent) of homicides in Trinidad and Tobago are committed using firearms, while 22 percent of weapons are sharp instruments, 7 percent are unknown, 4.5 percent are blunt objects, 3 percent are body force/strangulation, and less than 1 percent are other objects (Kuhns & Maguire, 2012). Homicides in urban areas are more likely to involve the use of firearms, whereas homicides in Tobago (the smaller of the two islands) and Central, Southern, and South Western Trinidad were more likely to be completed by other means (St. Bernard, 2009).

At times, homicides occur during the commission of a robbery. With robbery-related homicides, firearms were used in 58 percent of cases with another 21 percent of victims dying from stab wounds and 11.6 percent from bodily force/strangulation (Pierce & Kuhns, 2012). The demographic composition of robbery-related homicide victims differs from the majority of other murder victims. Robbery-related homicide victims are in the mean age of 44 years, 12 years older than the average age of all other homicide victims (Pierce & Kuhns, 2012). Additionally, although Afro-Trinidadians represented close to half of all robbery-related homicide victims (49.5 percent), Indo-Trinidadians were overrepresented in robbery-related homicide victimization as compared to their representation in other homicide categories (Pierce & Kuhns, 2012).

Robbery-related homicides are geographically most common in the nation's capital of Port-of-Spain with 23.3 percent of incidents occurring in this region between 2001 and 2005 (Pierce & Kuhns, 2012). The Northern division is a close second accounting for 21 percent of robbery-related homicides (Pierce & Kuhns, 2012). Higher robbery-related homicides in Port-of-Spain and the Northern division is understandable since these urban areas are more densely populated and attract many people who visit stores, restaurants, night clubs, and businesses for recreation, to make purchases, and engage in other commerce. Although most robbery-related homicides occur outdoors (44.7 percent) and happen either on

Friday (17.2 percent) or Saturday (18.4 percent), in comparison to other types of homicides, they were more likely to occur in a business or vehicle (Pierce & Kuhns, 2012). The relationship between the victim and offender is missing or unknown from 96 percent of robbery-related homicides (Pierce & Kuhns, 2012).

Although firearms are the primary weapon for homicides in Trinidad and Tobago, the process to purchase a gun legally is lengthy and cumbersome. The buyer first is required to acquire a gun permit that is only issued after a lengthy background check, interview, and completion of a gun safety course. Few applicants are successful in this process (Townsend, 2009). Outside the legal process, Trinbagonians – citizens of Trinidad and Tobago – can obtain firearms through two other sources. First, firearms are trafficked into Trinidad and Tobago from Venezuela, Guyana, Suriname, and the United States and are available for purchase in the underground market for as little as 2,000 TT dollars (US$320) (Adams, forthcoming; Townsend, 2009). Second, citizens rent guns from police officers and persons involved in the street economy. The rate of the gun rental is contingent on the profits earned from the crime committed; the higher profits to be obtained from the crime, the higher the cost of the rental (Townsend, 2009).

Homicide Categorization

Once a homicide is committed, it is assigned to one of eight categories – domestic, robbery, drug-related, gang-related, altercation, revenge, other, and unknown. Of these classifications, "domestic" and "robbery" are the most reliable (Kuhns & Maguire, 2012). Classifications related to drugs, gangs, altercations, and possibly even revenge are not mutually exclusive and are all connected to "street" homicides (Kuhns & Maguire, 2012; Pierce & Kuhns, 2012). Most homicides assigned to the "other" category are also "street" homicides linked to gangs and the illegal sale of drugs and guns (Kuhns & Maguire, 2012; Townsend, 2009). Here we see that five of the eight homicide classifications are related to gun and gang violence in Trinidad and Tobago.

Gang members fall victim to homicide for various reasons. First, securing government contracts for construction and other infrastructural improvements in their neighborhood is one of the most lucrative endeavors for gang members. If one gang is awarded a government contract in a disputed territory, the second gang claiming the "rights" to the area may shoot members of the first gang to demonstrate their objection (Townsend, 2009). Second, if members of gang A are found liming (hanging out) with members of a rival gang (gang B), members from gang A may kill members of their gang under suspicion that they are being disloyal (Townsend, 2009). Third, with limited available land in urban areas, gang-related murders result from turf wars between rival gangs (Townsend, 2009).

Murders classified as altercations are more likely to occur between acquaintances and be carried out through stabbings (Miller & Hendricks, 2007). A total of 45 percent of murders in Trinidad and Tobago could be considered organized killings with the perpetrator walking up to the victim in a public space to exact revenge or carry out a "hit" on them. Victims in these scenarios are more likely to be young, unemployed men, with a history of contact with the criminal justice system (Miller & Hendricks, 2007).

Murder Victimization and Drugs

On average, alcohol and drugs are detected in one-third of the persons killed; in addition, patterns emerge based on demographic factors and homicide categorization. Generally, persons involved in street violence – that is, killings related to gangs, drugs, altercations, revenge, and retaliations – are more likely to test positive for drugs, specifically marijuana and cocaine, than homicides classified as domestic or robbery-related (Kuhns & Maguire, 2012; Pierce & Kuhns, 2012). A total of 32 percent of robbery related homicide victims have alcohol in their systems at time of deaths but only 5.5 percent of victims are legally intoxicated (Pierce & Kuhns, 2012). These rates are lower than what is found in 61 locations across the United States and other countries (Pierce & Kuhns, 2012). Fewer than 20 percent of robbery-related homicide victims (18.4 percent) had at least one drug in their system at the time of their death (Pierce & Kuhns, 2012). Of the robbery-related homicide victims who had drugs in their systems, 20 tested positive for marijuana, 3 tested positive for cocaine, and another 3 tested positive for opiates (Pierce & Kuhns, 2012). Marijuana and cocaine were less likely to be present in robbery-related homicide victims as compared to all other homicide victims (Pierce & Kuhns, 2012). But, the presence of marijuana in robbery-related homicide victims was twice as high in Trinidad and Tobago as compared to other locations (Pierce & Kuhns, 2012). The fact that marijuana is present in robbery-related homicide victims in Trinidad and Tobago at a higher rate as compared to other nations could be due to the relaxed national culture around smoking the plant. Although marijuana possession and use are still illegal, many people still casually smoke. Here we see a connection between the category of murder victimization and the likelihood the victim was under the influence of a drug at the time of their death.

Based on legal intoxication levels, 11 percent of street-related homicide victims, 6.1 percent of robbery-related homicide victims, and 7.5 percent of domestic homicide victims are legally intoxicated at the time of their death (Pierce & Kuhns, 2012). These data are consistent with perceptions of alcohol and drug consumption in the nation. Indo-Trinidadians, who predominately do not reside in Northern urban communities, are known to consume alcohol at high rates. However, young Afro-Trinidadians who are more likely to reside in the Northern urban communities, burdened by high homicide rates, have a higher risk for gang involvement and access to drugs.

Between 2001 and 2007, cannabis was detected in 32 percent of homicide victims while alcohol was detected in 29.4 percent of victims; however, only 9.8 percent of victims met the legal level for intoxication (Kuhns & Maguire, 2012). Younger Afro-Trinidadian male victims are more likely to have cannabis in their systems while older Indo-Trinidadian victims are more likely to be legally intoxicated at the time of passing (Kuhns & Maguire, 2012). It is possible that alcohol and drug users are at an increased risk of homicide victimization in part due to vulnerability associated with being inebriated, frequenting dangerous locations where drugs are sold, and engaging in aggressive behaviors that are facilitated by drug and alcohol consumption (Pierce & Kuhns, 2012).

Politics and Murder

Political officials are often complicit to the violence occurring within underprivileged communities insomuch as they validate the presence of notorious gang leaders. In the years surrounding 2002, the United National Congress (UNC) political party secured support from gang leaders and the People's National Movement (PMN) political party relied on criminally involved persons to intimidate citizens who planned to vote for their opposition (Townsend, 2009). Additionally, in 2002, government officials met with gang leaders in an attempt to settle gang wars; however, in the years following these controversial meetings, known gang members such as Mark Guerra and Kerwin "Fresh" Phillip were appointed to positions within the government (Townsend, 2009). These appointments provided the foundation for increased economic strength of some gangs. Since then, gang members have been awarded lucrative government contracts to partake in infrastructural developments and to clean up their communities (Townsend, 2009). The revenue from these projects enabled gang members to purchase food, clothing, vehicles, and other items that help the community. Similar to what Hagedorn (2005) observed, neoliberalism often helps gangs become institutionalized into the infrastructure of a community and provide opportunities often neglected by the state, community, and governmental organizations.

At the turn of the twentieth century, community leaders and the government of Trinidad and Tobago made numerous attempts to broker peace treaties between warring gangs in an attempt to subdue criminal homicides (Miller & Hendricks, 2007; Townsend, 2009). With the meetings held in 2002, the government hoped to resolve gang wars and decrease murders (Townsend, 2009). The unfortunate resolve of these meetings however was solidification of the relationship between top gang leaders and government officials, which heightened citizens' suspicions of the government officials' involvement in gang initiatives (Townsend, 2009).

NEOLIBERAL ECONOMIC POLICY AND THE TWIN ISLAND REPUBLIC

Trinidad and Tobago is a relatively young nation, gaining independence from Britain in 1962. Situating this nation within the global economy is helpful when exploring the impact of economic policies on crime. Many nations, including Trinidad and Tobago, have moved toward neoliberal economic structures and practices, where free markets, free trade, and private property rights are considered desirable for the advancement of human well-being (Harvey, 2005). Beginning in the early 1980s, many Latin American and Caribbean countries were forced to implement free-market reforms. For example, banks threatened that Caribbean countries would be ineligible for loans and would experience trade and credit sanctions if they refused to implement reforms (Huddle, 1997; Hurt, 2003).

Financial challenges during the 1980s motivated the government of Trinidad and Tobago to implement structural adjustments in 1987 that fundamentally altered the scope of governance (Dodman, 2008). Structural adjustments are economic policies a nation is asked to implement as a condition for borrowing money from the International Monetary Fund (IMF) and the World Bank. These economic policies involve privatization, free trade, imposition of higher taxes, and deregulation. Before structural adjustments were instituted in Trinidad and Tobago, the Prime Minister of the nation and the International Monetary Fund – a leader in neoliberalist practices (Gayle, 1998) – agreed on the various policies to be implemented (Searle, 1991). Among the executed changes, government expenditure was reduced, government employees received a 10 percent reduction in compensation, cost of living allowances were eliminated, the price of utilities increased, and grants provided to parents to offset the cost of their children's school books and uniforms were eliminated (Searle, 1991). Many changes occurred after these structural adjustments including but not limited to the opening of the nation's economy to foreign products, public-sector layoffs, and a reduction of social services (Dodman, 2008). By December 1988, the unemployment rate rose to 23 percent, the price of goods increased by 12 percent in comparison to the previous year, and youth, particularly those living in destitute areas, were left with little prospects for upward mobility (Searle, 1991). Further, neoliberal policies supplied a decrease in public investment in community services in lieu of services offered to citizens through the private sector (Dodman, 2008). However, as neoliberal policies were being implemented in Trinidad and Tobago, investment from the U.S. declined precipitously. In 1977, US investment in Trinidad and Tobago was 971 million in US dollars. By 1987, US investment had decreased by 60 percent (Crichlow, 1998).

Poverty and inequality in many Latin American and Caribbean countries worsened after neoliberal reforms (Huddle, 1997). These trends operate in contrast to the traditional neoliberal view that globalization has a positive economic impact as a function of the newfound integration of international borders (Wade, 2004). Wade (2004) quotes past President of the World Bank James Wolfhenson who once stated confidently, "Over the past 20 years the number of people living on less than $1 dollar a day has fallen by 200 million, after rising steadily for 200 years" (p. 571). However, the impact of neoliberalism remains more complex in the case of Trinidad and Tobago. Although a great deal of research adopts a trickle-down economics perspective, what is often lacking is how wealth and austerity shape widening disparities between the rich and poor, how distribution of wealth becomes concentrated among a few, and how an obsessive focus on the GDP (Gross Domestic Product) fails to acknowledge the slow destruction of the welfare state (e.g., investment in education, jobs, etc.). Furthermore, experts concede that the data are equivocal (Wade, 2004); in some cases (e.g., China), globalization is associated with less inequality and in other cases (e.g., the United States) it is linked with more. Consistent with this mixed evidence, Gafar (1998) finds that in certain Caribbean countries, for the poor, the situation has deteriorated. For Trinidad and Tobago, economic stagnation occurred between 1971 and 1976, followed by some economic growth, and then negative growth between 1980 and 1990 (Gafar, 1998). Other works support the view that Trinidad and Tobago, like other Caribbean nations, experienced serious recessions followed by economic growth (Fields, 1984). Unfortunately, The World Bank early on concluded that,

"Poverty has increased in countries that have had low or negative growth rates for protracted periods such as Guyana, Haiti, Jamaica, Suriname, and Trinidad and Tobago" (Gafar, 1998, p. 605). Despite the growth, a clearer picture emerges. The income share disparity between the top 20 percent earners versus the bottom 40 percent earners varies significantly (Fields, 1984). This shows that even though economic growth is happening, only a fraction of the population is benefitting.

Trinidad and Tobago is uniquely situated among Caribbean nations since it is rich in energy resources, which serves as the nation's main export (Kedir & Sookram, 2013). This places the nation at significant advantage in comparison to other Caribbean countries (Pelling & Uitto, 2001). In 2008, The World Bank classified Trinidad and Tobago as a high-income country but poverty remains a pressing problem (Kedir & Sookram, 2013). As of 2014, 20 percent of the population was living below the poverty line (Central Intelligence Agency, 2017). Furthermore, poverty is concentrated by race: Afro-Trinidadians 46.7 percent, Indo-Trinidadians 35.7 percent, and mixed race 17.7 percent (Gafar, 1998). It defies logic that a country so rich in oil and natural gas, with impressive economic gains at various times, has so many people living below the poverty line (Canterbury, 2011; Mycco, 2006). Mycco (2006) finds that despite growth in GDP, social sector spending (e.g., public health and education) has remained virtually nonexistent and has contributed to pronounced poverty and crime.

On the one hand, Trinidad and Tobago opened the door to international trade with the implementation of neoliberal practices; Girvan (1997) finds that Trinidad and Tobago exports for about 1 million annually in steel. However, Girvan (1997) also acknowledges how high debt and structural adjustments have taken a toll on Caribbean countries like Jamaica, the Dominican Republic, and Trinidad and Tobago. This augmented plight for poor people, as a result of low public sector spending and demolition of the welfare state, contributes to the adoption and development of the narco-economy in Trinidad and Tobago (Crichlow, 1998).

The Narco-Economy in Trinidad and Tobago

The gap between the haves and have-nots in Trinidad and Tobago has widened as a function of neoliberal policy, a factor associated with increased violence and homicide rates in the island (Hernandez-Ramdwar, 2009). The World Bank as early as 1999 found that a whopping 37.4 percent of youth, ages 15–19 years, were unemployed and notes that these economic indicators were associated with increased violence (Mosner & Bronkhorst, 1999). Neoliberalism fosters the development and strengthening of an underground economy as citizens ensure their survival by supplying the illicit goods (i.e., drugs), triggered by an incredible demand by their global neighbors (Crichlow, 2003; Hagedorn, 2005). The proliferation of trafficking drugs and guns becomes viable given the island's proximity to South America (Mycco, 2006). New routes of drug trafficking through the Caribbean were created as a response to the United States of America's and Colombia's efforts to tackle Colombia's drug market (Griffith, 1997; McElroy, 2000).

Neoliberalism and globalization do not always produce the safety and security for nations that have been promised. Passas (2000) asserts that:

> Promises of more freedom, prosperity, and happiness for a larger number of people have turned out to be chimeral… economic and power inequalities have widened…enormous populations have become more vulnerable to exploitation, criminal victimization, and recruitment into illicit enterprises. (p. 17)

Trinidad and Tobago's incorporation into the global market has been identified as an influential factor associated with homicide rates in the nation (Miller & Hendricks, 2007). In fact, Ayres (1998) reports that in the late 1970s to early 1980s, the homicide rate in Trinidad and Tobago was 2.1 per 100,000, a rate that increased to 12.6 per 100,000 in the late 1980s and early 1990s. In the 1990s, despite this increase, the homicide rate in Trinidad and Tobago remained relatively low. At the turn of the twentieth century, the number of murders committed began to increase. In 2000, 119 were reported, with 370 in 2006 and 540 in 2008 (Maguire et al., 2016; St. Bernard, 2009). In 2008, the 540 murders translate to a rate of 42.3 per 100,000 (Pino, 2009). Contemporary local reports have dubbed Trinidad the world's fifth most "murderous" country per capita (Amani Williams, 2013; Prentice, 2012). The adoption of the narco-economy in the Caribbean, which prompted drug and gun trafficking through Trinidad and Tobago (Pino & Johnson, 2011) and other Caribbean nations, developments situated by the nation's introduction into the global economy, helps explain the alarming trends in street violence (e.g., murders) and victimization risk.

HOMICIDE CLEARANCE RATES

As the murder rate increased, several factors may have inhibited clearing these criminal cases. First, the majority of murders were committed with firearms and since homicides perpetrated by firearms are harder to solve, this may have influenced the clearance rate (Maguire et al., 2010; St. Bernard, 2009). For example, in 83.3 percent of the homicides committed between 2000 and 2006, the offender was not detected. St. Bernard (2009) notes that it is four times harder to detect the offender in a homicide associated with a firearm as compared to homicides committed with other weapons. Second, gang related homicides – a type of homicide that is hard to solve – increased (Maguire et al., 2010). Since gang-related and drug-related homicides are often associated with firearms (St. Bernard, 2009), the difficulty of clearing these homicides may be compounded. Finally, there were major obstacles associated with investigating homicides; these are addressed in the following section.

Citizens often report a low level of trust in police officers believing they are rude and discourteous in their interactions with civilians, use excessive force against them, and are incompetent in their official duties (Kuhns, Johnson, & King, 2011; Maguire et al., 2010). Citizens' perceptions of officers' excessive use of force are not unfounded. Arrested crime suspects were abused while being detained by the police or died during apprehension or in police custody (Mastrofski & Lum, 2008).

When homicide suspects have confessed to a crime in writing, they sometimes claim their confessions were coerced by police officers. So prevalent is the perception of police brutality that when this accusation was introduced in court, the case often resulted in an acquittal (Maguire et al., 2010).

Distrust in police officers also stemmed from citizens' belief that police officers were complicit to criminal activities and disclosed witnesses' identification to suspected offenders which then led to retaliation from suspected offenders (Adams, 2012; Maguire et al., 2010). As such, witnesses to crimes were unlikely to report their observations to the police (Adams, 2012; Maguire et al., 2010; Pierce & Kuhns, 2012). In one high crime community, only two out of 30 respondents agreed that they would inform the police if they witnessed a crime (Adams, 2012); further, residents cautioned each other about the danger of speaking with the police at homicide scenes in various neighborhoods (Maguire et al., 2010). As the homicide clearance rate declined, citizens feared that police officers were unable to apprehend offenders and they became more reluctant to cooperate with police investigations (Maguire et al., 2010). Since criminal convictions are still heavily reliant on eyewitness testimony, citizens' lack of willingness to cooperate with criminal investigations contributes to low clearance rates (Adams, 2012).

Challenges Involved in Investigating Homicides

There are infrastructural issues that make homicide investigation a challenge in Trinidad and Tobago. Investigative techniques in the collection, transportation, and analyzing of crime scene data are often littered with problems. Specifically, the Trinidad and Tobago Police Service (TTPS) was unable to properly collect and preserve physical evidence at crime scenes, transport evidence to the Forensic Science Centre (FSC), and then release the evidence to law enforcement officials for trial purposes (Maguire et al., 2010).

The inability to collect and process physical and DNA evidence at crime scenes has hindered the TTPS's ability to clear criminal cases. The crime laboratory in Trinidad and Tobago possess the necessary equipments to analyze DNA evidence from crime scenes, but the chain of custody from the scene of the crime to the submission of evidence is filled with contaminants (Maguire & King, 2013). Crime scene tape is infrequently used, civilians would sometimes wander inside the crime scene accidentally contaminating the evidence, and evidence would be improperly packaged (Maguire & King, 2013).

The FSC did not possess the technological apparatus to effectively process crime scene evidence, specifically firearms (Maguire et al., 2010). The processing of firearms was so limiting that in 2005 it would have taken the FSC 10 years to process the 2,058 firearm cases they had on file if they did not receive any new cases (Maguire et al., 2010). The backlog in analyzing evidence was so unsatisfactory that police officers stopped collecting and submitting evidence from crime scenes (Maguire et al., 2010). To aid the examination of firearms, the FSC obtained an Integrated Ballistic Identification System (IBIS) in 2004. The IBIS would enable analysts to automatically search for matches that can then be confirmed manually by a firearms examiner (Maguire & King, 2013). Due to the backlog in the analysis of firearms, the lab was only able to confirm very few matches (Maguire & King, 2013). In an effort to address the backlog, British, American, and new local firearm examiners were hired. Firearm analyses were expedited but once the contracts for the British and American examiners expired, the backlog began to accumulate again (Maguire & King, 2013). Here we see that the nation made concerted efforts to address violent crime, but problems associated with forensic evidence (e.g., ballistic examination and DNA collection) limited the availability of reliable information to clear criminal cases. Further, although officers from the TTPS and the FSC were involved in investigating homicides, no single organization was accountable for long-term homicide investigations (Maguire et al., 2010).

Photographs documenting the crime scene can be powerful tools when used in court cases. However, the photographs from crime scenes in Trinidad and Tobago were often out of focus while others failed to capture critical pieces of information (Maguire et al., 2010). Draftsmen – crime scene sketch artists – rarely attended the scenes of crimes and often produced sketches of static objects (e.g., roads and nonrelated objects found at the scene of the crime) absent of the deceased bodies (Maguire et al., 2010). Sketches may have also been of limited use since they lacked information such as case numbers and a compass rose (Maguire et al., 2010). Combined, photographs and sketches produced from crime scene data were often ineffective at helping clear criminal homicides.

Burdened by heavy caseloads, officers infrequently devoted sufficient time to investigate homicides (Maguire et al., 2010). Police investigators, at times, failed to canvas homicide scenes not wanting to put residents at risk of reprisals from the person(s) who committed the crime (Maguire et al., 2010). This might be understandable given that the majority of homicides were investigated by officers with limited experience investigating homicides and most homicide investigators did not receive formal training in investigating homicides until after 2006 (Maguire et al., 2010).

CONCLUSION

The goal of this chapter was to describe homicide trends in Trinidad and Tobago, document possible explanations, and detail challenges involved in addressing homicide. The political economy of drugs in the Caribbean, shaped by neoliberal trends and practices, contribute to the rates of homicide in the country. Homicide rates were low in the 1970s, 1980s, and 1990s, and then began to steadily increase despite population size. This nation, so rich in natural resources, should not have the levels of poverty, inequality, and criminality that it currently registers. Government and police corruption, along with the concentration of wealth among a few, contribute to these trends. Furthermore, neoliberal adjustments, which undermine the welfare state, only augment the levels of poverty and need of the poor. In conjunction with these neoliberal trends, the United States of America's and Colombia's war on drugs structured a pressing need to reroute drugs through Caribbean nations. In a context of extreme poverty and inequality, the narco-drug economy becomes a lucrative option for people in the most destitute areas in the nation. This is where the greatest amount of violence and homicide risk and perpetration exist, in low-income urban areas where Afro-Trinidadians tend to reside.

There are many challenges involved in combating homicide trends in Trinidad and Tobago. Police officers receive limited training in investigative techniques before they are assigned to investigate homicides, no one unit was in charge of investigating violent crime, vital evidence has been mishandled, and the FSC has experienced great difficulty in processing ballistic evidence from crime scenes in a timely manner. The technological infrastructure necessary to process homicide data has proven to be largely ineffective. Inappropriate transporting and holding of forensic evidence, documentation of critical crime information, and resources and training on how to analyze homicide data remain a challenge. In many cases, officers have been known to release witnesses' names to criminally involved individuals, fail to secure vital crime scene information related to the homicide, and even occasionally rent guns for the commission of crimes. It is these types of incidents that undermine the legitimacy of the police, and make homicides more difficult to solve.

This chapter shows an interconnection between neoliberal policies, poverty, gang violence, illegal drugs found in urban communities, and homicide. While neoliberal economic policies may offer significant benefits to a nation, at times, they present unintended consequences. Moving forward, it is important for the nation to combat poverty as it appears to be intimately intertwined with the risk of street violence and homicide victimization. Combating poverty does not only involve reallocation of resources, but also an effort to cultivate local economies and entrepreneurship that will help to produce jobs and opportunities. If the sole focus is economic development at the macro-level, then the concentration of wealth and privilege will remain unabated.

In addition to addressing poverty, concerted efforts need to be made to improve the infrastructure of forensics and the criminal justice system. More specifically, police officers need additional training in investigating homicides and securing crime scenes to ensure unauthorized persons do not accidently trample areas sectioned off by crime scene tape. Training on the proper collection, handling, and transportation of crime scene evidence is critical to prosecution of homicides. Facilities to analyze evidence are futile if evidence submitted are contaminated. Additional, permanent ballistic analysts should be hired to process firearm evidence in a timely manner. The nation could also hire temporary ballistic analysts to address the backlog in firearm analysis but once these contracts expire, there needs to be enough local analysts to keep up with the demand for firearm analysis. Draftsmen should be required to attend crime scenes to compose sketches. Further, sketch artists should be required to include vital information in sketches including the deceased body, a compass rose, the location of evidence to be collected for purposes of the investigation, etc. Finally, structured efforts are needed to increase citizens' trust in the police. If citizens do not trust the police, they are less likely to offer information that could be useful in investigating homicides. Trinidad and Tobago has made significant economic gains as a Caribbean nation, but has lagged in terms of poverty eradication and efforts to develop its criminal justice system. By implementing the suggested changes, some of the deficiencies that remain in homicide investigation and patterns of violent crime may be addressed.

REFERENCES

Adams, E. B., (2012). 'We are like prey': How people negotiate a violent community in Trinidad and Tobago. *Race and Justice, 2*(4), 274–303. doi: 10.1177/2153368712452434.

Adams, E. B., (forthcoming). Police legitimacy in Trinidad and Tobago: Resident perceptions in a high crime community.

Amani Williams, H. M. (2013). Postcolonial structural violence: A study of school violence in Trinidad and Tobago. *International Journal of Peace Studies, 18*(2), 39–64.

Ayres, R. L. (1998). *Crime and violence as development issues in Latin America and the Caribbean.* Washington, DC: The World Bank.

Canterbury, D. (2011). Globalization, inequality, and growth in the Caribbean. *Canadian Journal of Development Studies, 26*(4), 847–866.

Central Intelligence Agency. (2017). *CIA world factbook: Trinidad and Tobago.* Langley, VA: Central Intelligence Agency.

Crichlow, M. (1998). Reconfiguring the "informal economy" divide: State, capitalism, and struggle in Trinidad and Tobago. *Latin American Perspectives, 25*(2), 62–83.

Crichlow, M. A. (2003). Neoliberalism, states, and bananas in the windward islands. *Latin American Perspectives, 30*(3), 37–57. doi.org/10.177/0094582X03030003004

Dodman, D. (2008). Developers in the public interest? The role of urban development corporations in the Anglophone Caribbean. *The Geographical Journal, 174*(1), 30–44.

Fields, G. S. (1984). Employment, income distribution, and economic growth in seven small open economies. *The Economic Journal, 94*, 74–83.

Gafar, J. (1998). Growth, inequality, and poverty in selected Caribbean and Latin American countries, with emphasis in Guyana. *Journal of Latin American Studies, 30*, 591–617.

Gayle, D. J. (1998). Trade policies and the hemispheric integration process. In T. Klak (Ed.), *Globalization and neoliberalism: The Caribbean context* pp. (65–86). Lanham: Rowman and Littlefield Publishers, Inc.

Girvan, N. (1997). *Societies at risk? The Caribbean and global change* (pp. 3–14). Discussion Paper Number 17. Management of Social Transformations. Retrieved from http://economia.uprrp.edu/Societies%20at%20risk%20The%20Caribbean%20and%20Global%20Changes.pdf

Green, W. A. (1976). British slave emancipation: The sugar colonies and the great experiment 1830–1865. London: Oxford University Press.

Hagedorn, J. M. (2005). The global impact of gangs. *Journal of Contemporary Criminal Justice, 21*(2), 153–169. doi:10.1177/1043986204273390

Huddle, D. L. (1997). Review: Post-1982 effects of neoliberalism on Latin American development and poverty: Two conflicting views; crisis and reform in Latin America: From despair to hope; silent revolution: The rise of market economies in Latin America. *Economic Development and Cultural Change, 45*(4), 881–897.

Hurt, S. R. (2003). Co-operation and coercion? The Cotonou agreement between the European Union and ACP states and the end of the Lomé convention. *Third World Quarterly, 24*(1), 161–176.

Gayle, D. J. (1998). Trade policies and the hemispheric integration process. In T. Klak (Ed.), *Globalization and neoliberalism: The Caribbean context*. Lanham: Rowman and Littlefield.

Griffith, I. L. (1997). *Drugs and security in the Caribbean: Sovereignty under siege*. Pennsylvania, PA: Pennsylvania State Press.

Harvey, D. (2005). *A brief history of neoliberalism*. New York, NY: Oxford University Press.

Hernandez-Ramdwar, C. (2009). Shottas and cubatoneros: Badmanism, bling and youth crime in Trinidad and Cuba. *Caribbean Journal of Criminology and Public Safety, 14*(1&2), 285–305.

Hutchinson, G. (2005). Variation in homicidal and suicidal behavior within Trinidad and Tobago and the associated ecological risk factors. *West Indian Medical Journal, 54*(5), 319–324.

Kedir, A. M., & Sookram, S. (2013). *Poverty and household welfare in Trinidad and Tobago: Evidence from the survey of living conditions (SLC) 2005* (pp. 1–17). The University of the West Indies. St. Augustine Retrieved from https://sta.uwi.edu/salises/pubs/workingpapers/PovertyHouseholdWelfareTNT.pdf

Kuhns, J. B., Johnson, D., & King, W. R. (2011). Resident perceptions of police mistreatment and use of force in a troubled Trinidadian neighborhood. *Journal of Crime and Justice*, *34*(3), 234–249.

Kuhns, J. B., & Maguire, E. R. (2012). Drug and alcohol use by homicide victims in Trinidad and Tobago, 2001–2007. *Forensic Science, Medicine, and Pathology*, *8*, 243–251.

Maguire, E. R., Armstrong, T., & Johnson, D. (2016). The structure of citizens perceptions of crime and disorder: New insights from a Caribbean community. *Journal of Quantitative Criminology, 33*(4), 675–699. doi.org/10.1007/s10940-016-9307-8

Maguire, E. R., & King, W. R. (2013). Transferring criminal investigation methods from developed to developing nations. *Policing and Society*, *23*(3), 346–361.

Maguire, E. R., King, W. R., Johnson, D., & Katz, C. M. (2010). Why homicide clearance rates decrease: Evidence from the Caribbean. *Police and Society*, *20*(4), 373–400.

Mastrofski, S. D., & Lum, C. (2008). Meeting the challenges of police governance in Trinidad and Tobago. *Policing: A Journal of Policy and Practice*, *2*(4), 481–496.

McElroy, J., (2000). The Caribbean narco-economy. The Christian Science Monitor. Retrieved from: https://www.csmonitor.com/2000/0106/p9s2.html

Miller, J., & Hendricks, N. J., (2007). Applying the problem-solving model to a developing world context: The case of murder in Trinidad and Tobago. *Crime Prevention and Community Safety*, *9*(4), 275–290.

Mohammed, A., & Sookram, S., (2015). Impact of crime on tourist arrivals—a comparative analysis of Jamaica and Trinidad and Tobago. *Social and Economic Studies, 64*(2), 153–176.

Mosner, C., & Bronkhorst, B. (1999, August). *Youth violence in Latin America and the Caribbean: Costs, causes, and interventions*. Retrieved from http://documents.worldbank.org/curated/en/430541468772467666/pdf/multi-page.pdf

Mycco, M. (2006). The retreat of the upper and middle classes to gated communities in the poststructural adjustment era: The case of Trinidad. *Environmental and Planning A, 38*, 131–148.

Passas, N. (2000). Global anomie, dysnomie, and economic crime: Hidden consequences of neoliberalism and globalization in Russia and around the world. *Social Justice*, *27*(2), 16–44.

Pelling, M., & Uitto, J. I. (2001). Small island developing states: Natural disaster vulnerability and global change. *Environmental Hazards*, *3*, 49–62.

Pierce, R. K., & Kuhns, J. B. (2012). Alcohol and drug use among robbery-related homicide victims in Trinidad and Tobago. *Criminal Justice Policy Review*, *23*(2), 211–230.

Pino, N. W. (2009). Developing democratic policing in the Caribbean: The case of Trinidad and Tobago. *Caribbean Journal of Criminology and Public Safety*, *14*(1&2), 214–258.

Pino, N. W., & Johnson, M. (2011). Police deviance and community relations in Trinidad and Tobago. *Policing: An International Journal of Police Strategies and Management*, *34*(3), 454–478.

Prentice, R. (2012). Kidnapping go build back we economy: Discourses of crime at work in neoliberal Trinidad. *Journal of the Royal Anthropological Institute*, *18*, 45–64.

Searle, C. (1991). The Muslimeen insurrection in Trinidad. *Race and Class*, *33*(2), 29–43.

St. Bernard, G. C. (2009). Firearms and reported homicide in Trinidad and Tobago: A socio-demographic perspective. *Caribbean Journal of Criminology and Public Safety*, *14*(1&2), 81–109.

Townsend, D. (2009). *No other life: Gangs, guns, and governance in Trinidad and Tobago*. Geneva, Switzerland: Small Arms Survey.

Trotman, D. V. (1986). *Crime in Trinidad and Tobago: Conflict and control in a plantation society 1838–1900*. Knoxville, TN. University of Tennessee Press.

Wade, R. H. (2004). Is globalization reducing poverty and inequality? *World Development*, *32*(4), 567–589.

ABOUT THE AUTHORS

Mathieu Deflem is Professor of Sociology at the University of South Carolina, USA. His research and teaching interests include sociology of law, social control, policing, terrorism, popular culture, and sociological theory. He has published widely in journals and anthologies and is the author of four books, including *The Policing of Terrorism*.

Melissa J. Tetzlaff-Bemiller is Assistant Professor in the Department of Social Sciences at Augusta University, USA, and Treasurer of the Homicide Research Working Group. Her research and interests primarily focus on violent crime, particularly on child homicide, sex crimes, mass murder, and media perceptions of murder.

Denise Paquette Boots is Program Head and Associate Professor of Criminology and Criminal Justice at the University of Texas at Dallas, USA. Her research interests focus on violence against women, Title IX and sexual assault, youth violence, program evaluation, and capital punishment. Her research has been published in *Pediatrics* among other journals.

Laura M. Gulledge is Assistant Professor in the School of Criminal Justice at The University of Southern Mississippi, USA. Her research interests include intimate partner violence, intervention strategies for juveniles in diversion programs, and psychosocial risk factors associated with delinquency. Her research has appeared in various journals, including *Criminal Justice and Behavior*.

Timothy Bray is Director of the Institute for Urban Policy Research at the University of Texas at Dallas, USA, where he teaches in the Criminology and Criminal Justice Program. His research interests include the intersection of organizational structure and mission in empowering service agencies to make lasting change.

Jennifer Wareham is Associate Professor of Criminal Justice at Wayne State University, USA. Her research is in the areas of juvenile justice, domestic violence, and justice program evaluation. Her interests include cooking and science fiction.

Alesa Liles is Assistant Professor of Criminal Justice at Georgia College and State University, USA. She holds a PhD from the University of Arkansas at Little Rock, USA, and studies juvenile delinquency, female criminality, and mental health. Her recent publications appeared in *Social Work and Mental Health* and *Youth Justice*.

Stacy Moak is Professor of Social Work at the University of Alabama at Birmingham, USA. She holds a PhD in Urban Studies from the University of

New Orleans, USA, and studies issues of social justice. Her recent work appears in *Race and Justice* and *Criminal Justice Procedure* (8th edition).

Danielle Sutton is a PhD Candidate in Sociology at the University of Guelph, Canada. Her research concentrates primarily on homicide, policing, and intimate partner violence. She also serves as a Senior Research Assistant for various projects at the Centre for the Study of Social and Legal Responses to Violence.

Daniel Adrian Doss is Associate Professor at the University of West Alabama, USA. His career spanned both academia and commercial industry. His research interests include criminology and homeland security. He is the author of *Economic and Financial Analysis for Criminal Justice Organizations* and *The Foundations of Communication in Criminal Justice Systems*.

Kayla Allison is a Doctoral Student in the Departments of Sociology and Criminal Justice at Indiana University-Bloomington, USA. Her research focuses on multiple inequalities, gender and crime, bias crime, and communities and crime. Her work has appeared in journals such as *Justice Quarterly, Crime and Delinquency,* and *The Sociological Quarterly*.

Wendy C. Regoeczi is Professor and Chair of the Department of Criminology, Anthropology, and Sociology at Cleveland State University, USA. Her research interests include homicide, domestic violence, criminal investigations, and sexual assault. Her publications have appeared in journals such as the *Journal of Quantitative Criminology, Justice Quarterly,* and *Social Forces*.

Malcolm D. Holmes is Professor of Sociology at the University of Wyoming, USA. His research primarily analyzes the relationship of race to criminal justice outcomes, particularly how the racial and spatial composition of cities affects the police use of violence.

Paige Vaughn is a PhD Student at the University of Missouri – St. Louis, USA. Her research interests include law and society, race and inequality, and crime control policy. She examines violent crime and criminal justice reform efforts in disadvantaged Black communities.

James B. Pratt, Jr is a PhD Student in the Department of Criminology, Law and Society at the University of California, Irvine, USA. He is interested in the relationships among law, violence, and culture...within and between institutions in society. He studies violence, race, and desire in the Southern Black Belt (SBB) using mix-methods including phenomenology.

Mateus Rennó Santos is a PhD Candidate in the Department of Criminology and Criminal Justice at the University of Maryland, USA. His research interests include crime trends, comparative criminology, policy evaluations, quantitative methods, and data science.

Alexander Testa is a PhD Candidate in the Department of Criminology and Criminal Justice at the University of Maryland, USA, and is an incoming Assistant Professor at the University of Texas – San Antonio, USA. His research interests include the consequences of criminal justice contact, criminal justice decision making, and cross-national criminology.

Claire Chabot is a Doctoral Student in the School of Criminology at the Université de Montréal, Canada. She earned her first university degrees in France and is currently working on the racial disparities of violence in the USA as they relate to states's policy choices.

Marc Ouimet is Full Professor of Criminology at the Université de Montréal, Canada. He earned a PhD in Criminal Justice from Rutgers University, USA, in 1990. His latest book is *Les Causes du Crime*. He specialized in the study of the variations of crime across space and time. He leads the World Homicide Project.

Ericka B. Adams is Assistant Professor in the Department of Justice Studies at San José State University, USA. Her research interests center on the impact of violence on communities in Trinidad and Tobago, the exclusionary practices that accompany criminal records, and whether criminal record expungement alleviates the collateral consequences of incarceration.

Claudio G. Vera Sanchez is Associate Professor in the Department of Justice Studies at San José State University, USA. His research interests are centered on how Latino and African American juveniles, from underprivileged neighborhoods, are criminalized by both nurturing (schools) and nonnurturing (police) institutions.

INDEX